BACKWOODS UTOPIAS

THE SECTARIAN AND OWENITE PHASES

OF COMMUNITARIAN SOCIALISM

IN AMERICA: 1663–1829

THE ALBERT J. BEVERIDGE MEMORIAL FELLOWSHIP OF THE AMERICAN HISTORICAL ASSOCIATION FOR 1946 WAS AWARDED TO THE AUTHOR FOR THE REVISION AND COMPLETION OF THIS WORK

FOR THEIR ZEAL AND BENEFICENCE IN CREATING THIS FUND THE ASSOCIATION IS INDEBTED TO MANY CITIZENS OF INDIANA WHO DESIRED TO HONOR IN THIS WAY THE MEMORY OF A STATESMAN AND A HISTORIAN

AMERICAN HISTORICAL ASSOCIATION

BACKWOODS UTOPIAS

THE SECTARIAN AND OWENITE PHASES
OF COMMUNITARIAN SOCIALISM
IN AMERICA: 1663–1829

By

ARTHUR EUGENE BESTOR, JR.
ASSOCIATE PROFESSOR OF HISTORY
UNIVERSITY OF ILLINOIS

Philadelphia
UNIVERSITY OF PENNSYLVANIA PRESS

Published in Great Britain, India, and Pakistan
by the Oxford University Press
London, Bombay, and Karachi

To the memory of

MY FATHER,

who studied history

ere he made it.

PREFACE

COMMUNITARIAN socialism is an unfamiliar name for a familiar pattern of ideas. What that pattern is the opening chapter of this book attempts to make clear. But the terminology used to describe it requires, perhaps, some prefatory explanation.

The two words that writers have commonly applied to the experimental, co-operative communities here discussed are *utopian* and *communistic*. Though each term is appropriate enough in certain connections, neither is precise and objective enough for the purposes of historical description and intellectual analysis.

According to the definitions employed by such students of the sociology of knowledge as Karl Mannheim, all socialist systems are *utopian* in that they draw their ideals not from the realm of what is, but from the realm of what might be, and they use these ideals to "inspire collective activity which aims to change . . . reality to conform with their goals." [1] It is in this sense that the word *utopias* is employed in the title of this book. The use of the term *utopian* to discriminate between different schemes of social reform, however, has no more exalted origin than party polemics. Ever since the Communist Manifesto of 1848, Marxists have condescended to their "utopian" predecessors and arrogated to themselves the term "scientific socialism." To import such an obviously tendencious classification into a work of history is to prejudge every question which it is the scholar's duty to deal with critically.

For quite different reasons, the term *communistic* must be rejected as misleading. That it has meant different things at different times and places is obvious to all, but few have recognized the magnitude and complexity of the changes in signification that have occurred since the word *communism* was coined in 1840. To begin with, it has actually denoted two quite different things—a system in which property is held in common, and a system in which reform is attempted through small communities. Reference books have ordinarily been guided by the first concept in their definitions and by the second in their examples. It is only in the second sense, of course, that most of the experiments described in the present work can be characterized as *communistic*, for only a minority were based on complete community of property. *Communism*, moreover, has possessed connotations diametrically opposed to each other. In the last

[1] Karl Mannheim, "Utopia," *Encyclopaedia of the Social Sciences* (15 vols., New York, 1929–35), XV, 201.

thirty years, of course, it has connoted a philosophy more militant and revolutionary than other systems of social reform. There was a time, however, when *socialism* was contrasted with it as being "far more imperious and widesweeping than communism," far more concerned with "revolutionizing society." [2] Face to face with such deep-seated ambiguities of meaning, the scholar has little choice but to seek another word.

Fortunately he does not need to go outside the group of terms that were current in the early days of the socialist movement. The very year 1840 that saw the birth of the word *communism* saw also the creation of the terms *communitarian* and *communitarianism,* which were joined two years later by the useful variant *communitive.* These words derived immediately from *community,* and they soon came to signify primarily a system of social reform based on small communities. A clear-cut distinction in meaning from *communistic,* in the sense of holding property in common, was never completely established, because of the limited currency of these differentiated terms. But they enjoyed high literary sanction in the writings of Hawthorne, and they find their places today in the larger dictionaries. No better answer can be found to the problem of terminology which the present study poses than to revive these half-forgotten, and hence uncontroversial, terms and to endow them deliberately with the sharply discriminated meaning that earlier usage had begun to accept.

The author's research in the history of communitarian socialism began with a study of the Fourierist movement of the 1840's. The first results were embodied in a doctoral dissertation presented at Yale, which was awarded the John Addison Porter Prize in 1938. This manuscript was allowed to remain unpublished, pending a more adequate study of the origins and earlier manifestations of communitarianism. The present volume is the outcome of that additional study. It carries the narrative, however, only to the end of the Owenite period. The original study of Fourierism will be comprised in a subsequent work dealing with the communitarian movement of the 1840's and 1850's in its various aspects.

For financial assistance in the research and preparation of the present volume, I am indebted to the Committee on the Albert J. Beveridge Memorial Fund of the American Historical Association, which awarded me the Albert J. Beveridge Memorial Fellowship in 1946 on the basis of the uncompleted draft; to the Newberry Library, which granted me a Newberry Fellowship for research in 1946; and

[2] Theodore D. Woolsey, *Communism and Socialism in Their History and Theory: A Sketch* (New York, 1880), p. 9. For a detailed study of usage see the present writer's article, "The Evolution of the Socialist Vocabulary," *Journal of the History of Ideas,* IX, 259–302 (June 1948).

to the Research Committee of Stanford University and the University Research Board of the University of Illinois, which provided aid through several grants. Under the last-mentioned of these I have enjoyed the able assistance of Mr. Claude E. Fike, Jr., Mr. Philip I. Mitterling, and Mr. Pinckney Miller Mayfield during the final revision of the work.

Specific acknowledgment is made in the footnotes and bibliography to libraries and individuals who gave permission to use unpublished materials in their collections. I cannot hope to repay, by a mere acknowledgment, the invaluable assistance and the innumerable kindnesses I have received from the staffs of the libraries in which I have worked: those, first of all, belonging to the universities with which I have been connected, Yale, Columbia, Stanford, Wisconsin, and Illinois, and those also whose collections I have consulted over extended periods of time, Harvard, the Library of Congress, the public libraries of New York and Boston, the Newberry Library, the Henry E. Huntington Library, the Indiana Historical Society, the Indiana State Library, the New Harmony Workingmen's Institute, the State Historical Society of Wisconsin, the Massachusetts Historical Society, and the Chicago Historical Society. I am also indebted to the librarians and staffs of the Co-operative Union, Manchester, England, the British Museum, and the National Library of Wales for locating and reproducing documents in their collections. The Illinois Historical Survey, a department of the Graduate College of the University of Illinois, has generously co-operated by acquiring photostats and microfilm of many important bodies of manuscripts for my use.

Over the years I have accumulated, in connection with this study, a multitude of personal obligations the enumeration of which is now hopeless. To my teachers at Yale, particularly Professor Ralph H. Gabriel, who guided my original research, and to many faculty colleagues elsewhere, particularly Professor Merle Curti of Wisconsin, I am indebted for long and stimulating conversations on the questions with which I have attempted to deal, and, in many instances, for critical reading of portions of the manuscript. I am under obligation also to many correspondents who communicated valuable information, and to a number of men and women who permitted me to invade the privacy of their homes in quest of the material survivals of early communitarian life.

The manuscript has been read in full by the members of the Committee on the Albert J. Beveridge Memorial Fund as constituted at the time of the Fellowship award; by Professor Robert E. Spiller of the University of Pennsylvania in his capacity as special consultant to this Committee during the completion of the manuscript; and by Miss Livia Appel of the State Historical Society of Wisconsin. To them belongs the credit for many merits which will hereafter pass as my own, and for the absence of many faults which, save for them, would have hardened into type. I hasten to add, in the words of Job, "And be it indeed that I have erred, mine error remaineth with myself."

A. E. B., Jr.

University of Illinois
August 1949

CONTENTS

Chapter I

THE COMMUNITARIAN POINT OF VIEW

THE American Republic, remarked the aging James Madison to an English visitor, is "useful in proving things before held impossible." [1] Of all the freedoms for which America stood, none was more significant for history than the freedom to experiment with new practices and new institutions. What remained mere speculation in the Old World had a way of becoming reality in the New. In this process, moreover, the future seemed often to unveil itself. The evolving institutions of the United States, wrote Lord Bryce, "are something more than an experiment, for they are believed to disclose and display the type of institutions towards which, as by a law of fate, the rest of civilized mankind are forced to move, some with swifter, others with slower, but all with unresting feet." [2] A conviction of this gave motive and meaning to the journey of many a traveler in early nineteenth-century America. Urged on by hope or by fear, each sought diligently the unique and the portentous in the social patterns of the new republic.

Little wonder, then, that many visitors were struck with the cooperative and communistic colonies that dotted the northern and western states. Here the social dreams of the Old World were dreams no longer, but things of flesh and blood. Here the social problems of the nineteenth century were being confronted on the plane, not of theory, but of action. Here, perhaps, the answers would shortly be found. So at least it appeared to Harriet Martineau, into whose ubiquitous ear-trumpet Madison spoke the words with which this chapter begins. Her reputation as a writer on political economy, well established when she came to America in 1834, lent weight to the conclusions she drew from her observations of the Shakers and of the German sectarians at Economy, Pennsylvania:

If such external provision, with a great amount of accumulated wealth besides, is the result of co-operation and community of property among an ignorant, conceited, inert society like this, what might not the same principles of association achieve among a more intelligent set of people, stimulated by education . . . ?

[1] Harriet Martineau, *Society in America* (3 vols., London, 1837), I, 1.
[2] James Bryce, *American Commonwealth* (3d ed., New York, 1893), I, 1.

1

Whether any principle to this effect can be brought to bear upon any large class of society in the old world, is at present the most important dispute, perhaps, that is agitating society. It will never now rest till it has been made matter of experiment.[3]

Miss Martineau was not the only visitor stirred to reflections like these. Alexis de Tocqueville wrote of the Shaker community at Niskeyuna, near Albany, New York. Charles Dickens concluded his American tour by visiting the Shakers at Mount Lebanon in the same state. Some years earlier Mrs. Trollope, mother of another English novelist, underwent considerable hardship to view Fanny Wright's community at Nashoba, Tennessee. The Swedish author Fredrika Bremer visited and revisited the North American Phalanx, a Fourierist enterprise in New Jersey, and journeyed also to the Shakers. The German Duke of Saxe-Weimar-Eisenach was a guest, first of Robert Owen at his New Harmony experiment in Indiana, and then of Father Rapp at Economy. Friedrich List, the economist, looked appraisingly upon the latter. At least two Spanish-speaking travelers thought the Shakers significant enough to merit detailed description.[4] To such an international array it is hardly necessary to add the names of Americans, influential and numerous, who turned inquiring glances upon Brook Farm, the Shakers, and the other experimental colonies.

One's first thought is that these observers were misguided. No unresting feet have hurried the American people into co-operative communities like these. No one at present would suggest that such experiments hold the clue to the future social structure of the world.[5] In the past half-century or so, the small co-operative community has seemed backward- rather than forward-looking, a plan to stabilize life at a simpler level than that of contemporary society. Toynbee, in fact, discusses utopias in general among the "Arrested Civilizations,"

[3] Martineau, *Society in America*, II, 57–58; see also I, x–xiv, xvii–xviii; II, 54–65.

[4] Alexis de Tocqueville to his mother, Auburn [N.Y.], 17 juillet 1831, printed in his *Oeuvres complètes* (9 vols., Paris, 1864–67), VII, 34–36; Charles Dickens, *American Notes for General Circulation* (Everyman's Library; London, 1907), pp. 211–15 (first published 1842); Mrs. Frances M. Trollope, *Domestic Manners of the Americans* (2 vols., London, 1832), I, 38–42, 194–96; Fredrika Bremer, *Homes of the New World*, translated by Mary Howitt (2 vols., New York, 1853), I, 75–85, 556–71; II, 573–80, 611–24; [Karl] Bernhard, Duke of Saxe-Weimar-Eisenach, *Travels through North America, during the Years 1825 and 1826* (2 vols., Philadelphia, 1828), II, 106–23, 159–66; Margaret E. Hirst, *Life of Friedrich List* (London, 1909), pp. 35–36; Watt Stewart, translator, "A Mexican and a Spaniard Observe the Shakers, 1830–1835," *New York History*, XXII, 67–76 (Jan. 1941).

[5] The most that has recently been claimed for them is that they provide "the type of settlement that seems best suited to the pioneer task of breaking the ground for other types." Henrik F. Infield, *Cooperative Communities at Work* (New York, 1945), p. vii.

arguing that "the action which they are intended to evoke is nearly always the 'pegging', at a certain level, of an actual society which has entered on a decline." [6] With the example of recent experimental communities before them, historians have found it hard to treat the nineteenth-century enthusiasm for such enterprises as anything but escapism.

Contemporaries did not so regard it. The advocates of experimental communities did not think they were stepping aside from the path of progress into an arcadian retreat. They presented themselves in all earnestness as guides and pathfinders to the future. And nineteenth-century observers were serious as they weighed such claims and sought, either with expectation or foreboding, to measure the potentialities of the movement.

To understand this movement aright, it is necessary not only to view it in contemporary terms, but also to define, more clearly than has usually been done, its essential characteristics. In achieving such a definition the present-day student is impeded by his understandable preoccupation with strictly economic questions. The experimental communities were concerned, of course, with such matters, but the solutions they offered ranged from the complete community of goods practised by the Shakers to the elaborate joint-stock organization of the Fourierist phalanxes, avowedly designed to safeguard every type of vested property interest. The various socialistic colonies of the early nineteenth century cannot possibly be subsumed under any definition phrased in purely economic terms.

Contemporaries were better able than we to recognize the obvious. What these enterprises had in common was the idea of employing the small experimental community as a lever to exert upon society the force necessary to produce reform and change. The ends might differ, with economic, religious, ethical, and educational purposes mingled in varying proportions. But the means were uniform, consistent, and well defined. These enterprises constituted a *communitarian* movement because each made the community the heart of its plan.

The significance of this approach to reform is not apparent at first glance, because the means which the communitarian proposed are in large measure outmoded today. In the half-century following the Napoleonic Wars, however, communitarianism offered a method of reform that was peculiarly relevant to existing conditions and that apparently avoided the difficulties and dangers inherent in alternative programs of social change.

Communitarianism was, in fact, one among four such alternative

---

[6] Arnold J. Toynbee, *A Study of History*, abridgement of vols. I–VI by D. C. Somervell (New York, 1946), p. 183.

programs. Today we are apt to think of but three. Individualism, now largely associated with conservative thinking, we can recognize as an authentic philosophy of reform in the hands of an Adam Smith or a Jefferson, and in the ringing words of Emerson's Phi Beta Kappa Address of 1837, "If the single man plant himself indomitably on his instincts, and there abide, the huge world will come round to him." [7] Revolution, too, is a possible path to social change, as present to our experience as it was to the eighteenth or nineteenth century. In between we recognize, as a third alternative, the multitude of reform movements, best described as gradualistic, which employ collective action but aim at an amelioration of particular conditions, not a total reconstruction of society.

Communitarianism does not correspond exactly to any of these. It is collectivistic not individualistic, it is resolutely opposed to revolution, and it is impatient with gradualism. Such a position may seem no more than an elaborate and self-defeating paradox. To the communitarian it was not. The small, voluntary, experimental community was capable, he believed, of reconciling his apparently divergent aims: an immediate, root-and-branch reform, and a peaceable, nonrevolutionary accomplishment thereof. A microcosm of society, he felt, could undergo drastic change in complete harmony and order, and the great world outside could be relied on to imitate a successful experiment without coercion or conflict.

Such a bare statement of the communitarian point of view requires amplification and illustration. The sources of the idea must be traced. The distinctions between the alternative programs must not be allowed to rest upon the arbitrary dictum of the historian but must be verified in the contemporary writings of communitarians and their opponents. The relevance of the idea to the time and place in which it achieved its temporary prominence must be studied. Such is the threefold purpose of the present chapter.

For the first century and a half of its history in America, the communitarian point of view was peculiarly associated with religion. Its ultimate origin is to be found in the idea, so persistent in religious thinking, that believers constitute a separate and consecrated body set over against the sinful world—a Chosen People as the Hebrews phrased it, a City of God in the language of St. Augustine. When such a separation from the world is thought to afford not only a means to individual salvation but also an example of the life through which all men may be redeemed, then this religious concept approaches the communitarian ideal. It did so, for example, in St.

[7] Ralph Waldo Emerson, *Complete Works,* ed. by Edward W. Emerson (Centenary Ed.; 12 vols., Boston, 1903–4), I, 115.

Benedict's view of the monastery as "a little State, which could serve as a model for the new Christian society." [8]

The specific origin of the communitarian ideal, as it developed in America, is to be found in the religious ideology of the radical Protestant sects that arose in the Reformation. That great movement proceeded along lines which correspond to the four methods of secular social reform already analyzed and distinguished. An emphasis upon individualism in religion is perhaps the most enduring consequence of Protestantism. But the Reformation also betrayed revolutionary characteristics in the numerous uprisings and conflicts that marked its spread. And its method was essentially gradual in the remaking of such ecclesiastical structures as the Church of England. Fourthly, and for present purposes most significantly, it produced the religious sect, which, in Ernst Troeltsch's concise definition, is a "religious association or conventicle, which aims at realizing within its own circle, as far as possible, the ideal of love and holiness"; which seeks "to withdraw from all contact with the State, and with force and secular power, and in a voluntary union to realize the evangelical Law of God," thus creating "a society within Society." [9]

Certain specifically religious doctrines lie behind and continually reinforce the belief of sectarians in the high mission to be performed by small, separate, purified bodies of believers. The importance they attach to conversion or regeneration is one element, for it emphasizes the sharpness of the break that must be made with the evils of this world. In the American sects that became fully communitarian the idea of conversion was carried over explicitly from the individual to society itself. "The work of regeneration and salvation," said the official manual of Shaker theology, "respecteth souls in a united capacity; for no individual can be regenerated nor saved in any other capacity than in a Church-relation, any more than a hand or foot can be born separate or distinct from the human body." [10] And the

---

[8] Ursmer Berlière's interpretation, quoted in R. W. Chambers, *Thomas More* (London, 1936), pp. 138–39.

[9] Ernst Troeltsch, *The Social Teachings of the Christian Churches*, translated by Olive Wyon (2 vols., London, 1931), I, 363–67. Compare H. Richard Niebuhr's characterization of a sect as a body that accepts "the ethics of the New Testament not as a program to be forced upon civil society but rather as the constitution of a separate religious community." Article "Sects," *Encyclopaedia of the Social Sciences*, XIII, 626.

[10] [Benjamin Seth Youngs], *The Testimony of Christ's Second Appearing; Containing a General Statement of All Things Pertaining to the Faith and Practice of the Church of God in This Latter Day. Published by Order of the Ministry, in Union with the Church* (3d ed., Union Village, O., 1823), p. 464. Compare the statement of the Rappites: "A harmonious and united society of men may be said to be a Kingdom of God. Men are created for men. All devotees, who do not

founder of the Oneida Community, John Humphrey Noyes, recognized a close historical connection between revivalism and communitarianism. "Since the war of 1812–15," he wrote, "the line of socialistic excitements lies parallel with the line of religious Revivals. . . . The Revival periods were a little in advance of those of Socialism. . . . The Revivalists had for their great idea the regeneration of the soul. The great idea of the Socialists was the regeneration of society, which is the soul's environment. These ideas belong together, and are the complements of each other." [11]

A vivid and literal belief in the second coming of Christ reinforced these communitarian tendencies among the sects. In a world of sin and darkness, the perfect social order might be impossible, but if the world is about to pass away, then the attempt to create such a society is assured of swift and complete consummation. More than that, the attempt is part of the preparation that believers must make, and make quickly, to be ready to welcome the risen Christ. The Rappites, for example, believed "that they had formed their Society under the special guidance of God, whose kingdom was near at hand, and that life in their Society, as they planned it, was the best preparation for this kingdom. From their life of brotherly harmony to the kingdom of Christ would be an easy transition." [12]

In planning such a life, the communitarian sects turned naturally to the Scriptures. The Book of Acts provided a description of the society which they believed was enjoined upon them. "The Church," according to the Shakers, "is of one joint-interest, as the children of one family, enjoying equal rights and privileges in things spiritual and temporal, because they are influenced and led by one Spirit, and love is the only bond of their union: As it is written, 'All that believed were together, and had all things common—*and* were of one heart, and of one soul.' " [13] The concluding scriptural quotation —a combination of Acts 2:44 and 4:32—was the favorite text of the

practise the social virtues, deceive themselves." *Thoughts on the Destiny of Man, Particularly with Reference to the Present Times; by the Harmony Society in Indiana* ([Harmonie, Ind.], 1824), p. 82.

[11] John Humphrey Noyes, *History of American Socialisms* (Philadelphia, 1870), pp. 24–26.

[12] John A. Bole, *The Harmony Society: A Chapter in German American Culture History* (M. D. Learned. ed., *Americana Germanica*, n.s., reprinted from *German American Annals*, II; Philadelphia, 1904 [copyright 1905]), p. 37. Most of the communitarian sects in America held chiliastic beliefs in some form. The official name of the Shakers, for example, was the Millennial Church, or United Society of Believers in Christ's Second Appearing. The Perfectionists, who established the Oneida Community, taught that the second coming had occurred at the time of the fall of Jerusalem in A.D. 70. See J. H. Noyes, *A Treatise on the Second Coming of Christ* (Putney, Vt., 1840).

[13] Youngs, *Testimony of Christ's Second Appearing* (3d ed., 1823), pp. 397–98.

communitarians. In 1822, for example, the New York Society for Promoting Communities placed it on the title page of its *Essay on Common Wealths,* and went on to declare, "Such being the nature of God's kingdom, what would be the state of society most suitable to receive and promote it? We can conceive of none that is half so good as a christian community." [14]

A profound distrust of secular authority in every form followed from such beliefs as these, and was intensified by the persecution which most of the sects experienced. For the spread of their doctrines, accordingly, they did not look to the state, but relied upon preaching and example. The latter was peculiarly the method of the communitarian sects. The Rappites developed the idea with great explicitness: "Supposing their [*sic*] existed a rejuvenized, equitable and philanthropic society, which with its religious, christian & political sentiments formed *a united Whole,* . . . would not all good men of feeling conceive and acknowledge that by such united powers of the social spirit, a full restoration would be produced of all hitherto defective systems?" [15]

A small society, voluntarily separated from the world, striving after perfection in its institutions, sharing many things in common, and relying upon imitation for the spread of its system—such was the sectarian community. It offered a method for the religious regeneration of mankind. But might it not offer also a method for the social regeneration of mankind, apart from any specific religious doctrines? To many social reformers in the early nineteenth century it seemed to do so.

The communitarian idea was peculiarly attractive because alternative methods of social reform appeared to have reached a dead end during this particular period. Individualism seemed incapable of answering the nineteenth-century need for collective action. Revolution had revealed itself as a dangerous two-edged sword in the quarter-century of French and European history between 1789 and 1815. And the problems created by industrialization appeared to have so far outdistanced the ability of gradual methods to solve them that society itself was retrograding. Drastic reform was the demand, but drastic reform without revolution. Such a program the secular communitarians offered, and during the half-century following 1815 they were listened to with attention, only finally losing influence in

[14] New York Society for Promoting Communities, *An Essay on Common Wealths* (New York, 1822), p. 29. In 1736 the Moravians inaugurated their *Gemeinschaft* after reading Acts 2. See Adelaide L. Fries, *The Moravians in Georgia, 1735–1740* (Raleigh, N.C., 1905), pp. 135–37.

[15] Harmony Society, *Thoughts on the Destiny of Man* (1824), p. 52; see also pp. 7, 17, 24, 49, 65, 85–87.

the last third of the nineteenth century when gradual methods began at last to prove themselves effective.

That communitarianism was, in fact, a program different from individualism, from gradualism, and from revolution was fully recognized by contemporaries—by communitarians themselves, by their opponents, and by such observers as stood outside the controversy. Communitarians on both sides of the Atlantic rejected individualism as an ineffective answer to the problems facing society. "Ethics," said the French theorist Charles Fourier, "would give people good morals before giving them subsistence; it would lead men to the practice of truth before having found a means of rendering truth more profitable than falsehood." [16] No principle, declared the British communitarian Robert Owen, has ever "produced so much evil as the principle of *individualism* is now effecting throughout society." Consequently, "until the individual system shall be entirely abandoned, it will be useless to expect any substantial, permanent improvement in the condition of the human race." [17] In America Albert Brisbane was equally forthright in rejecting the individualistic idea that the evils of the world have their foundation "in the imperfection of human nature, or in the depravity of the passions." On the contrary, he wrote, "the root of the evil is in the social organisation itself; and, until wè attack it there, no permanent or beneficial reforms can be expected." [18]

The communitarian had little more respect for gradual methods of reform than for the individualistic approach. "The Error of Reformers," wrote Fourier, "is to condemn this or that abuse of society, whereas they should condemn the whole system of Society itself, which is a circle of abuses and defects throughout." [19] He was scornful of those who wished "to obtain piece by piece all these benefits, which should be introduced collectively and simultaneously by means of Association." [20] In similar vein Owen asserted that "Society has emanated from fundamental errors of the imagination, and all the institutions and social arrangements of man over the world have been based on these errors. Society is, therefore, through all its ramifi-

---

[16] *Publication des manuscrits de Charles Fourier* [tome IV], *Années 1857–58* (Paris, 1858), p. 356. Unless otherwise stated, translations are by the present writer.

[17] Owen, *A Developement of the Principles and Plans on Which to Establish Self-Supporting Home Colonies* (2d ed., London, 1841), p. 31; cited hereafter as *Home Colonies;* "Address . . . on Wednesday, the 27th of April, 1825, in the Hall of New-Harmony, Indiana," *New-Harmony Gazette,* I, 1 (Oct. 1, 1825).

[18] Albert Brisbane, *Social Destiny of Man: or, Association and Reorganization of Industry* (Philadelphia, 1840), pp. 2, 27.

[19] Charles Fourier, *Le Nouveau Monde industriel et sociétaire* (Paris, 1829), p. xv. The translation is that which Albert Brisbane used as a motto in his periodical *The Phalanx* (New York), p. 2 (Oct. 5, 1843).

[20] Fourier, *Traité de l'association domestique-agricole* (2 vols., Paris, 1822), I, 72.

cations, artificial and corrupt." Other reformers, Owen complained, plan "a change only in some of the *effects* necessarily produced by these original errors or causes of evil." For his part, he insisted that *"change must be made on principles the reverse of those on which society has hitherto been formed and governed."* This change "could not be one of slow progression, but it must take place at once, and make an immediate, and almost instantaneous, revolution in the minds and manners of the society in which it shall be introduced." [21] Similar words were written by Brisbane in America, "Whoever will examine the question of social ameliorations, must be convinced, that *the perfecting of Civilization* [i.e., the existing social order] is useless as a remedy for present social evils, and that the only effectual means of doing away with indigence, idleness and the dislike for labor is to do away with civilization itself, and organize Association . . . in its place." [22]

Communitarians, in other words, were demanding reforms as far-reaching, as drastic, and as rapid as those that appeared in any revolutionary program.[23] Yet they rejected completely the method of revolution. Fourier argued that "in themselves and by reason of the measures which they provoke, revolutions are incapable of creating anything which lives and lasts," [24] and he promised that his plan would "extirpate all the germs of revolution." [25] His leading disciple, Victor Considerant, laid down, as one of two fundamental conditions, "that every plan of social reform, if it is good, must seek not to impose itself through violence or by means of authority, but to make itself freely accepted by reason of the genuine advantages that it is capable of procuring for all classes." [26] Across the Channel, Robert Owen

---

21 Owen, *Book of the New Moral World* [Part I] (London, 1836), p. iv; *Lectures on the Rational System of Society* (London, 1841), pp. 19–20, 21; *Discourse in Washington,* Feb. 25, 1825, reprinted in *New-Harmony Gazette,* II, 241 (May 2, 1827). For complete bibliographical data on the discourse last cited, see below, p. 112, n. 71. In all quoted passages, italics are as found in the original, unless otherwise stated.

22 Brisbane, *Social Destiny of Man* (1840), p. 286.

23 In fact, Theodore D. Woolsey, a conservative critic of socialism, felt that the communitarian plan was more drastic than the revolutionary, for the latter "scarcely has had in view . . . so great a change and separation from the society of the present . . . as some of the communities . . . have introduced on the small scale." *Communism and Socialism* (1880), p. 9. Compare J. A. R. Marriott, *The French Revolution of 1848 in Its Economic Aspect* (2 vols., Oxford, 1913), I, xxvi.

24 Hubert Bourgin, *Fourier: Contribution à l'étude du socialisme français* (Paris, 1905), p. 237. See also the passages from Fourier's writings compiled under "Révolution" in E. Silberling, *Dictionnaire de sociologie phalanstérienne* (Paris, 1911), pp. 381–82.

25 Fourier, *Traité de l'association* (1822), II, 3.

26 Victor Considerant, *Exposition abrégée du système phalanstérien de Fourier* (3e éd., Paris, 1845), p. 15.

voiced the same ideas, "Extensive,—nay, rather, universal,—as the
re-arrangement of society must be, to relieve it from the difficulties
with which it is now overwhelmed, it will be effected in peace and
quietness, with the goodwill and hearty concurrence of all parties,
and of every people." [27]

Class struggle was explicitly rejected along with the other character-
istically revolutionary ideas. In 1819, in "An Address to the Working
Classes," Robert Owen stated, as his first conclusion, that "the rich
and the poor, the governors and the governed, have really but one
interest." Even after actively participating in militant labor unionism, Owen in 1841 was still criticizing the Chartists because they
"keep class divided against class." He presented his own communitarian plan as a direct contrast:

All former changes have had in view the supposed interest of some class,
some sect, some party, or some country;—some change for the particular
advantage of some portion of the human race, to the exclusion of, or in
opposition to, some other portion or division of it.

This change has no such exclusion or division of interest . . . ; but it
steadily contemplates the permanent high advantage of every child of man.[28]

This point of view was neatly condensed in the name that Owen gave
to the organization he founded in 1835—the "Association of All
Classes of All Nations." In similar language, Fourier boasted that it
was an "inherent property" of his system "to content all classes, all
parties." [29] The American Fourierites, for their part, quoted with
approval the words of Horace Greeley, one of their most influential
sympathizers:

Not through hatred, collision, and depressing competition; not through
War, whether of Nation against Nation, Class against Class, or Capital
against Labor; but through Union, Harmony, and the reconciling of all
Interests, the giving scope of all noble Sentiments and Aspirations, is the
Renovation of the World, the Elevation of the degraded and suffering
Masses of Mankind, to be sought and effected.[30]

Revolutionary reformers saw as clearly as did the communitarians
the sharp divergence between their systems. Much as Karl Marx ad-

[27] Owen, *Report to the County of Lanark* (Glasgow, 1821), as reprinted among
the appendices to *The Life of Robert Owen, Written by Himself* (2 vols. [numbered
I and I.A], London, 1857–58), I.A, 287. Quotations herein from Owen's publications
up to and including 1821 are taken from this work, hereafter cited as Owen, *Life
. . . Written by Himself,* or simply Owen, *Life.*

[28] Owen, "An Address to the Working Classes," March 29, 1819, in *Life,* I.A,
230; *Lectures on the Rational System* (1841), pp. 110, 145.

[29] Fourier, *Nouveau Monde* (1829), p. 15.

[30] Printed as a motto in Albert Brisbane, *A Concise Exposition of the Doctrine
of Association* (2d ed., New York, 1843), cover and title page.

mired some elements in Fourier's thinking, he and Friedrich Engels, when they composed the *Communist Manifesto,* classified all communitarian theories as "Critical-Utopian Socialism and Communism," an epithet that was half commendatory and half derogatory. As critics, the communitarians "are full of the most valuable materials for the enlightenment of the working class," said Marx and Engels, because "they attack every principle of existing society." But the "utopian" element in their thought, according to the *Manifesto,* vitiates all their teaching:

The undeveloped state of the class struggle, as well as their own surroundings, cause socialists of this kind to consider themselves far superior to all class antagonisms. They want to improve the condition of every member of society, even that of the most favored. Hence, they habitually appeal to society at large, without distinction of class; nay, by preference, to the ruling class. . . .

Hence, they reject all political, and especially all revolutionary action; they wish to attain their ends by peaceful means, and endeavor, by small experiments, necessarily doomed to failure, and by the force of example, to pave the way for the new social gospel. . . . The practical measures proposed . . . point solely to the disappearance of class antagonisms. . . . These proposals, therefore, are of a purely utopian character.[31]

After the failure of the great revolutionary efforts of 1848, when the revolutionary method itself seemed to many to be discredited, Marx felt obliged to denounce even more sharply the renewed tendency of the working class to throw itself "upon doctrinaire experiments . . . ; in other words, . . . into movements, in which it gives up the task of revolutionizing the old world with its own large collective weapons, and, on the contrary, seeks to bring about its emancipation, behind the back of society, in private ways, within the narrow bounds of its own class conditions, and, consequently, inevitably fails." [32]

31 Karl Marx and Friedrich Engels, *Manifesto of the Communist Party* (1848), translated by Samuel Moore in collaboration with Engels (1888), reprinted in Algernon Lee, ed., *The Essentials of Marx* (New York, 1926), pp. 62–63; cited hereafter as *Communist Manifesto,* with page references to this reprint. The authoritative German text is in Marx and Engels, *Historisch-kritisch Gesamtausgabe, Werke, Schriften, Briefe,* ed. for the Marx-Engels-Lenin-Institut by D. Rjazanov [pseudonym of D. B. Goldendach] and V. Adoratskij (projected in 4 multi-volume Abteilungen, but uncompleted; Frankfurt-am-Main, Berlin, Moscow, successively, 1929–35), I. Abteilung, VI, 523–57, with notes 682–86; cited hereafter as *Marx-Engels Gesamtausgabe.* For commentary see the critical editions of the *Communist Manifesto* by Charles Andler (2 vols., Paris, 1901), and by D. Ryazanoff [*sic*], translated by Eden and Cedar Paul (London, 1930).

32 Marx, *Eighteenth Brumaire of Louis Bonaparte* (1852), translated by Daniel De Leon (New York, 1898), p. 10. The quoted passage appears entirely in capitals in this translation.

The line between revolutionary and communitarian reform was so sharply drawn that contemporaries—even though bitterly opposed to both—never confused them. The task of communitarians in the nineteenth century was not to defend themselves against the charge of subversive activity, but to demonstrate to moderate-minded men the practicability of their plans. No one did so more persuasively than Albert Brisbane:

If we look around us, we see numerous Parties, laboring isolatedly to carry out various reforms—political, administrative, currency, abolition, temperance, moral, &c. &c.—which proves, *First,* the depth and extent of the evil that preys upon Society, and *Second,* the necessity of a fundamental Reform, which will attack that evil at its root and eradicate it effectually, instead of lopping off a few branches. . . . The reform we contemplate, although fundamental in its character, is not destructive, but constructive; it . . . will change quietly and by substitution, what is false and defective; it will violate no rights, injure no class; . . . but will improve and elevate the condition of all, without taking from any. It can moreover be tried on a small scale, and it will only spread, when practice has shown its superiority over the present system. Unlike political reforms, which, to effect the smallest change of policy, agitate and often convulse a whole country, and array one half of the People against the other half, it will not affect a space as large as a township and but a few hundred persons, and will not extend beyond these narrow limits unless its advantages— *practically demonstrated*—excite a strong and general approbation in its favor.[33]

There were several distinct points to the argument. First of all, the communitarian approach to reform could be thoroughly voluntary. Not only was membership in a community a matter of individual choice, but the whole process by which communitarianism was expected to spread and remake the world was conceived of in noncoercive terms. Voluntary imitation, the communitarian believed, would suffice. "And let us suppose only one such society to exist in the world, which possesses and exercises those principles, what is more natural than that many nations should become gradually in union with it," argued the leaders of the sectarian Harmony Society.[34]

Owen possessed the same confidence. "It may be safely predicted," he wrote, "that one of these new associations cannot be formed without creating a general desire throughout society to establish others, and that they will rapidly multiply." [35] The British socialist, in fact, was ready to begin with recipients of poor relief, quite confident that an improvement in their lot would occur so quickly as to make the

[33] Brisbane, *Concise Exposition* (2d ed., 1843), p. 4.

[34] Harmony Society, *Thoughts on the Destiny of Man* (1824), p. 24. See also John S. Duss, *The Harmonists: A Personal History* (Harrisburg, Pa., 1943), p. 60.

[35] Owen, *Report to the County of Lanark* (1820), in *Life,* I.A, 303.

erstwhile paupers "the envy of the rich and indolent under the existing arrangements." Of course, Owen argued, "no part of society will long continue in a worse condition than the individuals within such proposed establishments." Consequently "the change from the OLD system to the NEW must become universal." Moreover it "will proceed solely from proof, in practice, of the very great superiority of the new arrangements over the old." [36]

This faith was shared by Charles Fourier. In his first book he promised that the application of his societary principles to "a single canton will be imitated spontaneously in all countries, owing simply to the allurement of the immense advantages and the innumerable enjoyments which this order assures to all individuals." He asked his hearers "to prepare themselves for the most astonishing and most fortunate event which can take place on the globe, . . . the sudden passage from social chaos to universal harmony." He was deadly serious as he went on to advise his fellows to build no new buildings but to beget children, for, he argued, all the structures of the world will have to be altered, but three-year-olds will be the most precious assets of all in the coming order.[37]

In the second place, the communitarian program was more genuinely experimental than any of its rivals. Experiment, after all, involves the possibility of failure, and communitarians pointed out that the failure of revolutionary programs (or even gradual ones if applied to an entire nation) could be immensely dangerous. Dr. Charles Pellarin, disciple and biographer of Fourier, exclaimed that

an individual who should manage his business as nations in general manage theirs, when innovations are to be introduced, would rightly be considered as crazy. Suppose an agriculturist . . . wishes to make an experiment in cultivation, would he, unless evidently devoid of sense, apply it to the whole of his estate at once? The nations do this, however; they stake their fortune upon a single throw in the game of revolutions. The social experiments which they try are . . . enormously burdensome, because they are tried at once upon 33 millions of men, upon 28,000 square leagues of territory. If experimental chemistry should proceed in this manner, it would every day run the risk of blowing up our cities.[38]

[36] Owen, "Fourth Letter," Sept. 6, 1817, in *Life*, I.A, 126; *Report to the County of Lanark* (1821), *ibid.*, p. 310.

[37] Fourier, *Théorie des quatre mouvemens* (Leipzig [actually Lyon], 1808), pp. 19, iv, 421–22; cited hereafter as *Quatre Mouvements*.

[38] Charles Pellarin, *The Life of Charles Fourier*, 2d ed., translated by Francis Geo. Shaw (New York, 1848), p. 31. Pellarin elaborated the argument in an essay entitled "L'Expérimentation et l'empirisme en matière sociale," contained in his ed. of *Lettre de Fourier au grand juge* (Paris, 1874), pp. 87–88. See also Fourier's own statement that his plan was designed "to operate upon the entire world, savage, barbarian, and civilized; to metamorphose the whole by an experiment limited to a square league and 1800 persons. What a contrast with the philosophy

The communitarians were fond of describing their proposals in terms of experimentation. Even the religious communities did so. "True and real inlightning [sic]," declared the Harmony Society in Indiana, involves "many and every trial of practical, religious, as well as political experiments, to discover . . . the best . . . means . . . for the general welfare." [39] William Maclure, colleague of Robert Owen at New Harmony, and himself a distinguished man of science, stated the communitarian ideal of experimentation with perhaps the greatest clarity of all:

Each township might experiment on every thing that could conduce to their comfort and happiness, without interfering with the interests of their neighbors; thereby reducing all political, moral, or religious experiments to their [sic] simplicity, facility and utility of mechanism, manufactures and all the useful arts; that is, that a failure could only hurt the contrivers and executors of the speculation, forcing them to nullify their mistakes, and guaranteeing them against a perseverance in error.[40]

Experiment implies a well-formulated hypothesis, and the invention of methods to test it. This element of deliberate inventiveness and reasoned choice is a third characteristic of communitarian philosophy. Planning and choice must figure in any program of social reform, of course, but there is a marked difference in emphasis between the social inventiveness cultivated by communitarians, and the Marxist reliance upon historically generated social forces.

The Marxists themselves made much of the distinction. The *Communist Manifesto* condemned Owen, Fourier, and the other so-called utopians for their belief that

Historical action is to yield to their personal inventive action, historically created conditions of emancipation to fantastic ones, and the gradual, spontaneous class-organization of the proletariat to an organization of society especially contrived by these inventors. Future history resolves itself,

---

that throws empires into confusion from top to bottom without a single guarantee of good results!" *Nouveau Monde* (1829), p. xv.

[39] Harmony Society, *Thoughts on the Destiny of Man* (1824), p. 41.

[40] William Maclure, *Opinions on Various Subjects, Dedicated to the Industrious Producers* (3 vols., New Harmony, Ind., 1831–38), III, 9. Apropos of Owen's choice of New Harmony for his community the *Cincinnati Literary Gazette* commented: "There are no people, probably, in the world, who are so ready to make experiments respecting social relations and domestic arrangements, as those of the western country. . . . On this account we consider the location of Mr. Owen's theatre of operations, as exceedingly well chosen, if his object be merely to make an experiment of the feasibility of his plans." III, 193 (June 18, 1825). The experimental aspect of communitarianism is discussed in Merle Curti, *Growth of American Thought* (New York, 1943), pp. 263–65 (which quotes the foregoing passage), and Woolsey, *Communism and Socialism*, pp. 5, 22.

in their eyes, into the propaganda and the practical carrying out of their social plans.[41]

Friedrich Engels, coauthor of the *Manifesto*, elaborated this criticism in a later work, often reprinted in part under the title *Socialism, Utopian and Scientific:*

The solution of the social problems, which as yet lay hidden in undeveloped economic conditions, the utopians attempted to evolve out of the human brain. Society presented nothing but wrongs; to remove these was the task of reason. It was necessary, then, to discover a new and more perfect system of social order and to impose this upon society from without by propaganda, and, wherever it was possible, by the example of model experiments.[42]

Though a philosophy of history is by no means absent, communitarian writings are, in truth, concerned more with inventing solutions to social problems than with investigating deterministic historical trends. Charles Fourier was typically communitarian when he bewailed the three thousand years of felicity which the human race had missed because his system had not been discovered sooner, and when he announced that mankind could skip at least two definite and expected steps in its upward evolution by promptly adopting his proposals.[43]

The varied characteristics of communitarian thought were brought together in concise but comprehensive summary by Victor Considerant, Fourier's leading disciple, at the conclusion of a course of lectures he delivered in 1841:

The theory of Fourier may be deemed both *liberal* and *conservative* at once, for it aims at universal transformation, without directly or abruptly interfering with society. It proposes to substitute riches in lieu of poverty, liberty in lieu of anarchy and despotism, peaceful industry and progress in lieu of revolutionary change; to . . . substitute, in fact, a better and a different order of society without convulsive change or dangerous innovation: and to obtain these marvellous results, the simple combination of industrial series in Phalansterian association is deemed amply sufficient, under the protection of existing institutions. Industry is the basis of its operations, and superior wealth and morality its immediate aim. Nothing can be more simple, harmless, and legitimate. All parties are equally interested in its success, and nothing dangerous can be apprehended from

41 *Communist Manifesto*, p. 62.

42 Friedrich Engels, *Socialism, Utopian and Scientific*, translated by Edward Aveling (New York: International Publishers [1935]), p. 36. Originally published as part of his *Herrn Eugen Dühring's Umwälzung der Wissenschaft* (1878), these chapters were arranged by Engels for separate publication under the new title in 1880.

43 Fourier, *Traité de l'association* (1822), II, 426; see also his *Nouveau Monde* (1829), p. xii.

its failure, for its operations are confined to individual interests, and that on a very limited scale. In case of failure almost nothing would be lost; and if success attended the experiment, the most desirable change would be effected in the general condition of humanity. The poorest classes in society would be elevated to a state of moral dignity and industrial independency, while the rich would be secure in the enjoyment of their wealth, and all the human race, in time, would be improved and elevated to its real destiny.[44]

Each of the characteristics of communitarianism made a special appeal to Americans in the middle decades of the nineteenth century. Its faith that men can remake their institutions by reasoned choice evoked natural response in the United States, whose people believed they had done this very thing in their own constitution-making. The communitarian belief in social harmony as opposed to class warfare was certainly the prevalent hope of Americans generally. The communitarian emphasis upon voluntary action met exactly the American conception of freedom. The experimental aspect of communitarianism found ready echo in a nation of experimenters, in a nation that viewed even itself as an experiment.

Most significant of all, the group procedure that was the heart of the communitarian program corresponded to a like tendency that ramified through many American institutions and many fields of American thought. Government and law provide striking illustrations of this tendency. Students of Germanic institutions, notably Otto von Gierke, have traced this feeling for the group far back into medieval political philosophy and jurisprudence. Whereas the Roman codes were generally suspicious of associations and granted the privilege of incorporation grudgingly, Germanic law, Gierke points out, was remarkable for the encouragement it gave to the formation of an association or fellowship (Genossenschaft). Gierke glorifies "that inexhaustible Germanic spirit of association, which knows how to secure for all narrower members of the state an original, independent life, and . . . to create . . . , for the most general as for the most particular purposes of human existence, an incalculable wealth of associations which are not animated from above but act spontaneously." [45] In his translation of Gierke's work, Frederic William Maitland carries the argument over into the field of Anglo-American law, calling the roll of groups that might demand attention

---

[44] Considerant, Exposition abrégée (3e éd., 1845), pp. 54–55; employing the free translation by Hugh Doherty printed in London Phalanx, I, 252 (July 17, 1841). Doherty interpolated the word gradually in the second sentence; this has been omitted, using the customary indication.

[45] Otto von Gierke, Das deutsche Genossenschaftsrecht (4 vols., Berlin, 1868–1913), I, 3; as translated by John D. Lewis in an appendix to his Genossenschaft-Theory of Otto von Gierke (University of Wisconsin, Studies in the Social Sciences and History, no. 25; Madison, 1935), p. 114.

in an English treatise equivalent to Gierke's. "The English historian," he concludes, "would have a wealth of group-life to survey richer even than that which has come under Dr Gierke's eye." [46] The growth of this group-life was spontaneous and irrepressible. When formal legal doctrine was inhospitable to such self-constituted associations, as Maitland shows, they took shelter under the flexible English concept of the trust.

To America, then, the English settlers brought a habit of forming themselves freely into groups. The Mayflower Compact [47] is a classic illustration of the instinctive feeling that spontaneous associations possess an incontestable right to exist, in fact and in the eyes of the law. The conditions of frontier existence [48] and the progress of democratic ideas encouraged the formation of voluntary associations. Alexis de Tocqueville notes it as one of the outstanding characteristics of the American Republic:

The political associations that exist in the United States are only a single feature in the midst of the immense assemblage of associations in that country. Americans of all ages, all conditions, and all dispositions constantly form associations. They have not only commercial and manufacturing companies, in which all take part, but associations of a thousand other kinds, religious, moral, serious, futile, general or restricted, enormous or diminutive. . . .

I met with several kinds of associations in America of which I confess I had no previous notion; and I have often admired the extreme skill with which the inhabitants of the United States succeed in proposing a common object for the exertions of a great many men and in inducing them voluntarily to pursue it. . . .

Civil associations . . . facilitate political association; but, on the other hand, political association singularly strengthens and improves associations for civil purposes. . . . Thus political life makes the love and practice of association more general; it imparts a desire of union and teaches the means of combination to numbers of men who otherwise would have always lived apart.[49]

[46] F. W. Maitland, introduction to his translation of Gierke, *Political Theories of the Middle Age* (Cambridge, 1900), p. xxvii; see also pp. xxix–xxxvii.

[47] Cited in this connection by Maitland, p. xxxi.

[48] Compare Frederick Jackson Turner's observation: "From the first, it was evident that these men [of the backwoods] had means of supplementing their individual activity by informal combinations. One of the things that impressed all early travelers in the United States was the capacity for extra-legal association. . . . This power of the pioneers to join together for a common end, without the intervention of governmental institutions, was one of their marked characteristics." *The United States, 1830–1850: The Nation and Its Sections* (New York, 1935), p. 21.

[49] Tocqueville, *Democracy in America*, translated by Henry Reeve, revised by Francis Bowen, corrected and ed. by Phillips Bradley (2 vols., New York, 1945), II, 106, 115.

Federalism, in the sense opposed to consolidated nationalism, is an important complement of this respect for, and encouragement of, autonomous groups. It is therefore no accident that many close parallels to the communitarian argument may be found in the classic expositions of the role of states in the American federal system. According to Lord Bryce,

Federalism enables a people to try experiments in legislation and administration which could not be safely tried in a large centralized country. A comparatively small commonwealth like an American State easily makes and unmakes its laws; mistakes are not serious, for they are soon corrected; other States profit by the experience of a law or a method which has worked well or ill in the State that has tried it.[50]

President Franklin D. Roosevelt expressed the idea more colloquially to his Secretary of Labor: "The beauty of our state-federal system is that the people can experiment. If it has fatal consequences in one place, it has little effect upon the rest of the country. If a new, apparently fanatical, program works well, it will be copied. If it doesn't, you won't hear of it again." [51] In his famous dissent in the case of Truax *v.* Corrigan, Justice Oliver Wendell Holmes urged the Supreme Court not "to prevent the making of social experiments that an important part of the community desires, in the insulated chambers afforded by the several States, even though the experiments may seem futile or even noxious." [52]

This idea of political experiment on a small scale is a precise counterpart of the communitarian philosophy, with its conception of the community as an insulated laboratory for testing social measures. Communitive writers, in fact, sometimes presented their arguments as the final flowering of the federal idea. William Maclure, Owen's associate in the New Harmony community, insisted that federation had hitherto failed to reveal its full potentialities because it had been applied to political units that were too large and heterogeneous. Its greatest perfection would come when put into effect among small communitarian societies. "The uniting, by the federation system, any number of cooperative associations, would multiply and vary the enjoyments of the social order, ad infinitum." [53]

So ingrained in American experience was the idea of group pro-

[50] Bryce, *American Commonwealth* (3d ed., 1893), I, 353; see also p. 345.

[51] Frances Perkins, *The Roosevelt I Knew* (New York, 1946), p. 124. Compare Roosevelt's description of the Tennessee Valley project as "a laboratory for the Nation," in his *Public Papers and Addresses*, II (New York, 1938), 129.

[52] 257 U.S. 312, at 344 (Dec. 19, 1921); also printed in Holmes, *Dissenting Opinions*, ed. by Alfred Lief (New York, 1929), p. 13.

[53] Maclure, *Opinions*, I (1831), 40–42. For a similar argument from federalism, see Parke Godwin's address in *The Phalanx*, p. 113 (April 21, 1844).

cedure—of trying political and social experiments upon units of society less than the whole—that communitarians found little difficulty in winning a hearing for their own proposals, couched as they were in familiar terms. For many liberals and reformers, in fact, the communitarian approach had become almost instinctive in mid-nineteenth-century America. No clearer illustration can be found than a paragraph by an anonymous contributor to the antislavery *Liberator* in 1840:

Can society ever be constituted upon principles of universal Christian brotherhood? The believing Christian, the enlightened philosopher, answer —IT CAN. Will this organization commence with the entire race of man? with existing governments? or with small isolated communities. Doubtless, the principles of this new organization must be matured in the hearts and lives of individuals, before they can be embodied in any community, but when the new organization commences, it will doubtless be in small communities.[54]

This was the communitarian faith.

[54] "Co-operative Associations," *Liberator*, X, 207 (Dec. 25, 1840).

Chapter II

HOLY COMMONWEALTHS: THE COMMUNITIVE SECTS

THE communitarian idea came to fullest flower in the New World, but its seeds were brought from the Old. To be precise, they were brought not from Europe generally but from a restricted zone of religious radicalism that stretched from central Europe to the British Isles. Theological tensions were apparent in this region before the Reformation, but it was the struggle between Catholicism and Protestantism that made clear the existence and delimited the boundaries of this religious frontier. During the Reformation it constituted the borderland in which the great organized churches, Catholic, Lutheran, and Calvinist, battled for supremacy, and in which smaller sects sprang up amidst the tangle of conflicting ideas.

Beginning near the eastern boundary of the Holy Roman Empire in Moravia, this religious frontier circled the northern and western fringes of Bohemia, touching Saxony, Thuringia, and the Upper Palatinate. It reached the Danube near Ratisbon or Regensburg, and it comprised the entire triangle framed on south and west by the upper Danube and the upper Rhine—that is, Wurtemberg, and the Swabian and Franconian lands in general. The apex of this triangle rested on the borders of Switzerland, the country of Zwingli and later the center of Calvin's work. Down the Rhine to its mouth in the Low Countries ran the belt of religious unsettlement, taking in Alsace, the Rhenish Palatinate, Westphalia, and the northern Netherlands. The zone of conflict projected itself, finally, across the North Sea to include Great Britain.[1]

In this meandering borderland, the struggle between the major contending churches unloosed religious and social forces far more radical in tendency than Luther and the other reformers had bargained for. The very intensity of theological conflict encouraged speculation, and the absence of settled ecclesiastical authority made

[1] See Karl Heussi and Hermann Mulert, *Atlas zur Kirchengeschichte* (3e Aufl., Tübingen, 1937), plates X and XI, which picture the religious situation at successive dates between 1529 and 1740. Minor sects can only be shown impressionistically upon such a map, but their location with reference to the boundary line between the major creeds is clear.

20

Hx 654.B4

Remote Hx 654.B4 1950

possible (though nonetheless perilous) the preaching of novel and dissident faiths. The social implications of the new doctrines, moreover, proved oftentimes more radical than the theological.

The strength of Anabaptism lay in precisely this religious borderland. Its beginnings are conventionally associated with the "prophets" of Zwickau, on the German side of the Bohemian boundary, and with the preaching of Balthasar Hübmaier at Waldshut near the northern border of Switzerland. It spread rapidly to southern Germany, to Moravia (whither Hübmaier himself journeyed), then to the north German plain and the Netherlands. And it reached its most notorious climax in the millenarian kingdom at Münster in Westphalia in 1534–35, where communism and polygamy provided the high-water mark of social nonconformity.

In England, too, the religious ferment produced doctrines with radical social corollaries. Before the close of the sixteenth century, conservative English Puritans felt called upon to denounce the radicals in their midst who would "bringe in equalitie amonge all men, and woulde have all things in common and no man to be riche." [2] During the period of the Civil War and the Commonwealth, in the mid-seventeenth century, theological, political, and economic radicalism was made manifest in such religious groups as the Quakers, the Levellers, and the Fifth Monarchy Men, and reached a climax of direct economic action on April 1, 1649, when the followers of Gerrard Winstanley "began to digge, and to take possession of the commons for the poor on George-Hill in Surrey." [3]

Besides giving a stimulus to new ideas, the doctrinal conflict within this great religious frontier generated the most intense of social pressures—ferocious persecution and savage warfare. A century before Luther, the Hussite War had ravaged Bohemia. In Luther's day the Peasants' War spread through Swabia, Franconia, the Palatinate, Thuringia, and Saxony. The Thirty Years' War of the seventeenth century, which ultimately engulfed Europe, commenced in Bohemia and the Palatinate and seared the Rhineland with devastations that did not heal for generations. Finally in the long chronicle of religious strife came the Civil War in England, proving that even that island realm could not escape the armed struggle which religious and social tension had engendered in the ideological borderlands of the Continent.

After a century and a half of terror and suffering, it is no wonder that multitudes of men and women should have lost all hope for a

---

[2] Jo. Fieldus or Fielde, "A Briefe Confession of Faythe" (1572), in *The Seconde Parte of a Register,* ed. by Albert Peel (2 vols., Cambridge [England], 1915), I, 87.

[3] Gerrard Winstanley, *Works, . . . With an Appendix of Documents Relating to the Digger Movement,* ed. by George H. Sabine (Ithaca, N.Y., 1941), p. 392.

gradual reform of existing society, and should have placed their faith in the scriptural promise of new heavens and a new earth, where "they shall not build, and another inhabit; they shall not plant, and another eat: . . . They shall not labour in vain, nor bring forth for trouble." [4] The dawn of a complete new day was their prayer, not a mere sweeping away of the clouds that darkened the old. Even to the eyes of faith, however, there appeared little prospect of such a dawn in the lands prostrated by the wars of religion and by the later aggressions of Louis XIV. Emigration offered one way out, and a steady stream of Germans left the Palatinate and other parts of Germany for provincial Pennsylvania in the late seventeenth and early eighteenth centuries, carrying with them a heritage of religious radicalism, a vivid memory of trouble and injustice, and a profound millennial hope.

It was the experience of migration, in most instances, that caused these social yearnings to crystallize in communitarian form. Migration, after all, was a search for a new and better society, and it involved, in colonial America particularly, the temporary creation of new social institutions. To a certain extent every group settlement possessed some characteristics of a communitarian experiment. Among most migrating groups these communitive tendencies were superficial and fleeting, but among the sectarian immigrants forces of a peculiar kind were at work, strengthening such tendencies to the point where actual communitarian institutions came into being.

To begin with, the sense both of unity and of separateness was far stronger among the sects than among other types of immigrants. Transplantation further intensified this feeling. In leaving home the sect had deliberately detached itself from the larger whole to which it had once belonged, and it could not, even under the best of circumstances, expect immediate assimilation into the new society that surrounded it. In fact, it did not wish such assimilation. Its separation from the world was an article of faith, which was reinforced, not undermined, by opposition and difficulty. Difficulties were of many kinds—economic pressure, religious persecution, and the subtler forms of hostility that are visited upon immigrants of alien culture and foreign tongue. It was characteristic of the sect that its members responded to such pressures as a united group, coalescing rather than dispersing to meet the difficulties in their way.

In the new land, moreover, a process of natural selection began to operate upon the radicalism which the sect brought with it. The separateness of its life prevented it from contributing its social ideas to the general current of political and social agitation in the American colonies. That is to say, its idealism found no outlet in move-

4 Isaiah 65:22–23.

ments for gradual reform. On the other hand, revolutionary programs, to which the sect might once have inclined, became irrelevant in the new situation. The conditions and the authorities against which it might once have revolted belonged to the land it had left, and it possessed neither the motive nor the power to alter by revolution the institutions among which it now found itself. Only communitarianism remained as a distinctive program. The sect that clung with religious fidelity to its ideal of a completely reconstructed society became more positively communitarian in outlook and polity than it had been in Europe.

Before we take up chronologically the development of the sectarian communities in America, it will be well to look more closely at the process by which religious bodies were transformed into communitarian colonies. The histories of the Moravians and the Shakers in America illustrate fully and clearly the forces at work.

The "Renewed Church" of the United Brethren (Unitas Fratrum), otherwise known as the Moravians, dates from 1722, when fugitives from religious persecution in Bohemia and Moravia found refuge on the estate of Count Nicholas Ludwig von Zinzendorf, at Bethelsdorf in Saxony. These fugitives were remnants of the Bohemian Brethren, who, despite almost complete eclipse, had maintained Apostolic Succession from the fifteenth century. Under the pressure of persecution the Brethren on Zinzendorf's estate manifested collectivistic tendencies of two types. Within the community, which they called Herrnhut, they "rapidly developed an exclusive social and economic structure." In addition, their "deep-seated feeling of political and economic insecurity" led them to plant missionary colonies abroad, and they developed collective institutions to make such emigration practicable. "Wherever possible the Church bought land for these missionaries to form settlements. These colonies were societies or communities of missionaries." [5]

In 1741 the Moravians established their most important settlements, at Bethlehem and Nazareth in Northampton County, Pennsylvania. Communitarian tendencies, already manifested at Herrnhut, were intensified by the arrangements the Moravians made during the passage from Europe to America—the so-called "Sea Congregations." In the New World, faced by the difficulties of maintaining themselves and by the dangers of Indian attack, their communism crystallized at Bethlehem into the so-called "General Economy." This was explicitly formulated in 1744, and it lasted until 1762.

[5] Jacob John Sessler, *Communal Pietism among Early American Moravians* (*American Religions Series*, VIII; New York, 1933), pp. 18, 16, 17. For further information on the literature of the communitarian sects discussed in this chapter, see the Bibliographical Essay at the end of the present work.

Each member contributed his time and labor to the General Economy, which gave no wages in return, but provided food, clothing, and shelter for members and their children. Because the church purchased the land and the individual members brought almost nothing with them, there was no actual surrender of private possessions already existing. On the other hand, all the fruits of the members' labor—including the buildings and industries created by them—belonged to the General Economy, that is, to the church. The mingling of social and religious factors so characteristic of all American sectarian communities is brought out clearly in the Moravian experiment. The General Economy, says its most scholarly historian,

was the practical result of exigencies in the new situation; the Brethren bound themselves together for purposes of mutual support, protection against the Indians, missionary endeavors, the preservation of the customs of their Fatherland, and the continuance of their religious practices. Nevertheless there was a definite theological idea behind both the European and the American Moravian communities. After the renewal of the Church, they thought of themselves as a small theocratic republic. . . . Such a theocratic community did not allow extensive intermingling with outsiders. The community was a family of which Christ was the head, and their whole system of worship was built about this theocratic idea. It implied that the community life had to be exclusive.[6]

The communitarian organization of the Moravians had existed, in germ at least, before their migration, and the new American environment served simply to bring it to full fruition. Among the sects generally, however, it was more frequent for communitarian institutions to develop under the pressure of American conditions, without previous foreshadowing in Europe. Such was the case with the Shakers.

The little group of sectarians in mid-eighteenth-century England of whom Ann Lee became the leader appear to have developed no particularly collectivistic institutions in their mother country, and even after their migration to the United States in 1774 they at first found separate employment for themselves. Persecution, however, began; and during the Revolutionary War it was particularly intense because of the recent English origin of the sect.[7] Indeed, the fact that the Shakers, unlike the Moravians and most of the other communitarian sects, were an English-speaking group exposed rather than protected them. Their proselytizing activities were felt—correctly

[6] Sessler, *Communal Pietism*, pp. 86–87.

[7] See Victor H. Paltsits, ed., *Minutes of the Commissioners for Detecting and Defeating Conspiracies in the State of New York: Albany County Sessions, 1778–1781* (3 vols., Albany, 1909), II, 469–71, 504, 589, 592; and Henry C. Blinn, *Life and Gospel Experience of Mother Ann Lee* (East Canterbury, N.H., 1901), pp. 83–90.

enough—to be a greater menace to established denominations than the efforts of foreign-language sects.

Persecution and the hardship of making a living combined with the millennial hopes of the Shakers to impel them forward into a fully communitarian way of life. The forces at work, and the process itself, are revealed so clearly in the early official histories of the sect, that the story may properly be told in the Shakers' own words:

After Mother Ann and her little family arrived in this country, they passed through many scenes of difficulty, of a temporal nature. Being strangers in the land, and without any means of subsistence, excepting the daily labor of their own hands, they were obliged to seek employment where they could find it without hazarding the free enjoyment of their faith. . . .

They were led however, to make some arrangements, in the first place, for their future residence, where they could be united in the mutual enjoyment of their faith, and wait the call of God to more extensive usefulness. Accordingly William Lee and John Hocknell went up the river and contracted for a lot of land near Niskeyuna, in the county of Albany, and returned again to New-York. . . .

Thus, after passing through many trying scenes, Mother Ann and those who stood faithful with her, were collected together, and in the month of September, 1776, took up their residence in the woods of Watervliet, near Niskeyuna, about seven miles north-west of Albany. The place being then in a wilderness state, they began, with indefatigable zeal and industry, and through additional sufferings, to prepare the way for a permanent settlement, where they could enjoy their faith in peace, amid the tumults of the war, in which the country was then involved. . . .

A missionary journey through New England, lasting from 1781 to 1783, was followed by the death of Ann Lee on September 8, 1784. The official narrative continues:

The society being now deprived of the visible presence and protection of Mother Ann, Father James [Whittaker] saw and felt, with many others, the necessity of laboring for an increase of the substance of the gospel among the people, in order to maintain the testimony and protect them from the snares of wickedness which surrounded them, and the flood of opposition which now seemed ready to burst in upon them from every quarter. . . . And all those who had been faithful and honest hearted, being now firmly established in the increasing work of God, were led in their travel to see and feel the necessity of being gathered into a more united body, for the benefit of greater protection, and a further increase of their spiritual travel. . . .

To constitute a true church of Christ, there must necessarily be a union of faith, of motives and of interest, in all the members who compose it. There must be "one body and one bread:" [8] and nothing short of this union in all things, both spiritual and temporal, can constitute a true church, which

[8] 1 Cor. x. 17. [Footnote in original.]

is the body of Christ. And wherever that united body exists, it will bring into operation every individual talent for the general good of the whole body. . . . In this united capacity, the strength of the whole body becomes the strength of each member; and being united in the one Spirit of Christ, they have a greater privilege to serve God than they possibly could have in a separate capacity, and are better able to be mutual helps to each other; and they also find a greater degree of protection from the snares of a selfish and worldly nature. . . .

The first step was to gather the believers into a body, where they could enjoy all things in common, both of a spiritual and temporal kind, and in which their temporal interest could be united together, and be consecrated to religious purposes. . . .

The gathering of the society began at New-Lebanon, in the month of September, 1787, and continued to progress as fast as circumstances and the nature of the work would admit. Elders and deacons were appointed to lead and direct in matters of spiritual and temporal concern; suitable buildings were erected for the accommodation of the members; and order and regularity were, by degrees, established in the society: so that by the year 1792, the Church was considered as established in the principles of her present order and spirit of government. Those who were thus gathered into a united body, were denominated *The Church;* being a collective body of christians separated from the world, and enjoying, in their united capacity, one common interest.[9]

The Moravians and the Shakers illustrate the process that was repeated time after time in America in the seventeenth, eighteenth, and nineteenth centuries. The New World offered hospitality to the peculiar religious doctrines that predisposed a sect to communitarianism. At the same time it confronted such sects with social pressures of one sort or another that transformed these communitive tendencies from potentiality to actuality. The process, often repeated, gradually generated a communitarian tradition.

Chronologically, communitarian history in America began [10] in

[9] [Calvin Green and Seth Y. Wells], *A Summary View of the Millennial Church, or United Society of Believers, (Commonly Called Shakers.) . . . Published by Order of the Ministry, in Union with the Church* (Albany, 1823), pp. 14–16, 23–24, 51–52. The Bibliographical Essay has a section on the extensive literature by and concerning the Shakers; see below, pp. 255–58.

[10] Though sometimes discussed as a communitarian experiment, the settlement of the Pilgrims at Plymouth in 1620 is correctly described as a "common-fund-and-deferred-profit system." Charles M. Andrews, *The Colonial Period of American History: The Settlements,* I (New Haven, 1934), 265, see also pp. 123–26. William Bradford, it is true, regarded its experience as proof of the "vanitie of that conceite of Platos and other ancients, applauded by some of later times; that the taking away of propertie, and bringing in communitie into a comone wealth, would make them happy and florishing; as if they were wiser than God." *History of Plymouth Plantation, 1620–1647* (2 vols., Boston: Massachusetts Historical Society, 1912), I, 301–2. Bradford's reference to the applause of "some of later times" indicates that the Pilgrims were aware of the radical economic doctrines that were abroad in Holland and England, but not that they accepted them. The Jesuit *reducciones*

July 1663 with the arrival at the mouth of the Hoorn Kill, on the South (or Delaware) River, of a party of Dutch Mennonites under the leadership of Pieter Corneliszoon Plockhoy. The colony was the product of an interesting cross-fertilization of ideas between the radical sectarianism of the Low Countries and of England. Plockhoy, a native of Zierikzee, on the island of Schouven in the Netherlands, had gone to England in the latter days of the Protectorate. In 1659, ten years after the uprising of the Diggers under Winstanley, the Netherlander published two pamphlets, the second of which outlined a completely communitarian plan: *A Way Propounded to Make the Poor in These and Other Nations Happy, by Bringing Together a Fit, Suitable and Well Qualified People unto One Houshold-Government, or Little-Common-Wealth.*[11] By 1659, however, the tide in England had turned against such reforms. Back in his native land after the English Restoration, Plockhoy on June 9, 1662, obtained from the Burgomasters and Regents of Amsterdam a contract to establish a colony of Mennonites in New Netherlands.[12] He invited settlers by means of a new pamphlet, *Kort en klaer Ontwerp* (Amsterdam, 1662),[13] and the colony sailed in May 1663. The settlement they established at what is now Lewes, Delaware, enjoyed only a year of peaceful life, however, for in 1664 the English conquered New Netherlands and in the process plundered "what belonged to the Quaking Society of Plockhoy to a very naile." The colony that inaugurated communitarianism in America was obliterated too soon to influence the later history of the movement.

The first communitarian colony that achieved any degree of permanence within the limits of what is now the United States was

---

in Paraguay, founded in the early seventeenth century, did not influence the communitarian movement in what is now the United States and will not be discussed in this study.

[11] The author's name is given on the title page as Peter Cornelius, Van-Zurik-Zee. The original London edition of 1659 has been reprinted by John Downie in his *Peter Cornelius Plockboy [sic], Pioneer of the First Co-operative Commonwealth* (Manchester [England]: Co-operative Union, n.d.).

[12] The contract is printed in translation in E. B. O'Callaghan, ed., *Documents Relative to the Colonial History of the State of New-York* ([1st series], 11 vols., Albany, 1856–61), II, 176–77; see also XII, 429. The quotation concerning the destruction of Plockhoy's colony is from a report of 1684, *ibid.*, III, 346.

[13] In English, *Short and Clear Plan, Serving as a Mutual Arrangement to Lighten the Labor, Unrest, and Difficulty of All Kinds of Handicraftsmen by the Establishment of a Mutual Company or Colony . . . on the South River in New Netherlands.* The pamphlet is summarized and its title page reproduced in facsimile by Samuel Whitaker Pennypacker, "The Settlement of Germantown, Pennsylvania," Pennsylvania-German Society, *Proceedings and Addresses*, IX (1898), 229–63, whose account of Plockhoy leans heavily upon the earlier study by H. P. G. Quack, incorporated in his *De Socialisten: Personen en Stelsels* (3. Druk, 6 vols., Amsterdam, 1899–1901), I, 185–207.

established a score of years later. Its members came from the same center of religious and social radicalism as did Plockhoy—that is, the Netherlands and the adjoining lands of northwestern Germany. They were followers of Jean de Labadie, preacher of a mystical Protestantism, whose labors, begun at Geneva, were most extensive in the Netherlands. At Amsterdam about 1668 Labadie first developed his communitarian doctrines, and these were practised not only in that place, but in several subsequent communities of Labadists, such as those at Altona near Hamburg (where Labadie himself died in 1674), and at Wieuwerd in Friesland, in the Netherlands. From the latter place two emissaries were sent to America in 1679 to obtain land for a branch of the society, and in 1683 this project eventuated in a communitarian settlement of Labadists at Bohemia Manor on Chesapeake Bay, in what is now Cecil County, Maryland.[14]

The Labadist colony was authoritarian in its organization, and was closely enough connected with its parent community at Wieuwerd to share its declining fortunes. By 1698 a division within the group at Bohemia Manor foretold the end, though this was some years in coming. The dissolution of the Labadist experiment marked the end of Dutch and north German influence upon American communitism. The later waves of communitarian migration to America had their sources in southern and eastern Germany. As time went on, moreover, the sects were less closely connected with existing organizations in Europe, and their communitarian institutions were more definitely the product of American conditions.

A decade after the Labadists, a sectarian group from Wurtemberg and neighboring states set out for America under the leadership of Johann Jacob Zimmermann, a native of Vaihingen near Stuttgart and a teacher at the universities of Tübingen and Heidelberg. Leadership passed, after Zimmermann's death on the eve of departure, to Johann Kelpius, from the University of Altdorf in Bavaria, who had become acquainted with Zimmermann in Nürnberg. The newcomers first visited the Labadists at Bohemia Manor, but soon went on to Pennsylvania, where Quakerism seemed to possess something in common [15] with their own mystical doctrines, derived from the Rosicrucians and from Jacob Böhme. Settling in Germantown,

---

[14] The standard monograph is Bartlett B. James, *The Labadist Colony in Maryland* (Johns Hopkins University *Studies in Historical and Political Science*, vol. XVII, no. 6; Baltimore, 1899), whose author later re-edited the principal source relating to the preliminary Labadist expedition to spy out the land, *Journal of Jasper Danckaerts, 1679–1680*, ed. by B. B. James and J. Franklin Jameson (*Original Narratives of Early American History*; New York, 1913).

[15] On this point see Oswald Seidensticker, "William Penn's Travels in Holland and Germany in 1677," *Pennsylvania Magazine of History and Biography*, II (1878), 246–47.

Pennsylvania, Kelpius founded in 1694 a community, usually called the Society of the Woman in the Wilderness, on a ridge of land overlooking Wissahickon Creek, within the present boundaries of Fairmount Park. The community hardly survived the death of Kelpius in 1708, but its mystical ideas permeated other sects, and it had its own communitarian offshoots, such as Irenia, or the True Church of Philadelphia or Brotherly Love, founded by Henry Bernhard Köster at near-by Plymouth about 1697.[16]

The first community to enjoy a significant span of life was that at Ephrata, Pennsylvania, founded in 1732 by Johann Conrad Beissel. The founder was born at Eberbach in the Palatinate, a short distance above Heidelberg, on the Neckar. During young manhood he lived in various parts of southern Germany, including Heidelberg itself. He was deeply imbued with the Pietism of the region, and he seems to have had some contact with several of the sects that had betrayed, or were later to reveal, communitarian tendencies: with the Inspirationists, who founded the nineteenth-century community of Amana in the United States, with the disciples of Jacob Böhme, among whom the founders of the Woman in the Wilderness had been numbered, with the Anabaptists, perhaps even with the Labadists.

Migrating to America in 1720, Beissel became acquainted with the dwindling remnant of the Society of the Woman in the Wilderness, and apparently visited the Labadist community in Maryland.[17] The ascetic life which Beissel preached and lived in America culminated in 1732 in his withdrawal to the banks of the Cocalico Creek in Lancaster County, where in the succeeding years his followers gathered about him in the community which they called Ephrata. Its austerity of life—manifest even today in the buildings that have survived—caused Ephrata to be referred to as the Cloister, and its fame to reach even the pages of Voltaire's *Dictionnaire philosophique*.[18]

As settlement pushed farther west in Pennsylvania, across the

16 See Julius F. Sachse, *The German Pietists of Provincial Pennsylvania, 1694–1708* (Philadelphia, 1895), *passim;* and S. W. Pennypacker, "The Settlement of Germantown," *op. cit.*, pp. 264–85. Two important manuscripts, dealing principally with Kelpius' voyage to America, have been published: Oswald Seidensticker, translator and ed., "The Hermits of the Wissahickon," *Pennsylvania Magazine of History*, XI (1887), 427–41; and *The Diarium of Magister Johannes Kelpius*, translated and ed. by J. F. Sachse (Pennsylvania-German Society, *Proceedings and Addresses*, XXV [for 1914]; Lancaster, Pa., 1917). For additional references see Emil Meynen, compiler, *Bibliography on German Settlement in Colonial North America* (Leipzig, 1937), p. 90.

17 See Walter C. Klein, *Johann Conrad Beissel, Mystic and Martinet, 1690–1768* (Philadelphia, 1942), pp. 15, 20–33, 40–43. See also the section on Ephrata in the Bibliographical Essay.

18 Article "Église," in Voltaire, *Oeuvres complètes*, XVIII (Paris, 1878), 501.

Susquehanna and into the Cumberland Valley, converts were made by these German Seventh Day Baptists. One special group, along the East Branch of the Little Antietam Creek near what is now Waynesboro, Franklin County, Pennsylvania, came under the wing of Ephrata, from whom a pastor was sent to them. Toward the end of the eighteenth century these sectarians gathered into a community similar to Ephrata. From the donor of the land, Andreas Schneeberger, it derived its name, the Seventh Day Baptist Church at Snow Hill, or, more commonly, the Snow Hill Nunnery.[19]

Expansionist forces in the Ephrata Community were feeble, however, as compared with the missionary ardor that imbued the Moravians. The migration of the Unitas Fratrum was part of a general dispersion from Europe which, between 1732 and 1736, carried the Moravians not only to North America, but also to the West Indies and South America, to Greenland, and to South Africa. Their zeal to convert the Indians was in marked contrast with the apathy of most Protestant denominations, and the small band of Moravian missionaries played a role not unlike that of the Jesuits in penetrating the Indian frontier of the eighteenth century. The immediate result of their expansionist ardor was the widest diffusion that communitarian ideas had yet enjoyed.

In 1736, only four years after Beissel took up his abode at Ephrata, the Moravians worked out their first communitarian arrangements in America in their settlement on the Savannah River in Georgia.[20] They established their permanent community at Bethlehem, Pennsylvania, in 1741, and by the end of 1744 had elaborated the General Economy already described. This was promptly duplicated, not only at Nazareth, Pennsylvania, in 1744, but at the later settlements at Wachovia in North Carolina in 1753, and at Lititz in Lancaster County, Pennsylvania, in 1754. Though the General Economy was dissolved in 1762, it had spread over a wider area than any previous communitarian enterprise in America.[21]

The foreign-language sects lived a life apart. Their communitarianism, indeed, was partly designed to secure isolation from contacts that might dilute and weaken the religious zeal that had brought

[19] See J. F. Sachse, *The German Sectarians of Pennsylvania*, vol. II, *1742–1800* (Philadelphia, 1900), pp. 360–71; and Anonymous, *History of Franklin County, Pennsylvania* (Chicago, 1887), pp. 535, 614. The date of beginning is somewhat vague. A large stone house was built as early as 1793, but a later structure of 1814 is described by Sachse as "the first community house." P. 366.

[20] See Fries, *Moravians in Georgia*, pp. 135–37. In the same year, 1736, a group of Moravians visited Ephrata. Corliss F. Randolph, "The German Seventh-Day Baptists," in Seventh Day Baptist General Conference, *Seventh Day Baptists in Europe and America* (2 vols., Plainfield, N.J., 1910), II, 1009, 1031, 1036.

[21] See Sessler, *Communal Pietism among Early American Moravians*, pp. 17, 19, 20, 72–85, 186–87, 193–98.

them to America. Community life acted to preserve the mother tongue, and that too was useful in safeguarding the linguistic foundations of the faith. The barrier of language, however, affected not only incoming influences, but outgoing ones as well. Though the sectarian communities might eventually win the favorable opinion of their neighbors through the earnestness of their faith and the prosperousness of their affairs, their influence upon the life and thought of the American people in the eighteenth century was inconsiderable.

Only with the Shakers did communitarianism make a real impact upon American opinion at large. From the time of their coming in 1774, no barrier of language separated these English sectarians from their new neighbors. Persecution was quickly visited upon Mother Ann Lee and her followers, but this was at least a positive reaction, indicating (as indifference would never have done) that the new sect was making its impression. The missionary journey that Ann Lee and the elders of her church made through Massachusetts and Connecticut in the years 1781–83 was a momentous event in the history of communitarianism. American converts quickly outnumbered the original immigrants, for the first time in the history of such sects. The groups of believers that were won to the new faith in the various towns of New England therefore constituted the very first communitarian colonies of native-born, English-speaking Americans. Americanization of the Shaker sect proceeded rapidly. After Ann Lee's death in 1784, she was succeeded as head of the sect by James Whittaker, one of her original English followers. But when he died in 1787, leadership passed permanently into American hands, control being shared by Joseph Meacham and Lucy Wright, natives of Enfield, Connecticut, and Pittsfield, Massachusetts, respectively.[22] In less than fifteen years a small revivalistic band of dissenters in Manchester, England, had transferred their activities to the New World and had become a fully Americanized and growing sect.

The evolution, already described, of communitarian institutions within the sect paralleled its transformation into an American body. The first organization of the Shakers upon a fully communistic basis was effected at Mount Lebanon, or New Lebanon, in Columbia County, New York, in 1787. This community accordingly became, in Shaker phraseology, the "Mother-Church" or "the center of union to all the other societies." [23] The original settlement, however, had been at Niskeyuna or Watervliet, in Albany County, and the members there were gathered in "gospel order" the next year. The con-

[22] See *Testimonies of the Life, Character, Revelations and Doctrines of Mother Ann Lee, and the Elders with Her,* . . . *Collected from Living Witnesses, in Union with the Church* (2d ed., Albany, 1888), pp. 64–144; Youngs, *Testimony of Christ's Second Appearing* (4th ed., Albany, 1856), pp. 628–29.

[23] Green and Wells, *Summary View of the Millennial Church* (1823), pp. 68, 60.

verts scattered throughout New England were prompt to adopt the new communitarian pattern from Mount Lebanon, and nine additional communities were formed in the early 1790's. Two were just across the state line from Mount Lebanon, at Hancock and Tyringham, Massachusetts. One was in the Connecticut Valley at Enfield, Connecticut. Two others were in eastern Massachusetts, some thirty miles from Boston, at Harvard and Shirley. Another two were in New Hampshire, at Canterbury not far from Concord, and at Enfield near Dartmouth College. A final group were in the District of Maine. Two of these, at Alfred and at Sabbathday Lake or New Gloucester, were enduring; [24] the third, at Gorham, was quickly merged into the others.[25]

The Second Great Awakening, which got under way at the turn of the century, offered the Shakers an opportunity in the west, of which they quickly took advantage. Hearing of the great revival in Kentucky, the church at Mount Lebanon sent three missionaries to Kentucky and Ohio in 1805. Their preaching bore fruit in the founding of five new communities before the end of the decade. The first two were in Ohio, at Union Village in Warren County, some thirty miles from Cincinnati, and at Watervliet near Dayton. Two others were in Kentucky, at South Union or Gasper Springs in Logan County, and at Pleasant Hill, seven miles east of Harrodsburg. The farthest west which Shaker settlement reached was Indiana, where the community called West Union was established on Busseron Creek near the Wabash, sixteen miles above Vincennes.[26]

The last wave of expansion began in 1817, with the founding of a short-lived village at Savoy, Massachusetts.[27] The new enthusiasm lasted at least a decade. During this time two more communities were founded in Ohio, at North Union in what is now the Shaker Heights suburb of Cleveland, and at Whitewater in Hamilton County, a score of miles from Cincinnati. One more was founded in New York, locating first at Sodus Bay on Lake Ontario, and migrating ten years later to Groveland or Sonyea in near-by Livingston County.[28] No other expansion in the number of Shaker communities occurred

24 These were the eleven earliest communities as listed in the first official Shaker histories: Youngs, *Testimony of Christ's Second Appearing* (2d ed., Albany, 1810), p. 509; and Green and Wells, *Summary View of the Millennial Church* (1823), pp. 68–69. For the exact location and date of founding of the various communities, see the Checklist of Communitarian Experiments, constituting the appendix to the present work.

25 Anna White and Leila S. Taylor, *Shakerism: Its Meaning and Message* (Columbus, O., 1904), p. 95. Because the merger had already occurred, the Gorham community was not listed in the works cited in the preceding footnote.

26 Green and Wells, *Summary View of the Millennial Church* (1823), p. 75.

27 *Ibid.*, pp. 137–38.

28 *Ibid.* (2d ed., Albany, 1848), p. 84 n.

thereafter, except for the establishment of branches in Georgia and Florida in the 1880's and 1890's.[29]

In carrying communitarian ideas to the American people generally, the Shakers were more influential than all their sectarian predecessors combined. The establishment of their first full-fledged community in 1787 made that date as memorable in the microcosmic history of communitarianism as it is in the broader annals of the republic. In view of the regularity with which they organized the institutions of communitive life and set them forth in writing, and in view of the skill with which they provided for the westward expansion of those institutions, it is perhaps not too far-fetched to say that they were the makers of both the Constitution and the Northwest Ordinance of the communitarian movement.

The rapid expansion of the Shakers is not attributable solely to their own exertion. The scattered communitarian efforts of more than a century had at last begun to show a cumulative effect. By the final quarter of the eighteenth century small groups of native-born Americans were revealing the influence of such ideas. Contemporary with the rise of the Shakers was the development of certain other communitarian sects in America, significant not because of their numbers, but because they revealed a native communitarian tradition struggling into existence.

Most famous of these enterprises was the community of Jerusalem, which the prophetess Jemima Wilkinson, self-styled "Public Universal Friend," established in what is now Yates County in central New York in 1788, a year after the Shakers finally adopted communism farther to the east. Possessed of a Quaker background, Jemima Wilkinson was influenced by the New-Light Baptists in 1774,[30] but probably not directly by the newly arrived Shakers. Her

[29] On the White Oak colony in Camden County, Ga., see Alexander Kent, "Cooperative Communities in the United States," *Bulletin of the Department of Labor*, vol. VI, no. 35, p. 565 (July 1901); Federal Writers' Project, *Georgia: A Guide to Its Towns and Countryside (American Guide Series;* Athens, Ga., 1940), p. 289; and White and Taylor, *Shakerism*, pp. 213–14. On the colony at Narcoossee, Osceola County, Fla., see *The Manifesto, Published by the Shakers*, XXVII, 92, 141 (June, Sept., 1897), which precisely dates the founding as 1894.

[30] See David Hudson, *History of Jemima Wilkinson, a Preacheress of the Eighteenth Century* (Geneva, N.Y., 1821), p. 15. Robert P. St. John discusses Jemima Wilkinson and Ann Lee as manifestations of the same contemporary religious enthusiasm, but does not cite any direct connections between them. See his "Jemima Wilkinson," New York State Historical Association, *Proceedings*, XXVIII, 158–75 (April 1930), especially pp. 158–60. St. John provides an extensive bibliography with critical evaluations, thus making further discussion of the printed sources unnecessary here. Manuscripts in private hands are noted by him, and also in *Journal of American History*, IX, 263 (April–June 1915). In addition, a large collection has recently been acquired by the Collection of Regional History at Cornell University. See *Mississippi Valley Historical Review*, XXXIII, 519 (Dec. 1946).

career in New England and in Philadelphia had given her a notoriety that brought distinguished visitors to her community, among them the Duke of La Rochefoucauld-Liancourt, who described both her and the Shakers.[31]

No such glare of publicity surrounded the other communitarian groups—likewise with New England antecedents—who were her contemporaries, but whose histories are exceedingly obscure. Earliest were the Dorrilites, who in 1797 and 1798 adopted communitarian institutions in adjoining neighborhoods on either side of the Massachusetts-Vermont line.[32] Half a dozen years later a shoemaker named William Bullard led a group of Vermonters across the boundary into New York State, where from 1804 until 1810 they lived in a co-operative colony called "The Union," at Clark's Crossing, two miles north of Potsdam, between that town and Norwood.[33] In the next decade another Bullard, with the given name of Isaac, captained a group of so-called Pilgrims, who wandered into Vermont from Lower Canada, lived a life of theocratic communism for a time about 1817 at South Woodstock, and then started on farther journeyings that brought them into contact with the Shakers and took them eventually beyond the Mississippi.

More important than the spontaneous formation of these short-lived groups in the eastern states was the spread of communitarianism into the expanding west. Contemporary with the success of the Shakers in Kentucky in 1805 was the first crossing of the Appalachians by a German communitarian sect. This was the Harmony Society,

---

According to *New York History*, XXII, 248 (April 1941), a book on Jemima Wilkinson is being written by Mrs. Walter A. Henricks and Arnold J. Potter, who jointly contributed an article to the same journal, "The Universal Friend: Jemima Wilkinson," XXIII, 159–65 (April 1942).

[31] François Alexandre Frédéric, Duc de La Rochefoucauld-Liancourt, *Travels through the United States of North America . . . in the Years 1795, 1796, and 1797* (2 vols., London, 1799), I, 110–18, 389–94.

[32] The Dorrilites and the Pilgrims (discussed below) are described by Zadock Thompson, *History of Vermont, Natural, Civil and Statistical* (Burlington, 1853), II, 202–4; and by David M. Ludlum, *Social Ferment in Vermont, 1791–1850 (Columbia Studies in American Culture*, V; New York, 1939), pp. 239–40, 242–44. To the contemporary references on the Pilgrims cited by Ludlum should be added: Thomas Nuttall, *Journal of Travels into the Arkansa Territory during the Year 1819* (1821), as reprinted in Reuben Gold Thwaites, ed., *Early Western Travels, 1748–1846* (32 vols., Cleveland, 1904–7), XIII, 294–95; and Timothy Flint, *Recollections of the Last Ten Years, Passed in Occasional Residences and Journeyings in the Valley of the Mississippi* (Boston, 1826), pp. 275–80. Flint's is the most comprehensive account, and mentions the Pilgrims' relations with the Shakers.

[33] Richard C. Ellsworth, "Northern New York's Early Co-operative Union," New York State Historical Association, *Proceedings*, XXVII, 328–32 (Oct. 1929). The buildings are reported to be still standing. See *Watertown Daily Times*, Sept. 13, 1934.

which had migrated from southern Germany under the leadership of Father George Rapp, a Wurtemberger, and which settled in 1805 at Harmony in Beaver County, Pennsylvania, at the head of the Ohio Valley. The westward impulse that had carried them so far soon carried them farther, and in 1814 they established a new community of Harmonie on the banks of the Wabash in Posey County, Indiana. But the impulse had overshot its mark. Though successful in Indiana, the Rappites felt they had been unwise in venturing so far. In 1824–25, accordingly, they sold their property to Robert Owen, thus coming into direct contact with the opening phases of secular communitarianism in America. Their final migration to Economy, Pennsylvania, took them back to within fifteen miles of their original home, but at a more strategic location on the banks of the Ohio River, some eighteen miles below Pittsburgh. So located, their communal life attracted the notice—and sometimes influenced the opinions—of numerous westward-moving settlers, foreign travelers, and native-born social theorists. So well known did the Rappites become that as early as 1824 Byron was satirizing them in *Don Juan*.[34]

But fame brought misfortune also. Rival communitarian leaders, as well as travelers and poets, learned of the prosperous community at Economy. The second-adventist beliefs of the Rappites made them hospitable to a certain Bernhard Mueller, who, calling himself Count Leon, proclaimed that he was divinely sent to usher in the millennium. Coming direct from Germany, he wintered at Economy in 1831–32 and won many of the Harmonists to his leadership. Internal dissension came to a head in the spring of 1832, and 176 members of Economy went with Count Leon to found a schismatic community, which they called the New Philadelphia Society, at Phillipsburg (now Monaca), Pennsylvania, some ten miles downstream from Economy on the Ohio River. Though the original Harmony Society was forced to turn over a substantial part of its assets to the seceders, the success of the new colony was not thereby assured. In September 1833, Count Leon and his followers voyaged down the Ohio and Mississippi rivers, and in 1834 founded a new communitarian settlement at Grand Ecore in Natchitoches Parish, Louisiana. Two years later, after Count Leon's death, the community moved sixty-five miles north to Germantown in the same state.[35]

[34] Canto 15, stanzas 35–36. Among the travelers before 1840 who described the Rappites at Economy were Karl Bernhard, Duke of Saxe-Weimar-Eisenach (in 1825–26), Mrs. Basil Hall (1828), Charles Augustus Murray (1834–36), Harriet Martineau (1834–36), and James Silk Buckingham (1836–41). Titles and page references are given in other footnotes, which may be located through the Index. See also the Bibliographical Essay.

[35] See Karl J. R. Arndt, "The Genesis of Germantown, Louisiana: or The Mysterious Past of Louisiana's Mystic, Count de Leon," *Louisiana Historical Quarterly,*

By this time the westward movement was in full swing. A dozen years after the coming of the Rappites, a second group from Wurtemberg carried their sectarian ideas beyond the mountains. Under the leadership of Joseph Bäumler (who later anglicized his name to Bimeler), this group purchased land in Tuscarawas County, Ohio, in 1817. Two years later they organized themselves on a communistic basis as the Society of Separatists of Zoar. It was the members, rather than the leader, who, after a brief experience of American conditions, insisted upon community of property rather than a division of the lands as originally intended. In this decision equalitarian religious doctrines played a conspicuous part.[36]

Thus for a century and a half, from Plockhoy to Bimeler, the communitive movement developed in America under exclusively sectarian auspices. That the idea might eventually appeal to nonreligious, or at least nonsectarian, reformers was indicated by two enterprises that were projected in the eighteenth century but failed of realization.

The first was sponsored by a well-educated immigrant from Saxony named Christian Priber, who about 1736 went among the Cherokees in the southern Appalachians, learned their language, protected them from white exploitation, and finally planned a completely communistic society which he called "Paradise." Priber's plan had its roots in the ideas of Plato and More, not in religious sectarianism. In 1743 Priber, accused by British colonial authorities of aiding the French, was arrested and thrown into prison, where he died, his project unrealized.[37]

The humanitarian impulse of the Enlightenment did not exhaust itself with Priber. Half a century later other plans for emigrant colonies were in the air. In 1788, for example, J. P. Brissot de Warville, future leader of the Girondists in the French Revolution, visited America, in part to find a site for a model republic that M. Clavière was advocating. When Joseph Priestley, the English scientist, moved to Northumberland at the forks of the Susquehanna in Penn-

---

XXIV, 378–433 (April 1941); and *idem*, "The Life and Mission of Count Leon," *American-German Review*, vol. VI, no. 5, pp. 5–8, 36–37; no. 6, pp. 15–19 (June, Aug. 1940). Based on Louisiana records, these articles present a more favorable view of Count Leon than the narratives written from Rappite sources, which treat him, naturally enough, as a complete impostor. See Aaron Williams, *The Harmony Society at Economy, Penn'a. Founded by George Rapp* (Pittsburgh, 1866), pp. 72–81, 131–37; Bole, *Harmony Society*, pp. 124–26; and Duss, *The Harmonists*, pp. 79–90.

[36] George B. Landis, "Separatists of Zoar," American Historical Association, *Annual Report, 1898*, p. 174. See also the Bibliographical Essay.

[37] See Verner W. Crane, "A Lost Utopia of the First American Frontier," *Sewanee Review*, XXVII, 48–61 (Jan. 1919), and the same author's sketch of Priber in *Dictionary of American Biography* (20 vols., New York, 1928–36), XV, 210, where the principal sources are listed.

sylvania in 1794, it was with the hope of establishing there, in conjunction with Thomas Cooper, "a large settlement for the friends of liberty." Neither project was strictly communitarian, but together they influenced a proposal that was: the plan for a so-called "Pantisocracy," which Samuel Taylor Coleridge, Robert Southey, and others discussed in 1794. In Coleridge's words, "a small but liberalized party have formed a scheme of emigration on the principles of an abolition of individual property." The site chosen was on the Susquehanna, near Cooper and Priestley, but the plan fell through before any substantial steps had been taken.[38]

Though the nonsectarian plans of Priber and of Southey and Coleridge came to nought, the way was being prepared for purely secular forms of communitarian experiment. These reached the stage of actuality in 1825 when Robert Owen established his New Harmony Community in the old village of the Rappites on the Wabash River in southern Indiana. The date was epochal, for with Owen the communitarian movement in America came at last to stand on its own feet as an independent system of social thought, not a mere corollary of theological doctrine. Owen's accomplishment depended on the contributions that the sectarian communities had been making through more than a century and a half of effort. It depended, also, upon a transformation that was occurring during the early part of the nineteenth century in the thought of the sects themselves. This was the gradual secularization of the communitarian ideal among the very groups that had originally deduced it from religious postulates.

[38] The principal source materials bearing upon Pantisocracy are in the published correspondence of Coleridge and Southey; and the project is described in virtually all their biographies. Three recent articles describe the scheme and investigate its relationship to earlier plans of migration, such as those of Brissot, Cooper, and Priestley: Maurice W. Kelley, "Thomas Cooper and Pantisocracy," *Modern Language Notes*, XLV, 218–20 (April 1930); Sister Eugenia, "Coleridge's Scheme of Pantisocracy and American Travel Accounts," *Publications of the Modern Language Association of America*, XLV, 1069–84 (Dec. 1930); J. R. MacGillivray, "The Pantisocracy Scheme and Its Immediate Background," in Malcolm W. Wallace, ed., *Studies in English by Members of University College, Toronto* (Toronto, 1931), pp. 131–69. The statements of Priestley and Coleridge are quoted from MacGillivray, pp. 154, 165.

Chapter III

TRANSMITTING THE COMMUNITARIAN TRADITION TO THE NINETEENTH CENTURY

In America, and America alone, the religious socialism of the seventeenth century evolved without break into the secular socialism of the nineteenth. The communitarian sects were the links in this chain of continuity. The inspiration they drew from the Reformation and the Christian tradition in general, they passed on as a living force to the nineteenth-century leaders of social reform in the United States.

In Europe, by contrast, there was a definite hiatus. The rationalism of the eighteenth-century Enlightenment constituted a complete interruption, and the reactionary role played by the established churches engendered a far more militant anticlericalism among European reformers than among American. As a result, no genuinely formative intellectual relationship can be traced in Europe between the religious reformers of the earlier period and the outspokenly secular founders of modern socialism.

Thus, Charles Fourier called the Quakers and Anabaptists "political abortions,"[1] and regarded religious innovation in general as a source of discord to be charmed away by promises of quadrupled income.[2] Robert Owen discovered the communitive ideas of the seventeenth-century English sects only after he had formulated his own proposals.[3] Karl Marx's omnivorous reading included virtually nothing on the history of religious movements.[4] His colleague, Friedrich Engels, ridiculed the "very absurd and irrational opinions" of the communitarian sects, and remarked that if communism could

[1] Fourier, *Quatre Mouvements* (1808), 283 n.

[2] See Fourier, *La Fausse Industrie* (2 vols., Paris, 1835–36), II, 457–6 [*sic*]. In these erratically paged volumes, this is the sixth of a group of pages that follow p. 820, but bear the numbers 457–*1*, 457–*2*, etc.

[3] Francis Place first called Owen's attention to John Bellers' *Proposals for Raising a Colledge of Industry* (London, 1696), remarking, "I have made a great discovery—of a work advocating your social views a century and a half ago." Owen, *Life . . . Written by Himself*, I, 240. Owen reprinted the pamphlet in his *New View of Society: Tracts Relative to This Subject* (London, 1818), and in his *Life*, I.A, 155–81.

[4] See the elaborate index to books mentioned in the correspondence between Marx and Engels from 1844 to 1883. *Marx-Engels Gesamtausgabe*, III. Abteilung, IV, 593–612.

be successfully practised by them, "how much sooner must it be feasible for others who are free from such insanities." [5] Even the Christian Socialists owed little to the older radical sectarians,[6] however freely they might draw upon the same ultimate gospel sources. At the very end of the nineteenth century, it is true, socialist historians began to eye the sectarian reformers of the sixteenth and seventeenth centuries with approval and to claim them as forebears.[7] But this was too belated a gesture to be taken seriously as evidence of intellectual indebtedness, however useful it might be to the European movement in furnishing a coat of arms and a family tree.

In the United States, however, the older religious socialism retained its vitality throughout most of the nineteenth century. It existed side by side with, and influenced the development of, the newer nonreligious varieties of socialist thought. In point of fact, the communitarian tradition of the sects was not superseded but only secularized. Consequently in America religious radicalism played a real part in creating modern socialism. The communitive sects not only provided continuity with the religious past, they also participated in the process of secularization. For these reasons they occupy a unique place in the intellectual history, not merely of the United States, but of the modern world as a whole.

By the end of the first quarter of the nineteenth century the sects had accomplished their pioneer task. Continuing interrelations had drawn together the apparently scattered efforts of the Germans into a more or less unified tradition. That tradition had been translated into American terms by the Shakers. Under the leadership of both groups the new west had been invaded. And older regions had felt the influence of the movement sufficiently to produce native communitarian sects of their own.

[5] Engels, "Beschreibung der in neueren Zeit entstandenen und noch bestehenden kommunistischen Ansiedlungen," *Deutsches Bürgerbuch für 1845*, reprinted in *Marx-Engels Gesamtausgabe*, I. Abt., IV, 352.

[6] Fairly conclusive on this point is the silence of Charles E. Raven, *Christian Socialism, 1848–1854* (London, 1920), and James Dombrowski, *The Early Days of Christian Socialism in America* (New York, 1936).

[7] This interpretation was first presented on a comprehensive scale in the collective work edited by Eduard Bernstein and Karl Kautsky, *Die Geschichte des Socialismus in Einzeldarstellungen* (3 vols. [numbered I and III, the former being in 2 parts], Stuttgart, 1895–98), sections of which have been published in translation as separate works: Kautsky, *Communism in Central Europe in the Time of the Reformation* (London, 1897), and Bernstein, *Cromwell & Communism* (London, 1930). The same approach characterizes the subsequent writings of E. Belfort Bax and Max Beer, and, most recently, David W. Petegorsky, *Left-Wing Democracy in the English Civil War* (London, 1940). For a scholarly criticism of this type of interpretation, see Winthrop S. Hudson, "Economic and Social Thought of Gerrard Winstanley—Was He a Seventeenth Century Marxist?" *Journal of Modern History*, XVIII, 1–21 (March 1946).

This success was accompanied by a subtle but important change of emphasis. In 1825, when the followers of Father Rapp established the third of their villages, they called it not Harmony, as on both previous occasions, but Economy.[8] The choice of name was symbolic of what was happening in most of the religious communities. The economic and social implications of their way of life were thrusting theological concepts into the background, and the colonists were beginning to think of themselves as communitarians first and sectarians afterwards. This reversal of emphasis is clearly evident in the literature of the Shakers.

The first substantial work expounding Shaker principles, *The Testimony of Christ's Second Appearing,* often referred to as the "Shaker Bible," was published in 1808. Its introduction was pure theology, opening with the statement: "Whatever degree of natural wisdom may be attained by those who are without Christ . . . , the only true saving knowledge of God . . . is by and through the revelation of Jesus Christ." Not until the seventh of the eight parts into which the work was divided did the authors embark upon a description of their Church Covenant, by which "the whole body of Believers was placed in distinct societies or communities" and "possessed all things jointly." [9]

Fifteen years later, in 1823, the Shakers issued *A Summary View of the Millennial Church.* Beginning with history rather than theology, the authors reached the subject of Shaker communism at the opening of the second main division of their seven-part book.[10] And after another quarter-century had elapsed, the Shakers were ready to give their social and economic arrangements absolute priority in the literature they prepared for outsiders. When a second edition of *A Summary View* was called for in 1848, it was prefaced by a new section entitled "Introductory Remarks: Comprising a Short Review of the Formation of Associations and Communities," which began:

The present age of the world is an age of wonders. The most extraordinary changes, revolutions and remarkable events are rapidly rolling on, through the physical, political, moral and religious world, that were ever known on earth. . . . But among all the hopeful expectations, labors and desires of mankind, in the present age, none appear more evident than those which lead to the formation of associations in which all the members can

---

[8] Looking back upon the alteration in name, one of the later members felt that it had indicated "a slight but fundamental shifting in the subconscious ideals of the Society." Duss, *The Harmonists* (1943), p. 64.

[9] Youngs, *Testimony of Christ's Second Appearing* (2d ed., Albany, 1810), pp. xxi, 509.

[10] Green and Wells, *Summary View of the Millennial Church* (1823), Part II, chap. I, "Formation of the Society into a United Body, Possessing a Consecrated Interest," pp. 51–58.

enjoy equal rights and privileges, physical and moral, both of a spiritual and temporal nature, in a united capacity. . . . The great inequality of rights and privileges which prevails so extensively throughout the world, is a striking evidence of the importance of a reformation of some kind. . . .

During the present century, many attempts have been made to form associations upon the plan of a community of interest, in various parts of Europe and in the United States of America. Many societies have been formed in part or wholly upon this plan. But it is well known that with all their wisdom, skill, benevolent designs, unity of intention, convenience of location and confidence of success, they have soon failed in their expectations, and been scattered as before. . . .

But notwithstanding these general failures, we are prepared to show that there is a sure system, founded upon the principles of a unity of interest in all things, which has stood the test a sufficient length of time, to prove that it can be attained and supported. . . .

The United Society of Believers (called Shakers) was founded upon the principles of equal rights and privileges, with a united interest in all things, both spiritual and temporal, and has been maintained and supported in this Society, at New-Lebanon, about sixty years, without the least appearance of any failure. Is not this proof sufficient in favor of such a system? [11]

As the Shakers gradually shifted their emphasis from theology to social reform in the forty years between 1808 and 1848, public interest in them became more widespread and more sympathetic. As might be expected, the earliest response they had evoked had been a hostile one. During the Revolutionary period, anti-British feeling had been capitalized by Valentine Rathbun in *A Brief Account of a Religious Scheme Taught and Propagated by a Number of Europeans . . . Commonly Called Shaking Quakers. . . . The Whole Being a Discovery of the Wicked Machinations of the Principal Enemies of America* (Boston, 1781). The same mood prevailed west of the Appalachians thirty years later when James Smith published *Shakerism Detected: Their Erroneous and Treasonous Proceedings, and False Publications . . . Exposed to Public View* (Paris, Kentucky, 1810). Anti-Shaker propaganda also took the form of personal narratives, such as *A Brief Statement of the Sufferings of Mary Dyer, Occasioned by the Society Called Shakers, Written by Herself* (Boston, 1818).[12]

[11] Green and Wells, *Summary View of the Millennial Church* (2d ed., Albany, 1848), pp. 1–3. The substitution of a social for a theological emphasis permanently affected Shaker propaganda, as is shown by the titles of later nineteenth-century publications by their leading elder, Frederick William Evans, such as: *Shaker Communism* (London, 1871), *Shaker Reconstruction of the American Government* (Hudson [N.Y.], 1888), *Capital and Labor* (Mt. Lebanon [ca. 1890]), and *A Shaker on Political and Social Reform* (Mt. Lebanon, n.d.). See also Daniel Fraser, *Analysis of Human Society, Declaring the Law Which Creates and Sustains a Community Having Goods in Common* (Mt. Lebanon [ca. 1890]).

[12] Mary M. Dyer became Mrs. Marshall, but continued her attacks as late as 1847, when she published *The Rise and Progress of the Serpent from the Garden*

This flood of vituperation even led the New York legislature to consider hostile measures against the Shakers—a move which Thomas Jefferson denounced in 1817 as threatening to "carry us back to the times of the darkest bigotry and barbarism." [13]

Before long, however, unreasoning opposition began to be supplanted by intelligent curiosity. Scholars were in the van of those who about 1820 began to give serious attention to the social institutions of the Shakers. Representatives of Yale were first, despite the religious conservatism of that institution. President Timothy Dwight had observed the Shakers as early as 1799. He returned several times to their villages, read books by and about them, and in his *Travels in New-England and New-York,* published posthumously in 1821 and 1822, devoted a score of pages to them—critical, of course, but well-informed and never scurrilous. Benjamin Silliman, professor of chemistry and natural history at the same college, described the Shakers in his *Remarks Made on a Short Tour between Hartford and Quebec in the Autumn of 1819,* and thereafter returned several times to the subject, finally writing, in 1832, an entire volume on the *Peculiarities of the Shakers.*[14]

Interest soon spread from the meridian of Yale College (whence all longitude was reckoned in the map accompanying President Dwight's *Travels*) to the eastern provinces. In January 1823 Edward Everett, then professor of Greek at Harvard, published a long account of the Shakers in the *North American Review.* His article was remarkable for its shrewd, not to say cynical, analysis of the economic forces contributing to Shaker success. Without denying the role of religious enthusiasm, Everett frankly assumed that the theological and ascetic beliefs of the sect were handicaps to its program, overcome in the minds of the new converts only by its economic attractiveness. "Whoever supposes," he wrote, "that where a good farm is thus

of Eden to the Present Day, with a Disclosure of Shakerism (Concord, N.H., 1847). Other personal narratives of the same character were published by Eunice Chapman (Albany, 1817) and Abram Van Vleet (Lebanon, Ohio, 1818). In refutation of Dyer, Chapman, and Van Vleet the Shakers at Union Village, Ohio, published a volume entitled *The Other Side of the Question* (Cincinnati, 1819).

[13] Jefferson to Albert Gallatin, June 16, 1817, in Jefferson, *Writings,* ed. by A. A. Lipscomb and A. E. Bergh (20 vols., Washington, 1903–4), XV, 134.

[14] Timothy Dwight, *Travels in New-England and New-York* (4 vols., New Haven, 1821–22), III, 149–69; also (4 vols., London, 1823), III, 137–57; [Benjamin Silliman], *Remarks Made on a Short Tour between Hartford and Quebec in the Autumn of 1819* (New Haven, 1820), pp. 40–53; [Silliman], *Peculiarities of the Shakers, Described in a Series of Letters from Lebanon Springs* (New York, 1832). See also *Thomas Brown and His Pretended History of Shakers: Correspondence between Seth Youngs Wells of Shakers, N.Y. and Prof Benjamin Silliman of Yale College, New Haven,* ed. by A.G.H. (caption title, n.p., n.d.), containing letters dated 1823, but published (as internal evidence proves) subsequent to 1847.

offered, to any one that will come and live upon it, a few absurd peculiarities and positive requisitions will keep every body aloof, considers little the magnetic nature of meat and drink." [15]

Once initiated in the early 1820's, serious discussion of the Shakers continued unabated. *Niles' Register* and *Blackwood's Magazine,* as well as the *North American,* carried articles in 1822 and 1823.[16] Before the end of the decade local historians were beginning to record the development of the Shakers.[17] Belletristic writers, too, became increasingly interested. As early as 1824 Catharine Maria Sedgwick introduced a description of the Shakers at Hancock, Massachusetts, into her novel *Redwood.* Four years later, in 1828, Emerson visited the Shaker village of Canterbury, New Hampshire, and meditated on an ideal "protestant monastery." In the same year James Fenimore Cooper described the sect. In the 1830's Nathaniel Hawthorne found in Shaker life the material for two of his tales, and Horace Greeley wrote on the subject for the *Knickerbocker.* In 1843, when communitarianism was again at flood tide, the Transcendentalist *Dial* published "A Day with the Shakers." [18]

During the second quarter of the nineteenth century the Shakers were also becoming one of the sights to be seen by foreign travelers in the United States. Even before Silliman and Dwight published

---

[15] Edward Everett, "The Shakers," *North American Review,* XVI, 76–102 (Jan. 1823); the quotation is from p. 98.

[16] Jonathan Leslie, "The Shakers," *Niles' Weekly Register,* XXIII, 37–39 (Sept. 21, 1822); *Blackwood's Edinburgh Magazine,* XIII, 463–69 (April 1823).

[17] See, for example, [David D. Field], *History of the County of Berkshire, Massachusetts* (Pittsfield, 1829), pp. 285–86, 419–21; John W. Barber, *Historical Collections . . . Relating to . . . Massachusetts* (Worcester, 1841), pp. 73–74, 423–24 (first published 1839); idem, *Historical Collections of the State of New York* (New York, 1841), pp. 54–55, 120–22; Henry Howe, *Historical Collections of Ohio* (Cincinnati, 1847), pp. 501–2. See also such religious histories as John Hayward, *The Book of Religions* (Boston, 1842), pp. 75–85; and I. Daniel Rupp, *HE PASA EKKLESIA: An Original History of the Religious Denominations at Present Existing in the United States* (Philadelphia, 1844), pp. 656–62.

[18] [Catharine M. Sedgwick], *Redwood: A Tale* (author's revised ed., New York, 1850), pp. x, xiii–xv, 256–60 (first published 1824); R. W. Emerson, *Letters,* ed. by R. L. Rusk (6 vols., New York, 1939), I, 225–26; [James Fenimore Cooper], *Notions of the Americans, Picked up by a Travelling Bachelor* (2 vols., Philadelphia, 1833), II, 247–50 (first published 1828); Nathaniel Hawthorne, "The Canterbury Pilgrims," in *The Token and Atlantic Souvenir, 1833,* pp. 153–66; and "The Shaker Bridal," *ibid., 1838,* pp. 117–25; Horace Greeley, "A Sabbath with the Shakers," *Knickerbocker, or New-York Monthly Magazine,* XI, 532–37 (June 1838); [Charles Lane], "A Day with the Shakers," *Dial,* IV, 165–73 (Oct. 1843). This literary interest continued. See [Walt Whitman], "The Shakers," *Harper's New Monthly Magazine,* XV, 164–77 (July 1857), the authorship of which has been established by Charles I. Glicksberg, "A Whitman Discovery," *Colophon,* n.s., I, 227–33 (Oct. 1935); and William Dean Howells, "A Shaker Village," *Atlantic Monthly,* XXXVII, 699–710 (June 1876).

their descriptions, authors of travel books had made mention of the Shakers. But the earliest travelers, like Charles William Janson who toured the country from 1793 to 1806, noted only the extraordinary form of worship that had given the sect its name. Even as late as 1816 a traveler in the western country, David Thomas, could describe a Shaker village without mentioning its communistic arrangements.[19] After 1820, however, there was a decided change. Beginning with Silliman and Dwight, virtually every traveler dealt with the communitarian institutions of the Shakers as well as their theology. Many, in fact, showed no interest in the latter, subscribing to the view of Harriet Martineau: "The moral and economical principles of these societies ought to be most carefully distinguished by the observer. This being done, I believe it will be found that whatever they have peculiarly good among them is owing to the soundness of their economical principles; whatever they have that excites compassion, is owing to the badness of their moral arrangements." [20]

Discerning travelers perceived a unity behind the apparent diversity of these communities of English-speaking Shakers and German-speaking Rappites and Zoarites and others. They recognized that a single point of view animated them all, and they sought to understand and define this communitarian point of view through deliberate comparison and analysis. As early as 1826 the Duke of Saxe-Weimar-Eisenach undertook to compare Father Rapp's community at Economy with Robert Owen's at New Harmony. Captain and Mrs. Basil Hall visited both Shakers and Rappites in the years 1827 and 1828 and gossiped about Owen's experiment. Timothy Flint mentioned the Shakers near Vincennes and both the Rappites and the Owenites at New Harmony in his description of Indiana in 1828. Between 1828 and 1830, James Stuart visited the Shakers and the village of

[19] Charles William Janson, *The Stranger in America, 1793–1806*, ed. by Carl S. Driver (New York, 1935), pp. 103–4; David Thomas, *Travels through the Western Country in the Summer of 1816* (Auburn, N.Y., 1819), pp. 149–52. In 1795, it is true, the Duke of La Rochefoucauld-Liancourt was interested in the economic arrangements of the Shakers but could obtain little information. See his *Travels*, I, 389–94.

[20] Martineau, *Society in America*, II, 55. Fifteen descriptions of the Shakers by British travelers before 1835, and four more in the succeeding quarter-century, are listed, respectively, by Jane L. Mesick, *The English Traveller in America, 1785–1835* (Columbia University, *Studies in English and Comparative Literature;* New York, 1922), p. 267, n. 48; and Max Berger, *The British Traveller in America, 1836–1860* (Columbia University, *Studies in History, Economics and Public Law,* no. 502; New York, 1943), pp. 139–40, nn. 41, 42. Additional references are in: James Flint, *Letters from America* (1822), in Thwaites, ed., *Early Western Travels,* IX, 299–300; George Combe, *Notes on the United States of North America, during a Phrenological Visit in 1838-9-40* (3 vols., Edinburgh, 1841), II, 301–6; James F. W. Johnston, *Notes on North America, Agricultural, Economical, and Social* (2 vols., Edinburgh, 1851), II, 264–69.

New Harmony, learning all he could about Owen's recent community at the latter place. The scientific interests of Prince Maximilian of Wied-Neuwied brought him to New Harmony in the winter of 1832–33, and what he learned of the experiment that had been attempted there prepared him for a subsequent visit to the community at Zoar, Ohio. A Hungarian traveler, Sándor Farkas, visited both the Rappites at Economy and the Shakers at New Lebanon in 1834, and he discussed Robert Owen's experiment at New Harmony. During the years 1834–36 Harriet Martineau studied the Shakers and the Harmonists at Economy, in the most serious attempt yet made to understand the working of communitarian principles. James Silk Buckingham visited an even greater variety of communities between 1837 and 1841, including Economy and Zoar, as well as Shaker villages in New Hampshire, New York, and Ohio.[21]

At last there appeared, in the 1840's, travelers whose main purpose was to study and compare the experimental communities of various types that were to be found in the United States. Their efforts reflected, of course, the growing interest in socialism that preceded the revolutions of 1848, an interest that produced, in 1841, the first comprehensive historical survey of social experiments, Mary Hennell's *Outline of the Various Social Systems & Communities Which Have Been Founded on the Principle of Co-operation.*[22] Miss Hen-

[21] Karl Bernhard, Duke of Saxe-Weimar-Eisenach, *Travels* (2 vols., Philadelphia, 1828), II, 106–23, 159–66; Basil Hall, *Travels in North America, in the Years 1827 and 1828* (3d ed., 3 vols., Edinburgh, 1830), I, 111–12; *The Aristocratic Journey, Being the Outspoken Letters of Mrs. Basil Hall,* ed. by Una Pope-Hennessy (New York, 1931), pp. 40–44, 79, 253, 288; Timothy Flint, *A Condensed Geography and History of the Western States, or the Mississippi Valley* (2 vols., Cincinnati, 1828), II, 152–56, see also p. 317; James Stuart, *Three Years in North America* (2 vols., Edinburgh, 1833), I, 281–89; II, 403–20; Maximilian, Prince of Wied, *Travels in the Interior of North America* (1843), in Thwaites, ed., *Early Western Travels,* XXII, 163–97; XXIV, 154–56; Sándor Farkas, *Útazás Észak Amérikában [Travel in North America]* (Kolozsvár [Klausenburg], 1834), pp. 231–44, and chap. VI (reference supplied through the kindness of Dr. Henry Miller Madden); Martineau, *Society in America,* II, 54–65; James S. Buckingham, *America, Historical, Statistic, and Descriptive* (3 vols., London [1841]), II, 352–405; III, 219–20; *idem, The Eastern and Western States of America* (3 vols., London [1842]), II, 205–36, 292–93, 421–30.

[22] Originally published anonymously as an appendix to Charles Bray, *The Philosophy of Necessity; or, the Law of Consequences, As Applicable to Mental, Moral, and Social Science* (2 vols., London, 1841), II, 493–663; then republished as a separate volume (London, 1844), the author's name being given only in a note on p. iii. Four contemporary works published on the Continent ranged over the various types of socialist thought, but they were narrower in historical scope: [Jérôme] Adolphe Blanqui, *Histoire de l'économie politique en Europe* (2 vols., Paris, 1837); Louis Reybaud, *Études sur les réformateurs contemporains ou socialistes modernes* (Paris, 1840), originally published in 1837 in the *Revue des deux mondes;* Lorenz von Stein, *Der Socialismus und Communismus des heutigen*

nell's study, written in England, drew upon literary sources, not personal observation. The need for the latter was apparent to other leaders in the movement. In 1843, accordingly, John Finch, president of the Rational Society, the central Owenite organization in Great Britain, resigned his post in order to tour the United States. He visited many of the existing sectarian communities, a number of Fourierist phalanxes, certain independent enterprises, and, naturally enough, the site of Owen's experiment at New Harmony. Upon his return to England he published in the Owenite *New Moral World,* two series of "Notes on Travel in the United States," the first of which, comprising twenty-two letters, dealt with the communitive colonies he had visited.[23] Though never republished in book form, it deserves to rank as the first comprehensive work on the American communities.

When Finch came to America, an even more elaborate project than his was under way to gather for publication the original sources bearing upon all the American communities, existing and defunct. The projector of this work was A. J. Macdonald, a printer by trade, who had been interested in Owenism in Scotland, and who migrated to the United States about 1842. He spent some time at New Harmony in that year gathering reminiscences of the earlier experiment; he lived for four months among the Shakers at Watervliet, Ohio, in 1842–43; he attended Owen's lectures in New York in 1845; and before long he was making regular pilgrimages to existing communities to observe and inquire. He had originally planned a volume to be entitled *Travels in Search of Employment,* but his purpose gradually altered and with it his title, until in 1851 he printed a circular letter announcing a projected book on *The Communities of the United States,* which he hoped might "serve as a guide to all future experimenters," and for which he solicited information and documents from surviving participants in earlier communitive ventures. There was a gratifying response, and Macdonald was on the point of digesting his material into chapters when the cholera struck him down in New York, about the year 1854.[24] It remained for a later

Frankreichs (Leipzig, 1842); and Theodor Oelckers, *Die Bewegung des Socialismus und Communismus* (Leipzig, 1844).

23 *New Moral World,* XII, 232, to XIII, 10–11 (22 installments, Jan. 13–July 6, 1844). The section on the Shakers was reprinted in *Working Man's Advocate* (New York), April 27, 1844, p. 3.

24 The manuscripts and collections of A. J. Macdonald are preserved in the Yale University Library, where they were deposited by John Humphrey Noyes, who recovered them about 1865 and used them extensively in his own *History of American Socialisms* (1870). The circular letter is in the collection, and is reprinted by Noyes, who also gives a brief description of Macdonald. Some autobiographical information is furnished by the A. J. Macdonald MSS themselves.

generation to realize his plan for a comparative study of American communities based on first-hand observation. Three such volumes appeared at last between 1870 and 1878.[25]

As an investigator Macdonald exceeded his contemporaries in thoroughness, but he did not differ from them in the conception underlying his study. That the experimental communities were manifestations of a single movement was the unchallenged assumption of practically every observer in the second quarter of the nineteenth century. Indeed, though the founders of communities might differ from one another in their plans, they thought of themselves as participants in a well-understood and unified tradition. This they revealed by frequent references to their communitive predecessors.

The interrelations among seventeenth- and eighteenth-century German sectarians have already been examined. As the communitarian movement gathered momentum in the nineteenth century, intervisitation occurred on an even wider scale, and published cross-references became more frequent. In 1818, six years before he came to the United States, Robert Owen printed in pamphlet form a communication concerning the Shakers,[26] and a week after he landed in America he inspected the Shaker village at Niskeyuna, New York. This first-hand view of the Shakers, wrote his son, "made us all in love with a community." [27] The interest was by no means on one side only. The Shakers already knew of Owen's experiments at New Lanark,[28] and several members from societies in Indiana and Kentucky visited him at Harmonie after his arrival.[29] Other previous

As befitted one whom Noyes dubbed "the 'Old Mortality' of Socialism," Macdonald published a pamphlet entitled *Monuments, Grave Stones, Burying Grounds, Cemeteries, Temples* (Albany, 1848). At the opposite end of the sentimental scale, he edited a gift annual, *The Rainbow, 1847* (Albany, 1847).

[25] Noyes, *History of American Socialisms* (1870); Charles Nordhoff, *The Communistic Societies of the United States; from Personal Visit and Observation* (New York, 1875); and William A. Hinds, *American Communities: Brief Sketches of Economy, Zoar, Bethel, Aurora, Amana, Icaria, the Shakers, Oneida, Wallingford, and the Brotherhood of the New Life* (Oneida, N.Y., 1878). On these and subsequent publications see the first section of the Bibliographical Essay.

[26] W. S. Warder, "A Brief Sketch of the Religious Society of People Called Shakers," dated 1817, in Owen, *New View of Society: Tracts* (1818), reprinted in *Life*, I.A, 143–54.

[27] William Owen, *Diary . . . from November 10, 1824, to April 20* [actually 19], *1825*, ed. by Joel W. Hiatt (Indiana Historical Society *Publications*, vol. IV, no. 1; Indianapolis, 1906), p. 13; entry for Nov. 11, 1824.

[28] Donald Macdonald, *Diaries, . . . 1824–1826*, with an introduction by Caroline Dale Snedeker (Indiana Historical Society *Publications*, vol. XIV, no. 2; Indianapolis, 1942), p. 199; entry for Nov. 17, 1824.

[29] *Ibid.*, pp. 273–75, 290. See also Caroline Creese Pelham, ed., "Letters of William Pelham, Written in 1825 and 1826," in Harlow Lindley, ed., *Indiana As Seen by Early Travelers (Indiana Historical Collections* [III]; Indianapolis, 1916),

experiments were called to Owen's attention during his American travels,[30] and even the distant past of communitarianism was summoned up for him. An old disciple of Pantisocracy, for example, was stirred by the reports coming from New Harmony and published in the Owenite journal in London a sonnet he had composed in 1794 in honor of the earlier project.[31] In New York, moreover, Owen was given a first-hand account of the Jesuit *reducciones* in Paraguay by a South American general who knew them in boyhood.[32]

The most important and obvious connection between Owen and the American communitive past was furnished by the Rappites, whose colony at Harmonie, Indiana, he purchased outright as the laboratory for his own experiment. This was something more than an ordinary transfer of property. Owen had known of the Rappites for a decade at least, and in 1820 he had sent Father Rapp a set of his own publications, together with a request for full particulars on the latter's "two experiments" in Pennsylvania and Indiana.[33] Nor was Owen the only one to see a connection between his plan and the Rappites' practice. An Englishman named William Hebert visited Harmonie in 1822, and in 1825 he published the description he had written at the time, appending to it an expression of confidence that "an agricultural and manufacturing community," based "upon the plan of that benefactor of his race, Mr. Robert Owen, and somewhat similar to those of the Friends [i.e., the Shakers] and Harmonians," could not fail of success. "With the societies of the Harmonians and Friends of America before our eyes," he asked, "who can doubt it?" [34]

---

p. 397. This correspondence will be cited hereafter as "Pelham Letters," page references being to Lindley's volume.

[30] See W. Owen, *Diary*, pp. 62, 91; D. Macdonald, *Diaries*, p. 233. He visited Zoar in the summer of 1828. See Robert Owen to James M. Dorsey, Wheeling, July 14, 1828, MS in Indiana Historical Society. In 1841 Owen included descriptions of the Shakers, Rappites, and Zoarites in his *Home Colonies* (2d ed., 1841), pp. 153–59.

[31] *Co-operative Magazine and Monthly Herald*, I, 133 (April 1826); reprinted in *New-Harmony Gazette*, II, 120 (Jan. 10, 1827).

[32] D. Macdonald, *Diaries*, pp. 199–200; W. Owen, *Diary*, pp. 25–26.

[33] Owen to George Rapp, New Lanark, Aug. 4, 1820, MS in Chicago Historical Society, printed with minor verbal inaccuracies in George Flower, *History of the English Settlement in Edwards County, Illinois, Founded in 1817 and 1818, by Morris Birkbeck and George Flower*, ed. by E. B. Washburne (Chicago Historical Society, *Collection*, I; Chicago, 1882), pp. 372–73. In this letter Owen says he learned of the Rappites from John Melish, *Travels in the United States of America, in the Years 1806 & 1807, and 1809, 1810, & 1811* (2 vols., Philadelphia, 1812), II, 64–83. He probably read the extract from Melish in *The Philanthropist*, V (1815), 277–88; see below, p. 143, n. 37.

[34] William Hebert, *A Visit to the Colony of Harmony, in Indiana* (London, 1825), as reprinted in Lindley, ed., *Indiana As Seen by Early Travelers*, pp. 339–40.

Hebert wrote his description at the village of Albion, Illinois, in the midst of the English Settlement that Morris Birkbeck and George Flower had established in 1817–18 in Edwards County, a score of miles north of Harmonie, across the Wabash. This was a simple colony of immigrants, not an experiment in communitarianism, yet it provided important links between the Rappites and the Owenites,[35] and from its contacts with the two experiments it developed certain communitive tendencies of its own, which reveal how captivating the latter doctrine was in the 1820's.

The slavery issue was what first aroused the reforming zeal of the English settlers, and Rappite influences entered their thinking about the problem. As early as 1819 George Flower was turning over in his mind the idea of adapting "the Harmony plan" to Negro emancipation. Eventually, as we shall see, it was the New Harmony plan that he actually applied thereto, in collaboration with Frances Wright at Nashoba, Tennessee. In the meantime, communitarianism cropped up in other ways at Albion, for when Owen visited there in December 1824 several residents "seemed already to have commenced the community system." Owen's lectures drew some of the English settlers to New Harmony, and inspired an Owenite project on the English Prairie itself.[36]

The sense of common aims and values that was apparent during

[35] It was Richard Flower, father of George, who negotiated the sale of Harmonie to Owen. Moreover, the travelers who visited the English Settlement usually described the Rappites as well, thus advertising their principles in England. See the travel books of Thomas Hulme (1819), Richard Flower (1819), John Woods .(1820–21), William Faux (1818–19), and Adlard Welby (1819–20), as reprinted in Thwaites, ed., *Early Western Travels*, X, 53–61, 98–100, 312–16; XI, 248–51; XII, 260–67, respectively. See also Mesick, *English Traveller in America, 1785–1835*, pp. 294–97; and Jane Rodman, "The English Settlement in Southern Illinois as Viewed by English Travelers, 1815–1825," *Indiana Magazine of History*, XLIV, 37–68 (March 1948). The English settlers received inquiries from philanthropists elsewhere, many of whom were suspicious of Rapp. In 1817 a Quaker reported from Philadelphia that the German leader had "become the purchaser of a number of Redemptioners who are worn out with their confinement on board ship, and subscribe to his terms for the sake of release." The motive for writing was "an apprehension of the influence he may gain over a deluded people." Jeremiah Warder, Jr., to George Flower, The Hills [Philadelphia], 8th Month 28th, 1817, MS in Chicago Historical Society.

[36] W. Owen, *Diary*, pp. 79, 88–89, 91; *New-Harmony Gazette*, I, 268–69 (May 17, 1826). William Hall, who migrated to Wanborough in the English Settlement in 1821, was a fellow passenger and later a correspondent of Hebert's; he frequently visited the Rappites, attended Owen's lectures at Albion and at New Harmony, and was eventually secretary and treasurer of the Owenite society at Wanborough. "From England to Illinois in 1821: The Journal of William Hall," ed. by Jay Monaghan, Illinois State Historical Society, *Journal*, XXXIX, 35, 45–47, 51–57, 211, 215, 217, 221, 235, 238–45 (March, June 1946); cited hereafter as William Hall, "Journal." See also George Flower, *History of the English Settlement*, pp. 149–52, 282–83, and the more detailed accounts below, pp. 176, 214, 219–21.

the Owenite excitement of the 1820's became even more pronounced during the 1840's. Communitarians of all persuasions evinced an intense curiosity about one another's affairs. A Shaker sister who had lived at Mount Lebanon since 1826 compiled a "Sketch of Socialistic Experiments" covering the period—evidence in itself of Shaker interest. In it, moreover, she mentioned the visits and letters received by the Shakers from the leaders of other contemporary experiments—specifically William H. Fish of the Hopedale Community, Charles Sears of the North American Phalanx, Marcus Spring of the Raritan Bay Union, John A. Collins of the Skaneateles Community, John Orvis of Brook Farm, and Alcander Longley, sponsor of a sequence of communities in the vicinity of St. Louis.[37]

To the German sects, as to the Shakers, the founders of new communities turned for advice and assistance. The archives of the Harmony Society, reports a recent investigator, "provide ample unpublished evidence" that English-speaking communitarians "communicated with the Harmonists before their own groups were formed."[38] Financial aid was sometimes forthcoming, as when the Harmonites lent money during the 1870's to the Hutterians in South Dakota, and offered them lands in Pennsylvania.[39] Concerted action was occasionally taken by communitarian sects of different persuasions, notably by the Zoar and Harmony communities in the handling of applications for membership, and by the Bishop Hill, Oneida, and Rappite communities for more general purposes.[40] At one time in the 1850's an actual merger of Economy, Zoar, and the Shakers was contemplated.[41]

[37] Jane D. Knight, "Sketch of Socialistic Experiments," MS in Library of Congress, Papers of Shakers, no. 243, box 47. The catalogue describes this ten-page MS as having been written at Union Village, Ohio, in 1856, but date and provenience are manifestly in error, for events as late as 1872 are mentioned in the document and Sister Jane herself was a member of the Mount Lebanon community. See her *Brief Narrative of Events Touching Various Reforms* (Albany, 1880), an autobiographical narrative dealing principally with her conversion to Shakerism.

[38] Karl J. Arndt, "The Harmonists and the Mormons," *American-German Review*, vol. X, no. 5, p. 6 (June 1944). As the title of this article suggests, some influence was probably exerted by the Rappites upon the collectivistic institutions of the Mormons. The Owenite colony of Equality in Wisconsin borrowed details of its constitution not only from the Fourierist Wisconsin Phalanx, but also from the Separatists of Zoar. See *Herald of Progress* (London), p. 65 (Feb. 14, 1846).

[39] Arndt, "The Harmonists and the Hutterians," *American-German Review*, vol. X, no. 6, pp. 24–27 (Aug. 1944).

[40] Edgar B. Nixon, "The Zoar Society: Applicants for Membership," *Ohio State Archaeological and Historical Quarterly*, XLV, 348 (Oct. 1936); Michael A. Mikkelsen, *The Bishop Hill Colony, A Religious Communistic Settlement in Henry County, Illinois* (Johns Hopkins University, *Studies in Historical and Political Science*, vol. X, no. 1; Baltimore, 1892), p. 56.

[41] Bole, *Harmony Society*, pp. 126–27.

The Brook Farm community near Boston provides apt illustration of the varied influences that flowed into and out from such an enterprise. Two years and a half before the establishment of Brook Farm, George Ripley, its founder, visited the German sectarian community at Zoar, and his wife wrote enthusiastically of its way of life.[42] The first full-fledged prospectus of Brook Farm, published in the *Dial* in 1841, made allusion to the Herrnhuters, the Moravians, the Shakers, and the Rappites.[43] Nathaniel Hawthorne, who joined Brook Farm early in its career, had already shown an interest in the Shakers by publishing two tales about them in the 1830's. Brook Farm received visits from the Shakers,[44] and it maintained close fraternal relations for a time with the other Massachusetts communities of Hopedale and Northampton, despite the difference in their avowed principles.[45] The *Harbinger,* official organ of the Fourierist movement as well as of Brook Farm, reported on such non-Fourierist enterprises as the German sectarian community of Ebenezer near Buffalo, and the radically agnostic community at Skaneateles, New York.[46] The communitarian tradition influenced Brook Farm, and Brook Farm, in turn, passed the influence along. The Fruitlands experiment of Bronson Alcott at the near-by town of Harvard, Massachusetts, was in some measure its offshoot, for Alcott had participated in the original plans for Brook Farm, and inaugurated his own experiment only when convinced that the older community was "not sufficiently ideal." [47]

In the propaganda of other communities of the 1840's, as in that of Brook Farm, earlier experiments were repeatedly cited in justification, and contemporary efforts, even though ideologically different, were reported as part of the common enterprise. More remarkable even than the *Harbinger,* in this respect, was *The Communitist,* published by the Skaneateles Community at Mottville in Onondaga County, New York. Though committed to its own particular program, this periodical nevertheless published, within a period of ten

[42] [Sophia Ripley], "Letter," dated Zoar, O., Aug. 9, 1838, *Dial,* II, 122–29 (July 1841).

[43] [Elizabeth Palmer Peabody], "A Glimpse of Christ's Idea of Society," *Dial,* II, 222 (Oct. 1841).

[44] See George Ripley to Charles A. Dana, Brook Farm, March 18, 1842, in James H. Wilson, *Life of Charles A. Dana* (New York, 1907), p. 40.

[45] Representatives of all three communities sponsored conventions at Worcester, Leominster, and Boston in December 1843 and held periodic Associational Conferences at one another's domains in 1844. See A. E. Bestor, Jr., "Fourierism in Northampton: A Critical Note," *New England Quarterly,* XIII, 113–15 (March 1940).

[46] *Harbinger,* I, 319–30, 253–54; III, 208 (Oct. 25, Sept. 27, 1845; Sept. 5, 1846).

[47] Odell Shepard, *Pedlar's Progress: The Life of Bronson Alcott* (Boston, 1937), pp. 289, 293, 297, 343–80.

months in 1844–45, articles concerning no fewer than fourteen different Fourierist phalanxes, one Owenite community, and seven independent experiments.[48]

A few communitarians, it is true, looked disdainfully upon their predecessors. Albert Brisbane, for example, when he began to write in favor of Fourierism in 1840, asked his readers not to confound it with the "monotonous and monastic trials" of Owen, the Rappites, the Shakers, and others; [49] and he later rebuked a colleague for comparing Fourier to the Herrnhuters, Shakers, and Rappites.[50] A group of Fourierites in Rochester, New York, rejected even more emphatically the "peculiar ideas, some of them repugnant, and many hideous," of the Shakers, Rappites, and Zoarites,[51] though at the same time drawing favorable arguments from their prosperity. The mention is more significant than the disavowal, for the frequency of such allusions to other communities proves the communitarian tradition to have been a living thing both to the advocates of the new doctrines and to the audience they hoped to convert.

A narrow factionalism, moreover, was exceptional in early American socialism. Even the sectarian communities, narrow as their theology might be, proved surprisingly sympathetic to experiments that diverged widely from their own in purpose and plan. Thus, the Shakers felt themselves to be participants in a single great communitarian movement, and offered their experience as a guide and inspiration to those who were seeking by other roads to reach the promised land of community. Even the failures of other experimenters were embraced by the Shakers within the burgeoning tradition of which they felt themselves a part. "We view all labors of this kind," said their *Summary View* in 1848, "as providential and beneficial to mankind, and preparatory to the order of the true work." [52]

Like the Shakers, the Perfectionists who established the Oneida Community were devoted to a particular theological view that ostensibly brooked no compromise. Yet their founder, John Humphrey Noyes, was able and willing to view his whole enterprise as merely

[48] *The Communitist,* vol. I, no. 7, through vol. II, no. 1 (Aug. 21, 1844–June 18, 1845); see especially John O. Wattles, "History of Communities," II, 1 (June 18, 1845).

[49] Brisbane, *Social Destiny of Man* (1840), p. 29.

[50] *New York Weekly Tribune,* March 4, 1843, p. 3:2, commenting on Parke Godwin, "The Social Problem (An Outline)," *Pathfinder,* pp. 1–2 (Feb. 25, 1843). In page references to newspapers, the numeral following the colon indicates the column.

[51] *Labor's Wrongs, and Labor's Remedy* (Rochester [1843]), p. 8; not to be confused with John Francis Bray's work of the same title (Leeds, 1839).

[52] Green and Wells, *Summary View of the Millennial Church* (2d ed., 1848), p. 5.

one embodiment of an inclusive communitarian ideal, shared by even the nonreligious communities. Two decades of success at Oneida gave Noyes not a particularistic pride in his own system, but a sense of the reality and power of the communitive tradition as a whole. His *History of American Socialisms,* published in 1870, is a powerful affirmation of his belief that all the American experiments were organically connected:

> The great facts of modern Socialism are these: From 1776—the era of our national Revolution—the Shakers have been established in this country . . . [and] prosperous religious Communism has been modestly and yet loudly preaching to the nation and the world. New England and New York and the great West have had actual Phalanxes before their eyes for nearly a century. . . . The example of the Shakers has demonstrated, not merely that successful Communism is subjectively possible, but that this nation is free enough to let it grow. Who can doubt that this demonstration was known and watched in Germany from the beginning; and that it helped the successive experiments and emigrations of the Rappites, the Zoarites and the Ebenezers? . . . Then the Shaker movement with its echoes was sounding also in England, when Robert Owen undertook to convert the world to Communism; and it is evident enough that he was really a far-off follower of the Rappites. France also had heard of Shakerism, before St. Simon or Fourier began to meditate and write Socialism. These men were nearly contemporaneous with Owen, and all three evidently obeyed a common impulse. That impulse was the sequel and certainly in part the effect of Shakerism. Thus it is no more than bare justice to say, that we are indebted to the Shakers more than to any or all other Social Architects of modern times. Their success has been the solid capital that has upheld all the paper theories, and counteracted the failures, of the French and English schools. It is very doubtful whether Owenism or Fourierism would have ever existed, or if they had, whether they would have ever moved the practical American nation, if the facts of Shakerism had not existed before them, and gone along with them.[53]

Though Noyes emphasized the religious, and especially the Shaker, inspiration of communitarianism, he did not deny the creative role of even the secular experiments. To the Fourierist community of Brook Farm he acknowledged a direct and personal indebtedness, writing that "the Oneida Community owes much to Brook Farm. . . . The Oneida Community may be said to be the continuation of Brook Farm. Look at the dates. Brook Farm deceased in October 1847. Oneida Community commenced in November 1847. It is a simple case of transmigration, or in the latest language, persistence

[53] Noyes, *History of American Socialisms* (1870), pp. 191–92. This passage was originally published in *The Circular* (Oneida Community), n.s., V, 381 (Feb. 15, 1869), and it actually appears twice in the *History,* again on pp. 669–70, with minor verbal changes.

of force." [54] And Fourierism, in Noyes's view, was organically related
to the earlier Owenite movement:

> We must not think of the two great socialistic revivals as altogether
> heterogeneous and separate. Their partizans maintained theoretical op-
> position to each other; but after all the main idea of both was *the enlarge-*
> *ment of home—the extension of family union beyond the little man-and-wife*
> *circle to large corporations.* In this idea the two movements were one; and
> this was the charming idea that caught the attention and stirred the en-
> thusiasm of the American people. Owenism prepared the way for Fourierism.
> . . . The two movements may, therefore, be regarded as one. . . . The
> Communities and Phalanxes died almost as soon as they were born. . . .
> But the spirit of Socialism remains in the life of the nation, . . . as a hope
> watching for the morning, in thousands and perhaps millions who never
> took part in any of the experiments, and who are neither Owenites nor
> Fourierites, but simply Socialists without theory—believers in the possibility
> of a scientific and heavenly reconstruction of society.[55]

Noyes so greatly overstates the case for the organic unity of the communitarian tradition that he endangers his argument. Many communitive sects, of course, came to America long before the Shakers
existed. Even for nineteenth-century immigrants like the Rappites
and Zoarites, there is no evidence to support Noyes's assumption that
the Shakers influenced them before they came. Finally, Owen had
evolved his system before he learned of the Shakers, and Fourier
never had more than a vague impression of the sect, which he confused with the Quakers.

Nevertheless Noyes's thesis is significant if discriminatingly examined. That he believed in the unity of the communitarian tradition is, in and of itself, a fact of genuine historical significance, for
he was describing the influences that had played upon him as a leading participant in the movement, and he was in a position to know
how his contemporaries were affected by broadly diffused communitarian ideas. That Noyes should have erred in assuming a comparable influence abroad was the defect of his limited information,

---

[54] *Circular,* n.s., V, 348 (Jan. 18, 1869). This went farther than a previous statement by Noyes to the effect that Fourierism "broke the ice of intolerance" and
thus "rendered the formation of the Oneida Community practicable," and that
he himself had "adopted many of the external economies of Fourier." *Ibid.,* V,
114 (June 29, 1868); see also VI, 127 (July 5, 1869).

[55] Noyes, *History of American Socialisms,* pp. 23–24. The reciprocal influence
of the different communitarian enterprises in America is clearly the theme of
Noyes's book, despite an occasional inconsistent statement, e.g.: "we will lay aside
the antique *religious* Associations, such as the Dunkers, Moravians, Zoarites,
&c. . . . , which do not properly belong to the modern socialistic movement, or
even to American life. Having their origin in the old world, and most of them
in the last century, and remaining without change, they exist only on the out-
skirts of general society." *Ibid.,* p. 13.

and in no way invalidates his conclusions about purely American developments, which came under his direct observation and for which there is an abundance of independent corroborative testimony.

The most striking evidence of the reality, the unity, and the strength of the communitive tradition is furnished by the men and women whose loyalty to it impelled them from one community to another. The social idealism it inspired was often powerful enough to override religious preconceptions, permitting many adherents lightly to cross the line dividing theocratic communities from free-thinking, secular ones.

Robert Owen was notorious for his attacks upon organized religion, the Shakers for their almost fanatical sectarianism. Yet in 1825 two Shakers from Kentucky presented themselves at New Harmony to join Owen's community there,[56] and in 1827–28, after the failure of the Owenite experiment at Valley Forge, Pennsylvania, Shakerism made many proselytes among the disappointed members.[57] Two years later one of the most notable conversions to Shakerism occurred when Frederick W. Evans—active in the various reforms associated with Owenism, and a brother of George Henry Evans, later editor of the *Working Man's Advocate*—joined the sect, eventually to rise to its highest position of leadership.[58]

These shifts of allegiance were even more frequent in the 1840's and 1850's than they had been in the 1820's. The North American Phalanx, though decidedly secular in outlook, included among its members a former Shaker and a woman who had belonged to the religious community of Hopedale. Conversely, the theocratic Oneida Community attracted several persons from the earlier Skaneateles Community, the first article of whose creed had been "a disbelief in any special revelation of God to man." [59]

Not only the barrier of theology but also that of language was often crossed. The German-speaking community of Zoar included a former Shaker, and it received applications from several other members of that English-language sect.[60] The Swedish community

[56] "Pelham Letters," pp. 397, 411.

[57] White and Taylor, *Shakerism: Its Meaning and Message*, pp. 158–59. Sister Jane D. Knight, already mentioned, was one of these converts. See her *Brief Narrative* (1880), pp. 16–29.

[58] Frederick W. Evans, *Autobiography of a Shaker, and Revelation of the Apocalypse* (new and enlarged ed., Glasgow, 1888), pp. 5–17, 24–25. See also *Dictionary of American Biography*, VI, 198–99, 201–2. And see above, p. 41, n. 11.

[59] Noyes, *History of American Socialisms*, pp. 478–79, 175–79, 164.

[60] Nordhoff, *Communistic Societies of the United States*, p. 112; Nixon, "Zoar Society: Applicants," pp. 343, 347–49. A member of the Ebenezer community also applied for admission to Zoar. Such transfers from one German community to another were frequent. Examples of migration from Zoar to Economy, and from Economy via the New Philadelphia Society to Bethel, are given, respectively, by

at Bishop Hill in Illinois drew several members from the native New England community of Hopedale, and furnished several to the Shaker society at Pleasant Hill, Kentucky.[61]

A lifelong devotion to communitarianism was not uncommon. In the 1870's and 1880's the various socialist periodicals received contributions from many who had been active in the movements of the 1840's, and had subsequently taken part in experiments of different origin and design. One such veteran was Theron C. Leland, originally of Rochester, New York. From 1843 to 1845 he had been officially connected with three Fourierist phalanxes in that neighborhood. Next he had joined the community of Modern Times, devoted to the doctrine of "Individual Sovereignty," antithetical in many respects to Fourierism. Later he practised "communism, pure and simple," in a joint household of three or four families. When, in 1876, he recounted his experiences in the *American Socialist,* hospitable organ of the Oneida Community, he summed up his career thus: "In a word, Socialism, the dwelling together of brethren in unity, whatever form it may take, has been my dream, more or less realized, from youth to age." [62]

Another such lifelong communitarian was Alcander Longley. His father was a member of the Clermont Phalanx in 1844, when Longley was twelve. In 1853 the young man, now twenty-one, became a resident of the North American Phalanx in its closing years. Four years later, at the age of twenty-five, he founded his own Fourier Phalanx at Moore's Hill in Dearborn County, Indiana. Failures there and again in Michigan and Ohio did not discourage him, and eventually in 1867 he became a probationary member of the French-speaking community of Icaria. After withdrawing from it, he started a periodical in St. Louis, first entitled *The Communist,* then *The Altruist.* He conducted it for thirty years, from 1868 until 1917, the year before his death, and sponsored in its columns a succession of communitarian enterprises—the Reunion, Friendship, Principia, Mutual Aid, Relief, and Altruist communities—several of which enjoyed a brief span of actual existence in Missouri. As late as 1909, at the age of seventy-seven, Longley was still actively planning a venture of the kind.[63]

Duss, *The Harmonists,* pp. 120–21; and Robert J. Hendricks, *Bethel and Aurora* (New York, 1933), p. 8.

   [61] Mikkelsen, *Bishop Hill Colony,* p. 56.

   [62] *American Socialist,* I, 18, 73, 106 (April 13–June 29, 1876).

   [63] In addition to Longley's own periodicals, see the sketch of him in Albert Shaw, *Icaria: A Chapter in the History of Communism* (New York, 1884), pp. 178–82, supplemented, particularly for his later activities, by the article by Percy W. Bidwell in the *Dictionary of American Biography,* XI, 389–90. Shaw instances other careers of the kind and comments on the interrelationships between the different

Equally remarkable was the career of Stephen Young, who in 1886 contributed an autobiographical sketch to a periodical published in the interests of the experimental colony at Topolobampo in the state of Sinaloa, Mexico. Young reported that he had started out to join the Sylvania Phalanx in Pennsylvania, one of the Fourierist experiments of the early 1840's, but had been turned away for lack of room. Proceeding to another Fourierist phalanx, that at Leraysville, Pennsylvania, he found it in the throes of dissolution. He next tried unsuccessfully to enter the non-Fourierist community of Northampton, Massachusetts. At last he was admitted to the North American Phalanx in New Jersey, the leading Fourierist enterprise, but he was dissatisfied there and eventually became a member of Brook Farm. After its failure, other projects attracted him, and he made an effort to join, first, the Fourierist colony that Victor Considerant established in Texas in the 1850's; next the Kansas Vegetarian Company; then a so-called "Hygeiana" near Chillicothe, Ohio, founded by one Dr. Trall. Forty-odd years after his first venture, Young was writing because of his burning desire to join the newest communitarian colony, at Topolobampo.[64]

This intricate web of personal relationships attests the reality and power of the communitarian tradition, substantiating by historical evidence what would otherwise be mere inference. The likeness of the experimental communities to one another implies a common tradition, but only the interchange of ideas and of personnel among them proves its actual existence.

This continuing communitive tradition is the most important single factor behind the American enthusiasm for Owenism and Fourierism in the second quarter of the nineteenth century. It will not do to say, with those who view socialism in purely economic terms, that the religious communities "played but a secondary part."[65] Nor will it do to accept uncritically the dictum of Noyes that the various community experiments "were echoes of Shakerism, growing

---

ventures, and Noyes does the same. Shaw, *Icaria*, pp. 171–86; Noyes, *History of American Socialisms*, pp. 91–101.

[64] Stephen Young, "A Veteran Associationist," *Credit Foncier of Sinaloa* (Hammonton, N.J.), I, 551–52 (July 6, 1896). Topolobampo itself furnished members to even later communities, such as the Christian Commonwealth in Georgia in the years 1896–1900. According to Ralph Albertson, founder of the latter, "some of the people who joined us had previously been at Topolobampo," and others had come from the Willard Coöperative Colony in Tennessee and North Carolina. See Albertson, "A Survey of Mutualistic Communities in America," *Iowa Journal of History and Politics*, XXXIV, 414 (Oct. 1936). The quoted phrase is from a letter written by Albertson to the author, Cherrydale, Va., Nov. 9, 1936.

[65] Morris Hillquit, *History of Socialism in the United States* (New York, 1903), p. 24.

fainter and fainter, as the time-distance increased." [66] The tradition inaugurated by the sectarian communities was real and stimulating, but not all-powerful. The kind and degree of influence it exerted must be more accurately defined.

To begin with, the sectarian communities undoubtedly suggested to many Americans the possibility of social reform by means of communistic or co-operative colonies. An increasing interest in the religious experiments became evident about 1820 and contributed greatly to the success of the Owenite propaganda that began in 1824. Similarly, the even more widely diffused interest of the 1840's underlay the Fourierist enthusiasm of that decade.

Proximity to earlier sectarian communities, indeed, had much to do with the geographical location of mid-nineteenth-century communitarian enterprises. At the height of the movement, between 1840 and 1849, for example, twenty-four experimental communities of all types were founded in the three states of Massachusetts, New York, and Ohio, and exactly half were within thirty miles of a pre-existing colony of Shakers or German sectarians. Only two were more than sixty miles distant from such a center of communitive example and influence, and none was as far away as seventy-five miles.[67] In several instances, in various periods, the same site was occupied successively by different communities. New Harmony, of course, is the outstanding example. And there is abundant evidence that the rapid influx of members into Owen's community from the surrounding countryside was in part the consequence of the impression which the Rappites had previously made upon their neighbors.

It was the obvious prosperity of the Rappites, needless to say, that made the deepest impression. Undoubtedly the greatest contribution which the religious communities made to secular socialism was in demonstrating that communitarian establishments could be economically successful. Propagandists exploited this fact to the utmost. And it is clear that the continuing vigor and expansion of the communitive sects in the 1830's was what ultimately overcame the misgivings engendered by Owen's failures at New Harmony and thus made possible the great communitarian upsurge of the 1840's. The statistics are meager, but the total membership of the Shakers seems definitely to have climbed from a little over 4,000 in 1823 [68] to 5,400 in 1828 [69] (the year after New Harmony was abandoned), and to

[66] Noyes, *History of American Socialisms*, p. 192.

[67] See the Checklist of Communitarian Experiments.

[68] Green and Wells, *Summary View* (1823), pp. 68–69, 75–76. The figures given for individual communities produce a total of from 4,000 to 4,300, of which two-thirds are said to "have been added since the commencement of the present century."

[69] *American Almanac and Repository of Useful Knowledge* (Boston), *1830*, p. 228; *1836*, p. 152.

have reached a peak of about 6,000 [70] in the late 1830's and early 1840's.[71] Noyes was right when he said that "their success has been the 'specie basis' that has upheld all the paper theories, and counteracted the failures, of the French and English schools." [72]

Finally, the sectarian communities subtly shaped in their own image the ideals held by later communitarians. Owen elaborately depicted the architectural "parallelograms" he hoped to build, but in the end he used the edifices designed and constructed by the Rappites. Fourier drew up even more intricate and grandiose plans for his "phalansteries," but at least one American phalanx found a fitting and beautiful abode in a former Shaker village.[73] The same fate overtook the theoretical subtleties on which the European socialists believed their systems hinged. In American practice these principles, however basic in theory, were apt to be quickly discarded in favor of simpler procedures borrowed from the sectarian communities.

When Americans listened to Robert Owen or to the disciples of Charles Fourier, they reshaped the new doctrines to conform to a communitarian ideal that the religious communities had already made familiar. In effect, what these men and women thought they discovered in Owenism or Fourierism was a way of achieving the prosperity, the security, and the peace of a Shaker village without subjecting themselves to the celibacy and the narrow social conformity exacted by Shaker theology.

[70] This was the total given in the *American Almanac* each year from 1832 through 1843, and in John Hayward, *The Book of Religions* (Boston, 1861 [copyright 1842]), p. 84. Hayward had compiled and published a volume of religious statistics in 1836 before writing this book, the text of which was unaltered in the printings subsequent to 1842.

[71] The decline after the 1840's was at first slow, then rapid. Membership was between 4,400 and 4,700 in 1858; 2,415 in 1874; 1,728 in 1890; 516 in 1906; 367 in 1916; 192 in 1926; and 92 in 1936. See F. W. Evans, *Shakers: Compendium of the Origin, History, Principles, . . . and Doctrines of the United Society* (New York, 1859 [copyright 1858]), pp. 32–33, 36–37; Nordhoff, *Communistic Societies* (1875 [copyright 1874]), p. 117; and (for 1890 *et seqq.*) U.S., Bureau of the Census, *Religious Bodies: 1906*, vol. I, p. 514; and *ibid., 1936*, vol. II, Part 2, p. 1261.

[72] Noyes, *History of American Socialisms*, p. 670; a variant of the passage from p. 192, already quoted.

[73] This was the Sodus Bay Phalanx in New York State.

Chapter IV

ROBERT OWEN'S NEW VIEW OF SOCIETY

THANKS to the religious sects, social idealism in the United States took on a strongly communitarian coloring during the second quarter of the nineteenth century. The desire for reform arose, as it always must, out of actual conditions. The belief that reform could be accomplished through experimental communities rested upon the achievement of the sectarian communities. But the specific ideas that converted a vague aspiration into a systematic movement for social reform came from abroad. It is characteristic of American intellectual, social, and even political movements that they often bear the stamp of European theory even when the energies behind them are purely native. This is so, not because the Europeans are closer to the goal at which the American movement aims, but because, as a rule, they have wrestled with the problem longer and have therefore formulated it more clearly.

This was especially true of nineteenth-century communitarianism. What it proposed to solve were not the problems that had confronted the earlier sects, but the problems of a developing commercial and industrial society, in which insecurity was increasing, in which the gap between employer and worker was growing wider and more impersonal, in which the mechanisms of exchange were becoming so complex and gigantic as to threaten the independence of the small man everywhere. However clear these problems were beginning to be in the America of the Jacksonian Democrats, they were far clearer and more exigent in the England of the Chartists and the France of Louis Philippe. As an inevitable result, most comprehensive systems of social reform in the early nineteenth century were the products of European thinking.

Among European social theories two were especially significant for America because they embodied the communitarian approach which the religious sects had made familiar. These were the systems that Charles Fourier elaborated in France, and Robert Owen in Great Britain. The two men were born within a year of each other, in 1772 and 1771 respectively. Both experienced the vast upheavals that accompanied the French Revolution, the conquests of Napoleon, and the comprehensive countereffort by which Britain at last brought the conqueror low. And in the aftermath of the Napoleonic Wars both offered communitarian plans designed to transform the crisis-warped society of the nineteenth century into something more orderly and humane. Fourier, as a matter of fact, worked out his theories with fair completeness a dozen years before Owen, but they made no serious impression even in his native country until a decade after Owen's plans had swept Great Britain. And Fourierism did not reach the United States in force until the 1840's, more than fifteen years after the Owenite philosophy had created there the first communitarian movement of a purely secular character.[1]

To describe Owenism as a philosophy is to use the term in the loosest fashion. To be sure, Owen talked much of the new principles he had discovered, and as he grew older the list grew longer. But in the last analysis his was a system of logic with one sole postulate, *"that the character of man, is, without a single exception, always formed for him."* [2] As a rough generalization from experience this statement had considerable point. As a slogan for reform it revealed unexpected power. But as a philosophical principle, universally valid, it required critical examination such as its author never dreamed of giving it. The basic dilemma of any deterministic philosophy Owen never understood, for he never troubled to explain how he, alone among men, had broken the iron chain of cause and consequence.[3] He merely thanked God (or the Owenite equivalent) that the miracle had happened, and went on with the practical task of arranging circumstances so that the lives of other men might be steered in a direction as happy as his own. Owen, observed one of his contemporaries, "might live in parallelograms, but he argued in circles." [4]

[1] Fourier's leading ideas are to be found in germ in an article entitled "Harmonie universelle," published in the *Bulletin de Lyon*, 11 frimaire, an XII [3 déc. 1803], and reprinted in *Publication des manuscrits de Charles Fourier*, tome I, *Année 1851*, 52–53. His first book was the *Quatre Mouvements* of 1808. He won his first disciple, Just Muiron, in 1814, but a Fourierist school did not come into being until the late 1820's and the first Fourierist periodical was issued in 1832. See Bourgin, *Fourier*, livre 4, *passim*. A desultory American interest during the late 1830's did not develop into a Fourierist movement until the publication of Brisbane's *Social Destiny of Man* in 1840, a date which lies beyond the chronological limits of the present study. See Bestor, "Albert Brisbane—Propagandist for Socialism in the 1840's," *New York History*, XXVIII, 128–58 (April 1947).

[2] Owen, *A New View of Society*, Essay Third (1814), reprinted in his *Life . . . Written by Himself*, I, 292; see also I, 352; I.A, 68, 222.

[3] "Causes, over which I could have no control, removed in my early days the bandage which covered my mental sight. If I have been enabled to discover this blindness with which my fellow men are afflicted, . . . it is not from any merit of mine." Owen, *Address Delivered to the Inhabitants of New Lanark, on the First January, 1816, at the Opening of the Institution Established for the Formation of Character* (London, 1816), in *Life*, I, 350; cited hereafter as *New Lanark Address*.

[4] Quoted by Harriet Martineau in her *Biographical Sketches, 1852–1868* (2d ed., London, 1869), p. 313.

It is through biography, not logic, that Owenism must be approached. Robert Owen was born on May 14, 1771, at Newtown in northern Wales, whence he set out, at the age of ten, to seek his fortune in London. After making his way successfully in various retail drygoods establishments, he was eventually attracted to Manchester. There he found himself at the very center of the nascent industrial revolution, based on the new cotton-spinning machinery invented less than a score of years before by Hargreaves, Arkwright, and the others. In Manchester in the 1780's the new factory system was in process of rapid growth, exploiting both the new devices and the working population that gathered to operate them. Rarely has ingenuity, mechanical or managerial, been at such a premium. That Owen possessed the latter in abundance he quickly proved by his first venture in manufacturing, as partner of a young mechanic engaged in building cotton-spinning machines. The partnership was short-lived, but Owen took three of the machines and set himself up as a cotton manufacturer. The business ability he displayed was in such demand that by 1790, before the age of twenty, he had become manager of one of the largest mills in Manchester. The decade of the 1790's—which, incidentally, saw the ruin of Fourier's fortune in France—saw the creation of Owen's in Britain. Successive upward steps in the manufacturing world brought him finally, at the beginning of January 1800, to the managership of the New Lanark mills in Scotland, at a salary of a thousand pounds a year and with a one-ninth interest in the partnership that owned not only the factory but the village itself.[5]

For a quarter of a century New Lanark was the center of Owen's activities. It was there that he initiated the experiments in factory reform that gradually evolved into experiments in comprehensive social planning. It was there that he finally made his decision against programs that looked to a gradual amelioration of existing society and in favor of those that proposed a communitarian transformation of it. It was from New Lanark as a base that he first projected his ideas to the world at large, and it was to New Lanark that he constantly pointed as evidence that his plans were practicable. It was with good reason that he signed himself, on the title pages of most of his early books, "Robert Owen of New Lanark."

But Owen's achievements at New Lanark, impressive though they were, are not our present concern. His activities there are important primarily because they reveal so clearly the characteristic attitudes of mind that went into the making of Owen's new view of society.

To begin with, Owen saw clearly that the inhabitants of the little

---

[5] Owen, *Life*, I, 1, 11, 21–32, 56, 78. See also Frank Podmore, *Robert Owen: A Biography* (2 vols., London, 1906), chaps. I–III

mill town were caught in circumstances beyond their control. Their vices were the consequences of the life they were obliged to lead. Even their virtues were imposed upon them by the discipline of the factory. In the face of the facts that he observed, Owen's earlier doubts about individual responsibility hardened into the conviction that "character is universally formed *for* and not *by* the individual." [6]

Holding such a belief, Owen could be neither a moralist nor, in any fundamental sense, an individualist. He must operate upon society and his procedures must be practical and utilitarian. This pragmatic way of working—characteristic of all his efforts in social reform—was well described by Owen himself in an autobiographical passage written in the third person. New Lanark, he said,

> was a fair field on which to try the efficacy in practice of principles supposed capable of altering any characters. The manager formed his plans accordingly. He spent some time in finding out the full extent of the evil against which he had to contend, and in tracing the true causes which had produced and were continuing these effects. . . . He therefore began to bring forward his various expedients to withdraw the unfavourable circumstances by which they had hitherto been surrounded, and to replace them by others calculated to produce a more happy result. [7]

Throughout his career Owen was, in fact, more the enlightened manager than the social theorist. At times this gave him the characteristics of a benevolent despot. After his public meetings in London in 1817 he expressed surprise that anyone should imagine that he "wished to have the opinions of the ill-trained and uninformed on any of the measures intended for their relief and amelioration. No! On such subjects, until they shall be instructed in better habits, and made rationally intelligent, their advice can be of no value." [8] Eight years later he inaugurated the New Harmony experiment by declaring, "As no other individual has had the same experience as myself in the practice of the system about to be introduced, I must for some time, partially take the lead in its direction." [9] A judicious participant in that experiment attributed many of Owen's difficulties to his failure to recognize that "the materials in this country are not the same as the cotton spinners at New Lanark, nor does the advice of a patron go so far." [10] Time did not soften Owen's attitude. In 1844,

---

[6] *New Lanark Address* (1816), in *Life*, I, 352.

[7] *A New View of Society*, Essay Second (1813), in *Life*, I, 279.

[8] "Fourth Letter," Sept. 6, 1817, in *Life*, I.A, 119–20.

[9] "Address . . . on Wednesday, the 27th of April, 1825, in the Hall of New-Harmony," *New-Harmony Gazette*, I, 2 (Oct. 1, 1825).

[10] William Maclure to Marie D. Fretageot, Louisville, Ky., Sept. 25, 1826, in A. E. Bestor, Jr., ed., *Education and Reform at New Harmony: Correspondence of William Maclure and Marie Duclos Fretageot, 1820–1833* (Indiana Historical

for example, he bluntly told the Congress of the Rational Society, which he had founded, that

he could not accept of office in connection with the Society, unless he could have full authority to act as circumstances rendered it necessary, without reference to previous resolutions of Congress. If they desired his services, it would be necessary for them to rescind the resolutions which they had passed, . . . as he would not [sic] only act as circumstances appeared to him to render it necessary, and not according to the wishes of individuals who had no experience of what was necessary for the government to do.[11]

Owen was not always so dictatorial, but a certain distrust of popular control marked all his proposals for reform. Though he offered self-government to his proposed communities, he indicated his suspicion of conventional democratic machinery by recommending a substitute: "Their affairs should be conducted by a committee, composed of all the members of the association between certain ages—for instance, of those between thirty-five and forty-five. . . . By this equitable and natural arrangement all the numberless evils of elections and electioneering will be avoided."[12]

These characteristic ways of thinking and acting—all clearly manifested at New Lanark—explain some features of Owen's socialist system, but they do not explain why he should have developed a socialist system in the first place. Something deeper and more fundamental in Owen's character set him apart from his fellow manufacturers and filled his mind with the great dream that was to inspire the Owenite movement.

In the first place, Owen was unique among the cotton lords of his day in ascribing his personal success not to his own individual effort but to social forces of which he was the beneficiary. There was a normal amount of human vanity in Owen, as his autobiography reveals, but it was not the typical conceit of the self-made businessman. Though Owen appreciated the role of effective management, he did not attribute the increase of wealth in society to managerial or entrepreneurial skill. Without reservation he credited it to the increased productivity of the new machinery, or the new "scientific power" as he called it. Great Britain, he estimated in 1818, has "ac-

---

Society *Publications*, vol. XV, no. 3; Indianapolis, 1948), p. 371; cited hereafter as *Maclure-Fretageot Correspondence* or, where the context is clear, *Correspondence*.

[11] *New Moral World*, XII, 402 (June 8, 1844).

[12] *Report to the County of Lanark* (1821), in *Life*, I.A, 301. Two of the small communities established at New Harmony actually applied this principle. Macluria entrusted executive power to a Council of Fathers comprising the five eldest members under the age of sixty-five. Feiba-Peveli confided similar powers to the five eldest under fifty-five. See *New-Harmony Gazette*, I, 209, 225 (March 29 and April 12, 1826).

quired a new aid from science in twenty-five years, which enables her to increase her riches, annually, twelve times in quantity beyond what she possessed the power of creating prior to that period." [13]

Being under no illusion that he, as an efficient manager, was the personal creator of the new wealth that surrounded him, he was able gradually to evolve a new conception of the ultimate aims of management itself. His first conception, the foundation of his earliest success in Manchester, was conventional enough: to maintain "order and regularity throughout the establishment." [14] But as he became responsible for ever larger enterprises he grew increasingly aware of the importance of the human, as against the mechanical, constituents of the factory system. Addressing his fellow "superintendents of manufactories" in 1814, he wrote:

Experience has shown you the difference of the results between mechanism which is neat, clean, well-arranged, and always in a high state of repair; and that which is allowed to be dirty, in disorder, without the means of preventing unnecessary friction. . . .

If, then, due care as to the state of your inanimate machines can produce such beneficial results, what may not be expected if you devote equal attention to your vital machines, which are far more wonderfully constructed? . . . [It is] natural to conclude that the more delicate, complex, living mechanism, would be equally improved by being trained to strength and activity; and that it would also prove true economy to keep it neat and clean; to treat it with kindness, that its mental movements might not experience too much irritating friction; to endeavour by every means to make it more perfect; to supply it regularly with a sufficient quantity of wholesome food and other necessaries of life, that the body might be preserved in good working condition, and prevented from being out of repair, or falling prematurely to decay.[15]

This was, of course, an *argumentum ad hominem;* Owen was proposing a humanitarian program to those whose only measuring rod was a pecuniary one. He was not falsifying his argument, however, for he believed, and never ceased to believe, that such a program would be profitable according to even the narrowest definition of profit. But if it were not, then Owen, still speaking as a cotton manufacturer to cotton manufacturers, was ready to exclaim: "Perish the cotton trade, perish even the political superiority of our country, (if it depends on the cotton trade,) rather than they shall be upheld by the sacrifice of everything valuable in life by those who are the means of supporting them." [16]

[13] Owen, *Two Memorials on Behalf of the Working Classes* (London, 1818), in *Life,* I.A, 214–15.

[14] *Life,* I, 23.

[15] *A New View of Society,* address prefixed to Essay Third (1814), in *Life,* I, 260–61.

[16] "Observations on the Cotton Trade" (1815), in *Life,* I.A, 18.

The fact is, Owen refused to differentiate his responsibility as a manager from his responsibility as a citizen. Viewing wealth as a social product, he held that society was entitled to the fullest possible return for its effort, and that the primary duty of those in control of the industrial system was to secure this result. Without ceasing to regard himself as the manager of a business enterprise, Owen in the end made management identical with social and economic statesmanship:

It is the grand interest of society to adopt practical measures by which the largest amount of useful and valuable productions may be obtained at the least expense of manual labour and with the most comfort to the producers. . . .

The grand question now to be solved, is, not how a sufficiency of wealth for all may be produced; but how the excess of riches which may be most easily created, may be generally distributed throughout society advantageously for all, and without *prematurely* disturbing the existing institutions or arrangements in any country.[17]

By recognizing problems that others could not or would not see and devising pragmatic solutions to them, Owen started on the path of reform. By reaching out to understand and control the great forces that were molding society, he became a full-fledged reformer. But how came he to be, in especial, a communitarian reformer? The New Lanark experience is again the key.

This is not to say that New Lanark itself constituted a communitarian experiment. It was a cotton manufactory, set in the midst of a company town, and Owen never sought to change its primary character as a business establishment. "Let it therefore be kept in everlasting rememberance," he wrote, "that that which I effected at New Lanark was only the best I could accomplish under the circumstances of an ill-arranged manufactory and village, which existed before I undertook the government of the establishment." Far from being a model of his system, he declared, "its foundation is an error; and its superstructure could be amended only by an entire re-creation of new conditions."[18]

Even so, Owen's experiments at New Lanark bent his mind in the direction of communitarianism. The mill town itself was an isolated community with a population of approximately two thousand. As manager of the mills Owen could direct the entire population along the new lines he laid down, with a minimum of interference from outside. These were, after all, the distinctive preconditions that the

[17] *Two Memorials* (1818), in *Life*, I.A, 215–16. The first of the quoted paragraphs is printed in italics in the original.

[18] *Life*, I, 80, 79. He made a similar disclaimer publicly as early as 1816. *Ibid.*, I, 355.

communitarian always sought. From the very beginning, moreover, Owen analyzed the problems of the village in collective, social terms, not individualistic ones. He ruled out the idea of individual responsibility, and consistently viewed the thievery, drunkenness, falsehood, and prostitution in the town as the results of social maladjustment, not personal depravity. He devised a multitude of practical expedients to forestall the misdeeds rather than punish the wrongdoers. This philosophy of prevention, moreover, underlay the comprehensive educational program that he inaugurated at New Lanark, the bearing of which upon his development into a communitarian reformer must be considered in a later chapter.[19] The point to note here is that his educational plans focused upon the community rather than the individual. Time after time he used the phrase "train the young collectively." [20] And the name he applied to his educational enterprise, the Institution Established for the Formation of Character, referred to the collective character he expected to give to the population as a whole. In the end he laid claim to success on the ground that his program had "effected a complete change in the general character of the village." [21] And when he came to generalize, as he loved to do, he proposed the axiom: "Any character, from the best to the worst, from the most ignorant to the most enlightened, may be given to any community, even to the world at large." [22] His whole conception was unmistakably social.

It is hard to say when Owen first began to envisage his program as one to be imitated afar. The tendency of an old man is to read his ultimate purposes too far back into his youth, and Owen was guilty of this in the autobiography he wrote at the age of eighty-six. Contemporary documents suggest that it was not until 1812 or thereabouts that he turned his mind decisively outward from the specific problems of New Lanark to the general problems of society. That he did so then was probably owing largely to difficulties with his partners, whose reluctance to spend money on nonremunerative enterprises like the Institution Established for the Formation of Character impelled him to look for partners more sympathetic with his purposes. To aid him in this quest Owen prepared his first pamphlet, an anonymous *Statement Regarding the New Lanark Establishment,* printed in Edinburgh in 1812. He spent much of this year and the next in London, where he succeeded in inducing a group of distinguished reformers—among them Jeremy Bentham and the Quaker philanthropist William Allen—to join him in a

---

[19] See chapter VI, below.
[20] *A New View of Society,* Essay Fourth (1814), in *Life,* I, 309, 314, 316, 323.
[21] Essay Second (1813), in *Life,* I, 284.
[22] Title page of Essay First (1813), in *Life,* I, 255; see also pp. 265, 266.

partnership which purchased the New Lanark Mills in December 1813. From this time forward Owen's scope was national, not local. Recognizing his new role, he printed in 1813 and 1814 the four parts of *A New View of Society: or, Essays on the Principle of the Formation of the Human Character, and the Application of the Principle to Practice.*[23]

The communitarian tendencies that marked Owen's activity at New Lanark were born of local circumstances rather than deliberate choice. Whether he would develop, in the national arena, a communitarian or a legislative (that is to say, a gradual) program was an open question. His first proposals were neither decisively the one nor the other. *A New View of Society* described at length his various proceedings at New Lanark and suggested, by unmistakable inference, that one path to reform might well be the imitation of them in other small-scale experiments. On the other hand, the final essay was entitled "The Principles of the Former Essays Applied to Government," and therein Owen advocated national programs of education and public works.

In his next important move Owen leaned definitely to legislative, not communitarian, means. In January 1815 he publicly proposed that Parliament enact a drastic measure prohibiting the labor of children under ten in factories, restricting the hours of work to ten and a half for children under eighteen years, requiring four years of compulsory education for all children employed, and appointing paid inspectors (or "visitors") to enforce the act.[24] The fate of the proposal

[23] The four essays were first printed as individual pamphlets in London, the first two in 1813, the last two in 1814. They were not published until 1816. The title of the first edition, given above, was the same for each. The words "Essay Second" and "Essay Fourth" followed the title on those particular numbers only; the other two title pages were without such indication. The first two essays were originally issued anonymously, authorship being attributed to "One of His Majesty's Justices of Peace for the County of Lanark"; the last two carried Owen's name. The first edition of Essay Second bore the words "A Proof Copy" on the half-title; the last two essays, in their first editions, carried the printed notation "Not Published" at the foot of the title pages. A number of variations in imprint and pagination are recorded in existing bibliographies, and it is probable that Owen had copies struck off on different occasions before formal publication. Among the variants is a set of the four essays, bound together, in which Essay Second carries Owen's name, and Essays Third and Fourth have undated half-titles instead of full title pages. The typography and paper are inferior to the other early editions, and the set may represent a much later reprinting. The first *published* edition, London, 1816, is described on the title page as the second edition and carries a notice that "the profits of this edition will be given to the Association for the relief of the Manufacturing and Labouring Poor." The essays are reprinted (with the omission of one of the dedications) in *Life,* I, 253–332, to which all citations herein are made.

[24] The various documents are reprinted in *Life,* I.A, 11–45, 183–204; see also Owen's own narrative, *ibid.,* I, 112–21, and Podmore, *Robert Owen,* I, 184–211.

was disillusioning in the extreme to Owen. Though Sir Robert Peel, father of the Prime Minister of a later day, sponsored the measure in the House of Commons, Owen himself was subjected to a hostile, and in many respects unfair, cross-examination by the committee to which it was referred. He witnessed repeated postponements of the measure, and perceived, when an emasculated version was finally enacted in 1819, that most of the reforms he had envisaged were left unrealized, so to remain until the Factory Act of 1833.

The final effect of this experience with legislation—in other words, with a gradual approach to social reform—was to commit Owen definitely to communitarianism. The turning point was an address which he delivered on January 1, 1816, in New Lanark at the opening of the finally completed Institution Established for the Formation of Character. Though Owen had moved easily in parliamentary and ministerial circles, he now realized that the force he wished to exert required a definite, localized fulcrum. Politics would always remain a mystery to him, but at New Lanark he was back in a situation he thoroughly understood, and one where he had been able to work with singular effectiveness for upwards of a decade and a half. It is not surprising that he formulated, more explicitly than ever before, the idea of accomplishing reform through a small-scale experiment that might serve as a model for widespread imitation. "I wish to benefit all equally," he told the inhabitants of New Lanark, "but circumstances limit my present measures for the public good within a narrow circle. I must begin to act at some point; and a combination of singular events has fixed that point at this establishment." The means were local, but the end was nothing less than "to effect extensive ameliorations throughout the British dominions." Owen had not given up hope that legislation might make its contribution, but he placed his main reliance upon "an example in practice." And he pointed out the added advantages in this small-scale, communitarian way of proceeding. The various reforms would be rendered more beneficial, he said, "by their being *all brought into practice together*" instead of being undertaken piecemeal. The direction of Owen's thinking was clear, but he was not yet ready with a fully worked-out scheme. All he could promise was that "in due time communities shall be formed possessing such characters," the details to be "more particularly described in a future publication." [25]

The promise was soon fulfilled. Before the end of 1817 the national

---

Owen originally proposed that the labor of children under twelve should be prohibited, and that the maximum hours should apply to all employees. *Life,* I.A, 18. His draft bill, however, contained the provisions summarized above. *Ibid.,* pp. 23–26.

[25] *New Lanark Address* (1816), in *Life,* I, 344, 348 (two quotations), 353, 355, 356.

economic crisis elicited from Owen a full-fledged communitarian plan. The problem of the unemployed had concerned Owen in a general way as early as 1813,[26] but it was the condition of those actually at work that he had sought primarily to improve. By 1816, however, their misery was overshadowed by the plight of those who had been thrown out of work by the cessation of the Napoleonic Wars. All along Owen had confidently described his principles as "universal, and applicable to all times, persons, and circumstances." [27] Here were times, circumstances, and persons that would test them as they had never been tested before. Could the new machinery actually be made to produce abundance for all? Was education powerful enough in fact to check the demoralization of the unemployed and to create in them the qualities of character on which a harmonious and happy society might be built?

Owen could admit none but an affirmative answer. The principles were clear. As at New Lanark, the only problem was to devise suitable expedients and arrangements. This he undertook to do. By the summer of 1816 he was ready to suggest a few of them orally to a committee sponsored by the Association for the Relief of the Manufacturing and Labouring Poor. The committee desired to see the plan in writing, but by the time it was ready they had decided it should more properly go before the poor-law committee of the House of Commons. On March 12, 1817, accordingly, Owen submitted his proposal, complete with illustrative drawing, to the parliamentary committee. The rebuff he had experienced in connection with his factory bill was repeated, but more pointedly: the committee kept him waiting in an anteroom for two days and then decided not to take the testimony which they had summoned him to give.[28]

This time Owen took the matter to the country. It was a new departure for him. Previously he had sought only a select audience. His first three pieces of writing had been printed anonymously and had circulated in limited editions with the notations "Not Published" or "Proof Copy" on the preliminary pages.[29] Now he took an opposite tack and developed overnight a battery of devices for mass propaganda. He secured the publication of his report in full in both the **London *Times*** and **the *Morning Post*** of April 9, 1817. It appeared also in the *Philanthropist,* published by his partner William Allen. Before long Owen had issued it in at least two other forms, as a cheaply printed broadside and as one of the pamphlets which he

---

[26] See *A New View of Society,* Essay Second (1813), in *Life,* I, 285; and, for a more extensive statement, Essay Fourth (1814), *ibid.,* 325–30.

[27] Essay Second (1813), in *Life,* I, 283.

[28] *Life,* I, 121–33, 155.

[29] See above, p. 68, n. 23.

collected together in a volume entitled *New View of Society: Tracts Relative to This Subject.*[30] Having been denied a hearing by the poor-law committee, he wrote out a cross-examination of himself and published it in the *Times* and other papers on July 30. At the same time he announced a great public meeting, which was held in the City of London Tavern on August 14 and was followed by a second meeting a week later. The texts of his addresses, which took hours to deliver, were furnished to the newspapers and printed in full. In his spare time he composed lengthy public letters, which received equal attention in the press.[31] Of each newspaper he purchased thirty thousand copies, and "had one copy sent to the minister of every parish in the kingdom,—one to every member of both houses of parliament,—one to each of the chief magistrates and bankers in each city and town,—and one to each of the leading persons in all classes." As if this were not enough he reprinted the documents in three numbered broadsides, headed *New View of Society,* and distributed forty thousand copies.[32] The flood subsided on September 25, when the *Times* announced that it had decided not to publish his latest communication.[33] By this time Owen himself was ready to call a halt, for in two months he had expended four thousand pounds on propaganda. It was money well spent. He had made himself a national figure and had aroused such enthusiasm that he felt justified in opening a New State of Society Enrolment Office in Fleet Street, where those who would might sign the waiting list of the millennium.[34]

As this announcement proved, the plan already encompassed far more than poor relief. It was, in fact, the communitarian plan which —with important modifications that must be discussed later—Owen

[30] London, 1818. The various tracts bound up in this volume are independently paged and are frequently met with separately. They may have been so issued, though they carry half-titles rather than full title pages.

[31] The "Report to the Committee of the Association for the Relief of the Manufacturing and Labouring Poor," the four letters to the newspapers, and the two public addresses are reprinted in *Life,* I.A, 53–138. The brief running heads supplied in this collection are used herein in citing the individual documents, e.g., "Report on the Poor," March 12, 1817; "First Letter," July 25, 1817. The dates are those of writing or delivery. Headnotes in the reprint also give the dates of publication in the London newspapers, which have been verified in the *Times.*

[32] *Life,* I, 156; see also Podmore, *Robert Owen,* II, 656–57. Besides the numbered broadsides and the complete newspapers, Owen appears also to have distributed offprints from the latter. An "offsheet from the 'Sun' News-paper" is described in George Harding's Bookshop, London, *Catalogue* 54 (Winter 1939), p. 38, item 3464. This contains Owen's "Second Letter," published Aug. 9, 1817, but corresponds to none of the numbered broadsides.

[33] London *Times,* Sept. 25, 1817, p. 2:3–4. The communication was received in printed form; it was the "Address," dated Sept. 19, 1817, reprinted in *Life,* I.A, 138–41.

[34] "Address," Sept. 19, 1817, in *Life,* I.A, 141.

was to advocate for the remaining forty-one years of his life. The summer of 1817 was the most creative period in his intellectual development and the great turning point in his career. In those months his ideas crystallized finally in a communitarian pattern, and his leadership became that of a propagandist to the masses of men. The documents he published in 1817, though often neglected, are actually the key to his thought, his program, and his influence.

At the very outset Owen's solution for the problem of unemployment involved the use of small, self-sufficient groups. His original report of March 12, 1817, may not have offered a completely communitarian proposal, but it did reject explicitly the revolutionary, the individualistic, and the gradual methods of reform. After warning against the first, he went on to reject the second and third by denying that the necessary reforms could be applied "either to individuals or to families separately, or to large congregated numbers." They could, he continued, "be effectually introduced into practice only under arrangements that would unite in one establishment a population of from 500 to 1,500 persons, averaging about 1,000." [35] The very nature of the problem, it should be remarked, encouraged Owen to adopt a group procedure, for relief was traditionally handled by local agencies, and experiments had already been made by certain poor-law authorities with houses of industry that embodied at least some elements of self-sufficient community life.[36] More influential upon Owen than such precedents, however, was his experience at New Lanark. He was not proposing simply a means of self-support, as had those who were concerned only about the increasing cost of relief. He was proposing a whole group of reforms aimed at improving the condition of the unemployed, reforms which, like those at New Lanark, were integrated with one another and were designed to create a new social and educational environment.

In the report itself Owen stuck closely to the matter of relief for the unemployed poor. But the more he worked on the details of his proposed establishments the more he realized that his plan was of far wider applicability. How rapidly the proposal broadened out is revealed by the successive documents he published during the summer of 1817. Certain statements in his self-catechism of July 24 were straws in the wind. Asked (by himself, of course) whether the proposed villages might not ultimately compete with existing agricultural, manufacturing, and commercial enterprises, he conceded the possibility, but argued that the poor-law authorities could restrain them from doing so. Then came a significant afterthought: "When society

---

[35] "Report on the Poor," March 12, 1817, in *Life*, I.A, 57.

[36] Frank Podmore cites examples in his *Robert Owen*, I, 229–30, but attributes to them more influence upon the formation of Owen's plan than the evidence seems to me to warrant.

shall, however, discover its true interests, it will permit these new establishments gradually to supersede the others; inasmuch as the latter are wretchedly degrading, and directly opposed to the improvement and well-being of those employed either in agriculture or manufactures." [37] Two weeks later he amplified this idea by presenting some sixteen point-by-point comparisons between conditions "In the Manufacturing Towns" and "In the Proposed Villages." [38] So attractive did Owen make the latter that he fell in love with his own pictures. At his first public meeting on August 14 he exclaimed, "Should my life be longer spared, the utmost bounds of my ambition is to become an undistinguished member of one of these happy villages." [39] He hardly needed to add, in his second address a week later, that he had "no idea that these villages will be occupied by the present poor only." [40]

Clearly the plan had become, in Owen's mind, an all-embracing scheme of social reform. But he had not yet explicitly announced it as such. This he finally did in a fourth letter, dated September 6, 1817, and published on the tenth. It was the last of the great series of communications with which he stuffed the newspapers and blanketed the realm during those summer weeks. The series could well come to an end, for with this article Owen finally placed himself on record as the exponent of a definitively communitarian program for the reorganization of society and, as the title of his letter announced, "the emancipation of mankind." What he proposed was a whole hierarchy of villages. The parish paupers, for whom the plan had originally been designed, were now to constitute only the first class. There were to be villages as well for the working classes, with or without property, and, at the top of the scale, Voluntary and Independent Associations for those with property ranging from a thousand to twenty thousand pounds.

The demand for the latter, Owen believed, would become irresistible once the proposed arrangements were tried out upon paupers and their advantages demonstrated. Forthwith "the meanest and most miserable beings now in society will . . . become the envy of the rich and indolent under the existing arrangements." Then "it will be obvious to the meanest capacity that the OLD state of society will not bear one moment's comparison with the NEW; and *that the only real practical difficulty will be to restrain men from rushing too precipitately from one to the other."* The change must come gradually, he said, but what Owen called gradual most men would

[37] "First Letter," dated July 25, 1817, published July 30, reprinted in *Life*, I.A, 74; it was actually written on the twenty-fourth, as is indicated on p. 78.

[38] "Second Letter," Aug. 7, 1817 (published Aug. 9), in *Life*, I.A, 89–92.

[39] "First Address," Aug. 14, 1817, in *Life*, I.A, 102.

[40] "Second Address," Aug. 21, 1817, in *Life*, I.A, 118.

term abrupt. "The change," he said, "cannot be effected in a week or a month,—although much, very much, may be put into action next year." Apocalyptic passages from the Bible crowded into the closing paragraphs of his letter and dictated the phrasing of its peroration: "Thus, in the fulness of time, ere its commencement was well known, is the great work accomplished. The change has come upon the world like a thief in the night!" [41]

Taken together, Owen's publications of 1817 constituted a fully developed communitarian proposal. Though major aspects of his system underwent drastic alteration in the forty subsequent years that he kept it before the public, certain characteristics of it remained constant. These unchanging features should obviously be examined first.

To begin with, Owen believed that a healthy and happy society could not be based on the great overgrown cities that industrialism was spawning, or, at the other extreme, upon "single and detrimental solitude." He had observed, he reported in 1829, "the effects of a gradual increasing population, from a few families until they amounted to about twenty-five hundred souls," and had assured himself that "the true minimum and maximum had been passed." His conclusion was that "the best medium number, ranges between eight hundred and twelve hundred, and that all associations of men, when they become rational, will be composed of congregations never descending below five hundred, nor ascending above two thousand." [42] The exact numbers given by Owen varied somewhat—in the 1840's he was talking of communities of two thousand or twenty-five hundred members [43]—but the principle never. It is significant that twenty-five hundred has always been recognized as a critical point in measurements of local population. The United States Census, for example, makes use of precisely this figure to distinguish rural from urban settlements. Owen, in other words, was insisting that country life and agricultural occupations must form part of any truly balanced social existence. His personal observation had convinced him that

manufactures, when they constitute the exclusive employment of a population, cannot, by any possible arrangement, be made compatible with the

[41] "Fourth Letter," Sept. 6, 1817, in *Life*, I.A, 126, 125, 132, 137; the last sentence quoted was originally printed in capitals. The letter was entitled "A Further Development of the Plan for the Relief of the Poor, and the Emancipation of Mankind."

[42] *Robert Owen's Opening Speech, and His Reply to the Rev. Alex. Campbell* (Cincinnati, 1829), pp. 123–24. The same optimum had been mentioned in his *Report to the County of Lanark* (1821), in *Life*, I.A, 281–83.

[43] Owen, *Home Colonies* (2d ed., 1841), p. 37. In 1849 he spoke of a maximum of 3,000 persons, the highest figure he ever used. *The Revolution in the Mind and Practice of the Human Race* (London, 1849), p. 42.

possession of that degree of health and happiness to which human beings are entitled; and that this object can only be attained under a system, combining manufacturing with agricultural labour, and of which the latter is the basis.[44]

On the other hand, Owen was not beating a retreat from the industrial age. He firmly believed that men could master its problems and use its power to create a society richer in every respect than those of the past. The starting point of his plan in 1817 was his calculation that machinery had increased the productive power of Great Britain fifteen- or twenty-fold in the preceding quarter of a century. "Mechanism," he went on, "may be made the greatest of blessings to humanity" instead of "its greatest curse." [45] Far from minimizing industry, Owen proposed to "permit mechanical inventions and improvements to be carried to any extent," confident that under his arrangements "every improvement in mechanism would be rendered subservient to and in aid of human labour." [46] He foresaw and welcomed the application of machinery to household tasks which in his day had hardly been touched by the progress of invention. In the end, he promised, "MECHANISM AND SCIENCE *will be extensively introduced to execute all the work that is over-laborious, disagreeable, or in any way injurious to human nature,*" to such an extent as "to render MECHANISM AND SCIENCE *the only slaves or servants of men.*" [47]

In Owen's mind, moreover, the small size of the units which he wished to adopt—communities of twenty-five hundred inhabitants

[44] Quoted in Henry Grey Macnab, *The New Views of Mr. Owen of Lanark Impartially Examined* (London, 1819), p. 72. Owen's contemporary Fourier condemned him for ignoring agriculture. *Traité de l'association* (1822), I, 3. This was a misapprehension, arising possibly out of the assumption that Owen's plan was essentially the same as his practice at New Lanark. Owen constantly insisted that it was not, particularly as regards the combination of agriculture with manufacturing. See especially *Life*, I.A, 257.

[45] "Second Address," Aug. 21, 1817, in *Life*, I.A, 111.

[46] "Report on the Poor," March 12, 1817, in *Life*, I.A, 64. Owen's curious advocacy of spade cultivation in place of the plow—an aspect of his plan in 1819–21 —was not an intentional contradiction of this faith in applied science, for he firmly, however erroneously, believed that the change would "produce far greater improvements in agriculture, than the steam engine has effected in manufactures." *Report to the County of Lanark* (1821), in *Life*, I.A, 274. Spade husbandry, incidentally, was still a fad among British social reformers a quarter of a century later. See *People's Journal*, III, supplement (entitled "Annals of Progress"), 13–14, 28, 36 (Feb. 13, April 3, May 1, 1847).

[47] "Fourth Letter," Sept. 6, 1817, in *Life*, I.A, 124. The Owenites gave an earnest of what they intended at their community of Harmony Hall or Queenwood in Hampshire, where a visitor in 1842 noted the mechanical devices for delivering food from kitchen to dining-hall, and remarked that "there were very few kitchens so completely and expensively fitted up," even in London. Alexander Somerville, as quoted in Podmore, *Robert Owen*, II, 548.

or less—did not constitute an obstacle to the full utilization of the new "scientific power." This is a fact which it is vital to remember in connection not only with Owenism but with the entire communitarian movement of the second quarter of the nineteenth century. New Lanark did not exceed this size, yet the manufactory there was sufficiently large to keep fully abreast of technological advance. In America none of the sectarian communities approached the number of members which Owen set as a maximum, yet many of them, notably the Shakers and the Rappites, carried on a combination of agricultural and manufacturing operations that impressed contemporaries by their progressive methods as well as by their profitableness. So long as ninety per cent of the American people made their living in places with a population less than twenty-five hundred—which they did until 1840—the limitation of a community to that size could hardly be regarded as retrogressive. Until the middle of the century it was reasonable to believe that most of the advantages of the new machinery could be realized, while its disadvantages were avoided, in settlements of the size that communitarians, with striking unanimity,[48] were proposing. The decline of the communitarian doctrine was rapid once this belief began to be rendered untenable by the great increase in the size of successful industrial and business units in the last half of the nineteenth century.

Owen's views on the proper size for a community coincided with those of his contemporaries in the communitive movement. So too did his statements concerning the economies to be expected from co-operative living. Under the present system, he wrote, "each family must have domestic arrangements for cooking, &c., and one person must be wholly occupied in preparing provisions, &c., for a family of ordinary numbers," whereas in his proposed villages "the best provisions will be cooked in the best manner, under arrangements that will enable five or six individuals to prepare provisions for 1000." [49] Wasteful methods of exchange would also disappear when whole networks of communities began to trade directly with one another, eliminating the costly middleman. Strikingly similar passages may be found in the writings of Charles Fourier,[50] though their respective systems were worked out in almost complete independence of each other.[51]

The resemblance extended even to the physical arrangements

48 Fourier fixed upon 1,620 persons as the theoretical optimum and warned that a community of 2,000 would be hazardously large. *Traité de l'association* (1822), II, 17–21.

49 Owen, "Second Letter," Aug. 7, 1817, in *Life*, I.A, 90.

50 See, for example, Fourier, *Traité de l'association* (1822), I, 348–76, 462–96, 546–81.

51 Owen, to be sure, believed that it was from his own *Report to the County*

proposed. Both Owen and Fourier recommended the centralized grouping of the buildings, which were to be interconnected by enclosed passageways. Fourier's "phalanstery" was a great palace with wings, and Owen planned a closed "parallelogram" with living apartments around the four sides, and school, church, and dining hall across the center.[52] Owen wisely placed his workshops at a distance across the fields, whereas Fourier's were to occupy the wings of the main building—an arrangement justly criticized by the Owenites.[53] The likenesses, however, were more striking than the differences, and elaborate architectural drawings figured in the propaganda of both Owenites and Fourierites.

The details of community life just described were pictured in exactly the same way in all the proposals that Owen offered during his long career as a social reformer. In the economic aspects of his plan, however, there is no such consistency. His ideas on property, on the distribution of income, and on the question of social equality underwent changes whose magnitude few students of his doctrine have sufficiently grasped. Socialism today is so predominantly a matter of economic theory that consistent views on these matters have come to be almost the *sine qua non* of a socialist system. It is a falsification of history, however, to read the modern preoccupation with economics back into the socialist thought of the early nineteenth century—particularly into Owenism.

---

of Lanark, written in 1820 and published in 1821, "that Fourrier [*sic*] obtained all his knowledge respecting the formation of a society limited in number to form a *practical* community." *Life,* I, 234, see also p. 238. This was quite untrue, as shown above, p. 61. Fourier borrowed a few details of his educational plans from Owen, whom he heard of first in 1820, but that was all. See Bourgin, *Fourier,* pp. 106–15. On the other hand, Owen derived practically nothing from Fourier, despite the latter's priority. He probably first learned of the French socialist about 1824, when Fourier began to correspond with some of the English Owenites. *Ibid.,* pp. 106–7. Fourier's dream of "attractive industry" was faintly reflected in the *Articles of Agreement Drawn Up and Recommended by the London Co-Operative Society* ([London], 1825), p. 10. Fourier's proposal that disagreeable tasks be undertaken by children as a matter of honor was borrowed by Owen in 1830 in his *Lectures on an Entire New State of Society,* p. 148. In the 1840's the latter proposed a "civil army" similar to the *armées industrielles* that Fourier had described long before. Compare Fourier, *Traité de l'association* (1822), II, 108–13, with Owen, *Lectures on the Rational System* (1841), p. 162, and *Revolution in the Mind and Practice* (1849), p. 71. These, the only demonstrable borrowings, form an insignificant part of Owen's system.

[52] Owen, "Report on the Poor," March 12, 1817, in *Life,* I.A, 58, and accompanying illustration. For a later description see his *Home Colonies* (2d ed., 1841), pp. 37–40, and the two elaborate folding plates. The pictures and models that he used in propaganda are discussed below, pp. 128–29.

[53] See William Thompson, *Practical Directions for the Speedy and Economical Establishment of Communities* (London [1830]), p. 58.

Owen's major purposes were social, in a noneconomic sense of that term. Ethical, educational, and psychological principles were uppermost in his mind. The phrases by which he referred to his plans—a "new moral world," a "rational system of society"—were without economic content. His communities were designed to bring such a moral or rational society into being, and their economic organization was merely a subordinate part of the mechanism—a means, not an end. On secondary matters Owen never felt it necessary to commit himself, permanently and explicitly. To consult expediency in adapting means to ends, to modify subordinate details as need arose, was his normal procedure. Inconsistencies in economic detail were a natural consequence of his pragmatic approach.

Through disregard of this fact an oversimplified version of Owen's economic ideas has been commonly accepted. Contemporaries, of course, could hardly avoid taking a foreshortened view. Fourier, for example, denounced Owen as a believer in complete equality, "a political poison in Association," and as an advocate of "community of goods, which destroys emulation." [54] Modern scholars, on their part, have not escaped the danger. Charles Gide, for example, makes Owen's system hinge upon "the abolition of profit." [55] The inaccuracy of these interpretations becomes apparent if one follows chronologically the changes in Owen's economic thought, for it is by no means true, as G. D. H. Cole asserts, that "Owen said what he had to say in his earlier books; his later works are merely more and more elaborate and prosy repetitions of his better writings." [56] Prosy Owen certainly was, but his incessant repetition of familiar phrases must not be allowed to obscure the changes that his ideas actually underwent. By 1825, when he threw his resources into the experiment at New Harmony, his doctrine already differed significantly from that presented in his writings prior to 1821 (the closing date of Cole's selection). Again in the 1840's, when Owen returned to the United States to propagate his ideas in opposition to the Fourierist system that was then sweeping the reform movement, he offered a program that departed from earlier ones. Three distinct phases in the development of Owen's communitarian doctrine can in fact be recognized. And only during the second phase—from the middle 1820's to the middle 1830's—was he proposing anything like the drastic modifica-

[54] Fourier, *Traité de l'association* (1822), I, 3; *Piéges et charlatanisme des deux sectes Saint-Simon et Owen* (Paris, 1831), p. vi. The latter doctrine, said Fourier, is "so pitiable that it does not deserve refutation." *Nouveau Monde* (1829), in *Oeuvres complètes*, VI, 473.

[55] Charles Gide and Charles Rist, *History of Economic Doctrines*, translated from the 2d revised ed. of 1913 by R. Richards (London, 1915), pp. 239–44.

[56] G. D. H. Cole, introduction to his edition of Owen, *A New View of Society & Other Writings* (Everyman's Library, no. 799; London, 1927), p. vii.

tion of property rights or the thoroughgoing equalitarianism that has usually been attributed to him.

At first glance, it is true, his "Report on the Poor" of 1817 might seem to confirm the conventional analysis of his views. Let it be remembered, however, that the villages he proposed were to be built with public funds and were to be occupied by unemployed and propertyless paupers. In such a context community of property and abolition of profit were meaningless terms. As for equality, that was the natural condition among recipients of parish poor relief. That Owen had no intention of wiping out existing inequalities, economic or social, was clearly revealed the moment he extended his plan to include Villages of Unity and Mutual Co-operation for others than paupers. Not only were four distinct classes clearly recognized in his proposal of September 6, 1817, but each of the two highest classes comprised twelve divisions based entirely on property qualifications. The upper classes, moreover, were promised that "their accommodations of all kinds will be in proportion to the capital they can at first advance or may hereafter acquire." [57]

The different classes of society, in fact, were not even to mingle in the same village, save as the "Working Class, without Property" might be employed by the members of the wealthier communities. So fearful was Owen of breaking down existing social distinctions that he hesitated to bring together in one village any persons who had not "been trained in the same class, sectarian notions, and party feelings." To prevent such dangerous social mingling he drew up, in his methodically humorless fashion, a table of 140 different combinations of sect with party. The number 27, for example, was assigned to High Church adherents who were also violent Ministerialists, and the number 97 to Arminian Methodists who were at the same time moderate Whigs. Each applicant was told, in all seriousness, to sign his name in the numbered column corresponding to his own peculiar combination of convictions, and he was promised a Village of Unity and Mutual Co-operation especially suited to his prejudices as soon as five hundred others like him had registered.[58]

This cautious preservation of social distinctions marked all the plans that Owen put forward during the first phase of his career as an avowed communitarian, a phase extending roughly from 1817

[57] "Fourth Letter," Sept. 6, 1817, in *Life*, I.A, 128, 124. It seems to me a serious misinterpretation to say, as does Podmore, that Owen's September proposal "departed from the simplicity of his original plan," which had been "purely communistic." *Robert Owen*, I, 260, n. 1.

[58] "Fourth Letter," Sept. 6, 1817, in *Life*, I.A, 122, 128–32. As originally published in the London *Times*, Sept. 10, 1817, p. 2:1–5, this table had spaces for Bramins, Confucians, Mahometans, and Pagans, but these were left to fend for themselves when Owen reprinted the table, reducing its squares from 144 to 140.

until his departure for America in 1824. Throughout these years his propaganda was still largely directed to the upper classes, from whom he hoped to obtain the funds for an experimental village. In 1818 he addressed his appeal to the diplomats gathered at the Congress of Aix-la-Chapelle; in 1819 he made it at a meeting in London over which the Duke of Kent presided; in 1820 he laid it before the "Noblemen, Freeholders, Justices of the Peace, and Commissioners of Supply" for the County of Lanark; in 1822 he presented it under the auspices of a British and Foreign Philanthropic Society to which many members of the English aristocracy lent their names; and in 1822–23 he expounded it in Ireland under equally exalted auspices. In the one "Address to the Working Classes" which he published during this period, his tone was paternalistic in the extreme. He described the golden future that was in store for them, told them that the upper classes "have now a real desire to improve your condition," counseled them to be patient, and concluded: "What has been said is sufficient for your minds to digest at one time. When you are prepared to receive more, it shall be given to you." [59]

In view of these social and economic attitudes, it was easy enough for Owen's supporters to explain away the overtones of equalitarianism that sometimes accompanied his doctrine. This was done most explicitly by the committee appointed in 1819 at the "select meeting" over which the Duke of Kent presided:

Several . . . objections rest upon a supposition that Mr. Owen's plans necessarily involve a community of goods; this is a great mistake or misrepresentation. In the establishment which is now proposed there would be no community of goods nor any deviation from the established laws of property. Mr. Owen, it is true, has expressed on a former occasion some opinions in favour of a state of society in which a community of goods should exist, but he has never considered it as essential to the success of such an establishment as is now proposed, nor required it as the condition of his superintendence. . . .

It has also been said that these plans have a tendency to the equalisation of ranks. The notion is connected with, and depends upon, the erroneous one that they involve a community of goods. If the laws of property are preserved, and the plan rests, as it does, upon the supposition of its being a profitable mode of investing capital, it has no other tendency to equalisation than all plans which have for their object the extension of the comforts, the intelligence, and the virtues of the poorer classes of society.[60]

The radicalism which the committee so easily explained away had its origin in three ideas that Owen tentatively expressed between 1817 and 1824, but the implications of which were not fully de-

[59] "An Address to the Working Classes," March 29, 1819, in *Life*, I.A, 230.
[60] "Address of the Committee," Aug. 23, 1819, in *Life*, I.A, 245–46.

veloped until the next period of his career. Most tentative of them all were Owen's reflections on the disproportion between the wealth and influence of the various classes of society and their aggregate numbers. These reflections he expressed in symbols rather than words. Using as a basis the tables on distribution of national income compiled by Patrick Colquhoun in 1814, Owen prepared a set of cubes representing the different classes of society in sizes proportioned to their numbers, and displayed them as a pyramid, the aristocracy resting on the broad base of "the working and the pauper classes." Even without words of explanation, the privileged classes could see the point. When Owen showed the cubes to the Dukes of Kent and Sussex, "the whole party for the moment seemed confused, feeling and seeing the real weakness of their class as to numbers, compared with all the others." [61]

The second idea upon which Owen was later to base his more radical program was the conviction, amounting to positive certainty, that his proposed new arrangements would usher in a future of unlimited abundance. Under such conditions economic inequalities would not need to be abolished; they would literally be submerged. The relation of antecedent and consequent must be carefully noted. Unlimited production was a necessary prerequisite to equality and community of property:

As the easy, regular, healthy, rational employment of the individuals forming these societies will create a very large surplus of their own products, beyond what they will have any desire to consume, each may be freely permitted to receive from the general store of the community whatever they may require.

This expectation was not unlike Fourier's, who also believed that enormously increased production would render meaningless the perpetuation of existing inequalities. But whereas Fourier planned to retain the institution of private property under all circumstances, Owen went on to the conclusion—logical enough, granted his premises—that "individual accumulation of wealth will appear as irrational as to bottle up or store water in situations where there is more of this invaluable fluid than all can consume." [62]

Out of certain reflections of Owen's concerning the monetary

[61] *Life*, I, 151–52. The cubes are pictured in *Report of the Proceedings at the Several Public Meetings Held in Dublin by Robert Owen* (Dublin, 1823), p. 151. In 1826, when Owen had entered fully upon his more radical phase, he used the cubes to show "what a powerful burden rested on the labouring class, and how desirable an equal division of property would be." Karl Bernhard, Duke of Saxe-Weimar-Eisenach, *Travels* (1828), as reprinted in Lindley, ed., *Indiana As Seen by Early Travelers*, p. 435. See also Podmore, *Robert Owen*, I, 255–56, which cites Owen's later descriptions.

[62] *Report to the County of Lanark* (1821), in *Life*, I.A, 303, 302.

system came the third idea that held radical implications for the future. Such theoretical speculations were not characteristic of Owen, but he was led into them in 1820 by the apparent need for devising a circulating medium for his proposed communities. As he sought a basis for this he came to the conclusion, which he stated in his *Report to the County of Lanark,* that "the natural standard of value is, in principle, human labour, or the combined manual and mental powers of men called into action." This was not in itself a revolutionary notion. But as Owen developed its practical bearings he let fall dicta which, in combination, came close to being so: "Manual labour, properly directed, is the source of all wealth," and *"That which can create new wealth is of course worth the wealth which it creates."* [63] Had Owen pushed these statements to their logical conclusion at this time he would have been defending in 1820–21 an intellectual position that in reality he did not occupy until at least half a decade later. In point of fact, he seems not to have grasped the possible implications of what he had said, for in the next breath he shifted his ground completely by asserting that "the producer should have a *fair and fixed proportion* of all the wealth which he creates." [64] There was nothing in this to interfere with the "high profits" which Owen promised that his system would pay.

Unawares Owen had stumbled upon the basic propositions of a doctrine which Anton Menger has called "the right to the whole produce of labour." [65] Adam Smith, of course, had asserted that in the "original state of things, . . . the whole produce of labour belongs to the labourer," [66] but he believed essentially that rent and profit, developing out of the later complexities of economic life, were legitimate deductions from this original whole. The classical economists who followed him took the same position. Menger identifies Charles Hall, writing in 1805, as "the first socialist who saw in rent and interest unjust appropriations of the return of labour, and who explicitly claimed for the worker the undiminished product of his industry." [67] Hall's ideas may have been known to Owen when

[63] *Ibid.,* pp. 268 (in capitals in the original), 264, 278 (italics as shown).

[64] *Ibid.,* p. 278 (italics mine).

[65] Anton Menger, *The Right to the Whole Produce of Labour,* translated by M. E. Tanner, with an introduction and bibliography by H. S. Foxwell (London, 1899). The important contributions of the last-mentioned writer will be cited hereafter as Foxwell, "Introduction to Menger," and "Bibliography."

[66] Adam Smith, *An Inquiry into the Nature and Causes of the Wealth of Nations,* ed. by Edwin Cannan (New York: Modern Library, 1937), p. 64.

[67] Menger, *Right to the Whole Produce of Labour,* p. 48. See also Foxwell's comparison of Hall with William Godwin, William Ogilvie, Thomas Spence, and Tom Paine, who must also be reckoned among the founders of this particular tradition. "Introduction to Menger," pp. xxvii–xxxviii.

he made his *Report to the County of Lanark,* for they were criticized in the first Owenite periodical a few months later.[68] They came to real fruition, however, not in Owen's discourses, but in three writings published in 1824 and 1825: William Thompson's *Inquiry into the Principles of the Distribution of Wealth,* John Gray's *Lecture on Human Happiness,* and Thomas Hodgskin's *Labour Defended against the Claims of Capital.* These writers drew upon a wide and varied range of intellectual sources—upon Godwin and Hall, upon Bentham and the utilitarians, and so notably upon Ricardo that they can properly be described as Ricardian socialists.[69] But Thompson and Gray, at least, reflected also the influence of Owen. And the three men together contributed virtually all the genuine economic theory which Owenism ever possessed.[70]

William Thompson's connection with Owenism was the closest of the three. In his first work he praised Owen's "magnificent combinations, the result of a rare union of profound thought and unequalled practical knowledge." [71] Owen himself read the book aloud and distributed copies of it during his trip to America in 1824, immediately after its publication.[72] Until his death in 1833 Thompson devoted himself to communitarian projects, and in 1830 published his *Practical Directions for the Speedy and Economical Establish-*

[68] *The Economist: A Periodical Paper Explanatory of the New System of Society Projected by Robert Owen,* I, 49–64 (Feb. 17, 1821). See also Foxwell, "Introduction to Menger," pp. xxxiv, xxxvii.

[69] See, in addition to Foxwell and Menger, the dissertation by Esther Lowenthal, *The Ricardian Socialists* (Columbia University, *Studies in History, Economics and Public Law,* vol. XLVI, no. 1; New York, 1911).

[70] To the extent that socialism is viewed primarily as economic theory, Foxwell's conclusion is sound: "After 1830, the Ricardian socialism seems to have captured the Owenite movement. . . . The name Socialist was of Owenite origin, . . . But the ideas which we associate with the term to-day came not so much from Owen as from Thompson and his school. . . . The Ricardian socialism was the yeast of the Owenite movement, and the foundation of all the more able contributions to Owenite literature." Foxwell, "Introduction to Menger," pp. lxxxii–lxxxiii. Foxwell, however, seems to me to make the unconscious assumption that economic theory is the only significant type of theory which is involved in a socialist system. As I have tried to show, communitarianism is itself a theory, though not necessarily an economic one, and to it Owen made original and significant intellectual contributions. In this sense he brought more to the movement than the "ceaseless energy and unflagging enthusiasm" with which Foxwell credits him. *Ibid.,* p. lxxxv, see also pp. xxvii–xxviii.

[71] William Thompson, *An Inquiry into the Principles of the Distribution of Wealth Most Conducive to Human Happiness; Applied to the Newly-Proposed System of Voluntary Equality of Wealth* (London, 1824), p. 384.

[72] See Robert Owen to Messrs. Wheatley & Adelard, Liverpool, Sept. 30, 1824, British Museum, Additional MS 27952, folio 155; Donald Macdonald, *Diaries,* pp. 165–66, 211; "Pelham Letters," pp. 386, 387.

ment of Communities. Owen's plans were always in Thompson's mind.[73] The new contribution he made was to develop in connection with them a complete economic doctrine.

The doctrine was based on the hint that Owen had let drop in his *Report to the County of Lanark.* "The produce of no man's labor," wrote Thompson in 1824, "nor the labor itself, nor any part of them, should be taken from the laborer, without an equivalent *by him* deemed satisfactory." [74] The last phrase was important. Thompson, of course, recognized that one worker might produce more than another, but he believed that laborers would voluntarily agree to equal remuneration in view of the benefits and satisfactions that a state of equality would afford. Consequently, when he summarized his doctrine in the sentence "Wealth should be so distributed as to produce the greatest *equality,* consistent with the greatest production," [75] he had no real fear that the two would in fact prove inconsistent.

It was only in a community, Thompson believed, that these principles could be successfully applied. His *Practical Directions* of 1830 defined the economic concepts that should govern its organization. Two of his formal definitions contained the essence of the radical Owenite doctrine:

EQUAL DISTRIBUTION: *that which affords to every individual equally exerting, or equally willing to exert, his or her faculties for the common good, equal means of physical, intellectual, and social enjoyments.* . . .

COMMUNITY OF PROPERTY OR POSSESSIONS: By community of property or possessions, we do not mean, that no person shall possess any thing, *but that every adult person shall possess every thing, that is to say, all the lands, houses, machinery, implements and other stock of the Community, in as ample a manner as they are possessed by any other member whatever.* . . . This community, or union, of possession, is only limited by the individual use of such articles of food, clothing, &c. as are appropriated from the common stock, and are in the course of individual consumption by each member.

Community of property, however, did not imply confiscation, nor even that "those having now larger possessions should be called upon to unite them with those having smaller or having none." Thompson provided elaborate machinery for effecting the transition from private to community ownership. Members possessing capital would invest it, whereas the propertyless would perform extra labor for a

[73] See Thompson, *Practical Directions for the Speedy and Economical Establishment of Communities on the Principles of Mutual Co-operation, United Possessions and Equality of Exertions and of the Means of Enjoyments* (London [1830]), pp. i–ii, 22–23. Fourier is praised on p. 58.

[74] Thompson, *Inquiry* (1824), p. 5.

[75] Thompson, *Inquiry* (1824), p. xxi. This quotation, taken from the table of contents, summarizes the argument of pp. 90–103.

few months or years until they had made a contribution of equal value. The whole capital accumulated would be used for outright purchase of the estate, which would thereafter be held in common, no rent or profit being paid to individual members or to outsiders. In other words, "the possessions of all, within the community, should be united and equal, because all would have contributed equally, whether in money or labor, to the common stock." [76]

The ideas of Hodgskin, though important in their own right, had little connection with the communitarian aspects of Owenism except as they tended to reinforce the radical strain among the later Owenites. John Gray's association with Owenism, on the other hand, though it was to all intents and purposes limited to his one *Lecture on Human Happiness*, had a direct and immediate influence. This pamphlet, published in London in 1825 and republished in Philadelphia the next year, was an important link between the Owenite movements of the two countries.[77] And its arguments were among the most persuasive of those that were drawing Owen himself toward a more radical position on equality and the rights of property.

Like Thompson, Gray praised Owen's plan, at the same time reading into it his own conceptions. Its "grand feature," he said, is that *"it abolishes the circumstance which now limits production, and gives to the producers the wealth that they create."* In other words, Gray, like Thompson, saw in Owen's proposals a means of guaranteeing to the industrious classes their right to the whole produce of labor—the principle which Owen had barely hinted at, but which Gray stated explicitly: "The foundation of all property is LABOUR, and there is no other just foundation for it. . . . If a man can, in any case, say truly 'this is mine,' surely it is, when the thing spoken of is the produce of the labour of his hands." Gray developed his argument along different lines from Thompson's, however. Using Colquhoun's tables, upon which Owen had based his cubes, he emphasized the distinction between productive and unproductive (or useless) members of society, and came to the startling conclusion that "each man, woman, and child, in the productive classes . . . received . . . but a small trifle more than ONE-FIFTH PART OF THE PRODUCE OF THEIR OWN LABOUR!!!" [78]

[76] Thompson, *Practical Directions* (1830), pp. 4, 6, 9–10.

[77] See below, pp. 170–71, n. 35.

[78] John Gray, *A Lecture on Human Happiness . . . in Which Will be Comprehended a General Review of the Causes of the Existing Evils of Society, and a Developement of the Means by Which They May Be Permanently and Effectually Removed* (London, 1825), pp. 56, 34, 20 (reproduced in facsimile by the London School of Economics and Political Science in its *Series of Reprints of Scarce Tracts in Economic and Political Science,* no. 2, 1931). On Gray's relationship to Owenism, see his own account in his *Social System* (Edinburgh, 1831), pp. 337–74.

Although Gray announced at the end of his pamphlet that he would offer plans "altogether different from those proposed by Mr. OWEN," [79] his *Lecture on Human Happiness* was widely accepted, particularly in America, as an authoritative statement of official Owenite doctrine. This was partly because it carried as an appendix the articles of agreement for a community drawn up by the London Co-Operative Society, the leading organized group of Owen's disciples. So recommended, the document was naturally considered a model for Owenite constitutions, and it tended to tie Owenism securely to the economic doctrines of Thompson and Gray which it embodied—notably in the preamble, where the evils of the world were laid to "Individual Competition and Private Accumulation," and where the principles of "Mutual Co-operation, Community of Property, and Equal Means of Enjoyment" were listed as the three-fold objective of the community. [80]

Owen himself fell under the influence of the new doctrines that were circulating in his name. The teacher, for a period of time, became the pupil. This period was roughly the five years from 1824 to 1829, which he spent largely in America. His experiences there played an important part in reshaping his views, but it was primarily the radical Owenites who pointed the new direction of his economic thinking. The end result can be seen in the *Lectures on an Entire New State of Society,* which Owen delivered and published in London in 1830.

In these lectures Owen described his doctrine as a "Science of Society," the basic principles of which now included opposition to private property, to commercial competition, and to inequality of rank or condition. "Private property," he asserted, "is entirely the child of the existing system of the world; it emanates from ignorant selfishness, and perpetuates it." Commercial competition, to take up the second point, "creates a covered civil warfare . . . ; it takes the means of supporting themselves, by their utmost exertions, from many; it gives to [a] few accidentally favourable [sic] individuals, in every branch of industry, injurious advantages over the mass." Finally, asserted Owen, "without equality of condition, there can be no permanent virtue or stability in society."

Owen's conclusion was still communitarian not revolutionary. He insisted that the "very foundation [of society] must be laid afresh; its construction must be altogether different; no part of the new will

---

[79] Gray, *Lecture on Human Happiness* (1825), p. 71.

[80] *Articles of Agreement Drawn Up and Recommended by the London Co-Operative Society, for the Formation of a Community on Principles of Mutual Co-Operation* ([London], 1825), pp. 3–4; appended, with separate title page and pagination, to Gray's *Lecture.*

resemble any part of the old." But he argued, too, "that such a change can never be introduced through a revolution of violence." It must come through "harmony of thought, feeling and action." [81] So strong in fact was Owen's continuing faith in the harmony of classes that he was not yet ready to subscribe wholeheartedly to the distinction, of which Gray had made so much, between productive and useless classes. He did, it is true, expand greatly his earlier catalogue of the waste resulting from existing arrangements in production and distribution, and he did go so far as to classify the priesthood and the law as needless professions in a rational social system.[82] But it was another decade before he was prepared to relegate to the category of the useless the entire aristocracy, the civil and military professions, and all bankers, merchants, and others "trading for individual profit." [83]

This sweeping denunciation—the only aspect of Owen's thinking that was more radical in the 1840's than it had been in the previous decade—was primarily the lingering effect of his participation in the more class-conscious co-operative and trades-union movements of the early 1830's. During Owen's all but continuous absence in America from 1824 to 1829, his propaganda and that of Thompson and others bore fruit in a vigorous co-operative movement. Its members were drawn, not from the privileged classes to whom Owen had addressed his message in the first place, but from the rank and file of workingmen. However anxious they were for the millennium that Owen promised, they could not afford the luxury of waiting for it. The co-operative societies therefore became agencies through which laboring men sought immediate measures of amelioration as well as ultimate emancipation. In Owen's communitarian plans they found the elements from which they developed a program of gradual reform embracing consumers' co-operatives, "Exchange Bazaars" that employed labor notes instead of currency, and trades unions that looked

[81] Owen, *Lectures on an Entire New State of Society; Comprehending an Analysis of British Society, Relative to the Production and Distribution of Wealth; the Formation of Character; and Government, Domestic and Foreign* (London [1830]), pp. 15, 64, 68, 69, 73, 75–76, 85, 86. The date of the book (variously guessed at in standard bibliographical works) was given as 1830 by Owen himself in *Manifesto of Robert Owen, the Discoverer, Founder, and Promulgator, of the Rational System of Society, and of the Rational Religion* (6th ed., London, 1840), p. 42. See also *Revue encyclopédique* (Paris), XLVII, 679 (sept. 1830).

[82] See *Lectures on an Entire New State of Society* (1830), pp. 66–67. On pp. 21–22 Owen estimates the waste in production at £4–5 million daily; in distribution, at 49 parts out of 50.

[83] *The Book of the New Moral World*, Part Fifth (1844), pp. 16–17, 27–29. See also *Lectures on the Rational System* (1841), p. 184, and *Home Colonies* (2d ed., 1841), pp. 55–56. And compare Fourier's catalogue of *improductifs* in his *Traité de l'association* (1822), I, 468–72.

toward a system of producers' co-operatives.[84] Owen, ever one to work with the means at hand, assumed what he considered his rightful place at the head of these movements, as soon as he returned to England from his American venture. He rephrased their purposes in his own magniloquent rhetoric. And he emerged in the years 1832 to 1834 as the leader of two grandiose projects, the National Equitable Labour Exchange and the Grand National Consolidated Trades Union of Great Britain and Ireland, and as the editor of a periodical whose title, *The Crisis,* reflected his heightened sense of impendency. These ventures into gradual types of reform constituted Owen's only important retreat from communitarianism after he embraced it in 1817. The episode was of considerable consequence to trades unionism in Great Britain, and the attention it has received from historians of the labor movement is abundantly justified. Nevertheless, from the point of view of Owen's own intellectual development the activities of these three or four years were little more than an opportunistic digression. Communitarian propaganda was by no means discontinued, but only pushed temporarily into the background, to be resumed again after the Labour Exchange and the Grand National Consolidated Trades Union collapsed in ruins in 1834.

The revival of the communitarian element in Owen's thinking can be traced in the periodicals which he published in continuous sequence from 1832 to 1845. It was at low ebb in *The Crisis.* An expensive woodcut showing the "Design of a Community of 2,000 Persons, Founded Upon a Principle, Commended by Plato, Lord Bacon, Sir T. More, and Robert Owen" was prepared in 1833 to run at the banner head, but it was replaced after appearing on only eleven weekly numbers.[85] And in November 1833 a correspondent asserted that an experimental community in the present generation was not even to be thought of.[86]

The Crisis ceased publication with the issue of August 23, 1834, and the following week there appeared, in the same format, the first number of *The New Moral World.*[87] This proved to be a false start, but two months later, on November 1, 1834, another volume I, number 1, was issued, and this successfully launched *The New Moral*

---

[84] Podmore examines the history of several societies and shows how the original purpose of establishing communities faded away. See his *Robert Owen,* II, 382–91, 398–402.

[85] *The Crisis,* II, 33 *et seqq.* (Feb. 9–April 20, 1833). It was so costly that readers were asked to pay an extra penny for the first issue in which it appeared. *Ibid.,* p. 32.

[86] *Ibid.,* III, 85 (Nov. 9, 1833).

[87] London, Aug. 30, 1834. A copy, apparently unique, is in the Newberry Library, Chicago.

World upon a career of eleven uninterrupted years.[88] The old communitarian ideals came gradually to the fore. In an opening "Address to the Public," Owen revealed that he was hesitating between no less than seven different modes of accomplishing "the change from moral evil to moral good," involving everything from paternalistic leadership by the aristocracy to concerted effort "by the operatives and peasants united." [89] A slight leaning toward the old communitarian program was apparent, but two years were to elapse before *The New Moral World* set aside a regular portion of its space for a "Herald of Community." [90] This was in response to a correspondent's plaint, published on October 8, 1836, that the Owenites had "let too much time elapse without . . . attempting anything in the form of a first or model COMMUNITY." [91]

By the summer of 1837 the communitarian revival was in full swing. *The New Moral World* began to pay attention to the American communities in that year,[92] and in 1838 it inaugurated a series of expositions of the doctrine of Charles Fourier, who had died the year before.[93] Though fully committed to Owenism, of course, *The New Moral World* eventually became the medium through which communitive theories of all kinds were made known to the British public. Action went hand in hand with propaganda. In 1837 Owen's Association of All Classes of All Nations definitely avowed its purpose of "founding, as soon as possible, COMMUNITIES OF UNITED INTEREST." [94] Impatient Owenites began to talk of emigrating to

[88] 13 vols., in 3 series, Nov. 1, 1834–Aug. 23, 1845. After the latter date the periodical passed out of Owenite control, but continued to appear for a short time longer—until Sept. 13, 1845, Jan. 10, 1846, or Jan. 24, 1846, according to different authorities. See, respectively, Foxwell, "Bibliography," p. 256; Podmore, *Robert Owen*, II, 667; and Josef Stammhammer, *Bibliographie des Socialismus und Communismus* (3 vols., Jena, 1893–1909), I, 266. The file in the Seligman Collection, Columbia University Library, ends with the issue of Oct. 11, 1845.

[89] *New Moral World*, I, 6, 10–11, 17–18, 25–28 (Nov. 1–22, 1834).

[90] *Ibid.*, III, 4 (Oct. 29, 1836) *et seqq.*

[91] *Ibid.*, II, 394, see also p. 404 (Oct. 8 and 15, 1836).

[92] "Co-operative Settlements in America," *ibid.*, III, 348, 355–56, 361–62 (Aug. 19 and 26, Sept. 2, 1837).

[93] The most important before 1840 were: Victor Considerant, "Social Destiny," *New Moral World*, V, 6–7, through VI, 605–6 (16 installments, Oct. 27, 1838–July 11, 1839); Louis Reybaud, "Socialism in France: Charles Fourier," *ibid.*, VI, 707–8, through pp. 771–73 (4 installments, Aug. 31–Sept. 28, 1839); Amo [pseudonym of the translator of the preceding series], "Fourierism," *ibid.*, VI, 834–35, through VII, 1194–95 (11 installments, Oct. 26, 1839–March 28, 1840). An even earlier series by Jule L. Gay said a good deal about Fourier's plans, *ibid.*, II, 37–39, through pp. 106–7 (10 installments, Nov. 28, 1835–Jan. 30, 1836).

[94] *Ibid.*, III, 35 (June 10, 1837). With successive reorganizations, the name of the association and its affiliates began to indicate more clearly the communitarian emphasis: National Community Friendly Society (1837), Universal Community Society of Rational Religionists (1839), Home Colonization Society (1840).

America, and a few small groups actually set sail in the middle 1830's.[95] Finally, on October 1, 1839—the first day of 1st month, year 1, N[ew] M[oral] W[orld], according to the calendar of some enthusiasts—a great Owenite experiment, Harmony Hall or Queenwood, got under way in England itself, at East Tytherly in Hampshire. The new chronological era was of short duration. Harmony Hall lasted longer than New Harmony, but the old immoral world resumed its sovereignty over the little domain in 1845.[96]

Though Owen was past seventy years of age, his career was not yet over. He left England just before the final failure of Harmony Hall, and from 1844 to 1847 he preached his gospel intermittently in the United States. Hardly had he established himself once more in Great Britain when the Revolution of 1848 drew him to Paris, where his proclamations and pamphlets in French swelled the stream of reformist literature.[97] The excitement of those days remained with him when he returned to London, and his next book, published in 1849, was entitled *The Revolution in the Mind and Practice of the Human Race*. Still his pen did not falter. In the 1850's he edited a succession of four periodicals, wrote numerous new tracts, and completed a volume of his autobiography (with a documentary appendix that spilled over into a second volume) before death claimed him on November 17, 1858.

Save for the spiritualism that Owen, in his latter years, incongruously fused with the rationalistic views on religion he had always preached, his essential ideas underwent no striking changes in the last two decades of his life. The period from 1836 until his death constitutes a third well-defined phase of his communitarian propaganda. It was a far less radical phase than the one which preceded it in the late 1820's and early 1830's.[98] It represented, in fact, a return to substantially the principles he had enunciated at the very beginning.

The retreat began as early as 1833, when communitarian ideas were tentatively revived in *The Crisis:* "Instead of a community of common property some have proposed, as a first step at least, a

[95] See Lloyd Jones, "To Those Who Contemplate Emigrating to America," *New Moral World*, XII, 207–8 (Dec. 23, 1843), an unfavorable account of such ventures from 1834 on. See also *ibid.*, II, 173, 188–89, 224 (March 26, April 9, May 7, 1836), and A. J. Macdonald MSS (Yale University Library), folios 406–8.

[96] For a full account of Harmony Hall, which is beyond the scope of the present study, see Podmore, *Robert Owen*, II, 530–78. On the new method of dating see *ibid.*, II, 534.

[97] See Owen's six French pamphlets of 1848 listed in Bibliothèque Nationale, *Catalogue général des livres imprimés*, tome CXXVIII (Paris, 1934), columns 729–32.

[98] Except for his distinction between productive and useless classes in society, discussed above, p. 87.

society of united expenditure only, to be formed by families or individuals of moderate but certain incomes." [99] This was the key to Owen's new approach. He centered his attention neither upon paupers nor upon aristocrats, as he had in his first period, nor yet upon aggressive workingmen, as he had in his second, but upon members of the middle classes, particularly "the *most experienced minds,* in every department of life." [100] What he stood for in this third phase of his communitarian propaganda was set forth with particular clarity in two publications of 1841, his *Lectures on the Rational System of Society* and his *Developement of the Principles and Plans on Which to Establish Self-Supporting Home Colonies.*

A renewed cautiousness marked Owen's emphasis upon the obstacles that must be overcome before the quick transition to the millennium could occur. With convenient forgetfulness of the past he asserted that "the Founder of the new system has been always aware of the impracticability of . . . premature union between classes brought up from birth in totally different habits, manners, and feelings, and he has therefore never proposed to carry his principles into execution by any such inexperienced proceedings." This was the signal for a renewed paternalism. "The working classes," he said, "are too inexperienced to be able to effect the change for themselves." Consequently "the onus lies with the Founder and the supporters of this New System to convince a sufficient number of the wealthy and influential members of old society . . . to assist the former in carrying the measures into execution to create this very superior state of society." [101]

Owen still hoped ultimately "to terminate the distinction of *rich and poor,*" but this was to be the tenth of the twelve steps through which the millennium would finally come.[102] In the meantime he concentrated his attention upon the immediate establishment of

---

[99] *The Crisis,* II, 33 (Feb. 9, 1833).

[100] Owen, *A Developement of the Principles and Plans on Which to Establish Self-Supporting Home Colonies; as a Most Secure and Profitable Investment for Capital, and an Effectual Means . . . to Remove . . . Poverty . . . ; and Most Materially to Benefit All Classes of Society* (2d ed., London, 1841), p. 2; cited herein as *Home Colonies.* There were two editions, both published in the same year by the Home Colonization Society, and both illustrated with folding plates. The first was a quarto, with separately paged appendices; the second an octavo in which the appendices, somewhat rearranged, were paged continuously with the text.

[101] Owen, *Lectures on the Rational System of Society, Derived Solely from Nature and Experience, As Propounded by Robert Owen, Versus Socialism, Derived from Misrepresentation, As Explained by the Lord Bishop of Exeter and Others; and Versus the Present System of Society, Derived from the Inexperienced and Crude Notions of Our Ancestors* (London, 1841), pp. 173–74, 103, 157.

[102] *Home Colonies* (2d ed., 1841), p. 9. The word "millennium" is recurrent in Owen's writings of this period.

"home colonies." In these the distinction between the "working class" and the "wealthy and more highly educated class" was clearly marked, and Owen toyed with the idea of two distinct settlements near each other, before deciding finally upon a single colony comprising all classes. The function of the working class, whichever the arrangement, was "producing wealth for both, and performing the practical measures requisite for both," until the transitional period was completed. All that Owen promised was that the arrangements would "present the least appearance of inequality in the condition of the four classes, that the present state of education, minds, and manners, of the parties will admit." [103] These four classes comprised, first, the hired laborers or servants, who would not be considered candidates for membership except under exceptional circumstances; next, the mechanics and artisans, who could look forward to ultimate membership; third, the actual members, who as proprietors would superintend the labor of the colony; and finally, the wealthy, who would pay board and rent, while living in what Owen frankly called a "Family Club" and doing only what seemed "the most beneficial and agreeable to themselves." [104]

Owen was back at his starting point, so far as economic equality was concerned. These four classes were almost identical with the four he had recognized in his original plan of September 6, 1817. The only difference was that they would occupy quarters in the same village. They would hardly mingle, however, for he planned to segregate the different classes on different sides of his quadrilateral. Fourier, who condemned Owen for his supposed equalitarianism, was careful to intermingle costly and modest apartments in all parts of his phalanstery, and to bring together rich and poor in both the labors and the recreations of the community. Owen, by contrast, ended by promising to the colonists of the lowest order only "the use of a raised terrace walk, extending in front of their houses and public buildings, . . . with privilege to extend this walk around the whole square, as their manners and conduct shall improve." [105]

The danger in generalizing about Owen's economic views or his attitude on social equality is apparent. What Owen brought to America in 1824 was not a set of definite proposals on such matters, but a plan for social reorganization based on small experimental self-supporting communities. It was his communitarianism that appealed to Americans, fitting in as it did with a tradition already well developed in the United States. The plan made a wider appeal than previous ones, not because of any special novelty in its details, but

[103] *Lectures on the Rational System* (1841), pp. 174–75.
[104] *Home Colonies* (2d ed., 1841), pp. 41, 44, 47.
[105] *Home Colonies* (2d ed., 1841), p. 49.

because it was free of all narrow sectarian restrictions. With the advent of Owen, communitarianism became a social program which Americans could support without worshiping strange and uncomfortable gods.

Chapter V

THE RECEPTION OF OWENISM IN AMERICA

OWENISM was more gospel than theory, and it needed to be preached rather than explained. This being true, the vogue of Owen's system throughout its history was closely bound up with the personality of its founder. In the United States this was particularly true. The new view of society attracted little attention there until Owen himself disembarked in New York on November 4, 1824, and local movements thereafter waxed and waned with his comings and goings. Nevertheless, the trickle of Owenite ideas to the New World before 1824 was not entirely devoid of significance. Communitive thought in the early 1820's was leaving its sectarian origins behind, and even slight influences could help determine its new, nonreligious direction.

Owen's popular propaganda in 1817 and subsequent years reached only a British audience. For the export of his ideas he still relied hopefully upon diplomatic channels, and he sought to reach abroad the influential few rather than the many. He induced the Home Secretary to send two hundred interleaved copies of *A New View of Society* "to the leading governments of Europe, and America,—to the most learned Universities in Europe,—and to . . . individuals . . . best calculated to form a sound judgment upon them." [1] He took matters into his own hands as well. In 1816 or 1817, for example, he entrusted copies to John Quincy Adams, American minister in London, for distribution to the President and Cabinet, and to the governors of each of the states.[2] In 1818 he printed in three languages a "Memorial to the Governments of Europe and America, on Behalf of the Working Classes," and at the Congress of Aix-la-Chapelle he personally thrust a copy into the hands of all the reigning sovereigns there—all, that is, except the Czar, who was wearing tight-fitting

[1] Owen, *Life . . . Written by Himself*, I, 109–10. An exemplar is in the University of Illinois Library. It comprises Essays Third and Fourth, interleaved with paper watermarked 1813, and bearing the printed notation "Not Published" on the title pages.

[2] Owen, *Life*, I, 110–11, 202; compare John Quincy Adams, *Memoirs . . . Comprising Portions of his Diary from 1795 to 1848*, ed. by Charles Francis Adams (12 vols., Philadelphia, 1874–77), III, 551–52.

clothes without pockets and told Owen he had "no place to put it in."[3] To the end of his days Owen believed that these ventures into high diplomacy had been master strokes of propaganda, and he gave unhesitating credence to a tale that his writings had converted the defeated Napoleon from the ways of war to peace.[4] What wonder then that he believed that the volumes sent to America had prepared the nation for his later coming?

He was mistaken. The writings that traveled by diplomatic pouch had nothing to do with his personal reception in 1824–25 or with the acceptance of his ideas by the handful of avowed Owenites who greeted him on his arrival. For all their fine bindings, the books went unread. It was the great English and Scottish reviews that brought to well-informed Americans whatever information they possessed before 1824 concerning Owen's proposals.

Once Owen embarked upon his public campaign in 1817, his writings—hitherto passed over by the general British periodicals—began to receive critical notice. The first important review, in the *Eclectic* for February 1817, was a friendly one. It condemned those who "refuse to listen to the voices of the countless multitudes who deafen heaven and earth with cries of Reformation," and it recommended Owen's practical suggestions, if not his abstract theories, to "the attentive consideration óf those who are engaged in the important work of investigating the operations of the great machine of Society."[5] Equally hospitable was the *New Monthly Magazine*, which summarized Owen's plan very briefly in September 1817, but subsequently printed three longer contributions by "Amicus," who cited the Moravians, the Harmonists, the Shakers, and the Jesuit communities in Paraguay as evidence for the practicability of Owen's proposals.[6] Not until October 1819 did the *Edinburgh Review* turn its portentous critical attention upon Owen. The reviewer was Robert Torrens, and, as might be expected from one whose economic orthodoxy had been attested by Ricardo himself, the review was a dogmatic reassertion of classical theory. To Torrens there were three causes, and three causes only, for the existing distress in England. Unless Owen "could improve the quality of those inferior soils to which we are obliged to resort," or "repeal those enactments against foreign

<hr />

[3] Owen, *Life*, I, 185. The memorials are reprinted *ibid.*, I.A, 205–22. See also Albert T. Volwiler, "Robert Owen and the Congress of Aix-la-Chapelle, 1818," *Scottish Historical Review*, XIX, 96–105 (Jan. 1922).

[4] *Life*, I, 112, 202.

[5] *Eclectic Review*, n.s., VII, 150–61 (Feb. 1817); the quotations are from pp. 150 and 160.

[6] *New Monthly Magazine, and Universal Register*, VIII, 164–65; IX, 27–29, 116–18, 290–91 (Sept. 1817; Feb., March, May 1818). There was an unfavorable reply to "Amicus," *ibid.*, IX, 313 (May 1818).

trade which are a disgrace to the age," or "charm away the collector of taxes," then he could do nothing. To offer another diagnosis of the ills of society, as Owen of course was doing, merely proved to a classical economist like Torrens that "in his reasonings, as well as in his plans, Mr Owen shows himself profoundly ignorant of all the laws which regulate the production and distribution of wealth." [7]

For the repute of Owen's ideas in America the strictures of Torrens were probably of less moment than the fact that the *Edinburgh* had spoken of Owen at all. Thinking men were bound to pay some attention to matters which the great review saw fit to notice, but the obligation to swallow Manchester economics whole was somewhat less mandatory. In point of fact, what the British reviews did was to make Owen a vaguely familiar, but not a controversial, figure in the United States. When at last he crossed the Atlantic in person, many educated Americans could recall, as did the editor of the *National Intelligencer* in Washington, that they had once "endeavored to become acquainted with his system, as developed in the British periodicals." [8] In the absence of local controversy, however, Owen's ideas spread slowly from the circles that read the foreign journals to the groups of discontented or utopian-minded men among whom a real flame might be kindled. Only in Philadelphia and New York did this diffusion take place to any significant extent.

In Philadelphia it was the ardently Jeffersonian editor William Duane who gave the first push to Owenism. His newspaper, the *Aurora,* published extracts from *A New View of Society* in 1817,[9] apparently the earliest notice of Owen in the American press. Duane did not pursue the matter, but a few Philadelphians began to manifest an interest. A Quaker named W. S. Warder was moved to furnish Owen with a sketch of the Shakers.[10] Thomas Branagan, whose benevolent and prolific pen had already celebrated *The Excellency of*

---

[7] *Edinburgh Review,* XXXII, 453–77 (Oct. 1819); the quotations are from pp. 462–64 and 468–69. Torrens had spoken against the plan at Owen's meetings in 1817 and again in 1819. See Podmore, *Robert Owen,* I, 241, 247, 266. See also Walter A. Copinger, *On the Authorship of the First Hundred Numbers of the "Edinburgh Review"* (Manchester, 1895).

[8] Washington *Daily National Intelligencer,* Dec. 1, 1824, p. 3:2. This paper also published a triweekly edition, cited simply as *National Intelligencer.*

[9] Mentioned in Thomas Branagan, *The Pleasures of Contemplation* (2d ed., Philadelphia, 1818), p. 205; first published in 1817. I have not located the article in the *Aurora;* it may have been antedated by the review in the *Christian Observer* (Boston, "from the London edition"), XVI, 662–80 (Oct. 1817), quoted below, p. 124.

[10] Dated 1817, published by Owen in his *New View of Society: Tracts* (1818), and reprinted in *Life,* I.A, 143–54. This was doubtless the W. T. [*sic*] Warder whom Owen saw in Philadelphia on Nov. 20 and 21, 1824. William Owen, *Diary,* pp. 29, 32; Donald Macdonald, *Diaries,* p. 208.

the Female Character and *The Beauties of Philanthropy,* went on in 1817 to write of *The Pleasures of Contemplation,* a little volume in which he included not only a sympathetic reference to Owen but also an essay, by another hand, which anticipated in remarkable fashion some of the later arguments of the radical Owenites.

The author of the appended essay was Dr. Cornelius Camden Blatchly, a recent alumnus of the College of Physicians and Surgeons in New York.[11] Though he had not seen the excerpts from Owen that Branagan had read, he had already developed a social philosophy which he eventually recognized as correlative with Owen's. His contribution to Branagan's volume was entitled *Some Causes of Popular Poverty,* and in it he argued:

> If the labour and diligence of the hand and head produce the riches and prosperity of civilized nations; should not every wise, just, and humane governor and legislator, encourage and recompense the artists, scientifics, and labourers, who enrich the nations? And if their industry and labours are the *sole* causes of the opulence of nations, either remotely or immediately, they are the sole persons who ought to increase in opulence.

Rent and interest, in other words, were unjust—"probably the effects of ancient usurpation"—and inheritance should be so regulated as to acknowledge that society is a major factor in the creation of wealth and hence should be the ultimate beneficiary:

> The civil united interest of society is one of the great sources of civilization, and of wealth and property. . . . If we owe so much to social union, and if our individual all, is from it, is not our individual all in a measure due to it? does it not belong to it?—and consequently to its disposal, as soon as death severs any individual of us from social rights and privileges? [12]

Nothing shows more clearly the strength of the communitarian tradition in those years than the fact that Blatchly turned naturally to it, rather than to legislation, for the means of correcting the injustices he saw about him. By 1820 he had organized a New York Society for Promoting Communities,[13] and for it he undertook to

---

[11] Columbia University, *Alumni Register, 1754–1931* (New York, 1932), p. 78. As early as 1815 Blatchly sent President Madison a pamphlet he had written on war. Corn[eliu]s C. Blatchly to James Madison, 6th of 5 Month, 1815, MS in Madison papers, Library of Congress.

[12] Cornelius C. Blatchly, *Some Causes of Popular Poverty, Derived from the Enriching Nature of Interests, Rents, Duties, Inheritances, and Church Establishments, Investigated in their Principles and Consequences, and Agreement with Scripture* ([2d ed., Philadelphia], 1818), pp. 179–80, 187–88. This essay constituted "Appendices the First" to Branagan's *Pleasures of Contemplation,* with which its pagination was continuous. It had, however, its own separate title page, both in the first and second editions.

[13] The date 1819 is to be inferred from the reference in Paul Brown, *Twelve Months in New-Harmony* (Cincinnati, 1827), p. 4.

write an essay "On Common Wealths." Just as he completed the composition he came upon Owen's *New View of Society* for the first time, welcomed it as corroborative of his own ideas, and incorporated portions of it in the pamphlet, which his society promptly published, *An Essay on Common Wealths. Part I. The Evils of Exclusive and the Benefits of Inclusive Wealth. Part II. Extracts from Robert Owen's New View of Society. Part III. Melish's Account of the Harmonists.*[14] The three parts of the title indicate, with unconscious symbolism, the three streams that were flowing together to create the communitarian movement of the 1820's—native speculations on social justice, systematic theories worked out abroad, and the tradition built up by the sectarian communities.

Religious elements are still powerful in the *Essay on Common Wealths,* despite its quotations from Owen. The familiar verses from the second chapter of Acts are on the title page; the Kingdom of God is identified with "a pure and pious community"; and tribute is paid not only to the Shakers and Harmonists, but also to the Dunkers, Moravians, Mennonites, and even the Dukhobors. Nevertheless, the spirit of the *Essay* is not the spirit of the seventeenth- and eighteenth-century religious communities. The exclusiveness so characteristic of the sects is absent. In its place is an appeal to "the pious of all denominations . . . to institute and establish in *every religious congregation,* a system of social, equal, and *inclusive* rights, interests, liberties, and privileges to all real and personal property."[15]

Moreover, the secular doctrine of natural rights plays as pointed a role in the *Essay on Common Wealths* as do the Scriptures. Frequent quotations from Joel Barlow's *Advice to the Privileged Orders*[16] link the *Essay* to Jeffersonian liberalism. But Blatchly gives a new twist to the old argument from the rights of man in a state of nature, and reaches conclusions concerning property that are markedly at variance with those of John Locke and his successors:

In a *state of nature,* man would be in a *worse* condition than the *savages;* and could claim an *exclusive* title to nothing. . . . Hence the inference clearly arises, that all the property which men now possess *exclusively,* has been bestowed on them through the favour of *social laws, privileges, customs* and *advantages.* In other words, that real and personal wealth is derived from, and is the *gift* of society. . . . [Consequently] the productions and

14 New York: Published by the New-York Society for Promoting Communities, 1822. The copy in the Seligman Collection, Columbia University Library, bears the contemporary penciled notation "By Corn[eliu]s Blatchley, physician"; all available evidence supports this attribution. The author's discovery of Owen's "corroborative" ideas is recounted on p. 44; Owen is quoted on pp. 42–50, given a poetic tribute on p. 64, and otherwise mentioned on pp. 10, 24, and 38.
15 *Essay on Common Wealths,* pp. 28, 23, 36, 3.
16 *Ibid.,* pp. 7, 12–19.

wealth produced by society, should not be *individual, selfish,* and *exclusive property,* but *social* and *common* benefit and wealth. . . . If men lived in pure and perfect communities, where all things were as they should be, man's social rights would not *destroy,* as they now do, the *natural rights* he possessed in his wild and unassociated state. . . . And, as men claimed a right in their *natural* and *unassociated* state to *every thing around them;* so they should claim, in a pure community, a right to *all around them.*[17]

This was a novel use of the doctrine of natural rights, but it did not seem unduly heterodox to Thomas Jefferson, whose political philosophy derived from the same fundamental premises. Blatchly sent a copy of his pamphlet to Monticello and received a friendly acknowledgment, dated October 21, 1822. Though Jefferson believed that "communion of property" was feasible only in small societies, he acknowledged that the principle had at times produced "a state of as much happiness as heaven has been pleased to deal out to imperfect humanity." He praised the philanthropic temper of the *Essay* and wished every success to the society that sponsored it.[18] Blatchly treasured the letter, showing it to Owen and his party in New York in November 1824.[19] Finally in September 1825, when the discussion of Owen's ideas was at its peak in America, the letter was released to the press and was republished in newspapers from the seaboard states to Indiana.[20]

The *Essay on Common Wealths* reached a humbler audience as well. Those without access to the British reviews found in it their readiest approach to the ideas of Owen, for his writings were not separately printed in America until 1825, and were not previously obtainable from American booksellers.[21] Geographically, too, the

---

[17] *Ibid.,* pp. 24–25.

[18] Thomas Jefferson to Cornelius Camden Blatchly, Monticello, Oct. 21 [18]22, retained copy, signed, in Jefferson papers, series I, vol. 14, no. 258, Library of Congress; printed in his *Writings,* ed. by Lipscomb and Bergh, XV, 399–400. The recipient's copy is in the New York Historical Society, which, however, possesses no other papers of Blatchly. The latter's original letter to Jefferson, dated New York, 6th of the 10th Month, 1822, and signed by him as "Moderator of the N Y society for promoting communities," is in the Jefferson papers, series II, vol. 11, no. 69, Library of Congress.

[19] Donald Macdonald, *Diaries,* p. 183, see also p. 176.

[20] First printed, apparently, in the Philadelphia *Chronicle;* reprinted in Washington *National Intelligencer,* Sept. 22, 1825, p. 3:3; *Niles' Weekly Register,* XXIX, 72 (Oct. 1, 1825); Philadelphia *National Gazette and Literary Register,* Sept. 27, 1825; and Lawrenceburgh *Indiana Palladium,* Oct. 21, 1825. The last two citations are from Mary Louise Irvin, "Contemporary American Opinion of the New Harmony Movement" (unpublished M.A. thesis, 1932, University of Illinois Library), p. 4. Newspaper references derived from this study are indicated hereafter by the phrase "as cited by Irvin," followed by the page number of this thesis.

[21] See Paul Brown, *Twelve Months in New-Harmony,* pp. 1, 3.

circulation of the pamphlet was impressive. Some time before Owen manifested a personal interest in the Ohio Valley, the New York Society for Promoting Communities was known as far west as Cincinnati.[22]

In Philadelphia, as in New York, the Owenites maintained a small but active society. By the fall of 1823 they had projected a community, had interested some of the members of the Philadelphia Academy of Natural Sciences, and had found supporters as far away as Pittsburgh. In the Academy the warmest response appears to have come from Dr. Gerard Troost, the mineralogist, and John Speakman, one-time partner of the naturalist Thomas Say in the drug business. There was some correspondence on the matter with the president of the Academy, William Maclure, then in Europe. Though he poured cold water on the scheme, and though Say was inclined to ridicule it, the idea would not be quenched.[23] It smoldered until Owen himself came to Philadelphia, then burst into a flame of enthusiasm that eventually lighted the way to New Harmony, not only for Speakman and Troost, but also for Say and Maclure and the latter's educational colleague Madame Marie D. Fretageot.

The community proposed by the Philadelphians was only one of several Owenite colonies projected in the early 1820's.[24] The New York Society for Promoting Communities published a "Constitution for a Religious Community" and suggested that "a premium should be paid for the best constitution for every religious persuasion." [25] Prizes were hardly necessary, for constitution-drafting was ever a favorite avocation of reformers. Free of charge the New Yorkers secured a set of articles even from a visiting Englishman.[26] Action was harder than speech, and the colony which the society attempted

[22] *Cincinnati Emporium,* July 8, 1824, as cited by Irvin, p. 4.

[23] Marie D. Fretageot to William Maclure, Philadelphia, March 25, 1824, in *Correspondence,* ed. Bestor, p. 305.

[24] At the beginning of the decade there was also an attempt, quite independent of Owenism, to create a nonreligious communitive enterprise. In 1819 Heinrich Ludwig Lampert Gall came to America with a group of German immigrants for that purpose. Though an organization was formed in Harrisburg, Pennsylvania, in 1820, the attempt was a disastrous failure, and Gall returned to Germany in the winter of the same year, to devote the remaining forty-three years of his life to a more revolutionary brand of socialism. See Carl Stegmann and C. Hugo, *Handbuch des Socialismus* (Zürich, 1897), pp. 275–80. On the projects of the self-styled Rational Brethren, agitated as early as 1816, see below, pp. 207–8.

[25] *Essay on Common Wealths,* pp. 61–63.

[26] William Hebert, *A Visit to the Colony of Harmony* (1825), in Lindley, ed., *Indiana As Seen by Early Travelers,* pp. 353–59; cited hereafter as Hebert, *Visit,* page references being to this reprint. Hebert drafted his constitution "at the suggestion of a friend from New York, where a few gentlemen contemplated the formation of a society of this kind." The group may not have been the Society for Promoting Communities.

to establish in Virginia came to nothing. In 1822 a similar project drew at least one easterner to Kentucky, but he could find no trace of the community he hoped to join.[27] In 1823 a Scotsman named Brayshaw was touring the western states in search of a site for a communitarian experiment.[28] In 1824, on the eve of Owen's coming, a certain Edward P. Page lobbied Congress for a land grant in East Florida in aid of a "Scientific Commonwealth" which he proposed to establish.[29] The proliferation of such projects attests the prevalence of communitarian ideas. But the fructifying presence of Owen was needed to bring them into life.

It was not the efforts being made in his name, however, that attracted Owen to America. He probably knew nothing of them. Until 1824, indeed, he seems to have been less interested in the United States than were most contemporary European reformers. At New Lanark he received many visitors from across the sea, but he showed no curiosity about American institutions in general, and made only one or two desultory inquiries concerning the communitarian societies in that country.[30] His first transatlantic trip was the result not of a growing faith that the future lay with America, but of a specific opportunity that suddenly presented itself.

This was the opportunity to purchase complete the communitarian village which the Rappites had spent ten years in building at Harmonie on the Wabash River in southern Indiana. The Harmonists' earlier migration from the vicinity of Pittsburgh was felt, by their leaders at least, to have been a mistake, and in 1824 they decided to return to their original neighborhood. On May 21, 1824, all the members of the Harmony Society signed a power of attorney to Frederick Rapp to dispose of the property,[31] and two months later it was advertised for sale in Philadelphia.[32] About the same time the Rappites commissioned their neighbor Richard Flower to undertake in Great Britain the sale of their lands and buildings.[33] Flower called upon Owen at New Lanark in mid-August 1824. He came at a psychological moment. Owen had reached a dead end in the British Isles.

[27] Paul Brown provides the only contemporary reference to the Virginia and Kentucky projects. *Twelve Months in New-Harmony*, p. 5.

[28] Hebert, *Visit*, p. 352 n, which mentions a pamphlet by Brayshaw of which no copy can now be located. The British Museum possesses certain pamphlets on reform published by Joseph Brayshaw at Newcastle-upon-Tyne in 1819.

[29] *The Correspondent* (New York), III, 173–74 (April 5, 1828).

[30] Owen to George Rapp, New Lanark, Aug. 4, 1820, MS in Chicago Historical Society, printed in George Flower, *History of the English Settlement in Edwards County, Illinois*, pp. 372–73. Possibly Warder may also have sent his sketch of the Shakers to Owen in response to an inquiry.

[31] Posey County, Indiana, "Deeds," liber D, pp. 116–30.

[32] Philadelphia *National Gazette*, June 25, 1824, p. 4:3.

[33] George Flower, *History of the English Settlement*, p. 279.

Seven years of public propaganda had been exciting, and on his latest tour—in Ireland in 1822–23—he had hobnobbed with aristocracy as freely as ever. But he could hardly conceal from himself the obvious fact that the numerous subscription lists he had opened had never produced any actual cash, and that the projected community at Motherwell near Glasgow still remained only a project after several years of talk. Moreover, Owen's antireligious opinions were creating difficulty with his partners, who on January 21, 1824, finally forced him to accept a wholesale revision of his cherished educational program at New Lanark.[34] Owen could see no way out of the situation, for the cost of the property needed for a full-scale experiment in Great Britain would require more than twice the financial resources he could personally command.

The village of the Rappites, fully equipped for community life, could be purchased, however, for a quarter of the sum Owen had estimated for an establishment of minimum size in the British Isles. And at the same time it would provide fifteen to twenty-five times the acreage, for future multiplication of communities. Flower, or so it seemed to a skeptical American who was present at the interview, drew the long bow frequently as he described the property, and even intimated that frontier Indiana was "the most important State in the Union." [35] If Owen was credulous, it was not, however, because he swallowed tall tales like these, but because he succumbed so readily to the lure of cheap western land without considering the difficulty of assembling upon it a population appropriate to his purposes. He was neither the first nor the last reformer to make that mistake, as the history of the doctrine of the frontier as a safety valve was to show. But whatever the wisdom of his move to America, the motive, beyond question, was the opportunity to acquire, with the means he actually possessed, the facilities for a complete test of his plans.[36]

[34] Podmore, *Robert Owen*, I, 156–57.

[35] Chester Harding, *My Egotistigraphy* [ed. by M. E. White] (Cambridge, Mass., 1866), p. 90 (diary entry for Sat., Aug. 14, 1824).

[36] He made this quite clear in a speech to the London Co-operative Society on Aug. 28, 1825, just after the experiment was inaugurated. He told them that "he had purchased the colony at Harmony in the hope that the step would contribute to the dissemination of his principles of society more rapidly than any he could have taken in Great Britain," and he explained that he had previously intended to purchase 700 acres in Scotland for the price he actually paid for the 20,000 acres of Harmonie, including its already constructed village and factories. London *Examiner*, as reprinted in Washington *National Intelligencer*, Nov. 3, 1825, p. 4:2. The situation was roughly as follows: Owen's fortune amounted to about $250,000; he had estimated in 1817 and again in 1821 that the land, buildings, and equipment for a community of 1,200 persons would cost nearly $500,000 in Great Britain, or twice what he had; but he was able to acquire the land, build-

Once informed of the Rappites' terms, Owen's irrepressible enthusiasm bubbled up. He discussed the offer with Flower on August 14, 1824, and by early September he was in London on his way to America. His eagerness for the venture was so obvious that on the tenth his friend William Maclure reported as a settled fact that Owen had "decided to make the United States the field of his future experiments" and had already "purchased all the lands upon the Wabash, belonging to the Harmonists." [37] The London *Times* reported more accurately that Owen was about to go to the United States to negotiate for the property.[38] On October 2, a bare seven weeks after his interview with Flower, Owen sailed from Liverpool for his first visit to the United States, taking with him his second son William, and Captain Donald Macdonald of the Royal Engineers, who had been active in an Owenite "Practical Society" in Edinburgh in 1821 and who had accompanied Owen on his propagandist tour of Ireland in 1822–23.[39]

The voyage of almost five weeks provided ample leisure for Owen to expound his views to his shipmates. There was the usual talk about sea serpents, and there was an animated discussion of the newly promulgated Monroe Doctrine. But with relentless regularity the shipboard conversations came round to Owen's doctrines. He circulated his pamphlets, exhibited his drawings, and debated every aspect, theoretical and practical, of his plan. Two Anglican clergymen were aboard, and they provided a foretaste of the religious controversy that Owenism was to inspire in the United States in succeeding months. But the discussions at sea were friendly, and the clergymen parted from Owen with the reiterated promise, "We will support you as far as our principles will lead us." [40]

---

ings, and miscellaneous personal property of the Rappites for only $135,000, or approximately half the sum at his disposal. Owen's estimates of capital requirements (totaling £96,000) are in his "Report on the Poor," March 12, 1817, in *Life*, I.A, 60; and *The Economist* (London), II, 28 (Aug. 4, 1821). On the price paid Rapp, see below, p. 180, n. 74. Owen's fortune at the outset of the experiment is estimated by his son, Robert Dale Owen, *Twenty-Seven Years of Autobiography: Threading My Way* (New York, 1874), pp. 292–93. The last-mentioned work was also published in London the same year, with different pagination and with title and subtitle transposed; the American edition is cited herein, under the abbreviated title *Autobiography*.

37 Maclure to Benjamin Silliman, London, Sept. 10, 1824, in *American Journal of Science*, IX (1824–25), 161. See also Maclure to Mme Fretageot, same date, in *Correspondence*, ed. Bestor, p. 309.

38 London *Times*, Sept. 21, 1824, p. 2:3; Sept. 29, p. 2:3.

39 Donald Macdonald, *Diaries*, p. 159; *New-Harmony Gazette*, I, 173–74 (Feb. 22, 1826); Podmore, *Robert Owen*, I, 277–78.

40 D. Macdonald, *Diaries*, p. 166, see also pp. 161–62. The account of the voyage occupies pp. 159–73.

So precipitately had Owen acted that his decision to come was not generally known in America until he actually landed in New York on November 4, 1824.[41] The word had traveled more quickly in communitarian circles, of course, and Owen had barely set foot on shore when he was greeted and showered with pamphlets by Edward P. Page, the proponent of the "Scientific Commonwealth," [42] and, more significantly, by Dr. Blatchly of the New York Society for Promoting Communities. His first evening in the United States, in fact, was spent at a meeting of this organization.[43]

Wider entrée to New York society was provided by those who had become acquainted with Owen as visitors to New Lanark. Chief among these was John Griscom, whose interest in Owen as an educator will be discussed in the next chapter. Griscom was associated not only with secondary education but also with Columbia College, where he had served as professor of chemistry. He was therefore able to introduce Owen to members of the faculty and to a number of intellectual and political leaders who moved in the same circle. Griscom entertained Owen at breakfast the morning after his arrival, and promptly arranged for a small but distinguished group of his colleagues and friends to hear the visitor explain his proposals. At the end of the meeting David Hosack, vice-president of the College of Physicians and Surgeons, invited Owen to attend his Saturday evening literary soirée, which thereupon turned into a discussion of the "new view." These invitations led to others, and before the end of his first week in America Owen had been entertained in the homes of John McVickar of Columbia, who was about to publish his *Outlines of Political Economy*, and of William James MacNeven of the College of Physicians and Surgeons; he had discussed his ideas before William Harris and Charles King, present and future presidents of Columbia; and he had met Chancellor James Kent in the classroom where he was delivering the lectures that ultimately became the *Commentaries on American Law*. Those who joined with the faculty group in discussing Owen's plans included, moreover, Jonathan

---

[41] Owen's coming was announced only two days before he disembarked by the Washington *Daily National Intelligencer*, Nov. 2, 1824, p. 3:1, quoting the Philadelphia *Democratic Press*. It was not until after his arrival that the first items appeared in the *New-York Advertiser* (semiweekly ed.), Nov. 6, 1824, p. 2:2. On the same day the news was published in Baltimore in *Niles' Weekly Register*, XXVII, 150–51. As early as Oct. 21, it is true, Madame Fretageot in Philadelphia acknowledged two private letters informing her of Owen's coming. *Correspondence*, ed. Bestor, p. 311.

[42] D. Macdonald, *Diaries*, p. 175. See above, p. 101. This was probably the same eccentric Page who called again in Nov. 1825. See D. Macdonald, pp. 310–11, and R. D. Owen, *Autobiography*, pp. 265–67. See also Jane D. Knight, *Brief Narrative of Events Touching Various Reforms*, p. 17.

[43] D. Macdonald, pp. 175–76, see also p. 183.

Mayhew Wainwright, rector of Grace Church and later Bishop of New York; Cadwallader David Colden, former mayor of the city; Judge John Treat Irving, brother of Washington Irving; and such influential newspaper editors as Charles King, already mentioned, of the *American,* Theodore Dwight of the *Advertiser,* Sidney Edwards Morse of the *Observer,* and George Houston of the *Minerva.*

Owen had brought letters of introduction with him, of course, but his new acquaintances furnished him with more. One was to DeWitt Clinton. At the end of his eventful first week in New York, therefore, Owen took the steamer to Albany to make his call. Clinton, whose two years' absence from the governor's chair was about to end, thanks to the recent elections, received Owen cordially and provided him with letters to both Jefferson and Jackson. Before leaving Albany Owen and his party, together with Clinton, were dinner guests of General Stephen van Rensselaer. And Owen was forced to decline a similar invitation from the governor, Joseph C. Yates. For a fortnight all told, until his departure from New York City on November 18, 1824, Owen moved in the most exalted political and intellectual circles of the Empire State.

Owen's personal contacts, however, were by no means limited to those resulting from Griscom's original introductions. His own reputation was sufficient to induce the British consul to call on him the day after his arrival, and to entertain him at dinner later. To keep the record straight, His Majesty's official explained "that it was not customary for British consuls to make the 1st call, but as for some years he had entertained the highest opinion of him & of the utility & benevolence of his views, he considered it the duty of every man who wished to benefit his fellow creatures to step forward to receive him." [44]

Owen's position as a successful British manufacturer, moreover, opened the doors of the New York business community to him, despite the radicalism of his doctrines. Jeremiah Thompson, originator of the pioneer line of transatlantic packets, gave a dinner for him which was attended by several leaders in the mercantile and shipping world. On the trip back from Albany, Owen was cordially received by Peter A. Schenck, proprietor of a cotton and woolen mill at Matteawan, and later he was taken by Schenck's brother to an exhibition of American manufactures in New York. Owen's son, and presumably Owen also, were much impressed by both, and their host, in turn, was impressed by Owen—to the extent, at least, of discussing the "new views" until one in the morning. Some business callers, it is true, had axes to grind. Judge Thomas Ludlow Ogden, a trustee of Columbia and a son of the founder of Ogdensburg on the St.

[44] D. Macdonald, p. 181.

Lawrence, talked several times to Owen about his lands in northern New York, hopeful that the reformer might make his purchase there instead of at Harmonie. And a portly Quaker approached Owen with lands to sell in Ohio.

The first two weeks in New York State not only introduced Owen to American society but also gave him his first glimpse of the actual life of an American sectarian community. On the trip to Albany he and his party spent four or five hours in a minute inspection of the near-by Shaker establishment at Niskeyuna, Owen murmuring "very right, quite right" as the Shakers explained their practices, but turning a deaf ear to their warnings against founding a community on a diversity of religious beliefs.[45]

All in all, Owen's first fortnight in the United States provided an auspicious beginning to his new enterprise. Without a doubt he often interpreted as a conversion what was only a courtesy. Few of the distinguished men he talked with in New York could, by the wildest stretch of imagination, be considered potential supporters of his plans.[46] The attitude of conservatives was doubtless much like that which Supreme Court Justice Joseph Story expressed in a letter to his wife, after encountering Owen en route to Washington: "He thinks property ought to be held in common, and is so benevolent and yet so visionary an enthusiast that he talks like an inhabitant of Utopia. However, he is very simple in his manners and pleasant in his conversation, and gave a considerable interest to the residue of our journey."[47] Even though Owen's charm rather than his ideas attracted the intellectual leaders of the metropolis, the fact that they paid him such serious and friendly attention gave his theory a prestige that meant much when his propaganda began to penetrate to those groups which communitarianism had real power to attract.

By the time Owen left New York the newspapers had become fully

[45] Owen's activities in New York from Nov. 4 to 10 and from 16 to 18, 1824, are recorded by Donald Macdonald, pp. 174–84, 196–200. The intervening visit to Albany, to the Shakers, and to Schenck's factory, occupies pp. 184–96. Names are frequently misspelled by Macdonald, and no attempt at identification is made in the published diary. See my review in *New York History*, XXIV, 80–86 (Jan. 1943). Beginning Nov. 10, 1824, Macdonald's record is supplemented by William Owen's *Diary*, of which pp. 7–26 cover the period to Owen's departure from New York on Nov. 18.

[46] Theodore Dwight, for example, presumably penned the diatribe quoted on p. 132, below; and Jonathan M. Wainwright was one day to publish a discourse entitled *Inequality of Individual Wealth the Ordinance of Providence, and Essential to Civilization* (Boston, 1835). John McVickar, it is true, made friendly mention of Owen in the pamphlet he published in July 1825, but referred only to his improvement of working conditions in manufactories. *Outlines of Political Economy* (New York, 1825), p. 102 n.

[47] Joseph Story to his wife, Washington, Feb. 9, 1825, in William W. Story, *Life and Letters of Joseph Story* (2 vols., Boston, 1851), I, 485–86.

aware of his presence and purpose in America. On November 16, 1824, the day of their return from Albany, Owen's party were pleased to discover that their movements were reported.[48] On that very date, though they did not know it, news of Owen was being published in Cincinnati.[49] Moreover, the earlier statements of Owen's plan, derived from the British press, were gradually superseded by more accurate and sympathetic accounts based on Owen's personal explanations. Most important was an article in Charles King's *New-York American,* promptly reprinted in Baltimore and Washington:

> The means to be employed are, that certain communities should be assembled in any given district—each community living in common, though with separate and private dwellings for each family, and cultivating in common its allotted portions of earth, and prosecuting its own manufactures. These communities inhabit a large square of buildings, within which are the schools, refectories, dormitories, and other public rooms. A perfect equality to reign among all—the children above two years old, to be put under the government of the rules, and to conform to the general scheme, so that education may not vary according to the inexperience or indulgence of parents. Mr. Owen has with him drawings and plans carefully made, and exhibiting most ingenious combinations of a square of 1000 feet, presenting therefore four faces outward of those dimensions, capable of accommodating a very large number of families, who might subsist in community at a very small proportion of the expense they now separately incur, and become better, as well as more comfortable by the change.
>
> These plans, together with his general views of the subject, it is the intention of Mr. Owen to submit to the Congress of the United States—and whatever may be thought of their practicability, (and on that subject we will not presume to hazard an opinion) the praise of disinterested and persevering philanthrophy [*sic*] will certainly not be denied to Mr. Owen.[50]

It was as succinct and balanced a summary of Owen's proposals as could be given, emphasizing precisely those social and educational (as contradistinguished from economic) aspects of the plan that were uppermost in Owen's mind. And its friendly conclusion reflected the personal spell that Owen had cast over his hearers.

Owen enjoyed an equal personal triumph in Philadelphia, where he spent the better part of five days, from November 19 to 23, 1824.[51] Dr. James Rush, son of Benjamin Rush of Revolutionary fame,

---

[48] W. Owen, *Diary,* p. 24, mentioning specifically the *New-York Evening Post.*

[49] *Liberty Hall and Cincinnati Gazette,* Nov. 16, 1824, p. 2:5. Eleven days later there was an item on Owen in the Vincennes, Ind., *Western Sun and General Advertiser,* Nov. 27, 1824, p. 3:1.

[50] Washington *Daily National Intelligencer,* Nov. 16, 1824, p. 3:2, reprinting, from the Baltimore *American,* the article that originally appeared in the *New-York American.*

[51] The events in Philadelphia are recorded by D. Macdonald, pp. 202–11, and W. Owen, pp. 28–36. See also *Maclure-Fretageot Correspondence,* pp. 311–12.

hastened to invite him to dinner. Mathew Carey, the publisher and political economist, entertained him at breakfast. He lectured by invitation before the Franklin Institute; [52] he was a guest at the Athenaeum, where the members discussed his plans; and at a large tea he gathered all the guests in a circle to listen to him propound the new view of society. So busy was he that he was obliged to decline an invitation to address the "society of Commonwealth" that had been organized in the city. His engagements did not prevent him from cultivating the press, however, and in a call upon the editor of the *National Gazette* he presented a copy of William Thompson's newly published *Inquiry into the Principles of the Distribution of Wealth.*

In Philadelphia, moreover, Owen learned from John Speakman [53] of the community that had already been projected there, and he conversed with Thomas Say and Charles Lesueur of the Academy of Natural Sciences, within whose circle the earlier plan had been hatched. Finally, during this and subsequent visits, Owen drew tighter the lines of connection, to be discussed in the next chapter, between his own enterprise and the educational experiment that Madame Marie D. Fretageot was conducting in Philadelphia with the backing of William Maclure.

From Philadelphia Owen proceeded to the national capital, armed with letters of introduction to President Monroe and other national figures. Washington was in a political turmoil as the indecisiveness of the presidential elections of 1824 became increasingly apparent, but the general preoccupation with politics did not affect Owen's reception. On November 26, 1824, the morning after his arrival, he made the rounds. He was received first by John Quincy Adams, now Secretary of State, whom Owen had met as Minister to the Court of St. James. President Monroe made an appointment to see him the following day, and he was granted interviews at once by William H. Crawford, John C. Calhoun, and William Wirt. There were other conversations as well, but surely none so remarkable as the council ring in the Dennison Hotel, where Owen sat down with a group of

---

[52] Philadelphia *Democratic Press*, reprinted in *New-York Advertiser* (semiweekly ed.), Dec. 4, 1824, p. 2:1; *Christian Advocate* (Philadelphia), II, 560 (Dec. 1824).

[53] W. Owen, *Diary*, p. 30. This entry actually speaks of "Mr. Stuckman, a druggist," but proper names are so frequently misspelled in the document that there is no reason to doubt that this was John Speakman, who was, in fact, a druggist. Donald Macdonald mentions the episode and indicates that the visitor was a friend of Say's, but leaves the name blank. *Diaries*, p. 206. The careless rendering of names is doubly confusing here, for Owen's financial correspondent in Philadelphia (and later the agent for the *New-Harmony Gazette*) was Samuel Spackman. Both Speakman and Spackman are listed in the *Philadelphia Directory, for 1816*, but there is no Stuckman, Stackman, or Sparkman—names which appear in the diaries of D. Macdonald and W. Owen, but which must be simply erroneous spellings.

Choctaw and Chickasaw chiefs and gravely explained his new view of society through an interpreter.[54]

On November 28, 1824, three weeks and a half after disembarking in New York, Owen and his party set out for the west, to see Harmonie and to negotiate for its purchase. For the trip from Washington to Hagerstown they were forced to hire three hackney coaches, but at Hagerstown they caught the stagecoach on the National Road to Washington, Pennsylvania, whence another stage brought them to Pittsburgh on December 3, 1824. En route they encountered General Jackson, to whom Owen presented his letter of introduction.[55] John Speakman of Philadelphia had preceded Owen to Pittsburgh,[56] and promptly introduced him to the communitarians there, notably Benjamin Bakewell, the leading glassmaker of the city, who the next year became president of the local Owenite society. At Pittsburgh, too, Owen came closer to the objective for which he had crossed the Atlantic. Father George Rapp, with a portion of the Harmonists, was at the new community of Economy, eighteen miles down the river, and Owen drove out to share ideas with the German leader, to view the society in operation, and to gather further particulars about the property in Indiana that he proposed to purchase.[57]

The business affairs of the Harmonists, however, were under the control of Father Rapp's adopted son Frederick, who was still in Indiana. As soon as possible, therefore, Owen continued his journey by steamboat down the Ohio. On the afternoon of Thursday, December 16, 1824, he reached the village of Harmonie, which was to be the scene of his great experiment. Frederick Rapp greeted him at once, and for eight days they were engaged in a methodical inspection of the property, assisted by Captain Macdonald, whose training in the Royal Engineers was a valuable asset, and by young William Owen, whose practical knowledge of machinery almost equaled his father's. On Christmas Eve Owen journeyed to the English Settlement at Albion, Illinois, to visit Richard Flower, who had conducted him to America. Frederick Rapp followed him there and the negotiations continued.[58] On New Year's Eve Owen returned to Harmonie, and the next evening he informed his son "that he had decided on the

[54] On the visit to Washington, Nov. 25–28, 1824, see D. Macdonald, pp. 215–20, and W. Owen, pp. 39–46.

[55] For the journey see D. Macdonald, pp. 220–27, and W. Owen, pp. 46–56.

[56] See W. Owen, pp. 42, 51, 56; D. Macdonald, pp. 227, 232.

[57] For the visit to Pittsburgh and Economy, Dec. 3–6, 1824, see D. Macdonald, pp. 227–33, and W. Owen, pp. 51–56.

[58] Owen's stay in New Harmony from Dec. 16, 1824, to Jan. 3, 1825, broken by his trip to Albion from Dec. 24 to 31, is recorded by D. Macdonald, pp. 245–65, and W. Owen, pp. 71–94. The two diarists, however, preceded Owen to the English Prairie on Dec. 20, 1824. See also William Hall, "Journal," p. 238.

purchase." [59] On Monday, January 3, 1825, the papers were signed,[60] and in the afternoon Owen departed again for the east, the proprietor of a 20,000 acre tract of partially cleared land, with some 180 brick, frame, and log structures, comprising public buildings, factories, shops, and housing for approximately 700 persons.[61]

Judged by every outward sign the tour which Owen made from January 3 to April 13, 1825, was one of the greatest triumphs of his career. Heretofore he had discussed his plans in small, select groups, but from the beginning he had contemplated a great public campaign once the property at Harmonie was acquired, a propagandist effort that would culminate in the presentation of his plans to Congress.[62] His thoughts were upon Washington as he took leave of his son William and of Captain Macdonald, who were to remain in charge of affairs at New Harmony. By January 22, 1825, he was back in Pittsburgh, ready to hold his first public meeting. So enthusiastic was the response, according to reports reaching Britain, that even the court suspended its session during the hour of Owen's address.[63] In a whirlwind visit to Philadelphia in late January or early February he so effectively fanned the enthusiasm of those whom he had met the previous November that Troost, Say, and Speakman of the Academy of Natural Sciences were reported "making their preparations" to

[59] W. Owen, p. 92 (Jan. 1, 1825). On the following day, however, Robert Owen and Frederick Rapp continued their negotiations, and the latter presented his terms in writing. This apparently unsettled Owen's mind again, for he sent a hasty note that afternoon to George Flower at Albion saying: "It is . . . very desirable that you should be here as early tomorrow as you can come conveniently for important decisions may be made between 10 & 11 oclock & it is very uncertain whether they will be for or against a purchase." Robert Owen to George Flower, Harmony, Sunday [Jan. 2, 1825], 1 o'clock, MS in Eben Lane collection, Chicago Historical Society. See D. Macdonald, p. 264, which definitely establishes the date.

[60] George Flower arrived in answer to Owen's summons, a final agreement was signed in the afternoon, and Owen and Rapp together embarked on a keelboat for Shawneetown about 3 o'clock. W. Owen, p. 93; D. Macdonald, p. 265 (Jan. 3, 1825). Contemporaries believed the price to have been $125,000. See William Hall, "Journal," p. 239 (Jan. 16–23, 1825). The agreement signed at this time was apparently a binding one, but the terms were later revised. See below, p. 180, n. 74.

[61] Detailed physical descriptions of New Harmony are given in the diaries of Donald Macdonald, pp. 245 *et seqq.*, and William Owen, pp. 71 *et seqq.* The community as it was in Sept. 1822, before the Rappites decided to leave, is described in William Hebert, *Visit,* pp. 328–38. A "View of New-Harmony" at the beginning of Owenite occupation was published in the *New-Harmony Gazette,* I, 6–7, 14–15, 22, 30–31, 38–39 (Oct. 1–29, 1825). It was written by T. M. Bosson. See "Pelham Letters," p. 385.

[62] Washington *Daily National Intelligencer,* Nov. 16, 1824, p. 3:2; Dec. 1, 1824, p. 3:2.

[63] London *Times,* March 9, 1825, p. 3:5, reprinted from Edinburgh *Scotsman.* The date of the meeting is reported in D. Macdonald, p. 288; see also W. Owen, pp. 115, 120.

join him at New Harmony, and Madame Fretageot implored Maclure to transfer all his educational and scientific enterprises to Owen's colony on the Wabash.[64]

Owen reached Washington just as the House of Representatives brought the long presidential canvass to a close by choosing John Quincy Adams as the next occupant of the White House. It was a fortunate time for Owen. The electoral excitement was over, yet the capital was crowded with the leading figures of American public life. Owen's prospective visit had been announced long before in the papers, and at that time the *National Intelligencer* had welcomed Owen as one of those "who seem to have had no thought but how to lessen the sufferings of the unfortunate, and better the conditions of the human race, in every quarter of the world." [65] Even more enthusiastic was the communication which the *Intelligencer* willingly published on February 17, 1825, after Owen had actually reached the capital. In his experiments at New Lanark, the writer asserted, Owen

has realized, at his own expense, and from the pure emanation of his own unexampled resolution and mental and moral faculties, effects more extraordinary and rational than any lawgiver of ancient or modern times. . . . It is a fortunate event for the United States, that this gentleman has come among us with the express purpose of establishing an institution, in which all that has been here noticed, and more than what is here possible to be described, are meant to be carried into execution.[66]

An even more extraordinary tribute to Owen's personality and reputation was the fact that he was readily granted the use of the Hall of Representatives in the Capitol for two addresses, the first time by arrangement with Henry Clay, the Speaker, and the second time through the good offices of John Quincy Adams, the incoming President.[67] Adams, in fact, attended the first lecture on February 25, 1825, entertained Owen two evenings later, made a fruitless trip to the Capitol the day after his own inauguration to hear the second lecture,

[64] Madame Fretageot to Maclure, Philadelphia, Feb. 11, 1825, Feb. 18, and March [9]–13, in *Correspondence*, pp. 314–16. Also see below, pp. 154–56.

[65] Washington *Daily National Intelligencer*, Dec. 1, 1824, p. 3:2. At this time the editor knew only that Owen "is, or has been, and certainly will be" in Washington. More definite information was given after Owen had started back from Harmonie. *National Intelligencer* (triweekly), Feb. 8, 1825, p. 3:4.

[66] *National Intelligencer*, Feb. 17, 1825, p. 4:5, a communication signed D. and dated Feb. 15. The article was reprinted in the *Liberty Hall and Cincinnati Gazette*, March 15, 1825, p. 2:4.

[67] That Clay and Adams made the arrangements rests upon Owen's unsupported assertion ten years after the event. Owen also reported that the Supreme Court as a body had offered him its chamber for his second discourse. "Memoranda Relative to Robert Owen," *New Moral World*, I, 362 (Sept. 12, 1835), a series of articles based on information furnished by Owen.

only to discover that it had been postponed, and patiently returned on March 7 to sit through the whole three hours of Owen's final discourse.[68] His predecessor, James Monroe, was also in the audience,[69] as well as several members of the Cabinet, the Supreme Court, and the Congress. The complete texts of Owen's lectures were printed by the *National Intelligencer*[70] in the same conspicuous place that was assigned in due course to President Adams' inaugural address. Each discourse was also immediately printed in pamphlet form at Washington. And before the end of the year editions of the two addresses together had been published in Philadelphia, Pittsburgh, and London.[71] A New York publishing firm, moreover, brought out an American edition of *A New View of Society*, with supplementary writings, in time for Owen to read extensively from a copy during his second Washington lecture.[72]

[68] John Quincy Adams, *Memoirs*, VI, 512, 514, 522, 524–25.

[69] *Ibid.*, p. 524; *National Intelligencer*, March 8, 1825, p. 3:5.

[70] *National Intelligencer*, March 1, 1825, p. 2:1–5; March 15, p. 2:1–5. See also the brief notices in *ibid.*, Feb. 22, p. 1:2; Feb. 26, p. 3:4; March 3, p. 3:5; March 5, p. 3:5; and March 8, p. 3:5.

[71] Owen, *A Discourse on a New System of Society; as Delivered in the Hall of Representatives of the United States, in Presence of the President of the United States, the President Elect, Heads of Departments, Members of Congress, &c. &c., on the 25th of February, 1825* (Washington: Gales & Seaton, 1825); *A Discourse . . . on the 7th of March, 1825* (Washington: Gales & Seaton, 1825); *Two Discourses on a New System of Society . . .* (Philadelphia: Atkinson & Alexander, 1825); *Two Discourses . . .* (Pittsburgh: Eichbaum & Johnston, 1825); *Owen's American Discourses: Two Discourses on a New System of Society . . .* (London: Whiting & Branston; sold at the office of the London Co-operative Society, 1825). The Pittsburgh title page added "Judges of the Supreme Court" to the list of auditors. The two addresses are cited herein as *Discourses in Washington*, and page references are ordinarily given to the reprint in the *New-Harmony Gazette*, II, 225–26, 233–34, 241–42, 249–50, 257–58, 265–66 (April 18–May 23, 1827). Certain concluding passages dealing with the preliminary society "about to be commenced at Harmony" are omitted in the *Gazette*, however, and these are quoted from the pamphlets. John Speakman was responsible for the Philadelphia edition, and probably made the arrangements with Eichbaum, the publisher in Pittsburgh. See Speakman to Owen, Philadelphia, April 29, 1825, MS no. 67 in Robert Owen papers, in the library of the Co-operative Union, Ltd., Holyoake House, Manchester, England, a collection cited hereafter as Owen papers, Manchester. Quotations are actually taken from photostats in the Illinois Historical Survey at the University of Illinois, for whom the collection is being reproduced in its entirety.

[72] *A New View of Society* (First American from the Third London Edition, New York: E. Bliss & E. White, 1825). The forthcoming publication was announced as early as Jan. 22, 1825, in the Shawnee-Town *Illinois Gazette*, p. 3:4 (reprinted from *New-York Statesman*); it was advertised for sale in the *National Intelligencer*, March 12, p. 3:5, and reviewed in the *New-York Statesman*, March 17 (as cited by Irvin, pp. 28–29). See also Owen, *Discourse in Washington*, March 7, 1825, in *New-Harmony Gazette*, II, 249, 265. In addition there was a "First American from the Fourth London Edition" (Cincinnati: L. Watson, 1825). This was reviewed in *Cincinnati Literary Gazette*, III, 193–94 (June 18, 1825).

His views fairly before the public, Owen paid visits to Jefferson at Monticello and Madison at Montpelier in the middle of March, carrying personal letters of introduction from Monroe.[73] After a few additional days in the capital, he went on to Philadelphia. The enthusiasm he had previously aroused among the members of the Academy of Natural Sciences was as nothing to the excitement that met him this time, the laurels won at Washington fresh on his brow. At Madame Fretageot's, Owen wrote the first page of a joint letter to William Maclure, but it was a full day before the good lady was calm enough to continue it. She had been listening, she said, to "the best man explaining a plan which is the best calculated for human happiness. . . . I have heard and seen but what is positive in my mind as well as in the mind of all those who have had the same opportunity. It is that a great change is to take place on this part of our hemisphere." [74] From that time forward any other course than joining New Harmony was unthinkable to her.

Comparable enthusiasm greeted Owen on his progress back to New Harmony. At Cincinnati an Owenite society had been formed while Owen was in Washington, and two of its leaders were in his party when he finally reached New Harmony on April 13, 1825.[75]

In every outward respect, Owen's hundred days in the east—it was precisely that—had been a triumphant success. He had been received with undiminished courtesy by the most distinguished figures in the land. In addition he had this time attracted popular attention and made his doctrine a topic of newspaper discussion far and wide. The harvest, too, seemed substantial enough, for eight or nine hundred persons crowded into New Harmony in May 1825, the first month of community life. "The results of the proceedings," exulted Owen eight days after his return,

exceed the most sanguine anticipations that I had formed. The United States but particularly the States west of the Allegheny Mountains have been prepared in the most remarkable manner for the New System. The principle of union & cooperation for the promotion of all the virtues & for the creation of wealth is now universally admitted to be far superior to the

[73] James Monroe to Jefferson, Washington, March 9, 1825, MS in Jefferson papers, series II, vol. 58, no. 164, Library of Congress; Monroe to Madison, same place and date, MS in Madison papers, Library of Congress. See also J. Q. Adams, *Memoirs,* VI, 527; *National Intelligencer,* March 22, 1825, p. 1:3; "Memoranda Relative to Robert Owen," *New Moral World,* I, 362 (Sept. 12, 1835).

[74] Mme Fretageot to Maclure, Philadelphia, March 28, 1825, in *Correspondence,* pp. 317–19.

[75] *Liberty Hall and Cincinnati Gazette,* March 8, 1825, p. 2:4; D. Macdonald, *Diaries,* p. 292; W. Owen, *Diary,* p. 134; William Owen to George Flower, Harmony [April 13, 1825], MS in Chicago Historical Society, printed in Flower, *History of the English Settlement,* p. 373 (datable from internal evidence).

individual selfish system & all seem prepared or are rapidly preparing to give up the latter & adopt the former. In fact the whole of this country is ready to commence a new empire upon the principle of public property & to discard private property & the uncharitable notion that man can form his own character as the foundation & root of all evil. For years past everything seems to have been preparing in an unaccountable & most remarkable manner for my arrival. This new colony will be filled up to its full number before the end of this [sic] by useful & valuable families & individuals. . . . From present appearances I believe the whole of the district north of the Ohio River comprising all the free States will be ripe for the change before the [sic] of the year 1827. . . . Our operations will soon extend to the blacks & the Indians who by singular circumstances have been prepared in a peculiar manner for the change which I propose.[76]

In Owen's mind, no expedition in history had been so momentous.

Benefiting from hindsight, however, one must pronounce the campaign if not a failure then at least the precursor of later failures. Nothing that Owen did, in fact, really advanced the practical experiment to which he had committed himself, and much that he did was to prove detrimental. A truer index to what was happening during the hundred days is to be found in the diaries and letters of those who remained behind at New Harmony.

William Owen and Captain Macdonald were nominally in charge of preparations for the new community, but their terms of reference were so vague that in effect they were powerless. They did not know when to expect Owen back from the east. They did not know how he planned to recruit the population of his community. They did not know how he intended to reduce his general communitarian principles to actual community practice. They did not know how he expected to use the buildings at Harmonie or carry on the agricultural operations of the season that was about to begin.[77] All they could

---

[76] Owen to William Allen, New Harmony, April 21, 1825, MS no. 56 in Owen papers, Manchester. In his excitement Owen omitted two crucial words, indicated above by the word *sic*. Did he intend to write *month* or *year* in the first instance, *beginning* or *end* in the second? The larger figure for the influx into New Harmony is from Owen's speeches at Cincinnati, June 10, 1825, and at Philadelphia, July 6, 1825. *Cincinnati Literary Gazette*, III, 190 (June 11, 1825); Washington *National Intelligencer*, July 14, 1825, p. 3:1; *Niles' Weekly Register*, XXVIII, 325 (July 23, 1825). The *Cincinnati Literary Gazette* believed that Cincinnati had furnished "a large proportion" of the settlers in the new community. III, 193 (June 18, 1825). In September the town contained at least 800 inhabitants. See the committee report in Thomas Clinton Pears, Jr., ed., *New Harmony, An Adventure in Happiness: Papers of Thomas and Sarah Pears* (Indiana Historical Society Publications, vol. XI, no. 1; Indianapolis, 1933), p. 29; cited hereafter as *Pears Papers*.

[77] See especially William Owen to Robert Owen, Vincennes, Feb. 7, 1825: "We are anxiously looking for your return about the end of this month [i.e., a month and a half before Owen actually returned], as the season is advancing rapidly & much will require to be settled relative to the agricultural arrangements, before

do was parry the questions that were put to them on their trips through the neighborhood, or that arrived by mail.[78] It is true that they drafted and eventually published a notice about the community, but it did little more than specify the types of craftsmen that would be needed.[79] And Macdonald essayed an outline of the new social system, which was certainly as clear as any of Owen's but no more specific.[80] Even when most of the Rappites had departed and new families began actually to arrive in the town, the two deputies of Owen did not consider themselves authorized to assign lodgings. Under the circumstances a mood of discouragement enveloped those at the seat of the new experiment, contrasting strangely with the contemporaneous enthusiasm in the east. More than two months before Owen returned, his son was writing him: "I am quite tired of doing nothing here but talking. It is eternally the same thing over & over again. Always the same questions to be answered to every new face. I hope it will be otherwise when we begin to act." [81] After another six weeks had passed without news or instructions, young

---

the warm weather commences. You will likewise find many enquiries, which it will require much consideration to answer, but which must be settled before any one can be admitted." MS no. 58 in Owen papers, Manchester. The 4-page MS comprises a 2-page letter signed by William Owen, and a second letter of equal length, unsigned but indubitably written by Donald Macdonald; the latter is cited hereafter as Macdonald to Owen. William Owen's part of the letter, but not Macdonald's, was printed in *New Harmony Times*, Aug. 10, 1906.

[78] D. Macdonald, *Diaries,* pp. 268–92 *passim;* W. Owen, *Diary,* pp. 97–134 *passim;* William Owen to William Pelham, Harmonie, Jan. 22, 1825, in "Pelham Letters," pp. 416–17; William Hall, "Journal," pp. 238–39.

[79] A copy of the broadside, headed "Notice to Farmers, Tradesmen and Others," and dated Harmony, Feb. 1, 1825, is in the Owen papers, Manchester, no. 57; it has been reprinted in the *New Harmony Times*, Aug. 24, 1906. The circumstances of its printing were described by Macdonald in his letter of Feb. 7, 1825, to Owen: "So many enquiries had been made and all in so erroneous a point of view that we got hold of Dr. Müller & his printing press and struck off 100 copies of the Notice, modified according to your letter from Louisville relative to offering only food, clothes & habitations, and altered according to the impressions made upon the minds of the persons to whom we read it." MS no. 58 in Owen papers, Manchester. See also D. Macdonald, *Diaries,* pp. 268, 277, 282–83; W. Owen, *Diary,* pp. 97, 102, 109, 112, 113.

[80] Dated Feb. 1, 1825, reprinted from Vincennes, Ind., *Western Sun,* in Indianapolis *Indiana Journal,* March 22, 1825, p. 4:3. According to Macdonald's diary, p. 277, he wrote the article for the Shawnee-Town *Illinois Gazette.* It does not appear in the extant files of that paper, but the issues for Feb. 19 and March 5 and 12 are missing. In his letter of Feb. 7, 1825, to Owen, already quoted, Macdonald explained the reasons for this open letter: "As whatever is said or written about you seemed to interest the neighbourhood, and as the current ideas were all that you designed just to employ the people to your own gain, I sat down & wrote a letter simply giving the general views in distinct propositions with the consequences which would follow."

[81] William Owen to Robert Owen, Feb. 7, 1825.

Owen confided to his journal: "The enjoyment of a reformer, I should say, is much more in contemplation, than in reality. . . . I doubt whether those who have been comfortable and contented in their old mode of life, will find an increase of enjoyment when they come here." [82]

In the first quarter of 1825, appearances lent color to the optimism of Robert Owen, but realities justified the pessimism of his son. As a matter of fact, the purchase of Harmonie in January 1825 had completely altered the nature of Owen's task. Thereafter a condition confronted him, not a theory. For seven years he had been preaching his new doctrine, and the response had been all he could reasonably ask for. Now he had shifted his ground to practical experiment, and it behooved him to devote all his energy and skill to the specific job of making it succeed. Up to this time his achievements at New Lanark had sufficed as a warrant that he could carry his measures into successful operation when the time came. Now the time had come, and Owen was still talking, not acting.

Never, in fact, did he realize how much detailed planning still needed to be done to bridge the gap between theory and practice. He had talked about his plan for so long, and he had accompanied it with so many plausible calculations, that he had blinded himself to the fact that his "plan" was in reality a mere sketch, devoid of specifications on most of the material points. He believed, of course, and he told others, that he could fill in the details by solving specific problems as they arose in practice under his watchful managerial eye. If such was really his intention, nothing can justify his leaving the scene on the very day he committed himself finally to the experiment, and returning to it for less than two months out of the first twelve.[83] His triumph at Washington was his doom at New Harmony.

Of all the problems that cried out for practical solution, two were of transcendent importance. What system of property rights did he intend to establish at New Harmony? And what criteria did he intend to apply in the selection of members? The looseness of his thinking on these two questions is the most serious fault of his public utterances in 1825.

A preceding chapter has pointed out the difficulty of ascertaining what views Owen actually held on property and the possible holding of it in common. To historians the question is by definition an academic one. But to individuals who contemplated investing their

[82] William Owen, *Diary*, pp. 129–30 (March 24, 1825). Equally eloquent was Donald Macdonald's silence; the indefatigable diarist ceased his daily entries entirely between Feb. 12 and April 2, 1825.

[83] Between Jan. 3, 1825, when he signed the contract with the Rappites, and Jan. 12, 1826, when he returned to the community from Europe, Owen was present at New Harmony for only seven weeks and a half, April 13 to June 5, 1825.

capital and their labor in the experiment, it was of personal and compelling interest. And to Owen himself, who was actually staking his fortune on the venture, the matter should have assumed the highest and most immediate importance. How lightly he had considered it, however, was revealed by a speech he made at Albion, Illinois, on December 30, 1824, only four days before he signed the purchase papers. According to his son's report,

He told them also that it had occurred to him only this morning, that, perhaps, if he purchased Harmonie, the community might rent the houses and land from him and cultivate the land in common. . . . Mr. Clark wished to know what become [sic] of their present property. Mr. Owen thought if the soil was wet it might be laid down in grass, if dry in cotton or farmed for the private benefit of the individuals of the society.[84]

It would be difficult to compress into three sentences so much naive and confused thinking. Owen failed utterly to grasp the most obvious and at the same time the most crucial question that could be asked him. He had spoken of cultivating the land in common. It was natural to ask what that meant; in other words, what was to happen to property that members might possess when entering into a state of community. In effect, Owen's answer was an expression of airy unconcern: individuals might abandon their land or arrange to have it cultivated for them in absentia. To suggest the first alternative to a group of frontiersmen was an audacious folly. To propose the second was to strike at the roots of his own system, for how could community of property at home be reconciled with unearned income received individually from abroad?

A well-considered answer was of course hardly to be expected in view of the confession in Owen's opening sentence that he had only that morning given any thought to an even simpler and more immediate matter—the relationship between himself as owner of Harmonie and the members of the community to be established there. Incredible as it seems, he was on the point of sinking his fortune in an experiment without any notion of whether the subjects of it were to be considered employees or almsmen or partners or tenants of his. Each of these four possibilities had its precedent in what Owen had previously said or done—the first at New Lanark, the second in his poor-relief schemes, the third in his plans for "independent" communities. The fourth was proposed in his speech at Albion in too tentative a manner to dispel the ambiguity. As a consequence the persons who crowded into New Harmony in its first weeks included many who expected to find employment with Owen, others

84 W. Owen, p. 90. D. Macdonald's report of the speech, pp. 260–61, is almost identical.

who hoped to live off his bounty, still others who believed that Owen would pool his vast property with their little on terms of equality, and a final remnant who were prepared to form their own communitive groups and lease land from the founder. Beyond question Owen was thinking only of this last arrangement by the beginning of 1826, but he failed to make the fact clear during the crucial propaganda campaigns of 1825.

So far was Owen from adapting his general principles to the specific situation at New Harmony that the only "Rules and Regulations of a Community" which he had to offer were the ones he had drafted in 1823 in connection with his Irish tour.[85] Not only did he cite them in his informal talk at Albion, but he quoted them even in his formal addresses at Washington,[86] and allowed them to be printed in the *National Intelligencer* and in the pamphlets containing his two discourses without so much as altering pounds sterling to dollars.[87]

These thirty-nine rules gave a deceptive appearance of precision. On the vital question of property rights, however, they were not only vague in themselves but also inapplicable to the actual circumstances of the New Harmony experiment, for they assumed an already organized body of members to furnish or borrow the capital for the initial purchase. Members were to work for the common good and were to be "fully supplied with the necessaries and comforts of life," but whether their labor was to be balanced against their consumption, and how, was unexplained. The "surplus proceeds of the united exertions of the community" were not to be apportioned among the members, but kept as "a fund for the establishment of a second community," which appeared to mean that the members surrendered any right to participate in the profits on the basis of their investment or their superior productivity. And in case of withdrawal, the only recognition or protection of their property interests in the community was provided by a clause authorizing the committee in charge "to allow any such gratuity, as the circumstances of the case may re-

---

[85] Published in Owen, *Report of the Proceedings at the Several Public Meetings Held in Dublin* (Dublin, 1823), pp. 82–91, where the statement is made that the rules had already been printed at the conclusion of *A Report of the British and Foreign Philanthropic Society, with Other Statements and Calculations, Explanatory of Mr. Owen's Plan for the Relief of Ireland* (Dublin, 1823). The apparently complete copy of this pamphlet in the University of Illinois Library does .not contain the rules, but they may have formed a supplementary signature.

[86] D. Macdonald, p. 257; Owen, *Discourse in Washington*, March 7, 1825, in *New-Harmony Gazette*, II, 258 (May 16, 1827).

[87] Compare article VI as printed in Owen, *Report of the Proceedings . . . in Dublin* (1823), p. 83; in Washington *National Intelligencer*, March 26, 1825, p. 1:1–3; and in Owen, *Two Discourses* (Philadelphia, 1825), p. 45.

quire." [88] If these provisions be taken alone and at face value, then Owen was preaching community of property. On the other hand, his "Rules and Regulations" contained clauses inconsistent with this. Article VI, for example, gave greater powers at the outset to those who invested £100 or more, and provided for the eventual repayment to individual members of the capital they had advanced—which certainly implied that private ownership of capital was not to disappear even when the new society was fully under way.

Owen's speeches did nothing to clear up these contradictions. His two discourses at Washington, the most widely circulated and official of his statements, were as vague and ambiguous as the rules. On the one hand Owen proclaimed that inequality of wealth, individual competition, and the trading system as a whole must disappear, to be replaced by communities possessing "common property, and one common interest." [89] On the other hand, he invited those with capital to join the Preliminary Society as nonlaboring members, and he proposed a bookkeeping system which was far from providing complete community of property: "At the end of every year, a certain amount, in value, will be placed to the credit of each family . . . in proportion to their expenditure, and to the services rendered by them to the society." [90] How these arrangements were expected to lead gradually to a system of common property was not explained, and Owen's hearers were free to read into his proposals practically any economic doctrine they chose.

Only in proposing the last-mentioned Preliminary Society did Owen give evidence of truly constructive thinking. Such a "halfway house," as he called it, provided a common-sense way of deferring some of the problems that Owen had brought upon himself. It promised him two or three years of grace to evolve a plan that was really a plan, either by thinking through the fundamental questions he had hitherto ignored, or by improvising practical solutions in the course of day-to-day management as he had done at New Lanark. Let us see how he used his opportunity.

He worked up a constitution for the Preliminary Society during the last week of April 1825 and put it into effect on the first of May, two weeks and a half after his return to New Harmony from Washington. Despite the haste in drafting, the document was clearer than

[88] Articles XVI, XIX, XXXIV. That the profits were to be used to establish new communities was clearly understood at New Harmony. See *Pears Papers*, p. 25.

[89] *Discourses in Washington*, 1825, in *New-Harmony Gazette*, II, 234, 241, 258. See also his letter to Allen, quoted above, pp. 113–14.

[90] *Two Discourses* (Pittsburgh, 1825), p. 32.

any he had offered before, and the address he made in presenting it was somewhat more specific than usual.[91] Contrary to his own inclinations, he declared, he would be forced to "admit, for a time, a certain degree of pecuniary inequality." He would direct the experiment himself during the first year, the members would share in its control during the second, and then, "at the termination of the second year, or between that period and the end of the third year, an Association of Members may be formed to constitute a Community of Equality and Independence." Members of the Preliminary Society were to provide their own household furniture and small tools, but were to be credited on the books with any livestock they might contribute. Their daily labors would also be evaluated and recorded, and they would be debited for goods they consumed. Pending the annual casting up of accounts, the society would advance to each member a credit of fixed amount at the community store. Cash transactions were to be infrequent, and, except in case of withdrawal, members would receive their earnings only "in the productions of the establishment, or in store goods." Though far from liberal, these terms were at least clear —or would have been, had not Owen managed within a month to make several of them ambiguous.[92]

The constitution of the Preliminary Society, however, offered no clue to the kind of community that Owen planned ultimately to establish. The fact that he continued to point complacently to the vague and outmoded "Rules and Regulations," [93] drafted long before

[91] On April 20, 1825, exactly a week after Owen's return, a meeting was held at New Harmony to appoint a committee for drafting the constitution. The committee began work on Monday the twenty-fifth, Owen read the document publicly on the twenty-seventh, and Donald Macdonald took it to Evansville to be printed. D. Macdonald, *Diaries,* pp. 292–94. No copy of this printing is known, but the text of the constitution, dated May 1, 1825, and Owen's address of April 27 were printed in the first number of the *New-Harmony Gazette,* I, 1–3 (Oct. 1, 1825); quotations in the present paragraph are taken therefrom. The dates of events are not altogether clear, for William Owen's diary ceases on April 19 (misdated the twentieth in the printed text), and Macdonald's is somewhat confused, owing to the fact that he was coming to the end of one volume and commencing another. See p. 294 n, and note the complete gap from May 6 to June 5, 1825. During the week of April 17 to 24 William Hall "heard Mr Owens lecture on the establishment of his intended preliminary Society." See his "Journal," p. 242. It was on April 21 that Owen made his final bargain with the Rappites. See below, p. 180, n. 74.

[92] As early as June 2, 1825, Thomas Pears, who was employed in the bookkeeping department, wrote: "You will perceive by the report that no member of the society if put upon the maximum, can draw for provisions and clothing more than 180$ per year; . . . but in a discourse Mr. Owen delivered yesterday, he stated, I think, that each family were to be permitted to draw on the store sufficient for their support. But it is so variously understood that I am not certain about it." *Pears Papers,* pp. 13–14.

[93] The Constitution of the Preliminary Society stated that the future Com-

in Ireland, showed that he had no real intention of producing a better matured plan during the period for reflection provided by the Preliminary Society. Nor did he intend to use the breathing spell to gain experience by managing the enterprise on the spot, for on June 5, 1825, five weeks after officially launching the experiment, he left New Harmony again, to be absent for more than seven months.

In the end Owen likewise cast away whatever opportunity the Preliminary Society might have afforded him to select qualified members. Much was to be made, in later Owenite apologetics, of the irresponsible character of the persons who flocked to New Harmony. This undoubtedly contributed to the failure, but Owen had only himself to blame.[94] For months after he purchased the property, his closest associates had no idea how he intended to recruit the population for his experiment. At the beginning there was a widespread belief that he would "bring out nearly the whole town of Lanark in Scotland to settle it." [95] Yet when Owen was back in London in August 1825 one newspaper reporter was "pleased to observe that Mr. O. did not make use of a single expression to induce any of his hearers to emigrate to America." [96] Poor William Owen, in charge at New Harmony, never knew what to expect. In February 1825 he wrote a strong letter to his father in Washington cautioning him against admitting members from the immediate neighborhood and urging him to rely upon those who were to come from Europe.[97] The elder Owen paid no heed. A week after his return in April 1825 he

---

munity of Equality would "be governed according to the General Rules and Regulations contained in the printed paper, entitled *'Mr. Owen's Plan for the permanent Relief of the Working Classes.'*" *New-Harmony Gazette*, I, 3 (Oct. 1, 1825). The printed paper was perhaps the one which Macdonald procured in Evansville; the "General Rules and Regulations" were undoubtedly the old ones drawn up for Ireland, which were headed thus in the various republications in the United States.

[94] Utterly without foundation was the Owenite defense, first brought forward fourteen years after the event, that Owen had been forced to accept whatever persons he could get because Rapp had gone back on an alleged promise to leave his followers at Harmonie until they could be gradually replaced. See *New Moral World*, VI, 801–2 (Oct. 12, 1839).

[95] James O. Wattles to Azariah Smith, Albion, Ill., Jan. 15, 1825, MS owned by Mr. Wright Howes, bookseller, Chicago, and quoted with his permission. See also *Maclure-Fretageot Correspondence*, pp. 312–14, and "Pelham Letters," p. 417.

[96] London *Examiner*, reprinted in Washington *National Intelligencer*, Nov. 3, 1825, p. 4:2. See also London *Times*, Sept. 27, 1825, p. 2:6, and the editorial comment thereon in *National Intelligencer*, Nov. 12, 1825, p. 1:1.

[97] William Owen to Robert Owen, Vincennes, Feb. 7, 1825, MS no. 58 in Owen papers, Manchester. In his part of the same letter Donald Macdonald seconded this opinion: "We have not seen very many families in this country whom we expect would be found to your mind in any way, & therefore hope you will engage the most part before your return."

was reporting, with evident pride, that New Harmony would be completely filled by persons "accustomed to the climate & habits of the country without one coming out from Europe." [98] In June 1825 the young William Owen was left to deal alone with the eight or nine hundred persons who had been indiscriminately admitted by his father during the seven weeks he had spent at New Harmony. No use was ever made of the wise probationary features of the Preliminary Society, for the next year everyone at New Harmony was admitted to the supposedly permanent Community of Equality, on the simple condition of signing the new constitution.

During the whole of 1825, in effect, Owen acted in utter disregard of the fact that he had staked everything upon a crucial experiment. While time ticked away, he turned his back upon the reality which was New Harmony in order to chase the phantom which was public opinion.

Public opinion was bound to respond to propaganda as impressive as Owen's, and it did. But the reformer's public utterances furnished little solid meat for it to feed upon. Many of Owen's more or less irrelevant opinions were presented by him with far greater clarity and force than his basic proposals, and thus received the lion's share of attention. For every newspaper article that examined the strictly communitarian aspects of his plan, there were at least a score that hammered away at his views on religion.

To a surprising extent the American press conceded the economic feasibility of Owen's plan in the abstract, and questioned only its relevance to American conditions. The Washington *National Intelligencer,* at the very beginning, argued that "however applicable to a crowded population, abounding with paupers, it was not adapted to the present condition of any part of the United States." [99] And the Philadelphia *National Gazette* was willing to grant that the plan

[98] Robert Owen to William Allen, New Harmony, April 21, 1825, MS no. 56 in Owen papers, Manchester. On the later decision to admit all residents to the full organized community, without further tests, see below, p. 175.

[99] *Daily National Intelligencer,* Dec. 1, 1824, p. 3:2. See also *United States Literary Gazette,* II, 61–65 (April 15, 1825). Comparisons between the Old World and the New easily degenerated into nationalistic recrimination. A London paper bade farewell to Owen in 1824 with the remark "that this system of living will answer better among the savages of America than the enlightened people of England." Quoted in *New-York Advertiser,* Nov. 6, 1824, p. 2:2. American papers returned the bouquet, arguing that British reformers would find "more opportunities of doing good in England, than in this country, because objects of benevolence are more numerous there." Washington *National Intelligencer,* Nov. 12, 1825, p. 1:1. Within the United States sectional animosities were sometimes aroused by the controversy over Owenism. See Shawnee-Town *Illinois Gazette,* June 18, 1825, p. 3:2, where the Wabash Valley was defended against eastern slurs.

might "succeed in single instances,—with a few hundred or perhaps thousand persons; and this is all." [100]

Astonishingly few writers attempted to come to grips with the questions—seemingly so obvious and so fundamental—that were posed by community of goods. An unnamed member of Congress, writing in the *National Intelligencer* shortly after Owen's first discourse in Washington, did argue the point, though briefly. Even if community of property should be enforced and should succeed in ending "the distinctions created by inequality of estate," he argued, competition between men would not cease. "When all have enough, what is to be done? Will the mind be at ease? It will not. . . . As long as some men possess more intellect, more industry, and prudence, than others, there will be a difference of condition." [101] A few weeks later another correspondent returned to the theme of community of property, but merely to question the reformer's sincerity by asking "whether Mr. Owen be only *maximus inter pares*, eating at the same table with his disciples, drinking out of the same cup, working in the same field, &c; or whether he be indeed and in truth Lord of the Domain, enjoying a separate and splendid fortune . . . ?" [102]

It was actually the British newspapers, far from the persuasive example of sectarian communities like the Shakers, which discussed these issues most fully in 1825. On the basis of Owen's reports from America, the London *Times* thundered forth the arguments based on economic motivation that one seeks almost in vain in the American press. Its leading article on October 6, 1825, was respectful toward Owen's achievement at New Lanark, but declared flatly that his larger plans were

at variance with the course prescribed by Providence for the exertions and enjoyments of human beings in a state of society. The first moving power which impels mankind to work, is a desire to appropriate the fruits of their labour. This grand motive is cast aside at once by Mr. OWEN.

Economic motivation of this sort was even more essential in western America than in England, continued the *Times*.

Land, of the most productive quality, abounds in that quarter of the earth, and the labour employed upon it is sure of an ample recompense. . . .

[100] Philadelphia *National Gazette*, Nov. 27, 1824, as quoted by Irvin, p. 12. See also Washington *National Intelligencer*, March 22, 1825, p. 4:3; Nov. 12, 1825, p. 3:1.

[101] Washington *National Intelligencer*, March 22, 1825, p. 4:3, a communication dated Feb. 26.

[102] *National Intelligencer*, May 3, 1825, p. 4:3.

There will be more industry without his interference than with it; because individual existence in these self-dependent regions can be no otherwise supported than by daily toil; and an establishment where labour and the fruits of it were to be in common, would present less powerful stimulants to toil, than where the father of a family was conscious . . . that, for the preservation of his wife and children, he had no resource but in the vigour of his *own* arm.[103]

These are, of course, the doubts and queries that spring first to the mind of a modern man, steeped in the discussions of the past century and a quarter. Alongside them the questions raised in the American discussions of Owenism in 1825 seem far-fetched and irrelevant. But their very irrelevance is significant, not only because it reveals the influence which religious orthodoxy exerted upon social thought in the period, but even more because it reveals how congenial to American ways of thinking the communitarian point of view actually was. Only the latter fact can explain why the attack upon Owen was directed so largely not at the communitarianism that was the essence of his plan but at the religious views that were its accidentals.

The religious attack upon Owen began as early as 1817, in one of the very first American publications concerning his system. *The Christian Observer, Conducted by Members of the Established Church,* a London monthly regularly republished in Boston, reviewed Owen's *New View of Society* at great length in its issue of October 1817. It linked Owen with Voltaire, Condorcet, and Paine, and culled from his writings the principal passages that would sustain the charge of deism. These were of two sorts—Owen's denial of moral responsibility, which was a corollary of his doctrine that circumstances determine the characters of men, and his attack upon sectarian religious teaching as tending to inculcate false views of human nature and to perpetuate "superstition, bigotry, hypocrisy, hatred, revenge, wars, and all their evil consequences." No twisting of Owen's words was needed to establish the fact that he believed thus, for even stronger statements to the same effect could have been quoted from his addresses of 1817. To the reviewer the falseness of these propositions was self-evident. His purpose, he said, was rather "to expose, than to discuss or to refute the opinions of Mr. Owen." And since the reformer had woven these philosophical doctrines into every exposition of his social plans, it seemed pointless to examine the details of the latter. "Were a deadly poison to be presented to us, we should scarcely be reconciled to the draught, because the liquor in which it had been dissolved was delicious, or the vessel that contained it was framed with exquisite skill." [104]

103 London *Times,* Oct. 6, 1825, p. 2:2.

104 *Christian Observer* (Boston, "from the London edition"), XVI, 662–80 (Oct. 1817); the quotations are from pp. 663, 674, and 679.

Owen's theories were not a subject of controversy in America when the article was published, but its argument was not entirely forgotten, and quotations from it cropped up in the religious attacks upon Owen after his arrival in the United States.[105] The denunciations began, naturally enough, in the denominational journals. Dr. Ashbel Green, retired president of Princeton, was in the audience at Owen's lecture in Philadelphia on November 22, 1824, and he immediately published a critical note in the *Christian Advocate,* which he edited. The new scheme, he reported, "appeared not only exceedingly visionary, but in some particulars dangerous," for Owen "denied the doctrine of original sin, and seemed to us to build his system on the old and baseless foundation of the *Perfectionists.*" [106]

The secular press, however, did not begin to echo these arguments until after Owen's public appearances at Washington in February and March 1825. The discourses themselves did not especially emphasize the themes that were distasteful to the orthodox, but Owen there invited public criticism, and his wish was granted in overflowing measure. In the three months following Owen's Washington addresses, the *National Intelligencer* alone published twenty-four long communications on his plan, few of which failed to discuss its religious implications.[107]

Judging by the pseudonyms, it was a battle of giants. "Fenelon" led off the attack, while "Franklin" and "Nestor" sprang to Owen's defense. "Viator" was challenged by "De-Viator," and "A Freeman" by "A Citizen of the World." The defenders of Owen pointed out that he had guaranteed freedom of worship in his community [108]—as indeed he had [109]—and they labored to show that his enlightened purposes were in precise accord with the benevolent spirit of the gospels. One writer cited the Book of Acts to prove "that the first Christians adopted strictly" the very plan that Owen advocated.[110] And another argued that it was contrary to their own teachings for "Christians to withhold their aid from a scheme, whose promise is

---

[105] See *Church Register* (Philadelphia), I, 13–14 (Jan. 14, 1826), an Episcopalian periodical.

[106] *Christian Advocate* (Philadelphia), II, 560 (Dec. 1824).

[107] Washington *National Intelligencer,* March 22–June 7, 1825, *passim.* The earliest of these communications was dated Feb. 26, the day after Owen's first discourse in the Capitol.

[108] *National Intelligencer,* April 5, 1825, p. 2:2–3; April 21, p. 2:4; Shawnee-Town *Illinois Gazette,* June 18, 1825, p. 3:2.

[109] "That, as liberty of conscience, religious and mental liberty, will be possessed by every member of the Community, arrangements be made to accommodate all denominations with convenient places of worship." Owen, "Rules and Regulations," art. XXVIII, in *National Intelligencer,* March 26, 1825, p. 1:1–3.

[110] *National Intelligencer,* May 7, 1825, p. 2:1–3.

founded in rational calculations for the peace, order, and prosperity of society." [111]

The orthodox were outraged rather than conciliated by this appeal from the letter of Scripture to its spirit. To them it was little short of blasphemous that Owen's promises should echo those of the New Testament; it was further proof that "he comes among us, not to attack Christianity with the weapons of sarcasm and sophistry alone; but by pompous promises of alleviating our burthens and establishing our felicity." [112] In the last analysis it was not his plan but his theology that was wrong. Owen's indifference to immortality and his "denial of the moral agency and responsibility of man," according to one of the earliest reproofs, destroyed every incentive to virtue and constituted "a full apology for all vice." [113] It was Owen's rejection of the doctrine of human depravity and original sin, however, that broke open all the vials of wrath. He had attacked, exclaimed one critic, "the very corner stone" of Christianity; his scheme was "at war with revelation." [114] To another defender of the faith, Owen's doctrine threatened to bring upon the republic all the horrors of the French Revolution, for it was nothing else than "a revival, of the blasphemous tenets of the Illuminati, diffused over the continent of Europe in the last century; and the Ghost of Weishaupt has ascended from the Tartarean gulph, breathing the sulphurous flames of that pit from whence he has emerged." [115]

So bitter was the attack that one writer, signing himself "A Christian, disbelieving the doctrine of Original Sin," suggested, with considerable plausibility, that the orthodox were using Owen as a stalking horse while they waged war in reality upon the liberals within the theological preserve.[116] And another writer, admittedly hovering "between hope and fear" concerning Owenism, nevertheless confessed himself unable to discover any essential discordance between the new doctrine and conventional religion.[117]

To the distress of some of his fellows, one defender of Owen sallied forth to belabor the clergy with cheerful abandon. Their dislike of Owen, he asserted, was bred of fear—fear that "the 'kingdom of Satan' will lose power; and that the necessity of parsons, lawyers, &c. &c. (and, of course, their *salaries* with them) will be done away." He

---

[111] *Ibid.*, April 21, 1825, p. 2:4.

[112] *Ibid.*, May 7, 1825, p. 4:4–5. See also Shawnee-Town *Illinois Gazette,* May 13, 1826, p. 3:2.

[113] *National Intelligencer*, March 24, 1825, p. 4:1.

[114] Communications by "Viator," *National Intelligencer*, May 7, 1825, p. 4:4–5, and April 9, 1825, p. 1:1–2, respectively.

[115] *National Intelligencer*, April 30, 1825, p. 4:3–4.

[116] *Ibid.*, May 12, 1825, p. 2:3–4.

[117] *Ibid.*, June 7, 1825, p. 4:1.

would deny the name of Christian to at least one of Owen's antagonists, "for, if he was really a good man, or a Christian, he would exhibit a larger stock of that amiable quality called charity, of which he appears to be totally destitute." [118]

When personalities began to be bandied about like this, Joseph Gales, Jr., editor of the *Intelligencer,* felt obliged to step into the ring to enforce the Marquis of Queensberry rules. After his first admonition went unheeded he exclaimed, in a note appended to a later communication, "We most heartily wish our correspondents on Religious topics would forbear the pen and one another." [119] They did neither. Gales himself remained conscientiously neutral, and defended Owen's right to his opinions as eloquently after the debate as before.[120] Not so with other editors. After the middle of 1825 newspaper opinion was generally hostile, and defenses of Owen were occasionally refused publication.[121]

A curious feature of the debate was that it was conducted without reference to actual happenings at New Harmony itself. On June 7, 1825, the *National Intelligencer* printed the last original communication on Owen which it was to publish for several months.[122] Though the religious controversy was to flare up again, it is safe to say that all the arguments had been aired and most minds made up by that time. But no first-hand report from the scene of the experiment had as yet been printed,[123] and no effort had apparently been made by

[118] *Ibid.,* April 30, 1825, p. 4:1–2.

[119] *Ibid.,* May 12, 1825, p. 2:4; see earlier, April 30, p. 1:3.

[120] See *ibid.,* Nov. 12, 1825, p. 3:1; Dec. 6, pp. 1:1 and 2:1; Oct. 7, 1826, p. 3:1; July 22, 1829, p. 1:1. Hezekiah Niles maintained the same tolerant attitude. See *Niles' Weekly Register,* XXXI, 307 (Jan. 13, 1827).

[121] For example, by the *New-York Statesman,* Sept. 28, 1826, as cited by Irvin, p. 77.

[122] Aside from news items, the *National Intelligencer* published nothing on Owenism until Sept. 22, 1825, when it printed Jefferson's letter to Blatchly. In November, with Owen's return, discussion began again, but in greatly diminished volume so far as the *Intelligencer* was concerned. Another wave of religious polemics followed Owen's "Declaration of Mental Independence" on July 4, 1826. See below, pp. 222–23.

[123] The earliest appears to have been a letter of Thomas Pears, written at New Harmony on June 2, 1825, from which excerpts appeared in the Pittsburgh *Gazette* and the Philadelphia *National Gazette* prior to July 6. See *Pears Papers,* pp. 19–20 and n. 13. The account eventually reached the London *Times,* Aug. 22, 1825, p. 2:3, via a Charleston paper. Owen gave his own first report on affairs at New Harmony in an address at Philadelphia on July 6, 1825, reported in the *National Intelligencer,* July 14, p. 3:1. A favorable letter from a visitor circulated in eastern periodicals during the summer and was finally quoted in the Lawrenceburgh *Indiana Palladium,* Aug. 26, 1825, as cited by Irvin, p. 23. The earliest first-hand adverse report appeared in the St. Louis *Missouri Republican,* Sept. 19, 1825 (cited by Leopold, *Robert Dale Owen,* p. 27), and was reprinted in the Cincinnati *National Republican,* Oct. 7 (according to the *Liberty Hall and Cincinnati Gazette,*

any of the writers to discover the actual religious arrangements at New Harmony, or to determine whether their speculations concerning the effect of community life had any foundation in fact.

Owen himself took no direct part in the debate. It reached its height while he was at New Harmony, and was tapering off as he made his way eastward in June. His discourses en route were enthusiastic reports on what he had accomplished rather than answers to his opponents. He left New Harmony on June 5, 1825, held meetings at Mount Vernon, Louisville, Cincinnati, Marietta, and Pittsburgh, then veered northward from his usual route to lecture at Meadville, to view Niagara Falls, and to cross the state of New York by the completed portions of the Erie Canal. He reached New York City on the Fourth of July, and immediately journeyed to Philadelphia to deliver his most important address on the sixth. Another side trip took him to Boston, where he met the aged John Adams. He finally sailed from New York on July 16 and landed in Liverpool on August 6, 1825.[124]

Owen's associates at New Harmony expected him to devote his two months in England to practical preparations for the great experiment. Actually he was as much the propagandist as ever. Though he doubtless attended to business details at New Lanark, he brought no trained personnel from there, as had been expected. For the rest, he visited the new community at Orbiston and gave a few enthusiastic discourses in London,[125] then sailed for America on October 1, 1825.

The closest Owen came to a practical measure in England was to procure an elaborate model, six feet square, of the ideal community edifice he had been talking about. Its value, of course, was purely propagandistic, and its relevance to New Harmony remote, but it was a source of great satisfaction to Owen. He had long sought an adequate visual representation of his plan, particularly since a London paper in 1819 had commented that his proposed villages would be less suggestive of barracks if he would picture them "in

<hr>

Nov. 11, p. 2:1). The article was grist to the critical mill when it finally came to the attention of the eastern papers, notably the Philadelphia *Democratic Press*, Nov. 8, 1825 (cited by Leopold, *loc. cit.*), and the *New-York Advertiser* (semiweekly ed.), Nov. 23, 1825, p. 2:4.

[124] The details of the trip from New Harmony to Liverpool are covered by D. Macdonald, *Diaries*, pp. 294–306. Two letters introducing Owen to prominent citizens of Utica, both dated Sayracuse [*sic*], June 30, 1825, are in the Owen papers, Manchester, nos. 68 and 69. They were written by Robert Richardson, whom Owen met on the canalboat. See D. Macdonald, p. 309.

[125] See London *Times*, Aug. 24, 1825, p. 2:2; Sept. 26, p. 1:1; Sept. 27, p. 2:6; Washington *National Intelligencer*, Nov. 3, 1825, p. 4:2; Nov. 12, p. 1:1; Philadelphia *National Gazette* (triweekly ed.), Nov. 10, 1825, p. 1:2. Also see above, pp. 102, n. 36, 121, 123–24; and below, p. 181, n. 76.

a completer style," filled up "with trees and turf." [126] Owen brought
to America not only the model but also a live architect to explain it
—Stedman Whitwell by name.[127]

Whitwell and the faithful Captain Macdonald took charge of
handling the bulky masterpiece after the arrival of the party in New
York on November 6, 1825. It was displayed at Owen's public meetings in New York and Philadelphia in the course of the month, and
was exhibited briefly at Rembrandt Peale's museum in the former
city.[128] At the end of the month Whitwell and Macdonald left Owen
in Philadelphia, and took the model to Washington. It was unpacked
at the Patent Office and installed in an anteroom of the White House,
where the two deputies of Owen presented it to President John
Quincy Adams on December 3, 1825. After a short trip to Monticello
to visit Jefferson, Whitwell and Macdonald returned to the capital
for ten days, during which time they felt free to conduct visitors to
the White House for an examination of the model, even when the
President was out.[129] The newspapers gave considerable publicity to
the display and to Owen's promise that construction of the edifice
would soon begin on the higher lands commanding the Wabash,
some three miles from the village acquired from the Rappites.[130] The
news was duly reprinted in the *New-Harmony Gazette*, but it must
have added to the consternation of William Owen, who had just

[126] London *Examiner*, April 25, 1819, reprinted in Owen, *Life*, I.A, 233. Owen's
activity in procuring illustrations is narrated in his *Life*, I, 215, 222. One of the
most attractive was by Ramsay Richard Reinagle, R.A., reproduced in Podmore,
Robert Owen, I, facing p. 218. Owen displayed a hastily constructed model at
his second discourse in the Capitol at Washington on March 7, 1825. *New-Harmony
Gazette*, II, 257 (May 16, 1827). The large model he brought from England in the
fall was undoubtedly the basis for the folding plate that formed the frontispiece
to the first number of the *Co-operative Magazine and Monthly Herald* (London)
in Jan. 1826 (also reproduced in Podmore, *Robert Owen*, I, facing p. 290). Its
pointed arches and innumerable gables indicate a change of taste from the
simpler Georgian of Owen's earlier sketches, and foreshadow his son's later advocacy of Gothic architecture for the Smithsonian Institution. See Robert Dale
Owen, *Hints on Public Architecture* (New York, 1849).

[127] Whitwell eventually published a *Description of an Architectural Model from
a Design by Stedman Whitwell, Esq. for a Community upon a Principle of United
Interests, as Advocated by Robert Owen, Esq.* (London, 1830).

[128] D. Macdonald, *Diaries*, pp. 310, 313–14, 316.

[129] The journey of Macdonald and Whitwell from Nov. 28, 1825, when they
departed from Owen in Philadelphia, until Dec. 23, when they finally left Washington, is covered by D. Macdonald, pp. 317–32. See also J. Q. Adams, *Memoirs*,
VII, 68 (Dec. 2, 1825). The two men did not see Owen again until they reached
New-Harmony on Jan. 24, 1826.

[130] Washington *National Intelligencer*, Dec. 6, 1825, p. 2:1; *New-Harmony
Gazette*, I, 118 (Jan. 4, 1826). Some work was actually done at the proposed site
during the fall. See "Pelham Letters," pp. 365, 376, 394; *Pears Papers*, pp. 92–93. See
also D. Macdonald, *Diaries*, pp. 294–95.

written his father of the impossibility even of enlarging the existing accommodations in the town:

As for building houses, that is at present out of the question. We have *no lime, no rocks* (ready blasted), *no brick, no timber, no boards, no shingles*, nothing requisite for buildings, and as to getting them from others, *they are not to be had in the whole country*. We must ourselves produce the whole of them, before we can build, we must dig and burn the lime, dig and blast the rocks, mould and burn the bricks, fell and hew the timber, fell and saw the boards and split the shingles, and to do all these things, we have no hands to spare, or the branches of business in the Society must stop, and they cannot stop, or the whole Society would stop too.[131]

As a matter of fact, Owen's whole conduct after his return was exasperating to those at the seat of the experiment. His landing in New York was announced in the *New-Harmony Gazette* with the remark that his "arrival here is, therefore, daily expected." [132] Actually more than two months elapsed before he finally set foot in New Harmony on January 12, 1826. The interval was filled with ill-considered acts, not the least of which was his advertising in the Philadelphia newspapers for "Artificers and Mechanics," of no less than thirty-nine specified crafts, all of which, he announced, were "wanted immediately" at New Harmony.[133] William Owen, beside himself with the problem of housing those who were already in the village, exploded [134] when he heard of this step, taken in complete disregard of everything he had reported in his letters on the affairs of the community.

As if this were not enough, Owen threw stones again into the religious hornets' nest. On his sea voyage back to the United States he composed an open letter, vague in everything that concerned the practical details of community life and explicit only in its hapless reiteration of the charge that "all religions and laws" had hitherto been founded on error.[135] It was published in the newspapers on

---

131 William Owen to Robert Owen, New Harmony, Dec. 16, 1825, MS no. 54 in Owen papers, Manchester. The letter has been printed in *New Harmony Times*, Aug. 17, 1906.

132 *New-Harmony Gazette*, I, 87 (Dec. 7, 1825).

133 Philadelphia *National Gazette* (triweekly ed.), Nov. 22, 1825, p. 3:5, and subsequent issues. See also D. Macdonald, *Diaries*, pp. 312, 316. The advertisement, dated the fourteenth, announced that Owen himself would conduct interviews on the twenty-third. It was quoted as a news item in the *Liberty Hall and Cincinnati Gazette*, Dec. 20, 1825, p. 3:4.

134 In his letter of Dec. 16, 1825, quoted above. William Pelham offered an explanation of the advertisement, which, however, only underlined the fact that Owen was completely out of touch with affairs at New Harmony. See "Pelham Letters," p. 402.

135 The letter, dated "At Sea, . . . October, 1825," was given to the papers in New York on Nov. 7, 1825, and published the next day. See D. Macdonald, p. 308,

November 8, 1825, and the attack upon Owen began again.[136] It did not interfere with his propaganda in New York, where Governor DeWitt Clinton took the chair at the principal public meeting, held on November 18, 1825.[137] But in Philadelphia the religious critics lay in wait for Owen. Newspapers and denominational journals there had been particularly hostile, and opposition had even taken pamphlet form.[138] The climax was reached at the second of two lectures which Owen delivered in the Franklin Institute on Thursday and Friday, November 24 and 25, 1825. The newspapers carried a circumstantial account:

Mr. Owen has been pretty strongly suspected of infidelity, and attempts were made to bring his religious principles to some point by which they could be understood, during his lecture on Thursday. . . . But his answers were so evasive, that nothing satisfactory was elicited. On Friday, however, he was brought to the test by the following note, which was handed to him before he commenced his discourse:

"Mr. Robert Owen—Sir, . . . Would it be practicable to establish your system upon the *admission* of the following facts?

"That the Scriptures of the Old and New Testaments contain a Revelation of the mind and will of God to man.

"That our first parents were created perfect creatures, but that they fell from their original condition, and that mankind is now in consequence of this disobedience in a lapsed and falled [*sic*] state, 'shapen in iniquity and conceived in sin.' "

There was no room for evasion here, and Mr. Owen came out boldly, and spent nearly an hour in maintaining the reverse of these propositions.—He did not believe the old and new testament to be the word of God any more than he believed any other writings to be the word of God.[139]

The fat was in the fire. Some applause followed, but the defenders of orthodoxy manifested their displeasure by leaving the room and

---

and Leopold, *Robert Dale Owen,* p. 25, n. 4. It was republished throughout the country, e.g., in Washington *National Intelligencer,* Nov. 12, 1825, p. 2:4; *Niles' Weekly Register,* XXIX, 175–76 (Nov. 12, 1825); *New-Harmony Gazette,* I, 94–95 (Dec. 14, 1824); Shawnee-Town *Illinois Gazette,* Dec. 17, 1825, p. 2:2. See also "Pelham Letters," p. 398.

[136] See especially *Christian Advocate,* IV, 29–30, 72–77 (Jan. and Feb. 1826), and the observation by Karl Bernhard, Duke of Saxe-Weimar-Eisenach, *Travels* (1828), reprinted in Lindley, ed., *Indiana As Seen by Early Travelers,* p. 421. The *New-Harmony Gazette* also helped to stir up the religious controversy, for its first issues struck even Captain Macdonald as having been "written by Deists with a design of converting its readers." *Diaries,* p. 321.

[137] D. Macdonald, *Diaries,* pp. 309, 313–14.

[138] *A Letter to Robert Owen . . . , By A Son of the Mist* (Philadelphia, 1825).

[139] *New-York Spectator,* reprinted in Indianapolis *Indiana Journal,* Feb. 21, 1826, p. 4:1–2. See also *New-York Advertiser,* Dec. 3, 1825, p. 2:1, quoting the Philadelphia *National Gazette.* The incident is described by D. Macdonald, p. 316.

by filling the newspapers of the next few days with denunciations that echoed throughout the land. "This plan," wrote the editor of the *New-York Advertiser*, "appears to be a refinement of Godwinism; and the man who can invent any thing more absurd, more extravagant, more irreligious in its principles, or more mischievous in its tendency than Godwinism, must be possessed of no ordinary capacity." [140]

Owen himself was already on his way to the west.[141] The full irony of his propagandist effort of 1825, however, was summed up in this final episode. As he proceeded to the promised land along the Wabash, the anathemas hurled against him marked him out as a heretic—not in economics, but in religion.

---

[140] *New-York Advertiser*, Dec. 3, 1825, p. 2:1. On the intensity of feeling in Philadelphia at this time, see Philadelphia *National Gazette* (triweekly ed.), Dec. 3, 1825, p. 1:2; Washington *National Intelligencer*, Dec. 6, 1825, p. 1:1; *New-Harmony Gazette*, I, 142–43 (Jan. 25, 1826); Leopold, *Robert Dale Owen*, p. 27; Irvin, "Contemporary American Opinion," pp. 35–37.

[141] Owen was still in Philadelphia on Nov. 28, 1825, but had reached Pittsburgh by Dec. 7 or 8. Compare D. Macdonald, p. 317, and *Pears Papers*, pp. 45–46.

Chapter VI

EDUCATIONAL ALLIES OF
COMMUNITARIANISM

OWEN neared New Harmony in the early days of January 1826 with an intoxicating sense of victory already won. The nation, he fondly believed, was on the eve of a transformation compared to which "all former revolutions in human affairs scarcely deserve a name." As a consequence of his lectures, he announced, "a match has been applied to a train, that, if I mistake not, will dispel past errors, until old things shall pass away, and all shall become new, and beautiful, and delightful." [1] To appraise the results of his propagandist effort at such a rate was sheer illusion. But in one direction, as significant as it was unexpected, Owen's accomplishment had actually been as great as he supposed. That direction was indicated in Owen's first speech to the Harmonians who assembled to greet him on January 12, 1826, a speech whose theme was education.

After reporting that the rest of his party were still aboard a keelboat that was bearing them down the Ohio toward New Harmony, Owen proudly asserted that they represented "more *learning* than ever was before contained in a boat." And by learning he meant not "Latin & Greek & other languages but real substantial knowledge." Among the new arrivals, he announced, would be "some of the ablest instructors of youth that c[oul]d be found in the U.S. or perhaps in the world." [2] His hearers read into this an even grander promise: "In Harmony there will be the best Library & the best School in the United States." [3]

In his own statement Owen, for once, did not exaggerate. The "boatload of knowledge," so-called from the beginning,[4] was in truth one of the significant intellectual migrations of history. It represented the transfer to New Harmony—farther west than any existing Ameri-

[1] Owen, *Discourse in Washington*, Feb. 25, 1825, in *New-Harmony Gazette,* II, 241–42 (May 2, 1827).

[2] Owen's speech of Jan. 12, 1826, as reported by William Pelham in a letter to his son, New Harmony, Jan. 13, 1826, in "Pelham Letters," p. 405.

[3] Pelham to his son, Feb. 9, 1826, *ibid.*, p. 411.

[4] Mrs. Thomas Pears to Mrs. Benjamin Bakewell, New Harmony, March 10, 1826, in *Pears Papers*, p. 71.

can college [5]—of a group of educational and scientific enterprises that had been notable features of the cultural life of Philadelphia. In prevailing upon William Maclure, their sponsor and financial supporter, to join forces with him, Owen had achieved his most significant triumph in America. This acquisition alone seemed ample justification for the optimism with which he was preparing to launch New Harmony upon the climactic phase of its career as an all-inclusive experiment in communitarianism.

Even so, Maclure's decision to transplant his educational and scientific program to New Harmony was less a personal triumph of Owen's than a result of influences more perduring than momentary propaganda. In the last analysis Maclure's action was one of many manifestations—a particularly striking one—of the close affinity that existed in the early nineteenth century between educational and communitarian ideas. To a certain extent that affinity was the secular counterpart of the relationship, already noted, between sectarian religion and communitarianism.

This interpenetration of social and educational purposes is evidenced by the emphasis placed on education in so many nineteenth-century communitarian writings and experiments. Fourierism illustrates it quite as well as Owenism: more than two hundred pages of Fourier's principal work, the *Traité de l'association domestique-agricole,* were devoted to an exposition of his theory of *éducation unitaire ou intégrale composée.* Indeed, the first known mention of Fourier in the Western Hemisphere was a reference to him as "author of the two volumes on education." [6] And the first published announcement of Brook Farm, most famous of all the communitarian enterprises of the Fourierist era, described it as a school.[7] However great the interest of other social reformers in education as a means of indoctrination, none went so far as did the communitarians in making it an integral part of their plans and experiments.

More remarkable even than the communitarians' interest in education was the complementary tendency of educational reformers to think in communitarian terms. To begin with, schoolmen of the early nineteenth century were giving increased attention to the social context of education. So long as this wider outlook inspired no more than an adjustment of the curriculum to changes in society, it had

[5] See list of colleges in 1828–29 in *American Almanac,* vol. I, *1830,* pp. 226–27. The Indiana State Seminary at Bloomington opened its doors in 1824, but was not raised to the status of a college until 1828. See James A. Woodburn, *History of Indiana University,* vol. I, *1820–1902* ([Bloomington], 1940), pp. 17, 32, 110.

[6] William Maclure to Marie D. Fretageot [Mexico City, *circa* 1830], in *Correspondence,* ed. Bestor, p. 379, n. 10.

[7] *New England Farmer, and Horticultural Register,* XIX, 238–39 (Jan. 27, 1841), article entitled "Agricultural School."

few implications for the reform movement generally. But there were educationists to whom the relationship between school and society appeared a reciprocal one. The school should respond to social change, they held, but it should also be an instrument for effecting desirable alterations in society. In their hands educational reform became a branch of social reform.

The educator turned social reformer was, by virtue of a similar approach to his task, the natural ally of the communitarian. He was no revolutionary, as we have defined the term. Nor was he obliged to depend upon strictly gradual processes of change, for he had the opportunity to make immediate and fundamental reforms within the delimited sphere of his own particular activity. There are, moreover, important points of resemblance between the school, conceived of as an instrument of reform, and the model community. Each is a small, self-contained society that may be looked upon as a kind of laboratory. Each is, in some sense, a microcosm of the great world, so set apart from it that extensive social experimentation is possible without subverting its institutions, and yet so connected with it that the results of a successful experiment are bound to spread by voluntary imitation. More than one educational reformer became, by imperceptible stages, a communitive reformer, merely by opening out the walls of his ideal schoolroom.

To understand fully the communitarian movement of the early nineteenth century, then, one must understand the new trend of educational thinking. It is not, however, to Jean Jacques Rousseau that one should turn for the educational sources of communitarianism, despite the fact that he was both a social reformer and one of the fountainheads of modern pedagogy. In point of fact, modernity can be ascribed to only part of the program that Rousseau outlined in 1762 in his *Émile*. He set the tone of the new educational psychology, it is true, when he condemned teachers for devoting themselves to "what is important for men to know, without considering what children are in a position to understand." And he foreshadowed the new pedagogical technique in his dictum, "In general, never substitute the sign for the thing itself . . . ; for the sign absorbs the attention of the child and makes him forget the thing represented."

Respecting the social aspects of education, however, Rousseau spoke with the voice of the past rather than the future. What he actually proposed in the *Émile* was an education according to nature, which meant an education apart from society. And what he offered by way of illustration was the upbringing of a young man of independent fortune, favored with the undivided attention of a tutor. "The poor man," he wrote, "has no need of education; that belonging to his condition is forced upon him, and he can have no other." [8] This was the doctrine, not of the *Contrat social* but of the Enlightened Despots. It was no satisfactory doctrine for the nineteenth century, which was forced to think of education in wider terms. The "education of the lower orders" became an inescapable necessity—to the conservative who was interested in training them for permanent subordination, fully as much as to the liberal or reformer.

The man who developed the particular combination of ideas that the nineteenth century appropriated was Johann Heinrich Pestalozzi, the leading educational thinker of the generation between Rousseau and Owen.[9] Pestalozzi was imbued with the same respect for childhood as Rousseau, and like him was impressed with the educational importance of concrete objects. "The first rule," he wrote, "is, to teach always by THINGS, rather than by WORDS." [10] He differed from Rousseau, however, in that his chief concern was always the education of the poor. His first enterprise, conducted at Neuhof near Zurich from 1774 to 1780, was designed for twenty to forty poverty-stricken children of the area. Here he developed the same combination of schooling with labor in a cotton mill that Owen was later to work out at New Lanark, though with none of Owen's financial success. In his next experiment, at Stanz in 1799, Pestalozzi had an even lower level of poverty and distress to deal with, his pupils being orphans and the children of needy parents in a war-devastated town. Once again he combined instruction with manual labor, and so he continued to do throughout his migratory career in Switzerland— at Burgdorf, at Münchenbuchsee, and finally at Yverdon, where he remained from 1805 until 1825, two years before his death. Looking back in 1818 to the difficulties, discouragements, and failures of the past, he exclaimed, "I had not realized the moral destruction in the midst of which the poor live as convincingly as they must be realized if the causes of poverty, which are not in the poor themselves, are to be stopped—causes which so completely overwhelm all capacity for self-help that the poor man must go under." A possible way out, he felt—as Fourier and Owen were later also to believe—might be to combine farming and manufacture. "The highest development of popular education and culture," he believed, might come in precisely "those districts where the poverty of the soil or scarcity of population

[8] Rousseau, *Émile, ou de l'Éducation*, nouvelle éd. par François et Pierre Richard (Paris [1939]), pp. 2, 189–90, 27.

[9] The life spans of the leading persons discussed in this chapter were as follows: Rousseau, 1712–78; Oberlin, 1740–1826; Pestalozzi, 1746–1827; Maclure, 1763–1840; Owen, 1771–1858; Fellenberg, 1771–1844; Fourier, 1772–1837; Greaves, 1777–1842.

[10] Pestalozzi, *Letters on Early Education. Addressed to J. P. Greaves, Esq.* (London, 1827), p. 122.

makes it desirable to unite agricultural science with one or other town industry." [11]

The most widely read of Pestalozzi's writings, *Lienhard und Gertrud: Ein Buch für das Volk,* comes closest to the communitarian point of view. This novel, published in 1781, tells of the transformation of the village of Bonnal into a model community, largely through the agency of a new school, established with the deliberate purpose of reforming social conditions in the hamlet. The climax comes, in typical communitarian fashion, when the Duke appoints a commission to determine "whether it were possible to extend . . . [the] innovations to other villages, and so through the whole country." [12]

Such a transformation as Pestalozzi saw in imagination was wrought in actuality by his slightly older contemporary, Johann Friedrich Oberlin, pastor at Waldbach, some thirty miles southwest of Strassburg in the Vosges Mountains. When as a young man he settled in this poverty-stricken district, Oberlin set out to make his ministry economically and socially beneficial as well as spiritually fruitful. He worked for the improvement of roads, encouraged new farming methods, and established a depository for agricultural implements. For the promotion of education, which was a central feature of his program, he arranged for the older boys to receive training in the most useful trades, and instituted, long before Owen, a school for the infants of the community. At Waldbach, education and social improvement went hand in hand, in a community whose isolation was not unlike that which communitarians were to seek deliberately. Communitive ideas were hardly even implicit in Oberlin's mind, but in 1819 when the Société Royale et Centrale d'Agriculture in Paris awarded him its gold medal, his achievement was described in terms suggestive of the communitarian ideal: social experimentation on a small scale, followed by wide dissemination of its successful results. "We have already ascertained," read the report to the Society, "that there is in France uncultivated land sufficient for the formation of five thousand villages. When we wish to organize these colonies, Waldbach will present a perfect model." [13]

The combination of education with manual labor was developed most effectively and influentially by Philipp Emmanuel von Fellenberg in his institution at Hofwyl near Berne, Switzerland. Though for a time associated with Pestalozzi, Fellenberg was in many respects more like Owen, who was exactly of an age with him. Hofwyl was

[11] "Address to My House, 1818," in *Pestalozzi's Educational Writings,* ed. by J. A. Green and Frances A. Collie (New York, 1912), pp. 197, 202.

[12] Pestalozzi, *Leonard and Gertrude,* translated and abridged by Eva Channing (Boston, 1885), p. 179.

[13] Quoted in *Memoirs of John Frederic Oberlin, Pastor of Waldbach, in the Ban de la Roche* (London, 1829), p. 210.

managed with the same practical efficiency that Owen displayed at New Lanark. The temper of the two men's minds likewise—their distaste for rewards and punishments as educational stimuli, their tolerance, their resolute avoidance of artificial social distinctions— was so similar that Owen's eldest son was hardly conscious of a change when he left his father's home to become a student at Hofwyl.[14]

What linked Fellenberg most significantly with Owen, however, was his habit of looking at education in terms of a definite social purpose. By comparison, Pestalozzi's views were vague and inchoate. What Fellenberg stood for was summarized by a visitor to the Hofwyl institution:

> Fellenberg was convinced that every improvement must commence with the germ of society; that it was only in acting on the rising generation by improving the means of education, that any hope could be cherished of improving its condition. He believed that the efforts made for this purpose must be directed, at the same time, towards the two extremities of the social body; and that it would be in vain to reform those who are destined to labor and obey, without improving the character of those who consume and govern. He believed that no attempt should be made to disturb the order of the European community, by confounding classes of men whose lot Providence had so widely separated. . . . The poor were to be led by a rational and religious education, not only to be content with their own station, but to respect the order which Providence had assigned them. . . . The rich were to be taught to estimate the worth of industry, to feel how dependent they are upon the laboring classes, and to observe and revere the dignity of moral character which is often found among them.[15]

The "two extremities" of society were provided for on the Hofwyl estate by a Literary Institution (sometimes referred to as an Academy or College) for the upper classes; and an Agricultural Institution (or School of Industry or Rural School) for the poor. Certain schools intermediate between these two extremes existed for a time,[16] but the Literary and Agricultural Institutions dominated the enterprise. It was the latter, supervised by J. J. Wehrli, that attracted the widest attention and exerted the greatest influence, for there the combina-

[14] See Robert Dale Owen, *Autobiography*, pp. 146–66.

[15] [William C. Woodbridge], "Sketches of the Fellenberg Institution at Hofwyl, in a Series of Letters to a Friend," *American Annals of Education and Instruction*, I, 24–25 (Aug. 1830).

[16] The *Edinburgh Review*, XXXI, 154–55 (Dec. 1818), described an Agricultural Institution for young gentlemen in addition to the school for the poor, also a manufactory of farm implements. The latter, but not the former, was mentioned by Robert Dale Owen in his reminiscences of Hofwyl. *Autobiography*, p. 147. In 1829 Woodbridge described a Practical Institution for those destined for trade, which was intermediate between the Literary and Agricultural Institutions. *American Annals of Education*, I, 26 (Aug. 1830).

tion of manual labor with regular schooling was worked out so successfully as to make the Institution virtually self-supporting.

Though this plan of Fellenberg's was far from socialistic, it embodied many of the concepts that were basic to communitarianism.
It had an avowed social purpose, the heart of which was an improvement in the condition of all members of society, and a harmoniza-
tion of conflicting class interests. Fellenberg, it is true, would perpetuate a stratification of society more extreme than social reformers
could well tolerate, but it must be remembered that neither Fourier
nor Owen were opposed to the existence of social classes as such. Moreover, the combination of manual labor with intellectual pursuits,
which the communitarians favored, was part of the Hofwyl plan. In
so far as this combination, in Fellenberg's hands, produced a virtually self-supporting enterprise,[17] it added weight to the argument
of communitarians that their own, somewhat broader, social experiments would also prove economically feasible. Finally, though communitarians might differ with Fellenberg in matters of detail, the
institution at Hofwyl was in essence what they were talking about, a
miniature of a more perfect society.

Though Pestalozzi, Oberlin, and Fellenberg cannot be said to have
crossed the line from educational to communitarian reform, several
of their immediate followers did take that step. Aside from Owen and
Maclure, the most interesting was James Pierrepont Greaves. In
1817, the year of Owen's first great propagandist effort, Greaves went
to Yverdon and for four years worked with Pestalozzi. With his
publication in 1827 of the letters he had received from the Swiss educator,[18] he became the leader of the Pestalozzian movement in Great
Britain. The social implications of the new doctrine gradually assumed a paramount place in his thinking, and between 1838 and
1842 his correspondence was filled with discussions of what he called
"Sacred Socialism." [19] At the time of his death, in the latter year, his

[17] The *Edinburgh Review,* XXXII, 490–92 (Oct. 1819), which analyzed the
point with great care, concluded that although the board and education of the
students cost somewhat more than was realized from their labor, "the money
laid out upon such establishments, even where they do not entirely pay their
own expenses, may still be considered as *placed at high interest,* even in a worldly
sense of the word."

[18] *Letters on Early Education, Addressed to J. P. Greaves, Esq. by Pestalozzi,
Translated from the German Manuscript, With a Memoir of Pestalozzi* (London,
1827). This was retranslated from a French version in William Russell's *American
Journal of Education,* IV, 414–32, 548–55 (Sept.–Dec. 1829), and reprinted as
Letters of Pestalozzi on the Education of Infancy, Addressed to Mothers (Boston,
1830).

[19] [Alexander Campbell, ed.], *Letters and Extracts from the MS. Writings of
James Pierrepont Greaves* (2 vols., Ham Common, Surrey, 1843, and London,
1845).

followers were taking steps to convert their school, Alcott House, at Ham Common in Surrey, into an "Industrial Harmonic Educational College" or "Communitorium." [20] This institution, eventually renamed the "Concordium," was the one communitarian experiment of the 1840's in the British Isles that exerted a direct influence upon the American movement.

Greaves's development from an educational to a communitarian reformer was the work of a lifetime. Robert Owen's was a matter of a few years. It was, in fact, the rapidity with which Owen moved from the one position to the other, rather than the nature of the transition, that sets him apart from his contemporaries in educational reform. Actually he was one of them. His first important work, *A New View of Society,* despite its spacious title, was at bottom a description of what he had achieved in the education of the people of New Lanark. Like Oberlin at Waldbach, and like the fictional characters in Pestalozzi's *Lienhard und Gertrud,* Owen applied specific remedies to many of the obvious social ills he found in his little mill town, but it was to the school that he looked, as did they, for permanent amelioration.

The distress and the happiness of man, Owen said without qualification, "depend on the kind and degree of knowledge which he receives." The greatest evil is "that all men are . . . erroneously trained at present, and hence the inconsistencies and misery of the world." [21] Consequently "for some time to come there can be but one practicable, and therefore one rational reform, . . . that is, a reform in the training and in the management of the poor, the ignorant, the untaught and untrained, or ill-taught and ill-trained." [22] Education and social reform became practically synonymous in Owen's thrice-repeated summary: "Any general character, from the best to the worst, from the most ignorant to the most enlightened, may be given to any community, even to the world at large, by the application of proper means; which means are to a great extent at the command and under the control of those who have influence in the affairs of men." [23] Rarely, if ever, has education been given such unqualified primacy in social reform. Rarely, if ever, has it been conceived of so completely in social terms.

[20] *New Age, and Concordium Gazette,* I, 7–8 (May 6, 1843). For the American influence of Greaves and the Concordium, particularly upon Bronson Alcott's experiment at Fruitlands, see *Dial,* III, 227–55, 281–96, 421–26 (Oct. 1842, Jan. and April 1843); Dorothy McCuskey, *Bronson Alcott, Teacher* (New York, 1940), pp. 118–25; F. B. Sanborn, *Bronson Alcott at Alcott House, England, and Fruitlands, New England (1842–1844)* (Cedar Rapids, Iowa, 1908).

[21] Owen, *A New View of Society,* Essay Third (1814), in *Life,* I, 301, 302.

[22] Essay Second (1813), in *Life,* I, 285.

[23] Essay First (1813), in *Life,* I, 255, 265, 266.

As a social process, moreover, education does not begin or end with the years of conventional schooling. With unique emphasis Owen dwelt upon the educational significance of the everyday occupations of adult life. In one of the few statements of his that can be called succinct he declared: "Train any population rationally, and they will be rational. Furnish honest and useful employments to those so trained, and such employments they will greatly prefer to dishonest or injurious occupations." [24] Proper employment, in other words, is inseparable from proper education. This concept was what first impelled Owen to cross the line from educational to social reform. In the last essay of *A New View of Society* he proposed not only a national system of education, but also, as a necessary complement to it, a program of public works designed to guard the unemployed against the miseducative effects of enforced idleness.[25]

In his own enterprise at New Lanark, Owen put into practice this theory that education should extend from the cradle to the grave. His plan demanded facilities that only a new building could provide. Such a structure was begun in 1809, and on the first of January 1816 Owen opened the new Institution Established for the Formation of Character. As already noted, the address that he made on this occasion contained the first unmistakably communitarian pronouncement of his career.[26] This was no mere coincidence. The experimental communities that he envisaged would be, first and foremost, all-embracing schools of character. "Facts prove," he declared,

> That any community may be arranged, on a due combination of the foregoing principles, in such a manner, as not only to withdraw vice, poverty, and, in a great degree, misery, from the world, but also to place *every* individual under circumstances in which he shall enjoy more permanent happiness than can be given to *any* individual under the principles which have hitherto regulated society.[27]

As he elaborated his plan in 1817 and subsequent years, he continued to place education second only to actual subsistence among its objectives.[28] In becoming a communitarian Owen did not cease to be an educator. At least until the middle 1820's, contemporaries placed him in the latter category as often as in the former.

[24] Essay Second (1813), in *Life*, I, 285.
[25] Essay Fourth (1814), in *Life*, I, 324–31.
[26] See above, p. 69.
[27] *New Lanark Address* (1816), in *Life*, I, 352. In 1830 Owen drew an even more explicit analogy between school and community. He asserted that the evils of existing society are simply the evils of the old system of education writ large; in other words, that wealth and poverty are artificial rewards and punishments identical in nature with the pettier ones he would banish from the schoolroom. See his *Lectures on an Entire New State of Society*, pp. 61–64.
[28] See, for example, "First Letter," July 25, 1817, in *Life*, I.A, 70.

The educational principles for which New Lanark stood, and the communitarianism implicit in them, were summed up on the eve of Owen's departure for America in a pamphlet published by his son Robert Dale Owen in 1824. This *Outline of the System of Education at New Lanark* emphasizes the Pestalozzian technique of acquainting children with actual objects before teaching them "the *artificial signs* which have been adopted to represent these objects." [29] It describes, moreover, a utilitarian curriculum that understandably won the approval of Jeremy Bentham.[30] But young Owen gives a collectivist, not to say communitarian, restatement of Bentham's famous hedonistic axiom. "Whatever, in its ultimate consequences, increases the happiness of the *community*," says Owen, "is right; and whatever, on the other hand, tends to diminish that happiness, is wrong." The social objectives of the entire program are frankly avowed: "to raise all classes without lowering any one, and to re-form mankind from the least even to the greatest." And in a dedication to his father, young Owen makes clear that to him also communitarianism is the inevitable corollary of educational reform: "It gives me pleasure to know that you are about to commence a more perfect experiment, where practice may uniformly accord with principle. . . . But its success will scarcely create in my own mind a stronger conviction than I already entertain, of the certainty and facility, with which poverty and vice and misery may be gradually removed from the world." [31]

The enterprise at New Lanark, and the broader schemes of Robert Owen, attracted the attention they did because they fitted in so well with the growing interest in educational reform that agitated Great Britain in the years following Waterloo. The leading spokesman in public life was Henry Brougham. He it was who called attention to the educational experiments of Fellenberg, first through evidence presented to the parliamentary Select Committee on the Education of the Lower Orders, of which he was chairman from 1816 to 1818, then through two articles which he wrote for the *Edinburgh Review* in 1818 and 1819.[32] By a significant coincidence, the second of these articles appeared in the very number in which Owen's plans were first reviewed.[33] Brougham did not write the review of Owen, but he

[29] R. D. Owen, *An Outline of the System of Education at New Lanark* (Glasgow, 1824), p. 34; Pestalozzi is mentioned by name on p. 40. The *Outline* was reprinted at Cincinnati in 1825, and also in the columns of the *New-Harmony Gazette*, I, 49–51, through pp. 81–83 (5 installments, Nov. 12–Dec. 7, 1825). See D. Macdonald, *Diaries*, p. 296; "Pelham Letters," p. 383.

[30] R. D. Owen, *Autobiography*, pp. 200–2.

[31] R. D. Owen, *Outline*, pp. 12, 76, 4. The emphasizing italics in the first quotation are mine; actually that entire passage was printed in italics.

[32] *Edinburgh Review*, XXXI, 150–65 (Dec. 1818); XXXII, 487–507 (Oct. 1819).

[33] *Edinburgh Review*, XXXII, 453–77 (Oct. 1819), written (as already noted) by Robert Torrens, the economist.

did see a definite connection between the two men's ideas. In a speech in the House of Commons on December 16, 1819, he specifically compared Owen and Fellenberg. Though rejecting some of Owen's ideas as "wild or visionary," he felt that as an educational program Owen's was "much better than that produced in Switzerland." [34] Other contemporaries compared the two, though many were less favorable to Owen. Upon reading the first separate English work on Fellenberg, a writer in the London *Monthly Review* confessed that he had "more than once been lost amid anticipations of a sort of millennium, and fancied that we must be reading some scheme of Mr. Owen of Lanark. . . . We regard this as the more unfortunate, because we believe that much good has been actually effected by M. de Fellenberg when . . . pursuing his plan on a rational and moderate scale." [35]

Not only was Owen's propaganda facilitated by this growing interest in educational reform, but also he was himself thereby brought into closer association with the Continental educationists. At the outset of his experiment his acquaintance with advanced pedagogical thought seems to have extended no farther than the somewhat mechanical reforms of Joseph Lancaster and the Reverend Dr. Andrew Bell, whose monitorial systems of instruction received some financial contributions from him. [36] Owen's intellectual horizon was greatly widened by the new partnership which he formed in December 1813 for the conduct of the New Lanark mills, and which included such men as Jeremy Bentham and William Allen, the Quaker educator and benefactor. From Allen's periodical, *The Philanthropist*, Owen may well have first learned of Fellenberg, for one of the earliest English articles on Hofwyl was published in its pages in 1813 in immediate juxtaposition with a long review of Owen's own *New View of Society*. [37]

[34] *Parliamentary Debates* (Hansard), XLI, 1197–98. Note also the somewhat earlier linking of Owen and Fellenberg in the *Examiner*, April 25, 1819, reprinted in Owen, *Life*, I.A, 232.

[35] *Monthly Review; or Literary Journal*, XCIV, 196 (Feb. 1821). The twenty publications that Brougham had reviewed in the *Edinburgh* were all in French or German. In 1820 two expositions of Fellenberg's ideas appeared in English: John Attersoll, *Translation of the Reports of M. le Comte de Capo d'Istria and M. Rengger, upon the Principles and Progress of the Establishment of M. de Fellenberg at Hofwyl, Switzerland* (London, 1820), the work under review in the article here cited; and Count Louis de Villevieille, *The Establishments of M. Emmanuel de Fellenberg, at Hoffwyl* [sic] (London, 1820).

[36] See Owen, *Life*, I, 84–85, 106–7, 191–92, 249–52.

[37] "A Remarkable Institution for Education at Berne in Switzerland," *Philanthropist*, III (1813), 54–60, 119–27; review of *A New View of Society*, Essays First and Second, *ibid.*, pp. 93–119. A later article on Fellenberg appeared in *ibid.*, V (1815), 159–64. Owen may also have first learned of the Rappites from the same periodical, which in 1815 reprinted Melish's account of Harmony, Pa. *Ibid.*, V, 277–88. See above, p. 48, n. 33.

The article in the *Philanthropist* was based upon the reports of Fellenberg's work written by Professor Charles Pictet de Rochemont, a Councillor of State of Geneva, whom Brougham credited with having done most to inform the public of Fellenberg's significance.[38] It was Pictet who first brought Owen into direct personal contact with the Continental educators. His interest in schools drew him to New Lanark in 1817, and his enthusiasm for Owen's experiment led him to invite the British reformer to travel with him on the Continent. In 1818 the two men visited Pestalozzi at Yverdon, Fellenberg at Hofwyl, and possibly also Oberlin at Waldbach.[39] Owen was so impressed with Fellenberg that he sent his two older sons, Robert Dale and William, as pupils to Hofwyl that very autumn and in due course their younger brothers, Richard and David Dale.[40] In subsequent years the Owenite periodicals included frequent articles on Fellenberg, and one of them, as early as 1821, used the success of Hofwyl as an argument for Owenism, on the ground that it employed a "portion of the principles on which Mr. Owen's plan is founded." [41]

Such intervisitation of schools as Pictet and Owen engaged in was fairly common, and New Lanark was ordinarily part of the educational grand tour for visitors from the New World as well as from the Continent. Among Americans the most careful and comprehensive observer of European education during the period was John Griscom, the professor of chemistry at Columbia College who was to provide Owen with his most valuable introductions in New York in 1824. Griscom's interest in secondary education equaled his interest in science, as his founding of what became the New York High School for Boys made clear, and it was this interest that drew him to Europe. He visited New Lanark in March 1819, after having seen Hofwyl and Yverdon the previous October, and he clearly considered the schools

[38] See *Edinburgh Review*, XXXI, 151 (Dec. 1818). Pictet (1755–1824), one of the founders of the *Bibliothèque britannique* (later the *Bibliothèque universelle*), had published his first account of Fellenberg in 1812 in the form of a letter to his collaborators in that periodical.

[39] Owen, *Life*, I, 166–79, 186–87. Writing forty years after the event, Owen said he visited "Father Oberlin's, a Catholic school . . . at Friburgh." *Ibid.*, p. 174. It is obvious (though the discrepancy has hitherto gone unnoticed) that Owen is here describing the school of Père Grégoire Girard at Fribourg. Owen's mention of Oberlin's name, however, may indicate that he also visited the latter's school at some time, though this is far from certain.

[40] Owen, *Life*, I, 177–79; R. D. Owen, *Autobiography*, pp. 146–48; Walter B. Hendrickson, *David Dale Owen, Pioneer Geologist of the Middle West* (*Indiana Historical Collections*, XXVII; Indianapolis, 1943), pp. 6–9; Victor L. Albjerg, *Richard Owen* (*Archives of Purdue*, no. 2 [Lafayette, Ind.], 1946), p. 17. The two sons of Richard Owen bore the middle names Fellenberg and Pestalozzi.

[41] *The Economist*, I, 121 (March 17, 1821).

of Owen, Pestalozzi, and Fellenberg the most significant educational experiments of the day.[42] His two-volume account of the trip, published in 1823, helped prepare the way for Owen's enthusiastic reception in America the following year, just as Griscom personally helped open the first doors to the visitor.

Owen's initial propaganda in 1817 coincided with a growth of attention to Fellenberg; his activities in America in 1824, with a spurt of interest in Pestalozzi. Recognition of the older educator's work was curiously delayed in England until some years after the interest in Fellenberg had become widespread. As late as 1828 Brougham was able to write in the *Edinburgh Review:* "While the name of Pestalozzi is known as a familiar household word on the Continent, we in this island . . . are hardly acquainted with its sound, and know not that to him the world stands more deeply indebted than to any other man for the beginning of the sound and benevolent system, now making such rapid strides, the improvement of the poorer classes of the people." [43] The neglect of Pestalozzi was not so complete as Brougham implied, for a number of Pestalozzian pamphlets had already been published in English.[44] Nevertheless, in the main it is true that the discourse which Brougham reviewed, Charles Mayo's *Memoir of Pestalozzi, Being the Substance of a Lecture Delivered at the Royal Institution . . . May, 1826*,[45] inaugurated the period of widespread British interest in the educator of Yverdon. A revival of interest occurred simultaneously in America, where an address comparable to Mayo's was delivered before the New York Society of Teachers in 1825.[46] The speaker, Solyman Brown (famous as one of the founders of modern dentistry), was a living illustration of the connections between educational reform

[42] Griscom's longest visits were at Yverdon and New Lanark; his longest narratives were of Hofwyl and New Lanark. See his *Year in Europe . . . in 1818 and 1819* (2 vols., New York, 1823), I, 381–401, 415–24; II, 374–93.

[43] *Edinburgh Review*, XLVII, 118 (Jan. 1828).

[44] A partial list of American publications, beginning in 1806, is given by Will S. Monroe in his *History of the Pestalozzian Movement in the United States* (Syracuse, N.Y., 1907), pp. 205–13. He overlooks the earliest one, however, an anonymous translation, at second hand from the French, of Pestalozzi's *Leonard and Gertrude* (Philadelphia, 1801), and he mentions neither the discourse of Solyman Brown in 1825 nor the periodical articles it inspired. See below, n. 46. British and Irish publications from 1815 onward (including one item with the possible date of 1810) are listed under "Pestalozzi" in British Museum, *Catalogue of Printed Books* (London, 1881–1900).

[45] Second edition, London, 1828. No copy of the first edition, cited by Brougham under the title *Substance of the Principles of Pestalozzi*, has been located.

[46] Solyman Brown, *Comparative View of the Systems of Pestalozzi and Lancaster* (New York, 1825). This was reviewed in the *United States Literary Gazette*, in which appeared subsequent articles emphasizing Pestalozzianism. See I, 344–46, 372–74; II, 130–35 (Feb. 15, March 15, May 15, 1825).

and communitarianism. Three years before, he had been one of the sponsors of the New York Society for Promoting Communities, and as late as the 1840's he was to be active in the Fourierist movement.[47]

For communitarian history, however, the most momentous event of the Pestalozzian movement of the mid-1820's in the English-speaking world was the meeting of Robert Owen and William Maclure at New Lanark in July 1824.

William Maclure, born in 1763 in Scotland, was eight years older than Owen, and their early careers were parallel. Maclure too acquired a fortune through his own efforts before the end of the century. But whereas Owen's social radicalism found expression in projects connected with his regular business at New Lanark, Maclure's could be satisfied only by a complete break with the past. Just before the turn of the century he retired altogether from commercial activities, transplanted his home and his allegiance to the United States, and carved out for himself a new and significant career as a geologist and mineralogist. His repudiation of the past included a rejection of the educational principles upon which he had been trained. "In reflecting upon the absurdity of my own classical education, launched into the world as ignorant as a pig of anything useful, . . . I had been long in the habit of considering education one of the greatest abuses our species were guilty of, and of course one of the reforms the most beneficial to humanity." [48] In this frame of mind he stumbled

[47] See *Essay on Common Wealths* (1822), p. 4; and *Dictionary of American Biography*, III, 155–56.

[48] Maclure to Benjamin Silliman, Oct. 19, 1822, in George P. Fisher, *Life of Benjamin Silliman* (2 vols., New York, 1866), II, 41. For biographical information on Maclure, and professional evaluations of his scientific contribution, see Samuel G. Morton, *Memoir of William Maclure* (Philadelphia, 1841), also reprinted in *American Journal of Science*, XLVII, 1–17 (April–June 1844); George P. Merrill, *The First One Hundred Years of American Geology* (New Haven, 1924), pp. 31–37, 46–47, 91, 141–42; and J. Percy Moore, "William Maclure—Scientist and Humanitarian," American Philosophical Society, *Proceedings*, XCI, 234–49 (Aug. 1947), the latter based in part upon forty-two unpublished letters from Maclure in the Samuel G. Morton papers, American Philosophical Society. The record of Maclure's educational and reform activities from 1820 on is in the *Maclure-Fretageot Correspondence*, edited by the present writer from the original MSS in the Workingmen's Institute, New Harmony. There are occasional autobiographical passages in Maclure, *Opinions on Various Subjects, Dedicated to the Industrious Producers* (3 vols., New Harmony, 1831–38), especially II (1831), 624–28. The complicated bibliographical history of this work is discussed in *Maclure-Fretageot Correspondence*, pp. 407–8, n. 11. The variants among the different editions and issues affect citations only to volume II. As first issued this bore an undated title page, and its pagination was continuous from volume I, with which it was bound up. The first issue of this edition broke off at p. 592, the second continued to p. 640. The second edition (not so described on the title page, however) was dated 1837, and its pages were independently numbered, i–vii and 1–556. These two editions are cited hereafter as II (1831) and II (1837), respectively.

by accident upon Pestalozzi's school as early as 1805, and on at least six different occasions thereafter, while summering in Switzerland, he spent periods of some months at Yverdon.[49] The first visit sufficed to make him a convert, and to spur him to action. He hastened to Paris to see Joseph Neef, one of Pestalozzi's ablest coadjutors, and induced him to go to America, agreeing to pay his traveling expenses and to guarantee him an income of five hundred dollars a year while he learned the English language and established a Pestalozzian school.[50] The instruction that Neef offered in Philadelphia, and the *Sketch of a Plan and Method of Education* that he published there in 1808, were the effective beginnings of Pestalozzianism in the United States.

For the next ten years Maclure was fully occupied with his scientific work. Almost immediately he established his reputation with an epoch-making geological map of the United States, presented to the American Philosophical Society in 1809,[51] and before long he was in personal contact or correspondence with leading men of science in America and abroad. He was elected to the Academy of Natural Sciences of Philadelphia shortly after its founding in 1812, and began there his association with some of the naturalists who later accompanied him to New Harmony—notably Thomas Say, the entomologist and conchologist, and Gerard Troost, the Dutch geologist, whom Maclure succeeded as president of the Academy in 1817. In Paris in 1815 he became acquainted with Charles Alexandre Lesueur, who had already won a solid reputation as a naturalist, secured him as co-worker on a geological expedition through the West Indies and parts of the United States,[52] and finally induced him to settle in Philadelphia in 1817 as curator of the Academy. On similar field trips in 1817–18 and subsequent years, Maclure was accompanied by Say.[53] The scientific results of these expeditions were em-

[49] Joseph Neef, *Sketch of a Plan and Method of Education* (Philadelphia, 1808), p. 4; Maclure, *Opinions on Various Subjects*, I, 60–61.

[50] Neef, *Sketch*, p. 5; Monroe, *History of the Pestalozzian Movement*, pp. 70–71, which gives the text of the contract between Maclure and Neef.

[51] "Observations on the Geology of the United States, Explanatory of a Geological Map," American Philosophical Society, *Transactions*, VI (1809), 411–28; read Jan. 20, 1809. Eight additional years of research went into the revised and expanded paper on the same subject that he read on May 16, 1817, and that was published in *ibid.*, n.s., I (1818), 1–91.

[52] Agreement between Maclure and Lesueur, Paris, Aug. 8, 1815, MS in Twigg papers, Indiana Historical Society.

[53] Edward J. Nolan, *Short History of the Academy of Natural Sciences of Philadelphia* (Philadelphia, 1909), pp. 5–12. See also Harry B. Weiss and Grace M. Ziegler, *Thomas Say, Early American Naturalist* (Springfield, Ill., 1931), and the sketches of Say (1787–1834), Troost (1776–1850), and Lesueur (1778–1846) in the *Dictionary of American Biography*.

bodied in a revised geological map and accompanying paper, which the American Philosophical Society published in 1818.

Maclure's educational interests, forced into the background during this decade of scientific activity, were in no sense dead, and by 1819 he was in Spain seeking to establish there an industrial and agricultural school on the principles of Pestalozzi and Fellenberg. Though he invested heavily in the experiment, he did not commit all his resources, and gave support also to two Pestalozzian schools in Paris, one for boys conducted by Guillaume Sylvan Casimir Phiquepal d'Arusmont, and another for girls conducted by Madame Marie Duclos Fretageot. He also renewed his acquaintance with Pestalozzi by a visit to Yverdon in the summer of 1820. In a letter written there he explained the connections that he saw between educational and social reform:

From this 30 years I have considered ignorance as the cause of all the miseries and errors of mankind and have used all my endeavors to reduce the quantity of that truly diabolical evil. My experience soon convinced me that it was impossible to give any real information to men and that the only possible means of giving usefull knowledge to the world was by the education of children. About 15 years ago I stumbled upon the Pestalozzian system, which appeared to me to be the best that I had seen for the diffusion of usefull knowledge. I have therefore endeavoured to introduce it into the United States of America as the place I thought the most likely to succeed. . . . I once thought it might spread even in France, protected by the division of property and consequent division of knowledge, but in that I fear I was premature. Altho the property is divided, the knowledge is still monopolized and in the possession of that class who have a direct and immediate interest in the propagation of the most brutal ignorance.[54]

A radical social philosophy, it will be noted, was already part and parcel of Maclure's educational thinking. The year before, in fact, six essays of his had been barred from publication by the Paris censor as too democratic.[55] One would like to be able to trace in strict chronology the unfolding of his social ideas, but his earliest extant expressions of them belong to the years after 1819, when, as a man of fifty-five, his views were already fully developed. Whether his social philosophy was the corollary of his educational, or vice versa, it is impossible to say, but it is perfectly clear that both were formulated long before his association with Owen. So much of a piece are the ideas he expressed in his correspondence in the early 1820's and those he expounded over the years in the articles finally collected in the three volumes of *Opinions,* published from 1831 to 1838, that one may safely take the whole as a statement of the philosophy that

[54] Maclure to Mme Fretageot, Yverdon, May 22, 1820, in *Correspondence,* ed. Bestor, p. 301.
[55] Maclure, *Opinions on Various Subjects,* I [iii].

motivated his various enterprises from the one in Spain onward, and that finally drew him into association with Owen at New Harmony.

The first volume of Maclure's *Opinions on Various Subjects, Dedicated to the Industrious Producers* opened with a striking essay "On the Effects of Representative Governments"—presumably one of the pieces that roused the ire of the French royal censor in 1819. Society, he said, is divided into two classes, nonproductive and productive, whose interests are opposite and contradictory. It is, moreover, divided into the governors and the governed. The great difficulty is that the dividing lines in both cases tend to coincide, so that the governors belong to the nonproductive classes, and the governed to the class of those who labor with their hands. Checks and balances, Maclure believed, offer no remedy, for the same governing class is in control of the several branches charged with checking one another. Representative government, it is true, provides one counteracting influence in that it encourages rotation in office. In the long run, however, the permanent welfare of a nation depends on reducing the number of the nonproductive classes, and seeing to it that the "cake of liberty" is so divided that the industrious masses receive their just proportion of it. In the accomplishment of this, education has a vital role, for "KNOWLEDGE IS POWER in political societies, and it is, perhaps, as impossible, to keep a well informed people in slavery, as it is to make an ignorant people enjoy the blessings of freedom." In the end economic equality, education, and liberty are linked in a continuous circle of cause and effect, "for the equal division of property gives vigor to the great mass, and facilitates the acquiring of knowledge, which must be the foundation of all power." [56]

This introductory essay stated all the principal themes of Maclure's social philosophy. It was a philosophy far more radical than Owen's, closer, in fact, to that of John Gray. Maclure, indeed, hailed the latter's *Lecture on Human Happiness* as soon as it appeared in 1825,[57] and later credited it with first awakening in American working people a consciousness of the class divisions that separate producers and consumers.[58] Unlike Owen, who never altogether re-

[56] Maclure, *Opinions*, I, 1–6.

[57] Maclure to Benjamin Silliman, Paris, May 2, 1825, published in *American Journal of Science and Arts*, X (1825–26), 165–67.

[58] Maclure, *Opinions*, II (1837), 50–51. Though not primarily an economic theorist, Maclure wrote critical essays on the systems of Ricardo and Malthus. *Ibid.*, pp. 491–95. And he analyzed, in a remarkable passage long before Marx, the method by which the advantages of labor-saving machinery are garnered by the possessors of capital: "Where there is a great inequality of property, labor saving machinery gives additional advantages to the possessor of capital over the laborer, by affording the articles so much cheaper, that the greatest part of the profit gained by the use of machinery, is paid to the capitalist for the use of his money." *Ibid.*, p. 5.

linquished his paternalistic view that reform must be initiated from above, Maclure insisted that "none but the millions can benefit the millions." [59] Fortunately, so Maclure believed, there is a "strong propensity of nature to equalize property, and, consequently, knowledge and power, when not counteracted by force or unjust laws." [60] Such unjust laws he repeatedly enumerated—monopolistic land statutes, bank charters, indirect taxation, and the complicated, litigious, and uncodified common law borrowed from England.[61] During Jackson's administration Maclure placed himself squarely behind the President in his attack upon the Bank, in his veto of the Maysville road bill, in his advocacy of rotation in office,[62] in his "shirt-sleeve diplomacy." [63] He favored the distribution of land to actual settlers; he hoped for a codification of the laws on the lines of the Code Napoleon; and he seriously argued that "laws for the collection of debts ought to be abolished." [64] The industrious classes, he believed, must use their political power to correct the abuses of government, by uniting at the polls "to exclude all those from the legislatures who live or benefit by the abuses." [65]

In the last analysis, Maclure insisted, the effective use of political power rests upon knowledge: "Until the many shall be educated, they must continue to labor for the few." [66] In saying this, he was not mouthing vague platitudes about the efficacy of education in general. The school was but an instrument, which might be used for ends directly opposite to those he had in mind. In fact, it had generally been so employed; most public educational funds, he asserted, had been spent "to teach the children of the idle and non-productive" and thus "to increase the inequality of knowledge already pushed to a pitch dangerous to freedom." For this reason he opposed the creation of a national university at Washington, and told its supporters that he would rather "take all the revenues from all the colleges, universities, academies, &c. for the education of the rich, and divide them amongst parish and district schools, being the only schools entitled, in a free country, to the aid and support of a government bottomed on universal suffrage." [67]

[59] Maclure, *Opinions,* I, 68.
[60] *Ibid.,* I, 25.
[61] *Ibid.,* I, 25–29, 109–10, 155–61, 163–65, 172–78, 203–6, 450–58.
[62] *Ibid.,* II (1837), 40, 73.
[63] Mme Fretageot to Maclure, New Harmony, Dec. 19, 1828, MS in Workingmen's Institute. Though this specific statement was written to, not by, Maclure, it is in accord with the views expressed in his *Opinions,* I, 184–87.
[64] Maclure, *Opinions,* I, 142.
[65] *Ibid.,* II (1837), 6.
[66] *Ibid.,* II (1831), 561.
[67] *Ibid.,* I, 48, 113. See also pp. 68, 150; II (1831), 564.

To be socially effective, Maclure insisted, education must be consciously directed to that end. Its content, its organization, and its control were all significant in his educational philosophy, and his consideration of each of these three aspects provided a specific link with the thought of his contemporaries—with Pestalozzi, with Fellenberg, and with the communitarians.

With respect to the content of education, Maclure distinguished sharply between knowledge which was useful and that which was merely ornamental, and he insisted that a school concerned with the latter could serve only the nonproductive classes.[68] Useful knowledge he tended to equate with a knowledge of things rather than of abstractions, hence Pestalozzianism satisfied him as the best and likewise the most natural system.

To bring education within reach of the industrious classes, Maclure believed in the second place, its cost must be kept low, for public funds were in danger of being so largely diverted as to afford insufficient provision.

One of two things is . . . necessary to secure to the millions the necessary quantum of knowledge: either that more of the people's money be expended in furnishing instruction to their children, or, that instruction be so simplified, that the children could feed, clothe and educate themselves by their own labor; thus rendering them independent even of their own money, which they pay daily into the treasury.[69]

Justice indicated the first alternative to be the proper one, but practical experience suggested the second as the one to be relied on. And Fellenberg's institution at Hofwyl afforded the best demonstration that this alternative was feasible.[70]

Such schools as Maclure advocated could, in the third place, be kept to their true function only if they remained under the immediate control of the people. He had definite ideas on how this was to be accomplished, for he considered it "a political axiom, that the smaller the political society, the better every thing is administered for the interest of the many, and that the corruption and mal-administration of all nations is in exact proportion to the extent of territory and number of beings over whom their rulers domineer." Applying the axiom to education, he praised the free schools "made by the New-England townships; who were wise enough to retain the power of doing every thing for their own benefit, without depending on the State or general government for permission to spend their own money to the best ad-

---

[68] See especially *ibid.*, I, 48–59, where each of the fields of knowledge is analyzed according to this criterion.

[69] *Ibid.*, I, 69.

[70] *Ibid.*, I, 87.

vantage, for their own benefit." [71] The communitarian conclusions to which such an argument for local control easily led were stated in several passages of Maclure's *Opinions:*

> Under the management of the majority of the inhabitants of a township of six miles square, all radical reforms, comporting with their interest, might be tried without the risk of hurting, in case of failure, any one but themselves;—a losing game they would very soon tire of.[72]

And the success of the federal system in the United States encouraged him to hope that "thousands, or hundreds of thousands of small societies" might exist, separate yet federated, and might "traffic and deal with each other in the true spirit of equality, . . . exchanging labor for labor, without permitting avarice to introduce its poison in the form of coin—wasting none of their labor in counteracting or injuring one another." [73]

So comprehensive an educational program as Maclure's could obviously get its start only in a liberal atmosphere. This he hoped to find in Spain when he went there in 1819, but his hopes were short-lived. In October 1822 the Congress of Verona sealed the doom of liberalism in Spain, and with it the doom of Maclure's experiment. On April 7, 1823, French troops crossed the Spanish frontier. By October the death penalty had been decreed for those who supported the old liberal constitution. In that month Maclure was forced to abandon his school and flee the country, and in the following spring he visited the British Isles.

Britain had become in Maclure's mind an ultimate symbol of the aristocratic system he detested. Ever since he had renounced his British allegiance to become an American citizen a quarter of a century before, his contacts—scientific, educational, and intellectual —had been primarily with the Continent. What he now found in Britain therefore amazed him. Having considered "education as the most certain thermometer of all useful civilisation," he found himself "in a state of agreeable feelings approaching to extacey . . . to be an Eye witness of the immense progress made in civilisation in so short a time." Both in Dublin, where he first landed, and in London, he discovered that "schools for the lower orders are the rage of the day," and he felt "more encouraged and flattered by the concordance and union of more enlightened and liberal men than at any time or in any country I have visited." [74] The high point of his trip was a three- or four-day stay at New Lanark in July, "con-

[71] *Ibid.,* I, 83.

[72] *Ibid.,* III, 8. See also the quotations in chapter I above, pp. 14 and 18.

[73] *Ibid.,* I, 38–39, 40.

[74] Maclure to Mme Fretageot, Dublin, June 30, 1824; London, Aug. 25, 1824, Sept. 10, 1824, in *Correspondence,* ed. Bestor, pp. 305–9.

templating the vast improvement in society effected by Mr. Robert
Owen's courage and perserverance in spite of an inveterate and
malignant opposition." [75] Maclure had already known something of
Owen's educational endeavors, but this first-hand view exceeded any
expectations he had formed. His memories of despotism in Spain
were blotted out, and he was inspired to revive his plan for experimental farming schools, with the United States as the new location.
For some time, in fact, he had been looking with a more favorable
eye toward his adopted homeland across the Atlantic. As early as
1821 he had assisted Madame Fretageot, the Pestalozzian teacher
in Paris, to transfer her activities to Philadelphia, and in the fall
of 1824 he arranged for Phiquepal to follow her there.[76]

Owen, of course, was also looking toward America. His conference
with Richard Flower concerning the Rappite property took place on
August 14, 1824, only a few weeks after Maclure's visit. When the
latter heard of Owen's plan to go to America he expressed delight
that "the only man in Europe who has a proper idea of mankind and
the use he ought to make of his faculties is going to join the finest
and most rational Society on the Globe." [77] Though Maclure envisaged no direct connection between his own plan and Owen's, he
believed that the latter's "immense mecanizm" would clear away at
least "half the prejudice, superstition & bigotry we should have to
fight with unaided by him." [78]

By the time this latter comment was written, in January 1825,
Owen was already in America. His reputation as an educator contributed greatly to the warmth of his reception. Professor Griscom's
services in introducing him to the Columbia faculty have already
been described. In addition several schoolteachers sought him out in
New York to talk about Fellenberg and Pestalozzi or education in
general. William Channing Woodbridge came all the way from

[75] *Ibid.*, p. 307 (Aug. 25, 1824). Frank Podmore gives July as the date of Maclure's
visit, citing "Maclure's Diary, which is preserved in the New Harmony Public
Library." See his *Robert Owen*, I, 298–99 and note. The diary cannot be located
in the Workingmen's Institute; possibly the reference is to a letter.

[76] Mme Fretageot to Maclure, Paris, July 10, 1821; Le Havre, July 13, 22, and
27, 1821; New York, Sept. 22, Oct. 14, 1821; Philadelphia, Nov. 7, 1821, Oct. 12,
1824, Dec. 30, 1824, Jan. 3, 1825; MSS in Workingmen's Institute. See also *Correspondence*, ed. Bestor, pp. 302–3, 306, 313. Phiquepal had lived in the United
States at an earlier period, for in 1815 he signed himself "Gme Phiquepal de
Philadie" when witnessing the agreement between Maclure and Lesueur, Paris,
Aug. 8, 1815, MS cited above, p. 147, n. 52.

[77] Maclure to Mme Fretageot, London, Sept. 10, 1824, in *Correspondence*, ed.
Bestor, p. 309. See also Maclure's letter of the same date to Silliman, quoted
above, p. 103.

[78] Maclure to Mme Fretageot, Paris, Jan. 13, 1825, in *Correspondence*, ed. Bestor,
p. 312, see also p. 313 (Jan. 31, 1825).

Hartford to discuss with Owen the itinerary of a contemplated tour of European schools, the outcome of which was the propaganda for Fellenberg that Woodbridge inaugurated in the *American Annals of Education and Instruction,* which he founded upon his return.[79]

In Philadelphia Owen's educational reputation was an even more important element in the success of his propaganda. Madame Fretageot, the Pestalozzian teacher, appears to have been the principal intermediary. She had never been to New Lanark, but she brought with her to America in 1821 an account, just published in Paris, of Owen's educational principles. Among the Philadelphians who interested themselves in her school was a young physician, Dr. Philip M. Price, son of the superintendent of the Friends' Boarding School at West-Town. Early in 1822 he borrowed her book on New Lanark and became so enthusiastic over Owen's educational plans that he desired a first-hand report on them. Eventually he decided to make the trip himself, and he was in Scotland in 1824 at the time Maclure was meeting Owen and the latter was planning his venture in America.[80] Madame Fretageot was thus in touch with Owen before Maclure visited him. She was also in touch, of course, with the members of the Philadelphia Academy of Natural Sciences, of which her patron Maclure was president. It was apparently through her that Owenite ideas reached the latter group and inspired the communitarian project of 1823–24 in which John Speakman was prime mover.[81]

Even before he left England, Owen had planned to visit Madame Fretageot and her school, and on November 21, 1824, shortly after reaching Philadelphia, he did so. "When he entered in my house," she wrote Maclure, "I took his hands saying; there is the man I desired so much to converse with! And you are, said he, the woman that I wish to see. We are old acquaintances and in the mean time he gave me a kiss of friendship that I returned heartly." But it was not Owen's gallantry alone that won her; he went straight to her heart with his

[79] Donald Macdonald, *Diaries,* p. 179. Woodbridge's later articles are cited above, p. 138 and n. 15.

[80] See Mme Fretageot to Maclure, Philadelphia, March 16, 1822, Oct. 21, 1824, Feb. 11, 1825; Maclure to Mme Fretageot, Paris, Oct. 1, 1824, in *Correspondence,* ed. Bestor, pp. 304, 310–11, 314. The publication that Mme Fretageot lent to Dr. Price was Henry Grey Macnab, *Examen impartial des nouvelles vues de M. Robert Owen, et de ses établissemens à New-Lanark en Écosse,* traduit par Laffon de Ladébat (Paris, 1821). When Owen came to the United States in 1824, Philip M. Price remained in England, but his brother, Eli K., was among those who welcomed Owen to Philadelphia. See D. Macdonald, *Diaries,* pp. 208–9; and W. Owen, *Diary,* pp. 33–34 (where the name is sometimes given as Pierce).

[81] Mme Fretageot to Maclure, Philadelphia, March 25, 1824, in *Correspondence,* ed. Bestor, p. 305. See above, pp. 100, 108, 110–11, and 113.

remarks on the proper education of children.[82] For the time being he left the matter at that, but in the following January or February, when he again visited Madame Fretageot in Philadelphia, he pursued the educational argument to its communitarian conclusion. "It is necessary to observe," wrote Madame Fretageot, who quickly made his reasoning her own, "that in point of education the most essential is that children be surrounded by persons whose actions and speach be correct. . . . Then we can determine easely the situation the most convenient for the purpos; it is what said Mr. Owen." [83] And lest there be any doubt, Owen indicated clearly to Madame Fretageot the situation the most convenient for the purpose. She quoted his exact words: "We must, says he, work all at once on a spot where the difficulties are almost removed. Then it is only so that we are able to show what are the effects of a good education. He observed that I would devote 30 years of my life where I now am without being able to co[u]nterbalance the evils which surround my pupils." [84] New Harmony was obviously the place for her and for Phiquepal. From that time forward she devoted herself in her letters to persuading Maclure to transfer all his enterprises, educational and scientific, to the new community on the Wabash.

In her propaganda she found allies among Maclure's friends in the Academy of Natural Sciences, for Owen's charm had not been lost upon Say, Troost, Speakman, and Lesueur, with whom he conferred several times. By February 11, 1825, Madame Fretageot was reporting to Maclure that the first three of these, at least, were "making their preparations" to join Owen at New Harmony—an expression which she later qualified in the interest of strict accuracy: "I don't mean that they are going immediately but are terminating their business in order to be ready next fall." [85]

When Owen went to Washington in February 1825 to deliver his addresses in the Hall of Representatives, he sent for Phiquepal and

[82] Mme Fretageot to Maclure, Philadelphia, Nov. 28, 1824, in *Correspondence,* pp. 311–12. See also D. Macdonald, *Diaries,* p. 207, and W. Owen, *Diary,* p. 31.

[83] Mme Fretageot to Maclure, Philadelphia, Feb. 18, 1825, in *Correspondence,* pp. 315–16.

[84] Mme Fretageot to Maclure, Philadelphia, Feb. 11, 1825, in *Correspondence,* p. 314. Though she assured Maclure in this letter that she would "wait for your arrival before to fix my opinion," she confidently wrote Owen four days later: "Mr Maclure for whom I have the greatest esteem being informed by you and by me will join me in my opinion and I consider it would be a great acquisition." Mme Fretageot to Owen, Philadelphia, Feb. 15, 1825, MS no. 60 in Owen papers, Manchester.

[85] Mme Fretageot to Maclure, Philadelphia, Feb. 11, 1825, and March [9]–13, in *Correspondence,* pp. 315, 316. See also D. Macdonald, *Diaries,* pp. 206–9, and W. Owen, *Diary,* p. 34.

allowed him to see for himself the enthusiasm that had been generated in the national capital. Fresh from these triumphs, Owen, on his third visit to Philadelphia late in March, engineered a round-robin letter to Maclure from himself and the two Pestalozzian teachers, dated at "Madame Fretageot & Mr. Phiquepal's Academies." To Madame Fretageot fell the honor of expounding Owen's plan and its educational implications:

> The first society will be founded on the following principles. Those who will be received the first shall be choosen amongst the best principled being, in order to form by their example those who afterwards will be received indiscriminately. The town already built will be allowed to them for their residence, and [they] will remain there untill the community will allow them to take place in the new town, *which* plan would be to[o] long to detail. The first settlers by their wealth, their industry will establish all that is proper to accumulate prosperity, union, peace and consequently, happiness. The children's education is what will occupy the most, because from them depend the future prosperity not only of the community but of all. Those who will be witnesses of such happy result will of course be convinced that the present state of society is founded on such principles that it is quite impossible to be happy according its rules. This is but an imperfect sketch, but you'll be soon here; and not doubt remain in my mind that you'll join the plan as soon as you'll be informed of it as we are.[86]

Maclure tarried in France until June 1825, and his replies to Madame Fretageot's excited letters have unfortunately been lost. In a communication to Benjamin Silliman in May he voiced his sincere hope that Owen would succeed in his plan,[87] but Madame Fretageot's impatience makes it clear that he was by no means ready to merge his own projects with Owen's. On July 9, 1825, Maclure landed in New York, and before he could get to Philadelphia three more letters from her were in his hands.[88] Owen too was eager to influence Maclure. He had just made a fourth visit to Philadelphia and had brought Thomas Say at least part of the way back to New York with him. He was off

[86] Mme Fretageot to Maclure, Philadelphia, March 28, 1825, in *Correspondence*, p. 318. This forms the second and third pages of a letter of which the first page was written by Owen on the twenty-seventh and the fourth by Phiquepal on the twenty-eighth. For more than a month Mme Fretageot had been thinking about such a letter. "It is essential," she wrote Owen on Feb. 26, "that we could inform Mr. Maclure before he leaves france because he would collect every thing proper for the new Colony." Mme Fretageot to Owen, Philadelphia, Feb. 26, 1825, MS no. 64 in Owen papers, Manchester.

[87] Dated Paris, May 2, 1825, in *American Journal of Science*, X (1825–26), 165–67.

[88] Mme Fretageot to Maclure, Philadelphia, June 10, 1825, July 12, 1825 (two letters, one postmarked the twelfth, the other the thirteenth); Maclure to Mme Fretageot, New York, July 10 and 15, 1825, MSS in Workingmen's Institute, partially printed in *Correspondence*, ed. Bestor, pp. 321–23.

again on a flying trip to Boston at the time Maclure landed, but the two men managed to get together on July 15, 1825, the eve of Owen's embarkation for England.[89]

Maclure was not to be swept off his feet. He endeavored to restrain the impetuous ardor of Madame Fretageot, warning her that "when the imagination is exalted so as to leave room only for one favorite Idea in the mind, it approaches to insanity." For himself, he endorsed without qualification "the goodness and solidity" of Owen's theory, but was doubtful of the human materials with which he would have to work, "stubborn, crooked and too often bent in an opposite direction from their owne most evident interest." Communitarianism might be the logical sequel to what Maclure was attempting, but he still believed that for the present "the education of the children must be the chief support and foundation of the system." Time would be requisite, he told her, "and it's most probable that during that time both you and Phiquepal can be more usefully employed, both for yourselves and others, than joining Mr. O. in the commencement of his most arduous undertaking." [90]

The debate apparently continued throughout the summer. Maclure reached Philadelphia in mid-July, but Madame Fretageot had no immediate success in converting him to her views. Two letters written late in August show that the matter was still undecided. The first was a communication from Maclure to Silliman's *American Journal of Science,* which, under date of August 19, 1825, described the schools of Madame Fretageot and Phiquepal but said nothing of any contemplated removal of them from Philadelphia.[91] The second was an ambiguous letter of August 28 from Madame Fretageot to Maclure, then temporarily absent from Philadelphia. Rumors that he, she, and Phiquepal would go to New Harmony were in circulation, she reported, but since "people is much inclined talking without knowing what they say," she declined "to take notice of it." [92] Even as late as October 12, 1825, Say was writing that he expected to accompany Maclure "this winter on a western and southern tour," a plan that was clearly something different from joining New Harmony.[93]

[89] Maclure to Mme Fretageot, New York, July 15, 1825, in *Correspondence,* pp. 322–23; D. Macdonald, *Diaries,* p. 302. Owen arrived in New York from the west on July 4, 1825, left the same day for Philadelphia, returned on the eighth, immediately departed for Boston, returned to New York on the fifteenth, saw Maclure that day, and sailed for Liverpool the following morning.

[90] Maclure to Mme Fretageot, New York, July 15, 1825, in *Correspondence,* p. 322.

[91] *American Journal of Science,* X (1825–26), 151.

[92] Mme Fretageot to Maclure, Philadelphia, Aug. 28, 1825, in *Correspondence,* p. 324.

[93] Say to Nicholas Hentz, Philadelphia, Oct. 12, 1825, in Weiss and Ziegler, *Thomas Say,* p. 179.

Owen himself apparently turned the scale. He landed in New York on November 6, 1825, inspired anew by his summer in Great Britain. Dr. Price met him with good tidings from New Harmony and from Philadelphia, and accompanied him to the latter place on November 11. Owen stayed only until the fourteenth, but he was back again delivering lectures on the twenty-fourth and twenty-fifth. During these two visits he and his party conferred with Maclure, Say, Price, Madame Fretageot, and Phiquepal.[94] By the time of Owen's Philadelphia lectures, at the very latest, Maclure had made up his mind to join Owen, for less than a fortnight afterwards the two men were at Pittsburgh, ready to embark on the keelboat *Philanthropist,* which they had purchased for the voyage down the Ohio River to New Harmony.[95]

The party of forty composing the "boatload of knowledge" included, besides Maclure and Owen, the naturalists Say and Lesueur, the Pestalozzian teachers Madame Fretageot and Phiquepal and several pupils of the latter, Dr. Price and his family, Owen's son Robert Dale, and (though not at the beginning) his traveling companions Donald Macdonald and Stedman Whitwell.[96] The trip had scarcely begun when the vessel stuck fast in the ice some seven miles below Beaver, Pennsylvania, where it remained a full month, until January 9, 1826. Owen was not one to wait for either rivers or worlds to thaw of themselves, and he hastened to New Harmony by coach and (on the lower river) by steamboat. Maclure and Madame Fretageot also took to the land, spreading Pestalozzianism as they traveled, but eventually rejoining the party at Wheeling. The others, under the direction of Say, improved the time on board by stuffing

[94] D. Macdonald, *Diaries,* pp. 308, 310–13, 316–17.

[95] On Dec. 8, 1825, Benjamin Bakewell wrote from Pittsburgh: "At length he [Owen] and his party, consisting of forty, have arrived, and will at 12 o'clock be ready to embark." *Pears Papers,* p. 45. Owen had remained in Philadelphia when his traveling companions, Donald Macdonald and Stedman Whitwell, departed on Nov. 28, 1825. Presumably Owen, Maclure, and their party journeyed together from Philadelphia to Pittsburgh some time subsequent to that date. Lesueur, however, seems to have left Philadelphia as early as the twenty-seventh. See p. 77 of R. W. G. Vail's article cited below, n. 97.

[96] The only contemporary passenger list is in D. Macdonald, *Diaries,* p. 334. Slight errors crept into the lists compiled from memory by Victor Colin Duclos, "Diary and Recollections," in Lindley, ed., *Indiana As Seen by Early Travelers,* p. 537, and by Robert Dale Owen, *Autobiography,* pp. 267–68. Gerard Troost and John Speakman were already in New Harmony, having left Philadelphia in early October. See *Pears Papers,* pp. 44–45, 53; and Weiss and Ziegler, *Thomas Say,* p. 179. The evidence on Dr. Price is conflicting. Macdonald lists him in the party aboard the *Philanthropist* on Jan. 8, 1826, but the *New-Harmony Gazette* prints an address said to have been delivered by him at the community on Jan. 11. See I, 149–50 (Feb. 1, 1826).

fish and game for the museum of natural history that would soon enlighten New Harmony.

Even after the boat was freed from the ice, the trip was a leisurely one. Stops to interview prospective Harmonians were frequent. Maclure called on Joseph Neef at his home near Louisville, and made arrangements for him to join the Pestalozzian faculty at New Harmony in the spring. There was a slight delay even after the *Philanthropist* reached Mount Vernon on the morning of January 23, 1826, but the next day the party proceeded overland to New Harmony, reminding one observer of "a march with the baggage of a company of soldiers." [97]

They were a detachment from the army of educational reformers, marching as allies into the new encampment of the communitarians.

[97] D. Macdonald, *Diaries*, p. 337; on the incidents of the trip and the persons interviewed, see pp. 333–37. An equally important source for the voyage of the *Philanthropist* is the series of dated sketches by Lesueur, nos. 94–218 in the check-list of Robert W. G. Vail, "The American Sketchbooks of a French Naturalist, 1816–1837: A Description of the Charles Alexandre Lesueur Collection, with a Brief Account of the Artist," American Antiquarian Society, *Proceedings*, n.s., XLVIII, 49–155 (April 1938). Neef finally arrived in New Harmony on March 20, 1826. See his own statement in Paul Brown, *Twelve Months in New-Harmony* (1827), p. 107.

Chapter VII

NEW HARMONY: A STUDY IN DISSONANCE

WHEN Owen returned to New Harmony on January 12, 1826, to begin a continuous residence of nearly a year and a half,[1] the Preliminary Society was more than seven months old, but a sense that the experiment was yet to begin still pervaded the community. "All are in anxious expectation of Mr. Owen's return," wrote one member a week before his arrival. "Our store is in want of a great number of necessary articles, and nobody is sent on for goods, because they wished to consult Mr. Owen first." [2] Ironically enough, this mood of expectancy proved a stronger bond of union than any of the idealistic ties that community life was supposed to foster. The Preliminary Society actually enjoyed a longer life than any of the subsequent organizations at New Harmony. It was comparatively easy to bear with present difficulties when a *deus ex machina* was expected soon to descend and straighten them out. A general sentiment prevailed that "things will go on better soon after the return of Mr. Owen." [3]

As a consequence of this willingness to postpone crucial issues, the history of the Preliminary Society was comparatively uneventful. This was all to the good. The crucial issues, after all, were largely abstract and theoretical; the manifold problems of housing and feeding and employing a thousand persons gathered together close to the frontier of settlement were practical ones, better attacked without too much admixture of the kind of speculative talk that Owen indulged in so freely. On the whole the administration of the Preliminary Society, if not notably efficient, was at least realistic, and probably as successful as could be expected, given the overcrowding and indiscriminate admission of members that Owen had imposed upon it at the outset.

---

[1] To recapitulate, Owen had been at New Harmony from Dec. 16, 1824, to Jan. 3, 1825, and from April 13 to June 5, 1825, and had formally inaugurated the Preliminary Society during the latter visit, on May 1, 1825. After his return on Jan. 12, 1826, he remained until June 1, 1827. Subsequently he revisited the community from early April to June 27, 1828, and again for a few days beginning March 30, 1829, then did not see it again until Oct. 1844.

[2] Sarah Pears to Mrs. Benjamin Bakewell, New Harmony, Jan. 6, 1826, in *Pears Papers*, p. 52.

[3] "Pelham Letters," p. 393 (Nov. 27, 1825).

From June 1825 until January 1826 the responsibility devolved largely upon twenty-three-year-old William Owen. In theory the Preliminary Society was run by a committee, originally appointed by Robert Owen and subsequently enlarged and confirmed by vote of the community.[4] Its deliberations were supplemented by regular weekly meetings of the entire membership.[5] Despite this machinery of self-government, however, the final word in economic matters was almost certainly William Owen's. Conflicts of authority between the general meeting and the committee were resolved by the latter in their own favor,[6] and William Owen seems clearly to have dominated the committee. This was natural, and far from improper, for after all the entire property belonged to his father, who was likewise footing the bill for current expenses.

Despite his youth, William Owen apparently commanded respect; one member felt he possessed the "education, experience & general knowledge" of a man of thirty-five—an age that to the writer clearly signified maturity and wisdom.[7] Young Owen's letters give the im-

[4] The constitution clearly gave Owen the sole right to appoint the committee. *New-Harmony Gazette*, I, 2, (Oct. 1, 1825). He named four members to begin with, but during the first month permitted the members of the community to elect the entire committee. They chose Owen's four appointees and added three others. See *Pears Papers*, p. 15 (June 2, 1825); "Pelham Letters," p. 365 (Aug. 10); *New-Harmony Gazette*, I, 102–3, and correction, p. 135 (Dec. 21, 1825, Jan. 18, 1826). The committee was composed of William Owen, Dr. Elias McNamee, Judge James O. Wattles, John Schnee, T. M. Bosson, Robert L. Jennings, and Warner W. Lewis. "Proceedings of the Preliminary Meeting" (MS), Feb. 8, 1826 (see next footnote). Captain Macdonald, who had shared responsibility with William Owen in the spring of 1825, accompanied Robert Owen on his journey to England, and was therefore absent from June 5, 1825, until Jan. 24, 1826.

[5] The meetings of the community were held regularly on Wednesday evenings, apparently from the beginning. See *Pears Papers*, p. 28 (Sept. 2, 1825); "Pelham Letters," p. 370 (Sept. 7, 1825). Minutes, however, did not begin to be kept until Nov. 2, 1825. The original manuscript of these, headed "Proceedings of the Preliminary Meeting," and covering the period from Nov. 2, 1825, to Feb. 28, 1826, fills fourteen pages of a volume also containing the "Minutes of the Convention for Forming a Constitution for the Society of New Harmony Held January 25, 1826 [*et seqq*.]." It is owned by Mr. Thomas C. Pears III, of Pittsburgh; photostat copies are in the Indiana State Library, the Illinois Historical Survey of the University of Illinois, and the Workingmen's Institute, New Harmony.

[6] At the Wednesday evening public meetings the committee reported its transactions, which were discussed but apparently not put to a vote. See "Pelham Letters," p. 370 (Sept. 7, 1825). An attempt to instruct the committee was rebuffed by the latter in September with the statement "that no Resolution of ours [i.e., of the public meeting] was binding on the Committee." *Pears Papers*, p. 38 (Sept. 29, 1825). Repeated efforts to compel the committee to make public all its resolutions were blocked, the committee insisting upon its right to unfettered discretion. *Pears Papers*, p. 39 (Sept. 29, 1825); "Proceedings of the Preliminary Meeting" (MS), Nov. 9 and 23, 1825.

[7] "Pelham Letters," pp. 400–1 (Dec. 29, 1825).

pression of practical competence,[8] though they lack the powerful intellectual drive of his brother Robert Dale Owen, whose late arrival, in January 1826, deprived him of a role in the Preliminary Society. It is difficult to see how any decision which it was within William Owen's power to make could have improved the situation that existed at New Harmony in 1825.

The most obvious problem that beset the young community was housing. The Rappite accommodations could be enlarged but slowly, yet the new population was half again as large as that which had departed. The log cabins which the Rappites had begun to replace were pressed into service, and garrets were roughly finished off to serve as bedrooms. Prospective members were warned that living quarters might not be available for two years to come,[9] but the influx continued, until at last the *New-Harmony Gazette* gave public notice that friends of the social system were not to come without receiving previous assurance that they could be accommodated.[10]

An overabundant population, however, did not mean an adequate labor supply. There had been no scrutiny of members' qualifications, hence there had been no possible way of obtaining skilled craftsmen in either the number or proportion necessary to operate the manufacturing establishments which the Rappites had conducted so successfully, and the equipment for which they had left intact. With a frankness rare in its columns, the *New-Harmony Gazette* described the resulting situation in October 1825:

With the machinery now on hand, our operations in the wool business should turn out one hundred and sixty pounds of yarn per day, but the want of spinners reduces the business much below that amount. The fulling and dressing departments have, at present, neither regular superintendents or workmen; consequently they are not prosecuted with effect. The cotton-

[8] On the other hand, Robert Owen apparently complained that William's letters were "so unbusinesslike" that he was "at a loss how to act." See letter of William Owen in reply, New Harmony, Dec. 16, 1825, MS no. 54 in Owen papers, Manchester. The charge in this instance was most unfair, for it was the elder Owen who was disregarding every canon of business prudence. In 1830 William Owen had to be helped out of financial difficulties by his brother Robert Dale Owen, who expressed the opinion "that Wm's character is scarcely decisive enough" for the particular business venture in hand, "that he is too easily imposed upon, & too inactive in counteracting injustice or encroachment." R. D. Owen to James M. Dorsey, New York, Jan. 31, 1830, MS in Owen-Dorsey papers, Indiana Historical Society. From the other letters in the collection, however, it is impossible to determine whether William's misfortunes were the result of his own mistakes. It is unfortunate that the extant diary of William Owen breaks off in April 1825, before he assumed full responsibility at New Harmony.

[9] "Pelham Letters," p. 365 (Aug. 10, 1825), see also pp. 375, 393, 394, 397.

[10] *New-Harmony Gazette*, I, 270 (May 17, 1826). The notice was reprinted, as requested, in several newspapers, e.g., Xenia, O., *People's Press and Impartial Expositor*, June 14, 1826, p. 1:5.

spinning establishment is equal to producing between three and four hundred pounds of yarn per week, and is under very good direction; but skilful and steady hands are much wanting, which time will furnish from our present population. The dye-house is a spacious brick building, furnished with copper vessels capable of containing between 1500 and 2000 gallons; and will probably compare in convenience with any other in the United States. At present, this valuable establishment is doing nothing, for want of a skilful person to undertake the direction of it.

These various textile manufactories constituted what might be called the export industry of the place, and without them no adequate cash income could be expected, to balance the purchases necessarily made from outside. A marketable surplus of soap, candles, and glue, and some outside business at the cotton gin and the tavern were the only actual sources of income which the *Gazette* could point to, for its report on the flour mill and the sawmill mentioned only capacity, not production.[11]

To get the mills into operation was more of a task than to find work for individual craftsmen. Shops were set up in the log cabins and, before long, seventeen boot- and shoe-makers were busy, a hat manufactory employing eight was in production, and a ropewalk was supplying all the needs of the community. Carpenters, bricklayers, and stonecutters were immediately put to work making living quarters out of unutilized crannies in the various buildings. And the crafts of the butcher, the baker, the brewer, the blacksmith, the tailor, and the seamstress were, of course, in demand at once. Three tobacconists and two papermakers possessed talents which stumped the committee, but they alone were listed as "unemployed."[12] In the aggregate, however, the record of craftsmen actually at work was not impressive. Out of a population of at least eight hundred, an official report of October 1825 listed only 137 "in the employed professions."[13] Moreover, the output of all these craftsmen was absorbed

[11] [T. M. Bosson], "View of New-Harmony," *New-Harmony Gazette*, I, 30 (Oct. 22, 1825). On Sept. 2, 1825, Thomas Pears wrote that "our cotton factory,—has not yet, I believe, produced its expenses, for all was out of order. The woolen has not commenced." *Pears Papers*, p. 25. On Dec. 16, 1825, William Owen sent his father a long list of skilled trades in which the community was deficient. A superintendent and several journeymen for woolen spinning were still needed; the foreman cotton spinner was good, "but as he has rather a hasty and peculiar temper, some freak may carry him off without warning"; a dyer and a fuller had yet to be found. In other words, the situation in the major industries was unchanged. "But," young Owen added emphatically, "although I have said we want these men to make our workshops full and perfect, I would at the same time repeat and impress upon your mind that *we have no room for them.*" MS no. 54 in Owen papers, Manchester.

[12] Bosson, "View," *New-Harmony Gazette*, I, 30 (Oct. 22, 1825).

[13] *Ibid.* It is not clear whether these figures included the persons employed in the woolen and cotton mills, hence the total may have been somewhat larger.

by the community itself,[14] so that from their efforts nothing came to balance the external payments.

So far as industrial production was concerned, New Harmony was hardly a going concern. For the first year this was disappointing but not altogether unexpected. What was truly amazing was the slowness with which agricultural operations got under way. Presumably a large majority of those who drifted into New Harmony had had something to do with the land, yet in October 1825 the official roster listed only thirty-six farmers and field laborers and two gardeners among the "employed professions."[15] As far back as February 1825 William Owen had urged his father to make plans for the coming season, but nothing was done. During the precious months of April and May the new society was being organized, and its founders furrowed their brows rather than their fields. By the beginning of September the situation was critical in the extreme. "We are now, as we have been, without vegetables except what we buy," reported Thomas Pears, "and I believe that we shall go without potatoes, turnips, or cabbages this winter, unless they are purchased —which is but a slender thread to hang hope upon. Indeed until lately our committee gave up all idea of farming till Mr. Owen's return, except the sowing of fifty or sixty acres of winter barley, which they wisely concluded would be wanted for our beer the ensuing year." Pears, himself a manufacturer by training, got up a special meeting that prodded the committee into putting three or four plows to work,[16] but this was about all.

By and large, the low level of production at New Harmony was caused by a lack of competent foremen, supervisors, and skilled craftsmen. Here one comes squarely upon the problem of economic incentive in an equalitarian or socialist system. When Owen provided a measure of inequality in the Preliminary Society he was thinking primarily of attracting professional men. But in actuality such men were often drawn to the community out of intellectual sympathy with the ideas it stood for. Where New Harmony failed was in attracting and holding the superior workman, whose incentives were not professional but strictly economic, and whose abilities could command far more in the open market than in an equalitarian society.

In the end it was not the inhabitants of New Harmony, but Owen's pocketbook, that bore the brunt of all this. The store continued to supply the necessities of life to all the members of the community, and payment was nothing but a bookkeeping transaction, which could not in the nature of things be liquidated until actual produc-

[14] *Pears Papers*, pp. 25–26 (Sept. 2, 1825).
[15] Bosson, "View," *New-Harmony Gazette*, I, 30 (Oct. 22, 1825).
[16] *Pears Papers*, p. 26 (Sept. 2, 1825), see also pp. 29–32.

tion outdistanced consumption. The accounting procedure was as picturesque as it was complicated, the passbooks of the members exhibiting a "curious medley of items, bacon, chickens, eggs, melons, cucumbers, butter, tea, sugar, coffee &c &c with all the varieties of *store goods* on the debit side, while on the other are placed the credits of the individuals." [17] It took time to get the bookkeeping department running smoothly. To start with, the journal and ledger were far too small for the volume of transactions to be recorded, personal antagonisms arose in the counting house,[18] and the very idea of keeping books seemed "monstrous" to some who wanted to put behind them in community "all the depraved institutions of the trading world." [19] Ultimately, however, a fairly comprehensible system was evolved.

To each adult member, a fixed credit of $80 a year, or $1.54 a week, was immediately granted by the committee. It was entered on his passbook along with any sums he might deposit in cash. His purchases at the store, his weekly board bill, and the charges for various services were debited to his account. The credit was intended as a stopgap, since actual remuneration for services rendered was not to be calculated until the end of the year, or until the withdrawal of the member. The credit was not intended as a wage, but since it was made available weekly, it inevitably came to be looked upon in that light, and to be referred to as an "allowance." Demands for an increase in the allowance began immediately, and the cases of hardship were so obvious that individual requests could not be refused. The advancement of additional credits was at once the committee's greatest headache and its greatest potential lever of control. In a few months' time, however, the individual increases authorized by the committee had completely broken down any theoretical system of equality.[20]

The charges made by the committee for various items were moderate enough to occasion no particular dispute. Board was

[17] "Pelham Letters," p. 371 (Sept. 7, 1825). Thomas Pears complained that the system was complicated and that he "could not conceive that any system of bookkeeping in which double and single entries were combined could be correct." *Pears Papers*, p. 36 (Sept. 29, 1825). In the New Harmony Workingmen's Institute is a ledger with the pages ruled into some forty columns, each headed with the name of a commodity (coffee, tea, sugar, . . . beef, salt beef, pork, . . . potatoes, turnips, . . . sundries) or a service (clothing, furniture, . . . shoemakers, . . . washing). This was presumably made for the Preliminary Society, but no transactions and hence no dates were entered in it; later the volume was salvaged and used by Taylor, Fauntleroy & Co. The only account book in the collection that belonged certainly to the Preliminary Society is a "Journal A," with entries from May to Nov. 1825.

[18] *Pears Papers*, pp. 14, 36–37.

[19] Paul Brown, *Twelve Months in New-Harmony* (Cincinnati, 1827), pp. 16–18.

[20] *New-Harmony Gazette*, I, 3 (Oct. 1, 1825); "Pelham Letters," pp. 390, 393, 396; *Pears Papers*, pp. 13–14, 24.

originally fixed at $30 a year, or 57½ cents a week for adults (with graduated rates for children), and was later increased to 64 cents. The sum was charged on each member's passbook, and was credited to the boarding house or family where he took his meals.[21] A schedule of other charges was also announced, in which housing ranged from $10 a year for a log cabin to $40 for a brick or frame house. Various bases for calculating educational and medical expenses were announced,[22] but in the end the committee deducted 20 cents a week from each member's account for the school fund, 10 cents for the medical fund, and 5 per cent of his earnings as insurance against sickness.[23]

When it came to settling the accounts of individuals, wide discretion could be shown. "If it appeared that they have been prudent and economical and a balance still exists against them further allowance will be made, so as to balance the acct, on the principle that the services of every industrious, prudent man are equal to the necessary expenses of his living." From the improvident or the lazy, however, every farthing was to be exacted, even if this meant accepting his note of hand for the balance. In the last analysis, as one admirer of the system wrote, "it amounts to this simple fact, that whoever serves the Society faithfully and diligently whatever his occupation may be, gets his living and no more." [24]

Fortunately the account of one particular member has been recorded, and the actual operation of the system can therefore be examined. Joseph Walters was a member of the community from October 14, 1825, to February 7, 1826, a period reckoned at 15¾ weeks for accounting purposes. He had actually drawn $32.23 against his credit, for store goods, board, room, and sundries. The committee calculated his services in the tanyard at the rate of $130 per annum, which gave him an income of $39.37. Deductions for the school and medical funds and for insurance came to $6.69. On this basis he was entitled to a balance of 45 cents. He apparently needed some cash for his journey, however, and he was given $7.00. This was covered by a curious series of bookkeeping entries. The committee granted him a "further allowance" of $26 per annum, which amounted to $7.87, then turned around and charged him $1.32 "discount for cash." As all good accounts should, this balanced in the end, but not to the satisfaction of the individual concerned, for he caused the account to be published in a neighboring newspaper with the introductory

21 "Pelham Letters," pp. 386, 389, 396, 404; *Pears Papers,* p. 25.

22 *Pears Papers,* pp. 37–38.

23 This was the method used in settling the account of Joseph Walters, analyzed below. The printed text reads "per cent" instead of "cents per week" for the first two items, but the figures show that the latter was the actual basis of calculation.

24 "Pelham Letters," pp. 396, 389; see also pp. 383, 384–85, 392–93, 397.

motto, " 'Tis here, but yet confus'd—Knavery's plain face is never seen till us'd." [25]

Knavery was not part of the picture, however disappointing might be the return from weeks or months of labor. The community had operated at a heavy loss; this was the primary fact. Individual members may have received less than their exertions entitled them to, but taken as a whole the community had consumed far more than it had produced, and Owen had made up the difference. The various sources agree that he subsidized the living expenses of the Preliminary Society to the extent of at least thirty thousand dollars during its life of nine months.[26] Three more years at this rate would exhaust the remainder of his fortune.

The Preliminary Society was a total loss only in a financial sense. Owen had good reason to consider it an investment that had brought returns in other directions. His aim, after all, had been to create a new social environment, and in this a gratifying measure of success was obtained. Despite every hardship, there must have been many who could exclaim, as did William Pelham,

I have become a Harmonite and mean to spend the remainder of my days in this abode of peace and quietness. I have experienced no disappointment. I did not expect to find every thing regular, systematic, convenient—nor have I found them so. I did expect to find myself relieves [sic] from a most disagreeable state of life, and be able to mix with my fellow citizens without fear or imposition—without being subject to ill humor and unjust censures and suspicions—and this expectation has been realized—I am at length *free* —my body is at my own command, and I enjoy mental liberty, after having long been deprived of it.[27]

[25] Shawnee-Town *Illinois Gazette,* March 4, 1826, p. 3:2–3. When the affairs of the Preliminary Society were wound up and the Community of Equality launched, the services to date of the 232 full members of the society were evaluated, at amounts ranging from $234 to $45, but the methods of calculation were not indicated. "Proceedings of the Preliminary Meeting" (MS), Feb. 8, 1826; summarized and totaled in *Pears Papers,* p. 65 n.

[26] His bitter critic Paul Brown conceded as much. *Twelve Months in New-Harmony,* p. 24. This is corroborated by the Valuation List of Feb. 8, 1826, which allowed the members a total of $30,849.50 for services rendered to the Preliminary Society. *Pears Papers,* p. 65 n. Assuming that the Committee employed the same methods as in the cases previously examined, this sum probably roughly balanced the amounts charged against the members on the books for what they had consumed. Since the community had received negligible income from outside, this thirty thousand dollars' worth of goods represented purchases made with Owen's funds.

[27] "Pelham Letters," p. 373 (Sept. 8, 1825). Writing just after the failure of the community, Robert Dale Owen was confident "that three fourths of those who left Harmony, left it with regret for the social kindness and the quiet and perfect toleration it afforded." *Free Enquirer* (New York), I, 262 (June 10, 1829).

It was indeed a varied, enlightened, liberal, and, to all appearances, pleasant life which New Harmony afforded its members. The isolation that embittered the lives of so many on the western frontiers was absent. The weekly dance on Tuesday nights, the concert on Thursday or Friday, the public discussion on Wednesday, the frequent lectures on everything from the circulation of the blood to the circulation of wealth, the unhampered discussions of religious ideas, the meetings of the Female Social Society and the Philanthropic Lodge of Masons, the parades and the drills, provided a round of activities hardly to be matched in any other hamlet of a thousand west of the Alleghenies.[28]

Nor was this sheer frivolity, as some dour critics complained. A sense of high intellectual purpose differentiated the community not only from the typical western settlement, but also from the sectarian community that had preceded it at Harmonie. Education was in the forefront of Owen's plans, and even before the arrival of the Boatload of Knowledge the school had become a notable feature of New Harmony. From an initial enrollment of about a hundred, its pupils had increased by December 1825 to 140, all "boarded, clothed and educated at the public expense," as the *New-Harmony Gazette* proudly boasted.[29]

The *Gazette* itself, founded only five months after the establishment of the community, was another evidence that New Harmony took seriously its mission of enlightenment. The historian reading its files would be happy to dispense with many a long-winded philosophic discussion in favor of an additional factual report on happenings in the community, but he cannot miss the fact that the *Gazette* strove hard to keep open the vista to those larger intellectual horizons that were so easily obscured in the western forests. And he can recognize in its motto—"If we cannot reconcile all opinions, let us endeavor to unite all hearts"—a spirit of tolerance all too rare in journals pledged to a special cause.

Needless to say, liberality like this commanded less than universal admiration. Religious freedom, to many Americans in that day, did not include the toleration of antireligious opinions. Though the bitterest critics of Owen accused him of attempting to exclude religious influences from his community, his actual crime was to insist that religious teaching must face the free and fair competition of

[28] See "Pelham Letters," p. 370, *et passim; Pears Papers*, p. 28; *New-Harmony Gazette*, I, 38–39, 47 (advertisement), 58–59, 71 (advertisements), 149 (Oct. 29, 1825–Feb. 1, 1826); "Community Dances, 1826," MS volume in Workingmen's Institute.

[29] *New-Harmony Gazette*, I, 102 (Dec. 21, 1825); see also pp. 7 (advertisement), 22, 38, and the various discussions of education in general, pp. 14, 49–51, 57–58, 65–66, 73–74, 81–83, 89–90 (Oct. 1–Dec. 14, 1825).

other ideas. Sectarian doctrines formed no part of the instruction in the schools at New Harmony, as they form no part of the public-school curriculum of today, but this arrangement could hardly prove acceptable to those who, like the unnamed questioner in Philadelphia, demanded that Owen found his system on the twin doctrines of the depravity of man and the literal inspiration of the Scriptures.

The fact that Owen put the large brick church of the Rappites to secular uses was pointed to with horror by many who failed to mention that there was a second church at New Harmony, likewise the property of Owen, which was available without charge to any minister who chose to ask for its use, regardless of his creed.[30] A succession of preachers availed themselves of the privilege. On a single Sunday in September 1825 the pulpit of the church was occupied in the morning by the nonsectarian moral lecturer of the community, in the afternoon by a preacher of unidentified denomination who defended the authority of the Bible, and in the evening by a Methodist circuit rider who preached "about sin, and the devil, and heaven, and the straight [sic] and narrow way leading to salvation." [31] Freedom in these matters proved destructive neither of religion nor of the harmony of the community. Robert Owen had proved his point. "Whatever difference of opinion there may be, (and there is in reality a great difference in religious matters)," wrote one member, "I hear no illiberal remarks, I see no overbearing temper exhibited, but each one pursues his own course without meddling with his neighbor." [32] Though there were a few withdrawals for sectarian

[30] The official policy was clearly stated in the *New-Harmony Gazette*, I, 102 (Dec. 21, 1825). During the first month a member proposed to eject a visiting preacher who had attacked Owen as anti-Christ, and Owen himself rose to defend the clergyman's right to speak his opinions. Vincennes *Western Sun*, Sept. 24, 1825, as cited by Irvin, p. 25. Calumnies were occasionally circulated to the effect that the committee had refused the use of the church to particular religious groups, but no instance was ever substantiated. See "Pelham Letters," p. 398. Occasionally a member of the community would deliver a discourse in reply to a visitor's sermon. See "Pelham Letters," p. 370. This was apparently not a frequent practice, however, despite the statement published in England, which purported to summarize the policy of the community: "All preachers who come to New Harmony, for the purpose of preaching publicly, are permitted to live at the Tavern, free of all expense, as long as they please, provided that when they preach, any auditor, at the end of the sermon, may ask for explanation, proof, &c. of any thing the preacher may have advanced." Stedman Whitwell, "New Harmony," *Co-operative Magazine* (London), II, 48 (Jan. 1827). Whitwell was at New Harmony from January to August 1826, and this may possibly represent a policy that Owen introduced under the Community of Equality.

[31] "Pelham Letters," pp. 379–81; see also pp. 370, 371, 373, 387, 388, 392, 398.

[32] *Ibid.*, p. 377. Robert Dale Owen could still assert the same four years later. *Free Enquirer*, I, 262 (June 10, 1829).

reasons,[33] the storm of religious disapproval that raged in the east had little effect upon the members of the Preliminary Society, who were actual witnesses of what Owen intended.

Despite his blunders at the beginning, Owen still had much to build upon when he returned to New Harmony on January 12, 1826. Industry and agriculture could hardly fail to be more productive in the second year than in the first, and good management might bring them to the high level of efficiency they had enjoyed under the Rappites. The probationary characteristics of the Preliminary Society would make it possible to eliminate the malingerers who were obviously there, and this in turn would ease the housing shortage. The intellectual agencies of the community—school and press—were in good repute, and were about to be magnificently augmented by the Boatload of Knowledge. The social life was satisfying, morale was good, and personal confidence in Owen had, if anything, been heightened by his absence.

A prudent man would have prolonged the life of the Preliminary Society to its limit, concentrating his attention upon economical management and a gradual sifting of the membership. He would have recognized that whatever personal harmony had been achieved was a precarious thing, unlikely to survive any sudden change that tended to throw the members into permanent, closer, and therefore more inescapable association with one another. Finally, sensing the religious tensions that existed, he would have refrained from injecting into the situation anything new that might upset the balance.

Owen, however, returned to New Harmony filled not with prudence but with enthusiasm. Though his trip to England was not the same triumphal journey he had made to Washington, it affected Owen in much the same way. He witnessed the beginning of the Orbiston Community which the British Owenites had at last brought into being, and it was natural that he should wish his own experiment at New Harmony to be the first to reach the promised land of complete community. He also came more definitely under the influence of the radical Owenites than before. He had been interested in William Thompson's *Inquiry into the Principles of the Distribution of Wealth* during his first voyage to America,[34] but the terser and more outspoken *Lecture on Human Happiness* of John Gray had appeared while he was absent from Great Britain. Owen returned to America stimulated by its tone of immediacy,[35] and perhaps also by

[33] "Pelham Letters," p. 397.

[34] See above, p. 83, n. 72, and p. 108.

[35] Gray's *Lecture* was first advertised for sale in America in the same issue of the Philadelphia *National Gazette* that announced Owen's return to the United States. Nov. 10, 1825, p. 3:5. Thereafter Gray's name was frequently linked with

a sense of friendly rivalry induced by Gray's proposal to offer shortly a plan of his own, different from Owen's.[36] Finally, when William Maclure and his associates decided to join forces with him at New Harmony, Owen had further reason to believe that the new social system was sweeping everything before it.

Owen eventually convinced himself that he had thoroughly studied the situation at New Harmony in January 1826 and only then had decided to take the next step toward a complete community.[37] This was palpably untrue. Before he left New Harmony in June 1825 he had declared to the heterogeneous population: "Such is the progress which you have made, that what I did not think could be begun in less than three years from hence must be commenced next year." [38] When Owen passed through Pittsburgh in December 1825 on his way west he let it be known that the permanent community would be started "as soon as ever the Spring opens." [39] And the very day he set foot in New Harmony he began a series of public addresses that had the effect—and presumably the intention—of generating enthusiasm for the immediate transformation of the Preliminary Society into a full-fledged Community of Equality.[40]

On January 25, 1826, thirteen days after Owen's arrival, the fateful resolution was duly adopted "that a Community be [formed] as soon as practicable out of the present Society & that from the formation of this community the Preliminary Society do cease." [41] The public meeting immediately resolved itself into a constitutional convention and the next day elected a committee of seven to prepare a draft for discussion. The election was in effect a vote of confidence in Robert Owen. Some 158 members cast ballots, and his name appeared on

---

Owen's in American propaganda and discussion. In Philadelphia, for example, the Valley Forge community appended its constitution to an American reprint of Gray's *Lecture*. See below, p. 203, n. 3. Quotations from Gray preceded a reprint of the constitution of the New Harmony Community in a pamphlet entitled *Observations upon Currency and Finance. . . . With Some Remarks upon . . . Mr. Owen's New System . . .* , By a Looker On (Philadelphia, 1826). In the *New-Harmony Gazette* Owen and Gray were also mentioned together. See I, 269, 294, 301 (May 17, June 7 and 14, 1826). On Maclure's interest in Gray, see above, p. 149. The influence of Gray upon Owenite theory in Great Britain is also discussed above, pp. 85–86.

[36] Gray, *Lecture on Human Happiness* (London, 1825), p. 71.

[37] See *New-Harmony Gazette*, I, 262 (May 10, 1826).

[38] Quoted from memory by Thomas Pears in a letter to the editors of the *New-Harmony Gazette*, published in *Pears Papers*, p. 92. The communication is undated, but was a reply to an editorial in the *Gazette*, I, 100–1 (Dec. 27, 1826).

[39] Benjamin Bakewell to Thomas Pears, Pittsburgh, Dec. 8, 1825, in *Pears Papers*, p. 46.

[40] "Pelham Letters," pp. 405–6.

[41] "Proceedings of the Preliminary Meeting" (MS), Jan. 25, 1826.

136 of them.[42] In the end both he and William Maclure were excused from the detailed labor of drafting, but the actual committee included Owen's two sons, William and Robert Dale, and his traveling companion, Donald Macdonald. Four members (including William Owen) of the old governing committee of the Preliminary Society were chosen, hence six of the seven drafters of the constitution belonged to the inner group that had controlled affairs from the beginning.[43]

This did not mean, however, that there was unanimity of view. The committee duly reported a draft, which was printed as well as read,[44] but at the same time Captain Macdonald made a minority report and twice moved that the constitution be rejected, Robert Owen read a series of proposals that differed from those of the committee, and Robert Dale Owen offered an entirely new draft of his own. An attempt was made to induce Robert Owen himself to reconcile the various versions, but he declined. In the end the committee produced a revised constitution which, after amendment, was unanimously adopted on February 5, 1826, the twelfth day of the convention.

It was not economic policy, but questions of organization, that divided the convention. Robert Dale Owen merely wanted a more complex system of deliberative bodies than the committee had provided.[45] His father merely wanted a more elaborate hierarchy of officers charged with making reports on "the whole industry & daily conduct of every individual." [46] Donald Macdonald, at the opposite extreme, was distrustful of the "old suspicious system of written Constitution and Laws," and wanted to dispense with them entirely in favor of an "open family assembly" that would concert practical measures "unincumbered either by Creeds or Codes." [47]

[42] The votes were recorded in the margin of the "Minutes of the Convention for Forming a Constitution" (MS), Jan. 26, 1826. A total of 1,100 votes were cast for thirty-eight candidates. Assuming that each member was entitled to vote for seven, at least 158 ballots were cast, some being incomplete.

[43] The newcomer to the group was John Whitby, a former Shaker. See *Pears Papers*, p. 60. From the former governing body Judge James O. Wattles, Warner W. Lewis, and Robert L. Jennings were elected to the new committee, but the three other members of the old board stood low in the tabulation. Though the smallest vote that brought election was 63, John Schnee received only 21, E. McNamee only 15, and T. M. Bosson only 14.

[44] See "Minutes of the Convention" (MS), Jan. 26, 1826, Feb. 1 (text of draft); "Pelham Letters," pp. 406, 408. No printed copy is known to survive.

[45] "Minutes of the Convention" (MS), Feb. 3, 1826, which gives the full text.

[46] *Ibid.*, Feb. 1, 1826.

[47] Communication from Donald Macdonald, dated Feb. 16, 1826, in *New-Harmony Gazette*, I, 173–74 (Feb. 22, 1826). According to the "Minutes of the Convention," Jan. 30, 1826, "Capt Macdonald also read his declaration." This was probably the "plan of Arrangement of the affairs of the Society," mentioned

This sounds as if the members were of one mind concerning that "COMMUNITY OF PROPERTY" which the constitution proclaimed as one of its fundamental principles. Nothing could be farther from the truth. The simple yet well-nigh incredible fact is that the implications of a community of goods were completely lost sight of in the enthusiasm of the moment. Never was there a more convincing proof of the intoxicating power of Owen's eloquence. Not one of the various drafts came to grips with the fundamental issues, and no one from the floor called attention to the omission. The finished Constitution of the New-Harmony Community of Equality [48] was actually vaguer than the Constitution of the Preliminary Society in everything that pertained to economic matters. Some earlier provisions which permitted "a certain degree of pecuniary inequality" were eliminated,[49] but with them were swept away also all the specifications concerning credits and debits and the keeping of accounts, which, however defective, had underlain the practical operation of the Preliminary Society. In their place were vague provisions calling for "the Intendents' opinion of the daily character of each person attached to their Occupation," and requiring that "all the accounts of the Community shall be balanced at least once in each month." [50] Whether the members' income would depend on the results of this daily inquisition, and what the accounts were that should be balanced went unspecified. Members who withdrew could no longer expect to receive whatever balance stood to their credit on the books, but were thrown back upon a vague promise of "such compensation for

---

in "Pelham Letters," pp. 406–7, 408. The next day Macdonald called a public meeting of the Preliminary Society to carry through the arrangements he had proposed, but no action was recorded. "Proceedings of the Preliminary Meeting" (MS), Jan. 31, 1826. Three days later, after Macdonald had twice unsuccessfully moved the rejection of the draft constitution, another motion was made and defeated "That the further consideration of the Const be postponed for 3 weeks, & that during that time the present Society be arranged according to a plan proposed by Donald Macdonald." "Minutes of the Convention" (MS), Feb. 3, 1826. Macdonald was too unhappy to give more than a cursory account of these events in his diary, and he withdrew from New Harmony on March 4, 1826, in complete disillusionment. See D. Macdonald, *Diaries*, pp. 337–38, and the present writer's review in *New York History*, XXIV, 86 (Jan. 1943).

[48] The final text is in *New-Harmony Gazette*, I, 161–63 (Feb. 15, 1826), where it may conveniently be compared with that of the Preliminary Society, *ibid.*, pp. 2–4 (Oct. 1, 1825). The closest the convention came to deciding an economic issue was in deleting a promise to pay six per cent interest on deposited funds. "Minutes of the Convention" (MS), Feb. 5, 1826 (evening session).

[49] Notably the clauses permitting employment of "scientific and experienced persons" at higher salaries, and welcoming "persons who possess capital, and who do not wish to be employed."

[50] Article V, section 7.

previous services as justice shall require." [51] Silence and mystery descended once more over the disposition of the surplus which the community was expected to accumulate. And finally, though Owen certainly expected the community to purchase or lease the property of New Harmony from him, not a word was said in the constitution about this elementary relationship between founder and members.

The new voyage had begun, but the chartroom was empty. Owen had failed to deliver the large-scale maps he had promised, and the New Harmonites had thrown overboard the pocket atlas by which they had tried to steer themselves thus far.

Under the circumstances disillusionment was inevitable. Even so, its rapidity was startling. Two weeks to the day after adopting the constitution, the members gave up the attempt to make it work, and requested "the aid of MR. OWEN for one year, in conducting and superintending the concerns of the Community." [52] This was embodied in a formal agreement on March 4, 1826, the members putting themselves "under the sole direction of Mr. Owen until the 1st January 1827, and agreeing to be responsible for the loss if any, and to keep the gain if any." The new constitution had become "as nothing," [53] and even a retreat to the Preliminary Society was impossible, for it had all but completed the process of winding up its affairs. [54]

The crisis that destroyed the new community organization so quickly was a crisis of morale, not of economics. Doubtless the reorganization had disrupted the none too successful functioning of the New Harmony industries, but neither financial ruin nor starvation actually stared the members in the face in February 1826. Rather, as the intoxication of Owen's coming wore off, they suddenly realized how deeply they had now committed themselves to a way of life and a set of economic arrangements concerning which few were without misgivings. Even the most enthusiastic New Harmonites had noted the defects of the Preliminary Society, and all had looked forward to the return of Owen, the man of practical experience who would put affairs to rights. Now it suddenly dawned on them that he had

[51] Article VIII. Departing members, it is true, were guaranteed the return of any money they had deposited on arrival (an indication that community of property did not mean the pooling of members' assets), and they were promised their equitable share of the value of any real estate acquired during the period of their membership. Articles X, VII.

[52] New-Harmony Gazette, I, 175 (Feb. 22, 1826).

[53] Pears Papers, pp. 76 (March 21, 1826), 67 (March 4, 1826). See also D. Macdonald, Diaries, pp. 337–38, and New-Harmony Gazette, I, 190 (March 8, 1826).

[54] The final public meeting adjourned on Feb. 28, 1826, after fixing March 5 as the date on which the Preliminary Society would cease. It authorized the committee to continue its work beyond that date until all accounts should be settled. "Proceedings of the Preliminary Meeting" (MS), Feb. 28, 1826.

remedied no single defect, but had merely induced them to make the system permanent and to assume heavy responsibilities for maintaining it.

The first shock of realization came only three days after the constitutional convention adjourned. On February 8, 1826, the committee of the Preliminary Society brought in its report evaluating the labor which members had performed to date.[55] Any expectation that the community would soon produce an abundance for all was dashed to the ground. "They have not by their Valuation List of labor," wrote Thomas Pears, "allowed me and the children who work, enough to pay the board of the family according to the low rates of board established by the Committee themselves."[56] Hard work and meager living must clearly be the rule for months and years to come. Owen had talked of a land flowing with milk and honey; the valuation list was a reminder of the forty years in the wilderness.

As the members of the community glimpsed the long journey ahead they began to reflect more seriously upon the character of their fellow pilgrims. The casual associations of the Preliminary Society had been amiable enough, and, in the enthusiasm that came with drafting a constitution, universal brotherhood and equality were intoxicating abstractions. Unhesitatingly the convention welcomed all previous members into the new society, without discrimination or selection, and flatly rejected the moderate requirement that new arrivals should reside in the town a month before being elected to full membership.[57] In the days that followed, the members began to realize what they had done. "No one is to be favored above the rest, as all are to be in a state of perfect equality," wrote Mrs. Thomas Pears, reporting the idealistic sentiments of the convention. But in her next sentence she broke down: "Oh, if you could see some of the rough uncouth creatures here, I think you would find it rather hard to look upon them exactly in the light of brothers and sisters. . . . I am sure I cannot in sincerity look upon these as my equals, and that if I must appear to do it, I cannot either act or speak the truth."[58] The attempt to bring about equality and union at a single stroke had the paradoxical effect of opening wide fissures in the community. Social distinctions and religious differences had never been as sharp as they became in the months following this brief experiment in forced and premature social unity.[59]

[55] "Proceedings of the Preliminary Meeting" (MS), Feb. 8, 1826. See above, n. 25.

[56] *Pears Papers,* p. 65 (Feb. 16, 1826).

[57] "Minutes of the Convention" (MS), Feb. 5, 1826 (evening session); *New-Harmony Gazette,* I, 166 (Feb. 15, 1826).

[58] *Pears Papers,* p. 60 (Jan. 28, 1826).

[59] See especially the observations of Karl Bernhard, Duke of Saxe-Weimar-Eisenach, who visited New Harmony from April 13 to 21, 1826. *Reise Sr. Hoheit*

Owen's first problem, as the failure of the new constitution became evident, was to deal with the separate cliques into which the community had suddenly and unexpectedly crystallized. The earliest to demand attention was a group to whom Owen's religious views were peculiarly repugnant—"native back-woodsmen, strongly tinctured with methodism," according to one description. They had stuck it out under the Preliminary Society, but they refused to sign a constitution that would bind them irrevocably to a community where deistic ideas prevailed. By February 15, 1826, ten days after the adjournment of the convention, they had made arrangements to form a separate community. Though commonly referred to as Community No. II, they adopted officially the name Macluria, in tribute to William Maclure, whose unfavorable opinion of organized religion they obviously did not know. Before the end of March they had published their own articles of association, totally different from those of the parent community, but equally vague with respect to economic arrangements. Owen co-operated to the full, turning over to them twelve or thirteen hundred acres of uncleared land two miles from the village of New Harmony. By the middle of March they had erected nine log cabins, into which eighty persons crowded; and during the summer their numbers increased to perhaps 150. Though isolated from the disputes that agitated the village of New Harmony, they were not immune to the spirit of dissension. A public notice, dated October 24, 1826, announced the deposition of three officers of the Macluria Society, and gave outward sign of the schism that was to bring the community to an end the following month.[60]

A second separatist movement arose among a group of English farmers who had been attracted to New Harmony from Birkbeck's settlement in Illinois. The frontier experience had not erased their national self-consciousness, compounded partly of sheer prejudice

---

des Herzogs Bernhard zu Sachsen-Weimar-Eisenach durch Nord-Amerika in den Jahren 1825 und 1826, hrsg. Heinrich Luden (2 vols., Weimar, 1828), II, 134–54; English translation (2 vols., Philadelphia, 1828), II, 106–23; reprinted in Lindley, ed., Indiana As Seen by Early Travelers, pp. 418–37. This will be cited hereafter as Karl Bernhard, Travels, page references being given to the last-mentioned reprint.
60 The articles of association of Macluria were published in the New-Harmony Gazette, I, 209–10 (March 29, 1826), which also carried brief notices of its affairs from time to time: I, 166, 190, 227, 230, 262–63, 268; II, 7 (advertisement), 31 (advertisement), 207 (Feb. 15, 1826–March 28, 1827). Other contemporary descriptions or references are in Co-operative Magazine, II, 46 (Jan. 1827); Pears Papers, pp. 67, 70, 78, 80; Maclure-Fretageot Correspondence, p. 340; D. Macdonald, Diaries, p. 337; Paul Brown, Twelve Months, pp. 22, 61, 72, 122; and Karl Bernhard, Travels, pp. 428–29, 434.

and partly of well-justified contempt for the slipshod agricultural methods of their neighbors. Once Community No. II announced its independence, the English farmers came forward with proposals for a Community No. III. Owen was friendly to the idea, and granted them fourteen hundred acres—the best land, everyone agreed—for $7,000 on time.[61] The new project was announced on March 8, 1826, and in April it published its constitution, a document that followed very closely the one prepared for Macluria.[62] The only startling innovation was in its name, Feiba-Peveli. Stedman Whitwell, the architect, not content with designing the edifice of the new social order, devised for it also a new geographical nomenclature, in which latitude and longitude were translated into letters, and euphony was left to take care of itself. The English farmers paid tribute to their fellow countryman by adopting his scheme, and they came off pretty well, all things considered. If they had lived at Port Jackson, according to Whitwell's examples, they would have had to explain away the name Filts-Bubep.[63]

The new Community No. III erected frame houses as well as log cabins and enjoyed the luxury of glass in their windows. To the prejudiced eye of Whitwell, their agricultural methods were far superior to those of the American backwoodsmen at Macluria, whose labors betrayed "the slovenliness of the race"; but a more impartial observer thought that "the whole was attended to rather too much *en amateur.*" [64] There was less crowding than at Community No. II, for the population was only half as large. And national prejudice proved a more enduring bond of union than social idealism. One suspects that Owenism was quietly set aside, for the one public celebration at Feiba-Peveli to be recorded in print was an old-fashioned festival of harvest home.[65] Hardly noticed by the villagers at New Harmony, and untouched by their particular dissensions, the English farmers continued their group life long after the failure of New

[61] *Maclure-Fretageot Correspondence,* p. 340; *Pears Papers,* p. 78; Paul Brown, *Twelve Months,* pp. 22, 126; Donald Macdonald to George Flower, New Harmony, May 12, 1825, MS in Chicago Historical Society, printed in Flower, *History of the English Settlement,* pp. 373–74; see also *ibid.,* pp. 282–83.

[62] *New-Harmony Gazette,* I, 225–26 (April 12, 1826), see also p. 190 (March 8). The earliest references to the community are dated March 4, 1826. *Pears Papers,* p. 67; D. Macdonald, *Diaries,* p. 337.

[63] Stedman Whitwell, "New Nomenclature Suggested for Communities, Etc.," *New-Harmony Gazette,* I, 226–27 (April 12, 1826).

[64] *Co-operative Magazine,* II, 46 (Jan. 1827); Karl Bernhard, *Travels,* p. 435. See also *ibid.,* pp. 428–29; Paul Brown, *Twelve Months,* pp. 122, 126.

[65] *New-Harmony Gazette,* II, 342 (Aug. 1, 1827), frequently but erroneously said to have been the last published news of the community. See, for example, George B. Lockwood, *The New Harmony Movement* (New York, 1905), p. 174.

Harmony itself was complete,[66] and in the end the land passed quietly into their individual ownership.[67]

So rich was New Harmony in discords that it could suffer two substantial secessions without perceptibly diminishing its stock. Hard on the heels of Communities No. II and III came a project for No. IV. This was the most unexpected development of all, for its source was not dissent but hyperenthusiasm, and its leaders included Owen's own sons.

No group at New Harmony felt a greater attachment to its theoretical principles than did the young intellectuals. "This perfect equality," wrote Maclure in July 1826, "offers a charm which outweighs every idea of fortune and ambition." [68] The inescapable dilemma of the intellectual confronted each of them, however. The very ardency of their devotion to the cause often made them impatient of ordinary men and women who still clung to one or another fragment of the mores that were supposedly outmoded. Robert L. Jennings, a former Universalist minister, to take one example, had preached the most thoroughgoing equalitarianism from the pulpit of the Preliminary Society, but so disdainful was he of the masses who moved more slowly that the public meeting came to the verge of censuring him for having allegedly "treated the members with Ridicule." [69] The community introduced a distinctive costume, with

---

[66] On March 8, 1828, Community No. III held its last reported meeting and appointed a business agent. *New-Harmony Gazette,* III, 167 (March 19, 1828). A month later fire destroyed a "log building . . . , hitherto occupied by Community No. 3, as a brewery." *Ibid.,* III, 199 (April 16, 1828). The quoted phrase can be interpreted to mean that the community had already dissolved, and the public notice concerning a business agent may be taken as evidence of growing dissension, but an opposite interpretation of these, the last two published references, is equally possible. Feiba-Peveli was also mentioned, but very briefly, in *New-Harmony Gazette,* I, 230, 262–63, 268, 271; II, 206–7, 263, 342, 407; III, 39 (April 12, 1826–Nov. 7, 1827); and Paul Brown, *Twelve Months,* p. 34.

[67] Lockwood, *New Harmony Movement,* p. 176.

[68] Communication from Maclure, dated July 4, 1826, in *Revue encyclopédique,* XXXI, 801–2 (sept. 1826), also reprinted in translation in *Co-operative Magazine,* I, 373–75 (Dec. 1826); the quotation is from the latter, p. 375.

[69] "Proceedings of the Preliminary Meeting" (MS), Jan. 30, Feb. 1, 1826. Jennings left New Harmony in April 1826, was active in the Franklin Community at Haverstraw, N.Y., during the summer of that year, returned to New Harmony in 1828 to conduct a school, then left with Robert Dale Owen the following spring and became active in the free-thought movement in the east. See *New-Harmony Gazette,* III, 316, 320, 382 (July 30, Sept. 24, 1828); James M'Knight, *Discourse Exposing Robert Owen's System as Practised by the Franklin Community, at Haverstraw* (New York, 1826), pp. 10–15; *The Correspondent* (New York), I, 384 (July 7, 1827); Albert Post, *Popular Freethought in America,* pp. 39, 65, 78, 84, 175–77, 181. For contemporary characterizations of Jennings at New Harmony, see "Pelham Letters," pp. 370, 373, 376, 413, *et passim;* Karl Bernhard, *Travels,* pp. 423, 436; *Maclure-Fretageot Correspondence,* pp. 400–1.

pantaloons for men and women (the "Bloomer costume" of a later generation), and the "higher class of society" adopted it with such alacrity that what was intended as a mark of equality became a badge of aristocracy.[70] Despite their principles, the intellectuals found it difficult to be at ease with fellow members possessing different tastes and interests, and the embarrassed aloofness that resulted was hardly distinguishable from social snobbishness pure and simple, such as undeniably marked the conduct of a certain few at New Harmony.[71]

In the end this cleavage between the so-called Literati and the rest of the members produced the deepest and most enduring division within the community of New Harmony. Its first manifestation was the abortive project for a Community No. IV. Owen's eldest son, Robert Dale, played the leading role at the outset. In 1824 and 1825 he had fretted in England—"spoilt for every life but that of a community," he felt [72]—while his younger brother William took part in the great adventure. On January 23, 1826, at last, he reached New Harmony. When the constitutional convention began two days later, he threw himself wholeheartedly into its labors. But when the new society disintegrated, he, his brother William, and Robert L. Jennings impatiently organized Community No. IV early in March 1826, proposing to take over most of the buildings of New Harmony and to exclude all the summer soldiers and the sunshine patriots. It was doubtless a well-meant plan to make the new system work by unifying the efforts of those completely devoted to its principles. To persons outside the select group, however, it appeared nothing but an aristocratic *coup d'état*. Robert Owen saw the danger. By a convenient rationalization he had looked upon Communities No. II and III as cuttings from the vine, planted in different soil. But the new proposal called for the actual partitioning of the village of New Harmony, and Owen put his foot down. He offered the young enthusiasts a tract of virgin woodland in which they might "cut down trees and build log cabins as fast as they pleased," [73] and the movement quickly collapsed.

It was one thing for Owen to insist that Community No. I must remain a unit. It was another to make that unit into a workable society. The second reorganization, which Owen began on February 19, 1826, was particularly difficult because he had so long postponed coming to grips with basic economic and financial issues. With morale

---

[70] Karl Bernhard, *Travels*, pp. 424, 430; *Pears Papers*, p. 82.

[71] See Karl Bernhard, *Travels*, p. 430, and compare pp. 425–26, 431, 432–33.

[72] William Owen to Robert Owen, Vincennes, Feb. 7, 1825, MS no. 58 in Owen papers, Manchester.

[73] *Pears Papers*, pp. 67, 72 (quotation), 75, 78 (March 4–21, 1826); Paul Brown, *Twelve Months*, pp. 14, 18; D. Macdonald, *Diaries*, p. 337.

already at a low ebb he was now forced to reveal the frightening realities to the community.

Owen had paid $95,000 to the Rappites for their land and buildings in April 1825.[74] He had expended $30,000 in subsidizing the expenses of the Preliminary Society in 1825, and in January 1826 he had brought with him an additional $15,000 worth of goods for the store. The costs of more than a year of constant travel had been heavy. It is safe to say that Owen had already paid out three-fifths of his fortune of $250,000 on the experiment at New Harmony,[75] and he

[74] The agreement to purchase New Harmony that Owen signed on Jan. 3, 1825, apparently involved a price of about $125,000, payable in installments. On April 21, 1825, just after his return from Washington, he struck a new bargain, paying $95,000 in cash for all the real property, that is, 20,097.13 acres, with all buildings and improvements, expressly including "the Town Clock and Bells, all the furniture of every description in the Tavern, the Copper Brew Kettle, nine Dye Kettles, some of which are Iron and some Copper, thirty large & ten small Stoves & Pipes, the Cotton Gin, two woolen carding Engines, and One complete set of Blacksmith's tools." Penal bond, Frederick Rapp, for himself and as attorney for George Rapp and associates, to Robert Owen, April 21, 1825, MS copy in Owen papers, Manchester, nos. 66 and 129 (these two documents, now separated, apparently belong together). This bond promised, under penalty of $250,000, to deliver an unincumbered title in fee simple as soon as the bills of exchange tendered that day by Owen were honored. These bills, payable in London three days after sight, totalled £19,451, 5s., 5d.; in addition Owen bound the bargain with one dollar in American currency. The deed was actually delivered on Dec. 10, 1825, with the consideration stated (apparently on the basis of the superseded original agreements) as $125,000. Posey County, Indiana, "Deeds," liber D, p. 206 (recorded Jan. 18, 1826). On the day he made the payments, Owen notified his New Lanark partner William Allen of the transaction and added: "I have bought the flocks & herds & implements of husbandry & stock of store goods &c altogether as much in value including one years stock of provisions for a thousand people, as in England would have cost a princely fortune, for these articles I get 2 & 3 years credit if I do not find it more advantages [sic] to pay for them at the end of this year." Owen to Allen, New Harmony, April 21, 1825, MS no. 56 in Owen papers, Manchester. He actually signed notes totalling $40,000 for these additional chattels, payable in two equal installments on the first of May in 1827 and 1828. See *Address Delivered by Robert Owen, . . . at the Franklin Institute in . . . Philadelphia, on . . . June 25, 1827; To Which Is Added, An Exposition of the Pecuniary Transactions between That Gentleman and William M'Clure*, taken in shorthand by M. T. C. Gould (Philadelphia, 1827), pp. 30–36; cited hereafter as Owen, *Pecuniary Transactions*, with page references to the *New-Harmony Gazette*, in which the pamphlet was reprinted, II, 345–47, 353–54 (Aug. 8 and 15, 1827). See also *Maclure-Fretageot Correspondence*, p. 340. The $40,000 was eventually paid by Maclure, so does not figure among Owen's outlays. See below, p. 197.

[75] On Owen's $30,000 subsidy in 1825 see above, p. 167, n. 26; on the additional $15,000 expended in January 1826 see *Maclure-Fretageot Correspondence*, pp. 340, 376. Early in January 1825 the Flowers were prepared to lend Owen $15,000 at six percent, $5,000 of which represented the commission they received for negotiating the sale of Harmonie to him. See incomplete memorandum, initialed G.F., written on pp. 3–4 of Owen to George Flower, Harmony [Jan. 2, 1825], MS in Chicago Historical Society. There is no evidence that Owen took advantage of

still owed Rapp $40,000, due in equal installments on the first of May in 1827 and 1828. He never intended this as a gift to the inhabitants of New Harmony,[76] whatever some of them may have thought, but he had thus far failed to make clear the precise financial responsibility he expected them to assume. This he was at last obliged to do in March 1826.

Owen's plan was in reality simple and aboveboard. He offered to turn over to the community a part of his lands, their value to be assessed by a committee from the community itself, and payment would be accepted over a period of twelve years, with interest at five per cent. In the event of default the property would revert to him, on the stipulation, however, that it would never be appropriated to other than communitarian purposes.[77] Under the Preliminary Society, of course, the larger risks had all been Owen's. No member stood to lose more than the difference between what he might have earned elsewhere and what he received by way of subsistence at New Harmony. Now, however, the members were asked to accept an obligation that would weigh heavily even if the community were successful, and would involve them individually in ruin should the enterprise fail. Suddenly the shiftlessness of fellow members assumed a new importance. The lazy, the inefficient, and the irresponsible had constituted a drag on the community before, now they became a direct and personal liability to every subscriber.

The arrangement had been accepted without objection by Communities No. II and III, but their obligation had been small. The lands of Macluria were valued at less than $5,000, and those of Feiba-Peveli at only $7,000.[78] For Community No. I the situation was different. Its domain included practically all the buildings which the Rappites had left, and the valuation came to $126,520, including $88,000 for the land. Utter dismay greeted the announcement of this sum

---

this. In April 1825 he reported that he had drawn nearly £1,300, or about $6,000, during the spring, over and above the purchase price of New Harmony. Owen to William Allen, New Harmony, April 21, 1825, MS no. 56 in Owen papers, Manchester. This was probably the cost of his travel and propaganda during the hundred days in the east. These four ascertainable items of expenditure (purchase price, subsidies, and traveling expenses) totalled nearly $150,000, all before the end of the Preliminary Society. On Owen's total expenditure see below, p. 198.

[76] He made this perfectly clear in a speech while he was back in London: "Mr. OWEN, in reply to a question, said that the property of each community was to be invested in the members of it. For himself, he never would again invest property with a view to profit. Whatever he had done or would do in America, he would be content with the simple interest of his capital invested there." London *Times*, Sept. 27, 1825, p. 2:6.

[77] Paul Brown, *Twelve Months*, p. 22; *Pears Papers*, pp. 76–77.

[78] *Maclure-Fretageot Correspondence*, p. 340; Paul Brown, *Twelve Months*, pp. 22, 126.

on March 18, 1826. To make matters worse, Owen confused and antagonized the members by asking $20,000 for credit, over and above the interest to be charged.[79] The idea of making any payment at all infuriated extreme communists like Paul Brown, but even those who expected to assume some responsibility were appalled at the immensity of the risk. "Whatever may be the terms," wrote Thomas Pears, "I have no intention of making myself responsible, for I can see no prospect of producing enough to maintain us." [80]

The reorganization on which Owen had been laboring for a month was threatened with complete collapse. Hastily he selected twenty-four persons who were willing to go along with his plans, denominated them the "nucleus" of a permanent community, and entered into an agreement by which they assumed responsibility for the payments and in return were vested with authority to admit members on like terms, and to establish subordinate grades of membership. By March 21, 1826, the "nucleus" had assumed authority and the second reorganization in two months was completed.[81]

During the month of April 1826 the community enjoyed a period of comparative stability under its new organization. Meetings were incessant and changes of policy frequent, but New Harmony was for a time spared the turmoil of a complete reorganization such as it had already twice experienced, and was to experience twice again before the year was out. Accounts were being kept once more, according to a system (so far as one can judge) substantially like that of the Preliminary Society.[82] A breathing space was provided, too, for the varied social and cultural activities that gave to life at New Harmony its peculiar charm. In particular, the spring months of 1826 saw the organization and elaboration of the educational and scientific pro-

[79] Thomas Pears to Benjamin Bakewell, March 21, 1826, in *Pears Papers*, pp. 76–77. Paul Brown, who did not arrive until April 2, 1826, gives substantially the same account, but says the valuation was $140,000. Quite possibly Owen was asking, not $20,000 additional for credit, but repayment of $20,000 of the credit he had advanced to the Preliminary Society for subsistence. If so, he failed to make himself clear.

[80] *Pears Papers*, p. 77 (March 21, 1826). Thomas Pears and his family left New Harmony a month or so later.

[81] *Ibid.*; Paul Brown, *Twelve Months*, pp. 15, 19–20; Karl Bernhard, *Travels*, p. 430.

[82] Paul Brown, *Twelve Months*, pp. 16–17. Several account books belonging to 1826 are preserved in the Workingmen's Institute, namely: "New Harmony Community of Equality, March 6th 1826" (ledger, continued to May 31, 1826); "[Ledger No.] 6" (Oct. 3–Nov. 5, no year, but probably 1826); "Journal" (March 14, 1826–May 29, 1827); "Day Book" (Sept. 18, 1826–Jan. 1829); "Sales of Dry Goods for New Harmony Community, Commenced 7th March 1826" (and continued to Feb. 24, 1827); volume of printed forms (July 10–Oct. 12, 1826).

gram that William Maclure had transferred to New Harmony. The three or four hundred children of the community were not only receiving an education far above the general level but were also contributing substantially to their own support by the practical labors that were part of the curriculum.[83] Crates of books, specimens, and apparatus were constantly arriving, research in natural history and mineralogy was going forward, and scientific lectures were part of the public program.[84]

In economic matters, however, the "nucleus" was getting nowhere. It was trying to maintain the principle of equality of remuneration, and was running into the difficulties that every critic of economic equality and community of property had predicted. The work of the community was being done, reported an observer in mid-April, "as a statutory labor imposed on them," which they viewed "in the light of a corvée." [85] To prevent outright loafing the "nucleus" kept elaborate records of labor performed and then ranked the members "in certain degrees of character according to the number of hours' work that appeared against their names on paper." [86] This produced another crop of difficulties. To translate a quantitative measure of time into a qualitative measure of character was utterly unfair to the conscientious workman who "might do more in an hour than another . . . in four." Moreover, it did not reconcile the skilled craftsman to the idea that a day's labor of his was worth no more than the day of an unskilled worker, when he demonstrably contributed far more in the same amount of time to the real wealth of the community.

These conflicts of interest were noted by William Maclure, and he observed also a tendency even more inimical to the educational and scientific enterprise which was nearest his heart—a tendency to deny "that those who work with their heads, or mental labor, are

---

[83] *New-Harmony Gazette,* I, 166–67 (Feb. 15, 1826); William Maclure, "Notice of Mr. Owen's Establishment, in Indiana" (dated March 16, 1826), *American Journal of Science and Arts,* XI (1826), 189–92; *Co-operative Magazine,* I, 373–75 (Dec. 1826); *Maclure-Fretageot Correspondence, passim.*

[84] "Pelham Letters," pp. 407, 411; D. Macdonald, *Diaries,* p. 337; Karl Bernhard, *Travels,* pp. 422, 433, 436–37; *New-Harmony Gazette,* I, 270–71 (May 17, 1826); *Maclure-Fretageot Correspondence,* p. 338 *et seqq.*

[85] Karl Bernhard, *Travels,* p. 433, see also p. 434. As far back as Sept. 2, 1825, Thomas Pears gave his considered judgment to the same effect: "I do not think the men generally do work as well as they would for themselves. Many do, but not the majority, I think." *Pears Papers,* pp. 28–29.

[86] Paul Brown, *Twelve Months,* p. 17. See also William Maclure, "On the Easiest . . . Mode of Extinguishing the Spirit of Competition and Rivalry Which Is the . . . Degradation of the Old System of Society," *New-Harmony Gazette,* I, 268 (May 17, 1826). Quotations in the remainder of this paragraph and in the next are from Maclure's article.

as productive as those who work with their hands." Time was running out for the "nucleus" in May 1826,[87] and Maclure felt obliged to take a hand. In a communication to the *New-Harmony Gazette* on May 17, 1826, he supported unequivocally the principle of "equality in rights and property," but suggested dividing the population of New Harmony into different communities, each consisting of the persons engaged in a particular occupation. Individuals within each community would still be laboring for the common good, not for private profit, hence the rearrangement would not "bring them one iota nearer the individual system." The federated communities would exchange their products freely with one another. But the labor necessary to produce the total output expected of each community, Maclure believed, would be far more justly apportioned among the individual members when the group was small and homogeneous. Moreover, the financial responsibility of each community would be limited to paying for the property it actually used, a sum more "within the sphere of the previous habits of calculation" of the members.

Owen was impressed with the suggestion, and after some preliminary discussion he put it to the vote of the community on May 28, 1826.[88] The adoption of the proposal constituted the third reorganization of New Harmony in four months. After some shuffling about of occupations, three independent communities emerged—a School or Education Society, an Agricultural and Pastoral Society,[89] and a

[87] Though Owen radiated the most complete optimism in his "Retrospect of the Commencement and Progress of the New System of Society, for the First Year, in the United States," dated May 9, 1826, there is a marked difference between his reports of progress at Communities No. II and III and his cautious statement concerning affairs in the village itself: "The great experiment in New-Harmony is still going on to ascertain whether a large heterogeneous mass of persons, collected by chance, can be amalgamated into one community." *New-Harmony Gazette*, I, 262–63 (May 10, 1826).

[88] Paul Brown, *Twelve Months*, pp. 18–19, 23–25. The *New-Harmony Gazette*, II, 294–95 (June 7, 1826) printed the first part of Owen's speech of May 28, 1826, and concluded with a promise to publish at the first opportunity certain regulations "of the highest importance" which Owen had proposed at the meeting and which had "at length received the sanction of the whole society." It never published them. Maclure and Owen both suggested a choice between two alternatives: a single community with separate departments for the different occupations, and a federated group of communities. Only the latter seems to have received serious consideration at this juncture.

[89] The Agricultural and Pastoral Society adopted a constitution on July 30, 1826, but it is no more illuminating than its various predecessors. Text in *New-Harmony Gazette*, I, 362–63 (Aug. 9, 1826). Other contemporary references are: *ibid.*, I, 390, 397; II, 206; Shawnee-Town *Illinois Gazette*, Nov. 11, 1826, p. 3:1–2; *Co-operative Magazine*, II, 46–47 (Jan. 1827); Paul Brown, *Twelve Months*, pp. 24–25, 28, 35–36; *Maclure-Fretageot Correspondence*, pp. 343, 352, 357, 359–61.

Mechanic and Manufacturing Society.[90] They were bound together by a Board of Union, and they traded with one another by labor notes —apparently the first use of that mechanism of exchange which Owen had suggested in 1820, which he was later to elaborate in England, and which Josiah Warren was to employ in "Time Stores" at Cincinnati, at Modern Times, and elsewhere.[91] The most important aspect of this third reorganization was the creation of a separate School Society. For the moment Maclure and his associates had a free hand to order the educational affairs of New Harmony as they pleased, while Owen wrestled with the problem of organizing its economic life.

The third reorganization had made Owen's task no whit the easier. In fact, it tended to make him the focus of all antagonisms. The basic economic difficulty, of course, was simply that the community as a whole produced less than it consumed. It produced no more and consumed no less when divided into three. Previously, however, the store had been part of the community, and the accounts (under the Preliminary Society, at least) had been adjusted in favor of the members so that their remuneration at least equaled their withdrawals. The tavern, too, had produced a steady cash income, which presumably went into the community funds. Upon the partition of New

[90] At first there was apparently a Mechanic Society and a separate Manufacturing Society. Paul Brown, *Twelve Months*, p. 25. The latter was perhaps the "cut off mill society" referred to by Maclure on Sept. 25, 1826. *Maclure-Fretageot Correspondence*, p. 371 [the reading "cut off *mile*" given there, is, I now believe, incorrect]. The two societies united, probably immediately as Paul Brown says (p. 25), though the shifting combinations make the other sources somewhat ambiguous. No constitution was published, but there are contemporary references in *New-Harmony Gazette*, I, 390, 397; II, 206; Shawnee-Town *Illinois Gazette*, Nov. 11, 1826, p. 3:1-2; *Co-operative Magazine*, II, 46-47 (Jan. 1827); Paul Brown, *Twelve Months*, pp. 24-25, 27-28, 35, 36; *Maclure-Fretageot Correspondence*, pp. 343, 352, 354, 359-61. Both the Agricultural and the Mechanic Societies were located in the village of New Harmony, and the latter had about twice as many members as the former. *Co-operative Magazine*, II, 46-47.

[91] The fullest description of the Board of Union and of the labor notes is in an article from the *Louisville Courier*, reprinted in Shawnee-Town *Illinois Gazette*, Nov. 11, 1826, p. 3:1-2. See also *Co-operative Magazine*, II, 47 (Jan. 1827), and Paul Brown, *Twelve Months*, p. 24. The idea of using labor-time as a medium of exchange was propounded by Owen in 1820 in his *Report to the County of Lanark*, reprinted in *Life*, I.A, 266-69. On his later development of the scheme in the National Equitable Labour Exchange of 1832-34, see Podmore, *Robert Owen*, II, 403-22, and the illustration facing p. 418. On Josiah Warren's "Time Stores," see the poem reprinted from the Cincinnati *Saturday Evening Chronicle* in *New-Harmony Gazette*, III, 94 (Dec. 26, 1827), and the accounts in Lockwood, *New Harmony Movement*, pp. 294-306 (with illustrations facing pp. 296, 300, 304), in William Bailie, *Josiah Warren, the First American Anarchist: A Sociological Study* (Boston, 1906), pp. 9-24, 42-49, and in Noyes, *History of American Socialisms*, pp. 95-101.

Harmony into Agricultural, Mechanic, and School Societies, however, Owen properly kept in his own hands both the store, with the $30,000 stock of goods he had purchased for it, and the tavern. Though no one but Owen had the shadow of a claim to the properties, and though there was no logical reason for attaching them to any one of the separate communities, the cry immediately went up that Owen was shifting "into the characters of a retailer and tavern keeper, to save by nine-penny and four-pence-half-penny gains, after the manner of pedlars, the money which he had lost." To appease the clamor, Owen gave a half interest in the store to the Mechanic Society and turned over the tavern to the Agricultural Society. The latter immediately raised the price for board and lodging fifty per cent, while the former decided to keep on losing money for Owen at the old rates. But neither was satisfied.[92]

The farmers and the mechanics did not exhaust their ill feeling upon Owen, but vented some on each other and on the School Society. There were quarrels about boundaries, and in the disputed areas crops were allowed to run to weeds. When plots of land were allotted to individual families, extremists denounced the action as a violation of the principle of common property.[93] Eventually the two other communities refused to make payment to the School Society for the education of their children, and reciprocity between the organizations broke down completely.

The fact seems to be that Macluria, Feiba-Peveli, and the School Society had siphoned off most of the responsible and devoted members of the community, leaving under Owen's immediate direction mainly the drifters, the parasites, and the fanatics. There had always been plenty of these. Long before the Preliminary Society got under way William Owen warned his father that many prospective members had been "long accustomed to be dilatory in business & to be thinking only of overreaching others & acting an insincere part." Robert Owen was so far from suspecting duplicity, however, that he seemed to Maclure "to require nothing to found unlimmited confidence upon than a perfect coincidence with all his opinions, which few but rog[ue]s and hypocrites would even pretend to." Under such circumstances the selective process operated in reverse. In the fall of 1826, after the many secessions of the spring and summer, Maclure took issue with a competent observer who estimated that only a quarter of the remaining population at New Harmony were "good for

[92] Paul Brown, *Twelve Months*, pp. 24 (quotation), 25; *Maclure-Fretageot Correspondence*, pp. 343, 350, 354, 358–59, 361, 376 and n. 7. Brown asserts that Owen originally proposed a Society of External Commerce as one of the communities after the partition, but there is no other evidence of this. *Twelve Months*, p. 24.
[93] Paul Brown, *Twelve Months*, pp. 26, 31.

nothing." His own estimates ran from three-fourths to nine-tenths.[94] Whatever the proportion, it was disastrously high.

Malingering and incompetence ruined the community and Owen financially, and in the long run they were the significant facts. But the venom of doctrinaire extremists was destroying the *esprit de corps* of the community during 1826 and must have been at least as hard for Owen to bear. The central figure in this was Paul Brown,[95] who arrived on April 2, 1826. His coming had been heralded by a series of contributions to the *New-Harmony Gazette,* preaching the idea of community of property in its most extreme form.[96] At New

[94] William Owen to Robert Owen, Vincennes, Feb. 7, 1825, MS no. 58 in Owen papers, Manchester; *Maclure-Fretageot Correspondence,* pp. 377, 346. For other characterizations of the population by Maclure, probably the most disinterested of those who had a real opportunity to observe, see *ibid.,* pp. 337, 339, 343, 350, 354, 370, 378, 388. On Owen's inability to judge men, see also his son's matured conclusion: "His weak point always was, to believe in every body & every thing, that favored, or professed to favor, his peculiar views. . . . Again & again he has given his confidence to the most undeserving persons, merely because they professed unbounded admiration for, & implicit faith in, his system." R. D. Owen to Nicholas P. Trist, New Harmony, June 10, 1853, MS in Trist papers, Library of Congress.

[95] Paul Brown's *Twelve Months in New Harmony; Presenting a Faithful Account of the Principal Occurrences which Have Taken Place There within That Period; Interspersed with Remarks* (Cincinnati, 1827) is, by default, the principal source for events between April 2, 1826, and June 2, 1827. The bulk of it was completed at New Harmony on April 22, 1827 (hence the "twelve months" of the title); a postscript, entitled "Five Weeks More," was added in Cincinnati in July. It appears to be based on a diary, or at least on memoranda contemporaneous with the events, and in chronological and other strictly factual matters its accuracy can be demonstrated wherever an independent source exists. On the other hand, its interpretations are warped, sometimes into self-contradiction, by the author's extreme bias. The Education Society, to take one example, "clearly carried the marks of an aristocratical and exclusive spirit" when it separated from the rest of the community, but as soon as it developed an antagonistic attitude toward Owen it became, for Brown, the nearest approach to "a republican community" at New Harmony. *Twelve Months,* pp. 28, 83. Brown's communistic principles, however, were maintained with rigid consistency throughout his life. Before coming to New Harmony he had published *A Disquisition on Faith* (Washington, 1822), and *An Enquiry Concerning the Nature, End, and Practicability of a Course of Philosophical Education* (Washington, 1822). Immediately after his departure he produced not only *Twelve Months in New-Harmony* but also *A Dialogue on Commonwealths* (Cincinnati, 1828). Subsequently he published *The Radical: and Advocate of Equality* (Albany, 1834), and he left an unpublished MS entitled "The Woodcutter or a Glimpse of the 19th Century at the West" (original in Illinois State Historical Library), which contains material on New Harmony. As late as 1844 he was contributing to communitarian and reform journals. See *Regenerator* (New York), I, 92, 104 (June 1, 22, 1844).

[96] Paul Brown discusses these contributions in *Twelve Months,* pp. 11–12, 37–40, 70–74. The facts he gives about publication correspond exactly to the series entitled "Gray Light," signed S. or $, which appeared in thirty numbered installments in the *New-Harmony Gazette* between Dec. 21, 1825, and Sept. 20, 1826.

Harmony he was immediately offended by the very existence of book-keeping in a community. Before long he had convinced himself that Owen was nothing but a "speculator in land, power, influence, riches, and the glories of this world." At once he embarked upon a crusade against the "lord proprietor." Though the majority of those who had been at New Harmony could recollect nothing of the kind, Brown insisted that in 1825 Owen had promised the members to divide his property with them. This, Brown insisted, was the only possible basis of a community, and he wanted Owen and Maclure to turn over, not only their holdings at New Harmony, but all the money and property they might possess elsewhere. When, instead, Owen insisted that the separate communities should agree to purchase the lands they occupied, Brown's cup of wrath was filled to overflowing:

> When any man, who, having presented himself in the character of a philanthropist, . . . asks pay for his land or houses which he has destined for the foundation of such establishment, either principal or interest, to be secured as private property to himself or his heirs, from that moment he forfeits the confidence of all considerate persons who are in pursuit of realizing a true commonwealth upon earth. This was the beginning of Robert Owen's iniquities.[97]

Brown filled the columns of the *Gazette* with this doctrine until, after thirty numbers, the editor felt obliged to stem the flow of words. Brown, convinced that freedom of the press had been annihilated at New Harmony, took to holding sparsely attended public meetings, to nailing theses on doorways, and to heckling Owen at the end of his lectures by asking, "Would you be willing to make common stock of all your property . . . ?"[98] "That is," wrote Maclure in a sarcastic paraphrase of the question, "we are here in expectation of making all the benifit from your property as the principle motive that keeps us here."[99]

It is difficult to measure the actual influence of this Thersites. His book makes him appear a central figure in the conflicts at New Harmony, yet in several passages he admits the smallness of his following.[100] Few, indeed, were likely to be attracted to the Spartan

Vol. I, nos. 13–52 (excepting only nos. 21, 30, 34, 37, 43, 45–48, and 51), beginning at p. 100 and concluding with pp. 412–13.

[97] *Twelve Months*, pp. 10, 27, 15.

[98] *New-Harmony Gazette*, I, 365 (Aug. 9, 1826), reporting the public meeting of July 30. The questioner was unnamed, but the doctrine was unmistakably Brown's. The discourse which Paul Brown read on Sept. 10, 1826, and the argument he wrote out and posted in early October are printed in *Twelve Months*, pp. 41–50, 67–70.

[99] *Maclure-Fretageot Correspondence*, p. 357, see also pp. 342, 360.

[100] See, for example, *Twelve Months*, pp. 27, 41, 55–56, 70.

regime he sought to impose. He delivered a public harangue against card-playing. He deplored the fact that "persons were spending their time in teaching music and dancing." He was outraged because a "profusion of musical instruments were provided, and great quantities of candles burnt at their balls." And when a puppet show was opened at one of the boarding houses, with a charge for admission, he knew that the social system was doomed.[101] It would be hard to believe, furthermore, that many at New Harmony were ready to follow his economic leadership and, "without wavering or delay, render all their private possessions if they have any, into a common stock." They could hardly have been encouraged or reassured by an argument like this:

What can a person lose, as an individual? He can lose what he owns. How much does one own? That which makes him comfortable; and nothing more. . . . If he has more than this, it does not belong to him. . . . All that this man, then, would have lost as an individual, would be *his comfortable living in a community for the present moment*.[102]

A mere bagatelle!

If Paul Brown influenced events, it was because he was fishing in troubled waters. By September 1826, when he made his greatest oratorical effort at New Harmony, the Owenite experiment was in chaos. Reorganizations and recombinations had failed to make the Agricultural and Mechanic Societies viable.[103] An effort to form another community on the prairies across the Wabash had failed.[104] Owen was faced with the necessity of reorganizing the community for the fourth time. In a public meeting on September 17, 1826, he proposed that all the existing societies (except the school) in the village of New Harmony be dissolved and a new "energetic government" instituted

[101] *New-Harmony Gazette*, I, 292–94 (June 7, 1826); *Twelve Months*, pp. 25, 96, see also pp. 18, 21. Contrast Maclure's opinion in *Maclure-Fretageot Correspondence*, p. 347.

[102] *Twelve Months*, pp. 47, 52.

[103] See Paul Brown, *Twelve Months*, pp. 25, 35; *Maclure-Fretageot Correspondence*, pp. 357, 359–60, 370–71.

[104] A brief reference by Stedman Whitwell makes it clear that the community referred to as "the prairies," located in Illinois some twenty-five miles from New Harmony, was distinct from the Agricultural and Pastoral Society, from Feiba-Peveli, and from the short-lived Owenite organization at Birkbeck's English Settlement. *Co-operative Magazine*, II, 45–46 (Jan. 1827). I overlooked this passage in editing the *Maclure-Fretageot Correspondence*, where the only other references to "the prairies" occur, and consequently offered conjectures that now prove incorrect. Pp. 345 and n. 23, 352, 359–60 and n. 37, 371. Whitwell also mentions an experiment of his own in Illinois, which may have been distinct from "the prairies." *Co-operative Magazine*, II, 48; compare *Maclure-Fretageot Correspondence*, p. 345.

in their stead. By October 2 the new agreement was ready to be signed, and New Harmony Community No. I (as the four-times reborn society was still officially called) began to operate under a board of trustees comprising Owen, his son William, and three associates.[105]

Reorganizations were by this time so frequent that the precise terms became largely meaningless. The truly fateful development during the summer and fall of 1826 was the widening breach between Owen and Maclure. Its origin—simple and understandable enough—was Maclure's abrupt realization that his associate lacked every qualification of an efficient administrator. Personal animosity played no detectable part. Nor did the divergence of the two men represent an abandonment by either of the social radicalism that had brought them together. Maclure stated his position not once but many times: "I must repeat that the cooperative System has rose in my esteem and strong conviction of its utility in exact proportion as the positive conviction of Mr. O's mode being the ruin of it for some time in this country, and that he has been working hard to defeat his own views." [106]

In Maclure's opinion, Owen was not only dissipating his resources by his extravagant subsidies, but was actually corrupting the members of the community. The population of New Harmony had been un-promising to begin with, but their faults had been aggravated "by the force of money, which has produced nothing but waste and destruc-tion of property." A year and a half of Owen's paternalistic manage-ment, wrote Maclure in February 1827, had undermined the fitness of the inhabitants "for cooperative society, as all their instruction has been to consume not to produce, money having been sub-stituted for industry, negligence for care, wastefulness for econ-omy." [107]

Maclure could not be indifferent to Owen's mistakes; too much of his own property was at stake. To be sure, he himself had been care-less at the outset in neglecting to reach a precise understanding with Owen concerning the extent of his financial responsibility at New Harmony. He definitely agreed to assume half the losses that Owen might sustain at New Harmony, up to a limit of $10,000, but he managed to give Owen the impression that he was entering into a full-fledged partnership. In the spring of 1826, after witnessing Owen's

[105] Paul Brown, *Twelve Months*, pp. 59–67, 75–77. The text of the covenant or agreement is given *ibid.*, pp. 61–66. The *New-Harmony Gazette* alluded vaguely to this fourth reorganization on Oct. 11, 1826, and mentioned it again, when it had passed into history, on March 28, 1827. Vol. II, pp. 15, 206 (twelfth paragraph).

[106] *Maclure-Fretageot Correspondence*, p. 366 (Aug. 30, 1826), see also pp. 358, 388.

[107] *Maclure-Fretageot Correspondence*, pp. 339, 388 (June 20, 1826, Feb. 24, 1827), see also pp. 343, 344, 346, 350.

management at first hand, he tried strenuously to disabuse him of this idea. "In all Mr. O's money operations," he wrote,

I thought different and disaproved of them, but was told unless he was allowed his way he could not act, to which at last I so far dissented as to tell him I would back out at the risk of loosing the 10,000 dollars, but that loss must be on transactions that had taken place since our agreement, and that I could not consider the money wasted by the preliminary society or expended in any other way as making a part of his advance, to which he only said he was sorry for it, as he would have confined his plans to his own capital, which I told him he was not too late to do.[108]

As reorganization followed reorganization, Maclure's misgivings grew, and at the third reshuffle, in May 1826, he seized the opportunity to put his educational enterprise beyond Owen's control. By establishing the School Society as an independent entity, and formulating in writing its specific obligations, Maclure felt that he was extricating himself from entanglements that threatened to grow steadily more dangerous. Definite agreements were signed in late May or early June 1826. Maclure received a ten-thousand-year lease to a large segment of the village of New Harmony, including several of its principal public buildings, and some nine hundred acres of land. He turned over $24,500 to Owen at the time, and by the end of the year he had paid all but $11,000 of the total sum of $49,000 that he had agreed to.[109] Once the Education Society was established, Maclure made it perfectly clear to his immediate associates, and did his best to make it equally clear to Owen, that his financial support would be given exclusively to the new organization, and that he would accept no further financial responsibility at New Harmony except for the $10,000 "forfeiture" provided in his first informal understanding with Owen.

As financial co-operation between the two men ceased, co-operation in other matters became more difficult. Differences over educational policy were magnified by mutual distrust until an open break occurred. Maclure had always been more deeply impressed than Owen with the difficulty of educating adults for a new social order, and the latter's successive failures intensified the feeling. "My experience at Harmony," Maclure remarked before the end of 1826, "has given me such a horror for the reformation of grown persons that I shudder

[108] Maclure to Mme Fretageot, Columbus, O., July 9, 1826, in *Correspondence,* p. 342, see also pp. 357, 385. The conversation took place some time before June 8, 1826, when Maclure left New Harmony for a four months' trip.

[109] The lease is not extant, but the above terms were stated both by Paul Brown and by Maclure himself in a letter of Jan. 3, 1827. Brown, *Twelve Months,* p. 27; *Maclure-Fretageot Correspondence,* ed. Bestor, p. 382. But compare *ibid.,* pp. 337, 339, 340, 350, 356, where sums as high as $60,000 were mentioned by Maclure. See also the editor's discussion of the matter, *ibid.,* pp. 334–35.

when I reflect having so many of my friends so near such a desperate undertaking." Moreover, he carried his conclusions one step further: "I have so far lost the little confidence I had in adults or parents that I believe no good system of education can have a fair tryal but with orphans," he wrote Madame Fretageot, "and when I come home we shall consult on the best mode of taking 50 or 100." [110] Such a plan, of course, would put an end to any functional connection between the enterprises of Owen and Maclure at New Harmony.

It was not Maclure, however, who destroyed the reciprocal relation between school and community. The initiative came from the Agricultural and Mechanic Societies. The tendency to undervalue intellectual effort, previously noted by Maclure, became acute once the other inhabitants of New Harmony were asked to pay the School Society for the education of their children, even on the basis of labor for labor. Early in August 1826 the Agricultural Society flatly refused any longer to furnish goods, services, or money by way of tuition, and the Mechanic Society went a step further by repudiating the obligation it had already incurred.[111]

Owen entered the situation not to restrain but to encourage the separation. Despite his reputation as an educator, he actually had little interest in the larger aspects of his colleague's educational program. Maclure, a scientist in his own right, envisaged a close connection between teaching, research, and publication. He would replace the old classical curriculum, but he would replace it with a program in the sciences that would be intellectually significant because pupils would study under men actually engaged in research. Owen, however, took a purely functional view of the School Society. It was a department of the New Harmony enterprise, designed to serve the immediate, practical end of indoctrinating the population for community life. Like certain present-day advocates of "progressive education," he acted as though he believed that facility in newer techniques of instruction was an adequate substitute, in a teacher's qualifications, for the intellectual stimulus that comes from actual participation in the advancement of knowledge. Owen wanted to adapt the curriculum to modern life by emphasizing the sciences, but he regarded the entertaining presentation of a body of ascertained results as the equivalent of a laborious and painful discipline in scientific thinking.

Owen revealed his educational notions in a series of discourses in

[110] *Maclure-Fretageot Correspondence*, pp. 377, 351 (Nov. 28, Aug. 11, 1826), see also pp. 301, 362, 365.

[111] Paul Brown, *Twelve Months*, pp. 34–36. The pupils had been withdrawn by Aug. 11, 1826, when Mme Fretageot reported the fact to Maclure. *Correspondence*, ed. Bestor, p. 352. Maclure's remark about orphans was written the same day, but probably before he learned of these events.

August 1826, and ended by proposing a new system of "social education." The heart of his plan was a thrice-weekly meeting of the entire
community, adults and children alike, to be held in the evening after
the regular hours of schooling were over. Visual aids, in the form
of maps and globes, were to be displayed in the Hall for the teaching
of geographical names. Lectures on various trades and occupations
were to be delivered in place of systematic discussions of mineralogy,
chemistry, or mechanics, on the theory that "one useful thing is as
much a part of science as another." Practical experience was to be the
sole qualification of the lecturer, consequently "no distinction of
teacher and pupil" would be necessary. The scheme, Owen told the
New Harmonites, "requires no more than an honest endeavor on
your part to attend regularly, take your seats quietly, and listen atten-
tively. By this simple process, you will acquire a better education,
and more valuable knowledge than has been given by any system of
instruction heretofore put into practice." [112] Maclure showed considerable restraint when he called this quackery "the parrot method."
But the community promptly adopted the plan.

The educational reorganization worked no better than Owen's
numerous economic reorganizations. He was forced to raid Maclure's
faculty to conduct his day school, and this produced additional bitter-
ness.[113] The community-wide educational sessions in the Hall lasted
only a few weeks. Before long some of the children were being sent
again to the School Society.[114] Maclure had been absent while these
things were happening, but he returned on October 7, 1826, and
threw himself into the task of bringing order into the affairs of the
school and petitioning the legislature for a charter [115] that would,
among other things, put the Education Society beyond Owen's reach.
Maclure's health forced him to leave New Harmony for the south
on November 25, 1826, and four days later Owen knifed him in the
back by demanding part of the land of the Education Society on the
pretext that there had been a "misconception" about the boundary
line.[116]

[112] Owen's three discourses on education, delivered on Aug. 6, 13, and 20, 1826,
were fully reported in the *New-Harmony Gazette*, I, 366–67, 372–75, 382–83, 390–91
(Aug. 9–30, 1826). The quotations are from the final one, p. 390. See also *Maclure-
Fretageot Correspondence*, pp. 356, 359, 361–72; Paul Brown, *Twelve Months*,
pp. 40–41.

[113] See *Maclure-Fretageot Correspondence*, pp. 361–75, 383–86; Paul Brown,
Twelve Months, pp. 75, 82, 116–17; "Pelham Letters," pp. 414–15.

[114] See sources cited and discussed in *Maclure-Fretageot Correspondence*, ed.
Bestor, pp. 374, n. 4, and 375, n. 5.

[115] The bill was tabled on Jan. 17, 1827, and never revived. See *New-Harmony
Gazette*, II, 62, 157, 158–59 (Nov. 22, 1826, Feb. 14, 1827); Indiana *Senate Journal,
1826–27*, pp. 182–83.

[116] *New-Harmony Gazette*, II, 70 (Nov. 29, 1826); Paul Brown, *Twelve Months*,

By the end of the year the stage had been set for the last act of the tragicomedy at New Harmony. Each of three separate but intertwining plots reached its denouement during the first four months of 1827, and the curtain finally came down at the end of April.

To begin with, Owen was forced to undertake his fifth general reorganization of the community, for the trust set up in October 1826 had been no better able than its predecessors to cope with the situation. "The establishment," said a terse report of March 1827, "did not pay its own expenses." [117] Centralization having failed, Owen again tried decentralization. There were two phases to this final effort at reconstruction, one involving the main settlement at New Harmony, the other the outlying parts of Owen's domain. In January 1827 the village population was subdivided once more by occupations.[118] By the end of March the *New-Harmony Gazette* announced that the new system was in operation, with each occupation supporting itself, "paying weekly a small percentage towards the general expenses of the town . . . , determining its own internal regulations, and distributing or exchanging its own produce." Even the *Gazette* had to admit that this arrangement was not the new social system in operation. It continued, "New-Harmony, therefore, is not now a community; but, as was originally intended, a central village, out of, and around which, communities have formed." [119]

To form such outlying communities was, in fact, Owen's principal hope in this fifth and final reorganization. He described his plan in a letter of February 6, 1827. He now believed

that it would promote the real object in view to lay out the lands of Harmony suitably for Communities to encourage such of the members as could not be usefully employed in the Town, to settle in some of these detached Communities according to their respective predilections. . . .

With this view notice was given last week to many of those whose services could not be beneficially employed here, that land, provisions to serve until

pp. 78–83 (which includes a statement by Neef in behalf of the Education Society); *Maclure-Fretageot Correspondence*, pp. 380–83.

[117] *New-Harmony Gazette*, II, 206 (March 28, 1827).

[118] At the beginning of the month the formation of a society of iron founders and steam-engine manufacturers at New Harmony was announced, probably part of this reorganization. Philadelphia *National Gazette*, Jan. 2, 1827, p. 2:1; *Niles' Weekly Register*, XXXI, 307 (Jan. 13, 1827).

[119] *New-Harmony Gazette*, II, 206 (March 28, 1827). On May 6 Owen described the town merely as "the place for the reception of strangers," where "the occupations have formed among themselves a kind of preparatory society." *Ibid.*, 255 (May 9, 1827). By May 27 he had nothing to say of the arrangement by occupations. *Ibid.*, p. 279 (May 30, 1827). As early as April 1, 1827, he was leasing lots in New Harmony, with restrictive clauses that vaguely suggested the continuance of the social system but were without real substance. See Owen's lease to Jonathan Rodgers, April 1, 1827, MS in Lucius C. Embree papers, Indiana State Library.

the next crop, & such other aid as could be afforded from the parent Community would be given to them to form societies of common property, equality & kindness . . . , but that it became necessary for the good of the whole that those among them who could not so unite should remove from Harmony.[120]

Paul Brown screamed that February 1, 1827, when certain residents received their "walking papers," was "DOOMSDAY." [121] There were demands that Owen should pay their traveling expenses, and in general he went through an unpleasant three months, without in the end accomplishing anything toward making the village an efficient economic unit.[122]

The belief that the new communities would soon fill all the surrounding territory was also sheer illusion. During April 1827 Owen drew up grandiose ten-thousand-year leases, released the texts to the papers,[123] and entered into agreements with seven projected societies. Actually not a single group went out from New Harmony as a community, and Owen was in reality entering into arrangements with unknown persons at a distance who proposed to come as colonists. In doing so he made his property fair game for confidence men. His grant of fifteen hundred acres for a Community No. IV was announced with great fanfare on January 21, 1827, but its projector, William G. Taylor of Ohio, proved to be a sharper, from whose toils Owen extricated himself only with heavy losses and after protracted litigation.[124]

[120] Owen to James M. Dorsey, New Harmony, Feb. 6, 1827, MS in Indiana Historical Society. The offer was made orally to the inhabitants but was not published in the *New-Harmony Gazette,* which merely hinted at the new arrangements in early March, and did not describe them fully until the twenty-eighth. See II, 190, 198, 206–7 (March 14, 21, 28, 1827).

[121] Paul Brown, *Twelve Months,* p. 85, see also pp. 92–94.

[122] See Owen's addresses of May 6 and 27, 1827, in *New-Harmony Gazette,* II, 254–55, 278–79 (May 9, 30, 1827); and *Maclure-Fretageot Correspondence,* pp. 388, 391 (Feb. 24, March 2, 1827).

[123] *Co-operative Magazine,* II, 450–54 (Oct. 1827); see also *Niles' Weekly Register,* XXXII, 325–26 (July 14, 1827).

[124] *New-Harmony Gazette,* II, 142, 207; III, 375 (Jan. 31, March 28, 1827; Sept. 17, 1828); Posey County, "Deeds," liber E, pp. 35–39; Posey County Circuit Court, "Complete Record," liber B, pp. 485–500, see also the subsequent suits of Taylor and Owen against each other as listed in the "General Index to Civil Causes" of the same court; Mme Fretageot to Maclure, New Harmony, Oct. 10, 1828, Feb. 13, 1829, MSS in Workingmen's Institute; William Owen to James M. Dorsey, New Orleans, April 5, 1830, MS in Indiana Historical Society; letter of Richard Owen, quoted in Lockwood, *New Harmony Movement,* p. 156; Paul Brown, *Twelve Months,* pp. 83–85; A. J. Macdonald MSS, Yale University Library, folios 606–8, which are quoted in Noyes, *History of American Socialisms,* pp. 47–48; Leopold, *Robert Dale Owen,* pp. 55–56; *Maclure-Fretageot Correspondence,* ed. Bestor, p. 396.

Though Taylor did make his disastrous appearance, most of the colonists who were expected to people the new paper communities never arrived. When Owen on May 6, 1827, bravely asserted that "eight independent Communities of common property and equality, have been formed upon the New-Harmony estate, exclusive of Mr. Maclure's or the Education Society, and of the town of New-Harmony," [125] Paul Brown came back with a merciless, but probably accurate, description of the reality. Feiba-Peveli, he admitted, was still in existence. "Three or four poor families of German emigrants, just arrived in the country" constituted another of the communities; "one log cottage containing four families," a third. But the Marylanders who were to occupy the buildings of defunct Macluria had not arrived. And beyond these, "except one or two huts where single families live," no trace of an inhabitant, let alone a community, could be found on the entire estate.[126] Brown's statement was never refuted. When Owen bade farewell to New Harmony three weeks later, on May 27, 1827, he still addressed himself to the "Ten Social Colonies of Equality and Common Property," but he was careful to speak of them as "forming" not "formed" and to refrain from specifying them individually.[127] He knew full well that they were phantoms. There is more significance in the fact that Owen did not revisit the community for nearly a year than in the fact that he postponed until that time his admission of failure.[128] Actually the experiment came to an unequivocal end in April 1827.[129]

[125] New-Harmony Gazette, II, 255 (May 9, 1827). Owen included Feiba-Peveli among the eight.

[126] Paul Brown, Twelve Months, p. 122.

[127] New-Harmony Gazette, II, 278–79 (May 30, 1827). This address was delivered on May 27, and Owen departed on June 1, 1827.

[128] Owen returned to New Harmony early in April 1828, and on the thirteenth addressed a public meeting of the inhabitants. Even then his speech was something less than a forthright acknowledgment of failure. His leases to the new communities, he said, "have been, with a few exceptions, applied for individual purposes and . . . must return again into my hands." He announced that he was "still fully occupied" in devising arrangements "that will prepare a solid foundation for the social system" by enabling its supporters "to live in separate families on the individual system and yet to unite their general labor or to exchange labor for labor." Owen, "Address . . . on Sunday, April 13, 1828," New-Harmony Gazette, III, 204–5 (April 23, 1828).

[129] Newspaper reports of failure in this month were fully justified. See, for example, Vandalia Illinois Intelligencer, April 7, 1827, p. 3:1; Ohio State Journal and Columbus Gazette, April 12, 1827, p. 3:2. In later years Robert Dale Owen asserted that the editorial written by himself and his brother William and published in the New-Harmony Gazette on March 28, 1827 (II, 206–7) constituted an admission of failure. R. D. Owen, Autobiography, pp. 288–89. If so intended, it was a well-disguised admission, for Owenites elsewhere reprinted the article as a refutation of reports to that effect, and succeeded in inducing some editors to

A second plot in the complex drama of New Harmony also reached its denouement in the early months of 1827. The financial relations between Owen and Maclure were at issue. Owen had paid no heed to repeated and explicit warnings that he could expect no more funds from Maclure save the amount the Education Society had still to pay, and the $10,000 "forfeiture." Instead of reaching an understanding with Maclure, Owen began to play fast and loose with his agreements. In November 1826 he called in question the boundaries of the school property. In January 1827 he applied to Maclure's brother for additional funds while Maclure was in New Orleans.[130] The request was refused, but Owen continued to act as if a full and unlimited partnership existed. Maclure did not return to New Harmony until April 20, 1827, but he came with a fixed determination to settle the matter once and for all.

Events played into his hands. Frederick Rapp arrived in New Harmony to collect an installment of $20,000 due the Rappites on May 1, 1827, and to offer a discount in return for immediate payment of a final installment, of like amount, due a year later. Owen, however, lacked the necessary funds, and Maclure made the payments, receiving from Rapp the bonds that Owen had signed in the amount of $40,000. Having become Owen's creditor, Maclure was in a position to compel a settlement. Owen was willing to give him a deed instead of a lease to the property of the Education Society, but insisted on incorporating the complicated restrictive clauses that he had just devised for his grants to the new communities. Maclure wanted no more entanglements, and on April 30, 1827, he sent Thomas Say to the county seat to file suit against Owen for $40,000 on the basis of the bonds which he held. Owen countered with a suit for $90,000, a claim founded on the alleged existence of a partnership. Public notices were posted, the sheriff was called out, and the episode was gleefully reported in hostile papers throughout the country. Within three or four days, however, the matter was settled by arbitration. The arbiters apparently found that some sort of partnership existed, and they awarded Owen half of what he claimed. Maclure promptly turned over the bonds for $40,000, plus $5,000 in cash, and received from Owen on May 3, 1827, an unrestricted deed to 490 acres. The account was finally settled and the suits were withdrawn.[131]

---

retract. See *Co-operative Magazine*, II, 243–45, 315–25 (June, July 1827); *Correspondent*, I, 186–87 (April 14, 1827), quoting the *New-York Evening Post*.

[130] *Maclure-Fretageot Correspondence*, p. 385. For Maclure's warnings, see *ibid.*, pp. 337–89 *passim*.

[131] See Owen, *Pecuniary Transactions* (1827), in *New-Harmony Gazette*, II, 353–54 (Aug. 15, 1827); Paul Brown, *Twelve Months*, pp. 97–98, 127; Posey County

So far as one can tell from the extant evidence, Maclure paid over to Owen a total of $82,000, whereas he had expected to sink no more than $60,000. He came out as the owner of property valued in the deed at $44,000. Depending on the way he looked at the matter, he would have to charge from $22,000 to $38,000 to experience. This was not ruinous to Maclure, and for the remaining thirteen years of his life he continued to support generously the educational enterprise he had founded at New Harmony. Of Owen's financial losses it is hard to speak with assurance. The land he purchased from the Rappites was ultimately worth all that he paid for it. On the other hand, at least two-fifths of his capital was tied up there, producing little income; and eventually he turned over most of the property to his children in lieu of the sums he had earlier settled upon them in England. In subsidizing the living expenses of the New Harmony Community, moreover, Owen spent not only the money he received from Maclure in 1826, but also cash of his own amounting to at least $55,000, and probably to as much as $100,000. After his return to England his expenditures in the socialist and co-operative cause showed that he still possessed means. But his fortune of $250,000 had dwindled to little more than $50,000 in available funds as a result of his experiment in America.[132] Fifteen more years of propaganda and experiment exhausted the remainder. From 1844 onwards he was dependent upon remittances from his sons, part of which repre-

---

Circuit Court, "Order Book," liber C, p. 172; Posey County, "Deeds," liber D, p. 390; liber L, p. 65. Maclure made no public statement on the episode.

[132] On June 25, 1827, Owen said, "I cannot make a very accurate estimate of the expenses; but I dont think it has cost me a sacrifice of more than 80 or 100,000 dollars, since I came to this country." *Pecuniary Transactions,* in *New-Harmony Gazette,* II, 346 (Aug. 8, 1827). Further losses were still to come, especially through litigation. In this statement Owen was clearly not including his investment of $95,000 in real estate, which, five years later, was in fact valued at $95,849.50, almost exactly what he had paid down for it. James M. Dorsey and R. D. Owen, "Rough Estimate of New Harmony Real Estate, January 1832," MS in Workingmen's Institute. Owen's son, on the other hand, included this investment when he estimated that his father "expended . . . upwards of two hundred thousand dollars" at New Harmony. R. D. Owen, *Autobiography,* pp. 292–93. Thus the two statements would agree in placing Owen's *loss* at about $100,000. This is consistent with the figure of $51,000 for ascertainable expenditures before March 1826, as reached above, pp. 180–81. Owen's expenditures in 1826–27 were doubtless heavy, and he lost much in litigation thereafter. See *Maclure-Fretageot Correspondence,* p. 336, n. 17; pp. 393–94, n. 22. Additional study of the documents leads me to the conclusion, slightly different from the one I reached in the work just cited, that Owen's outright losses in the New Harmony experiment approximated $100,000. An almost equal amount was tied up in the New Harmony property, so his available funds could not have greatly exceeded $50,000 after 1827. Of this, £6,000 was still invested in the New Lanark mills, but his other shares and those of his family had been liquidated to pay for the American venture. See Podmore, *Robert Owen,* II, 394; R. D. Owen, *Autobiography,* p. 294.

sented income on the property at New Harmony, part their generosity.[133]

Though Paul Brown looked upon the controversy between Maclure and Owen as "a sort of contest or squabble about individual property, between two rich men," [134] there was much more to it than that. The educational policies of the two men were also at issue. They constituted the third snarl that had to be disentangled in the early months of 1827. Owen had been persistently undercutting Maclure's efforts ever since August 1826, when he proposed a "social education" for all the members of the community in the New Harmony Hall. That scheme had failed, but Owen had shown no disposition to turn the responsibility back to the Education Society. In fact, as affairs went from bad to worse, he began to find in the latter a scapegoat upon which the responsibility for failure might be loaded. Finally on May 6, 1827, at the end of the week in which the financial controversy reached its climax, Owen gave public utterance to his feelings in an address that lacked his usual bland amiability. He had, he said, placed "unlimited confidence" in Maclure and his associates, but the Education Society had failed to produce a "well-digested arrangement" for educating the scholars *en masse*. Instead the children had been divided into classes, "by which arrangement they were prevented from associating with the other pupils." He had hoped "that *all* the children should be educated in similar habits and dispositions, and be brought up truly as members of one large family." But the "error" of the School Society had frustrated this, the most important part of his plan, and, in consequence, had prevented him from bringing unity to the discordant population of New Harmony and "amalgamating the whole into a Community." [135]

Owen was no more ready to concede defeat in educational matters than in others. Before he left New Harmony on June 1, 1827, therefore, he instructed James M. Dorsey, newly arrived from Miami University at Oxford, Ohio, to assume charge of educating "the young Harmonians," and authorized him to spend $3,000 the first year. The money was to come from the rent paid by the ten "young Colonies" just established.[136] But there were no colonies, conse-

---

[133] On Owen's finances in his latter years, see Podmore, *Robert Owen*, II, 394-95; and Paul H. Douglas, "Some New Material on the Lives of Robert and Róbert Dale Owen," unpublished paper presented to the Chicago Literary Club, Feb. 2, 1942, typescripts in Library of Congress and Newberry Library.

[134] Paul Brown, *Twelve Months*, p. 127.

[135] Owen, "Address Delivered . . . the 6th of May, 1827, in the New-Harmony Hall," *New-Harmony Gazette*, II, 254 (May 9, 1827). See his earlier querulous statement of Aug. 6, 1826, and his later remarks on May 27 and June 27, 1827. *Ibid.*, I, 367; II, 278-79, 353 (Aug. 9, 1826; May 30, Aug. 15, 1827).

[136] Owen to Dorsey, New Harmony, May 31, 1827, MS in Indiana Historical

quently there was no rent and, so far as the records show, no school. Dorsey proved to be the ablest adviser that Owen, a poor judge of character, had chosen at New Harmony, and he rendered valuable service in business matters, but he could not bring to life the communitarian and educational enterprises whose dry stalks Owen left behind.

As Owen's project withered away, Maclure's was coming into flower. On May 14, 1827, two weeks after the financial settlement, he publicly announced that his school would be open to orphans,[137] and thus put into effect his oft-considered plan for freeing the enterprise from any dependence on the population of New Harmony. In June 1827, after Owen's departure, he began to publish his educational views in the *New-Harmony Gazette,* and before the year was out the series had run to twenty-five articles.[138] On January 16, 1828, he established his own periodical, *The Disseminator of Useful Knowledge,* bearing the imprint of the School of Industry. Gradually the ambitious program of scientific research and publication began to produce results. From the beginning Maclure had been assembling a technical staff comprising the scientists Say, Lesueur, and Troost, and an engraver of note, Cornelius Tiebout.[139] At the same time he had been building up a library and a number of collections in natural history, and had been accumulating the necessary equipment for printing, engraving, and coloring. The vocational curriculum of the School of Industry included the trades connected with publishing. Once all these were organized and directed toward the common end that Maclure had envisaged, the School Press began to issue its notable series of scientific publications, beginning with the five plates of Lesueur's *American Ichthyology* in 1827, continuing with the seven numbers of Say's *American Conchology* from 1830 to 1838, and concluding at length with the three-volume republication of François André Michaux's *North American Sylva,* with its 156 colored plates, in 1841. And social radicalism continued to be an ingredient in the philosophy of the school, as its publication of Maclure's *Opinions on Various Subjects* made clear.[140]

Society; see also *New-Harmony Gazette,* II, 8 (list of agents in col. 3), 270, 279, 353 (Oct. 4, 1826; May 23, 30, Aug. 15, 1827). Later letters in the Owen-Dorsey papers record his assistance to Owen and his sons in business matters. On Dorsey see below, p. 207 and n. 11a.

137 *New-Harmony Gazette,* II, 263 (May 16, 1827).

138 *New-Harmony Gazette,* II, 292, through III, 68 (June 20–Dec. 5, 1827).

139 *Maclure-Fretageot Correspondence,* pp. 371, 388, 401–2, 405. On Tiebout, "the first American-born professional engraver to produce really meritorious work," see David McNeely Stauffer, *American Engravers upon Copper and Steel* (New York, 1907), I, 271–72.

140 See *Maclure-Fretageot Correspondence,* chapters I and V.

New Harmony as an experiment with Owen's system was dead when its founder departed in June 1827. New Harmony as a community set apart from others, dedicated to high intellectual and social ends, and more or less consciously offering itself as a model for the future, was still alive. It was no longer a communitarian colony in the strict sense of the term, but elements of the communitarian ideal had become part of its life.

Chapter VIII

THE OWENITE LEGACY

THE fate of Owenism in America hinged on the experiment at New Harmony. Owen had deliberately made it the supreme test of his theories, and had thrown all his resources into the enterprise. What happened elsewhere could hardly affect the outcome. Sensing this, the most ardent converts to the new system were inclined to say, with William Pelham, "I will go to *Head Quarters*." [1] Many, however, were unable to cut established ties and make the long journey to Indiana. Local projects appeared to be the answer for them. After all, did not the Owenite gospel promise that the nation would soon be dotted with communities no less happy and prosperous than the pioneer one at New Harmony?

The enthusiasm that Owen aroused had a clearly defined geographical locus. No communitarian movement in America was ever to make headway in the cotton states. Owen, moreover, attracted no such attention in New England as the Fourierites were to do in the 1840's. But the seaboard cities of New York and Philadelphia responded to the new ideas, and enthusiasm spread throughout the Ohio Valley from Pittsburgh and Cincinnati to the mouth of the Wabash. From all this region men and women were drawn to New Harmony,[2] but in each of these four great cities enough Owenites remained behind to constitute a respectable nucleus for a local community.

Enthusiasm was probably greatest in Philadelphia, where John Speakman and others in the Academy of Natural Sciences had talked of a community before Owen's coming. Their project never materialized as a separate enterprise, for most of them joined the trek to New Harmony. At the very moment, however, when they lay locked in the ice aboard the *Philanthropist* en route to New Harmony, another group of Philadelphians, with a few supporters from Wilmington, Delaware, were organizing a Friendly Association for Mutual Interests, to be located at Valley Forge. Fifteen members met on December 22, 1825, and on January 19, 1826, they produced a

---

[1] "Pelham Letters," p. 400.

[2] The Preliminary Society comprised persons "from every state in the union, except two, and from almost every country in the north of Europe," according to *Niles' Weekly Register*, XXIX, 244 (Dec. 17, 1825).

preamble and constitution, which was in print in March. William Maclure, already at New Harmony, was induced to subscribe, but in the end was not called upon for payment. The community moved into Washington's headquarters on the historic campground in the spring of 1826. But it was immediately subjected to bitter religious attack, and by September it had broken up. Among the disappointed members the Shakers claimed a number of converts.[3]

New York City, too, had been stirred by the ideas of Owen. Communitarians there naturally looked up the Hudson River for a site, and two communities were actually organized in the valley during 1826. The first of these was the Franklin Community, which drew up its constitution in New York in March 1826 and at the end of April selected for its site a farm of 120 or 130 acres, two miles back from the river, near Haverstraw, in Rockland County, some thirty-five miles from the metropolis. Though the New York Society for Promoting Communities had been in existence for several years, it was not the sponsor of the Franklin Community. The leaders were drawn, rather, from among the militant freethinkers of the city. Most active of these was George Houston, who had suffered imprisonment in England for publishing atheistic writings, who had frequented Owen's gatherings in New York in 1824 and 1825, and who was to found a rationalistic journal, *The Correspondent,* on January 20, 1827, a few months after the failure of the New York Owenite communities. Associated with him was Abner Kneeland, whose trial and imprisonment for blasphemy in the 1830's was one of the *causes célèbres* of the period, and Henry A. Fay, a lawyer who defended cases of this kind though he was not actually Kneeland's counsel in the later trial.[4] Houston was secretary of the Franklin Community, Fay was one of its resident directors, and Kneeland was chosen to expound its principles from his Universalist pulpit in New York.

---

[3] John Gray, *A Lecture on Human Happiness;* . . . *To Which Are Added the Preamble and Constitution of the Friendly Association for Mutual Interests, Located at Valley Forge, (near Phil'a.)* (Philadelphia, 1826). The *Preamble and Constitution* was also issued separately. The publication was noted in the *New-Harmony Gazette,* I, 214 (March 29, 1826). On the formation of the community, see *ibid.,* p. 159 (Feb. 8, 1826); *Niles' Weekly Register,* XXIX, 244, 275 (Dec. 17 and 31, 1825); Macdonald, *Diaries,* pp. 308, 312 (Nov. 7 and 14, 1825); Karl Bernhard, *Travels,* p. 430. On its dissolution, see Maclure to Mme Fretageot, Springfield, O., July 24, July 31, 1826; Louisville, Ky., Sept. 19, 1826, MSS in Workingmen's Institute; Jane D. Knight, *Brief Narrative of Events Touching Various Reforms,* pp. 16–19; and Anna White and Leila S. Taylor, *Shakerism: Its Meaning and Message,* pp. 158–59. There is an undocumented account of the community, containing demonstrable errors, in Harry E. Wildes, *Valley Forge* (New York, 1938), pp. 287–89.

[4] On Houston, see Macdonald, *Diaries,* pp. 179, 183, 197, 315; Albert Post, *Popular Freethought in America,* pp. 45–48. On Kneeland and Fay, see *ibid.,* pp. 52–55, 80, 103–7, 215–18.

From New Harmony itself Robert L. Jennings hastened to the new community to give it the benefit both of his communitarian experience and of his rationalistic preaching.

It was not until June 23, 1826, that the community was able to pay down the necessary one-third of the purchase price of $16,000 or $18,000 demanded for its lands. In the meantime, however, a number of families had moved to the domain in early May, and had begun to farm the land, thinking to invest their labor in lieu of capital, which later comers would bring. When, however, the constitution was altered in June or July without consulting them, the resident members felt defrauded, and there were mutterings of discontent. These swelled to a full chorus when Houston, Jennings, and Fay arrived and began to put their deistic ideas into practice by secularizing the schools, establishing a Church of Reason, encouraging labor on the Sabbath, and quoting with approval the more outspoken of Owen's discourses on religion and marriage. A laxness in financial matters, perhaps amounting to dishonesty, hastened the end, which came five months after the venture began.[5]

In the upper Hudson Valley, near Coxsackie in Greene County, a second Owenite experiment, the Forestville Community, was organized as early as December 16, 1825. Its sponsors were apparently local men, though they were doubtless in communication with the Owenites in New York City. The Forestville Community printed its constitution in March 1826 and shortly thereafter moved to a 325-acre tract known as Lapham's Mills, seven miles back from the river.[6] Although smaller in membership than the Franklin Community, it was considerably longer-lived. When the latter disbanded, in fact, a number of its members moved to the community at Coxsackie. And when this in turn decided to sell its property in October

[5] The principal source is James M'Knight ("late a member of the community"), *A Discourse Exposing Robert Owen's System, as Practised by the Franklin Community, at Haverstraw* (New York, 1826), first delivered Aug. 26, 1826, and enlarged on Oct. 4. There is a single notice in the *New-Harmony Gazette*, I, 287 (May 31, 1826). J. H. Noyes, *History of American Socialisms*, pp. 74–77, prints all the material gathered by A. J. Macdonald in the 1840's and preserved in his MSS, Yale University Library, folios 391–92, 417. There is some additional information in David Cole, *History of Rockland County, New York* (New York, 1884), pp. 156–57.

[6] The *New-Harmony Gazette* furnishes most of the available information on the Coxsackie Community: I, 318; III, 34, 70, 141 (June 28, 1826, Nov. 7 and Dec. 5, 1827, Feb. 13, 1828). Noyes, *History of American Socialisms*, p. 77, prints the material preserved in A. J. Macdonald MSS, folios 418–19. Both Noyes and Macdonald paraphrase the article in the *New-Harmony Gazette*, III, 34, but label it as pertaining to a Forrestville [sic] Community in Indiana [sic]. Additional information is supplied by William S. Pelletreau in his chapter in the anonymous *History of Greene County, New York* (New York: J. B. Beers and Co., 1884), p. 242.

1827, after more than a year of communitarian life, half its members made an arduous winter journey to join the Kendal Community in Ohio.[7]

The Friendly Association for Mutual Interests at Kendal, Ohio, to use its official title, was the most successful of all the lesser Owenite experiments. By January 1826 the new view of society had inspired such enthusiasm in northeastern Ohio that a group of men in the vicinity of Canton and Massillon were contemplating a community there.[8] By March 17, 1826, they had drafted a statement of principles, thoroughly communitarian in spirit but differentiated from other Owenite documents by frequent allusions to the deity and the gospels. On May 15, 1826, the constitution was completed and the first organized meeting held, and the next day twenty-nine heads of families signed a "Bond of Social Compact" by which they agreed to buy a tract of over two thousand acres and assumed responsibility for the purchase price of $20,000. Shortly thereafter the community moved to its domain in Kendal, Perry Township, Stark County, a location now within the city limits of Massillon, Ohio.[9]

The comparative success of the community must be attributed to the mutual confidence of the members, grounded in long acquaintance. By contrast with New Harmony, whose population was gathered from the ends of the earth, and with the Franklin Community, whose aggregation of city-bred colonists knew even less of one another than of farming, the Kendal Community was composed of substantial citizens of the neighborhood who so understood and trusted one another as to be willing to turn over their existing farms in down payment on the larger tract, which they proposed to manage cooperatively. There were some withdrawals, and occasional expulsions, but on the whole the stake each one had in the enterprise gave him

---

[7] *New-Harmony Gazette*, III, 141 (Feb. 13, 1828); William H. Perrin, ed., *History of Stark County, with an Outline Sketch of Ohio* (Chicago, 1881), p. 388. There were negotiations for an actual merger of the two organizations but these fell through, and a published announcement that the Coxsackie Community had purchased the property of the Kendal Community was incorrect. *New-Harmony Gazette*, III, 70 (Dec. 5, 1827).

[8] Donald Macdonald, *Diaries*, p. 333 (Jan. 3, 1826); Cleveland *Herald*, Jan. 6, 1826, p. 3:4, as abstracted in Works Progress Administration in Ohio, *Annals of Cleveland, 1818–1935*, IX (Cleveland, 1938), 36, abstract no. 163; Maclure to Mme Fretageot, Springfield, O., July 21, 1826, MS in Workingmen's Institute.

[9] The record book of the Kendal Community, including constitution, minutes, and final balance sheet, is preserved in the McClymonds Public Library, Massillon, O., and has been printed in full by Wendall P. Fox, "The Kendal Community," *Ohio Archaeological and Historical Quarterly*, XX, 176–219 (April–July 1911). A little information is added by the *New-Harmony Gazette*, I, 349; III, 70, 141 (July 26, 1826, Dec. 5, 1827, Feb. 13, 1828); Noyes, *History of American Socialisms*, pp. 78–80; and W. H. Perrin, ed., *History of Stark County*, pp. 387–88.

sufficient incentive to keep going and sufficient common sense to avoid the petty bickerings and the ideological intrigues so characteristic of New Harmony. Furthermore, the members who came from distant Coxsackie had been tested by more than a year of communitarian life and had demonstrated their seriousness by their persistence.

As a consequence, the Kendal Community was carrying on, inconspicuously but with modest success, in the summer of 1828, more than a year after the collapse of New Harmony. It was at work on new buildings, it was planning an expansion of certain industries, it was entering in its minutes regular weekly reports of the income from its various businesses. The community, to be sure, had been unable to pay interest on the funds its members had invested, but no crisis had resulted, for on January 1, 1828, the relinquishment was amicably agreed to. Even the drafting of a revised constitution brought no such hubbub as at New Harmony, and the new instrument was put quietly into effect on May 17, 1828. Robert Owen visited this last surviving community in July 1828 and reported—in a patronizing tone he certainly had no right to adopt—that the Kendal Community "is a good scite with fine localities, & with a few practical leaders in agriculture & manufacture will do well in a few years. Dr Underhill is a zealous supporter of the social principles to their full extent but prudent in not urging their practice prematurely." [10]

The end of the community, however, was only six months away. It came unspectacularly. More than two years of steady labor had not created a millennium and seemed unlikely ever to do so. Individualism offered prospects that grew ever brighter as those of communitarianism grew dim. One by one the leading members asked release, and at a series of meetings in September and October 1828 the necessary settlements were agreed to in a friendly spirit. Finally on January 1, 1829, the society appointed an agent "to make deeds of the Kendal Community land," and on January 3 it voted "to discontinue business as a Company." The final accounts were presented on January 6, 1829, and the community ceased. According to the inventory the property of the association had a value of $26,522.25 and its debts to outsiders amounted to $22,539.37 (including $19,350.59 still unpaid on the land). The balance of $3,982.88 was not sufficient to cover the total of $5,642.00 owing to members of the community, but the loss to each was a moderate one, and occasioned no personal bitterness. [11]

[10] Robert Owen to James M. Dorsey, Wheeling, Va., July 14, 1828, MS in Indiana Historical Society. Dr. Samuel Underhill, a physician, was the leader of those who came from Coxsackie.

[11] Appended to the account of assets and liabilities summarized above is a schedule giving the "sum total of household goods and clothing" of each member. Fox, "Kendal Community," pp. 218–19. Its bearing upon the other accounts is not clear. It may represent personal property for which the community owed

Despite the relative success of the Kendal Community, the real focus of communitarian activity in the west was not northeastern but southwestern Ohio. The Shakers had first made it so in 1805 with their settlement at Union Village in Warren County, and by 1825 no less than three of their communities lay within sixty miles of Cincinnati. Gradually communitarian ideas began to influence the thinking of a small group of rationalists at Oxford, in near-by Butler County. Their leader was James M. Dorsey, principal of the "Select School" which the trustees of Miami University had opened there in 1811 as the first step in establishing a full-fledged university. Though Dorsey was eventually to become the most reliable associate of Owen at New Harmony, he could hardly have known of Owenism in 1816, when he developed his first communitarian project, a society called the Rational Brethren of Oxford. Dorsey's devotion to free thought was indicated by the title, as it had already been more dramatically illustrated by the name he bestowed on his second son, Godwin Volney Dorsey. Rationalism was not the only element, however, in the articles of association which he and his associate William Ludlow drew up for the organization and which they formally deposited in the archives of county and state. Manufacture of pot and pearl ash was one of its avowed purposes, and a vaguely communitarian plan was hinted at. The society itself was formally dissolved in 1817, but the record book remained in the possession of William Ludlow, and in it were eventually inscribed the documents of a communitive enterprise in which the earlier ideas came to fruition.[11a]

This was the Coal Creek Community and Church of God, which experimented with communitarian life in Fountain County, Indiana, from 1825 to 1832. The location was determined by the availability of land, for the society itself was actually born at Lebanon in Warren County, Ohio. William Ludlow, after separating from Dorsey, had settled in that town, some thirty miles away. By 1819 he

---

compensation in addition to the listed "debts due members of community." If so, the losses were heavier than here stated. On the other hand, it may represent personal property which the members were taking with them, in which case the losses may have been less.

[11a] The MS volume, with some pages missing, is now in the Indiana State Library. It begins with several documents of the Rational Brethren of Oxford, Sept. 10, 1816–Aug. 23, 1817, certain of which, it is indicated, were recorded in Butler County, Ohio, "Deeds," liber F, pp. 41–45, 113–14, and deposited in the office of the Secretary of State of Ohio. The only names mentioned are James M. Dorsey and William and Israel Ludlow. See note 11c below for a description of the second set of records contained in the volume. On Dorsey see *History and Biographical Cyclopaedia of Butler County, Ohio* (Cincinnati, 1882), pp. 60–61; Miami University, *General Catalogue of the Graduates . . . 1809–1909* ([Oxford, Ohio, 1909 ?]), p. xvii; Harry W. Newman, *Anne Arundel Gentry* (Baltimore, 1933), p. 17; and also above, pp. 199–200.

was attempting to revive the old project as the Rational Brethren of the West.[11b] He achieved success in 1823 under a strikingly different name. On May 1 of that year twelve persons besides himself signed "A Manafest [*sic*] of the fundamental principles of the Church of God," and by April 24, 1824, they had purchased from the government over a thousand acres along Coal Creek, near Stone Bluff, Indiana. The land could be acquired only in the names of individuals, but these executed a formal agreement for common ownership, making it clear that they were to be considered "only equal inheritors, enjoyers and partakers with the members in moral order in said Church." [11c]

Gratified by this start, William Ludlow on July 30, 1824, wrote Thomas Jefferson of their plans, presenting them as the culminating step in the long progress of society. These reflections drew from Jefferson one of his most remarkable letters, anticipatory, even in its figures of speech, of Frederick Jackson Turner:

Monticello Sep. 6. [18]24.

Sir

The idea which you present in your letter of July 30. of the progress of society from it's rudest state to that it has now attained seems conformable to what may be probably conjectured. Indeed we have under our eyes tolerable proofs of it. Let a philosophic observer commence a journey from the savages of the Rocky mountains, Eastwardly towards our seacoast. These he would observe in the earliest stage of association living under no law but that of nature, subsisting and covering themselves with the flesh and skins of wild beasts. He would next find those on our frontiers in the pastoral state, raising domestic animals to supply the defects of hunting. Then succeed our own semibarbarous citizens, the pioneers of the advance of civilisation, and so in his progress he would meet the gradual shades of improving man until he would reach his, as yet, most improved

[11b] *Cincinnati Literary Gazette*, III, 162 (May 21, 1825). No records of this project are in the volume described in the preceding footnote.

[11c] The records of the Church of God, subsequently the Coal Creek Community and Church of God, occupy a separately paged section of the MS volume described in note 11a above. They include the "Manafest," May 1, 1823, with thirteen signatures, and a supplementary article dated Oct. 23, 1823 (pp. 1–10); the "Constitution of the Coal Creek Community and Church of God," Dec. 10, 1825 (pp. 19–25); "A Record of withdrawal," Dec. 15, 1825–March 10, 1832 (p. 11); "A Record of money laid out or advanced by members," Oct. 23, 1823–Sept. 16, 1831 (pp. 132–39); and other minor records. The basic documents were recorded Aug. 28, 1828, in Fountain County, Ind., "Deeds," liber 1, pp. 121–23, the quotation in the text coming therefrom. The breakup of the community is reflected in documents of May 3, 1832, and Sept. 13, 1833, recorded in *ibid.*, liber 2, pp. 369–71, and liber 4, p. 264. The principal secondary account is in J. Wesley Whicker, *Historical Sketches of the Wabash Valley* (Attica, Ind., 1916), pp. 116–25, which utilizes certain court records in addition to the deeds already mentioned, but which does not cite the MS volume of records.

state in our seaport towns. This in fact is equivalent to a survey, in time, of the progress of man from the infancy of creation to the present day. I am 81. years of age, born where I now live, in the first range of mountains in the interior of our country. And I have observed this march of civilisation advancing from the seacoast, passing over us like a cloud of light, increasing our knolege and improving our condition, insomuch as that we are at this time more advanced in civilisation here than the seaports were when I was a boy. And where this progress will stop no one can say. Barbarism has in the mean time been receding before the steady step of amelioration; and will in time I trust disappear from the earth. You seem to think that this advance has brought on too complicated a state of society, and that we should gain in happiness by treading back our steps a little way. I think myself that we have more machinery of government than is necessary, too many parasites living on the labor of the industrious. I believe it might be much simplified to the relief of those who maintain it. Your experiment seems to have this in view. A society of 70. families, the number you name, may very possibly be governed as a single family, subsisting on their common industry, and holding all things in common. Some regulators of the family you still must have, and it remains to be seen at what point of your increasing population your simple regulations will cease to be sufficient to preserve order, peace and justice. The experiment is interesting; I shall not live to see it's issue but I wish it success equal to your hopes and to yourself and society prosperity and happiness.

Th[omas] J[efferson].[12]

Thus encouraged, the members moved to their domain in Indiana, some hundred and fifty miles up the Wabash Valley from New Harmony. On December 10, 1825, they adopted a revised "Constitution of the Coal Creek Community and Church of God." Ludlow himself withdrew shortly afterwards, visited and lectured at New Harmony, but resumed his membership in October 1826.[12a] Little is recorded of the life of the community, but it was sufficiently prosperous to make a mutually satisfactory refund of property to certain members who withdrew in 1827 and 1831. The secession of William Ludlow, who returned to New Harmony in January 1830, produced a serious crisis, however. In October the community tendered him the sum he had originally contributed, but he was dissatisfied and on February 4, 1832, took the matter into court. An agreement was reached on May 3, but the community does not seem to have long survived the litigation.

Communitarianism was thus a familiar idea in Cincinnati long

[12] Original draft, initialed, in Jefferson papers, series I, vol. 14, no. 303, Library of Congress; printed in his *Writings*, ed. by Lipscomb and Bergh, XVI, 74–76. Ludlow's letter, dated Lebanon, O., July 30, 1824, is entered in Jefferson's Epistolary Record under the date of receipt, Aug. 28, but the document itself is missing.

[12a] *New-Harmony Gazette*, I, 156–57, 186–87 (Feb. 8 and March 8, 1826); Coal Creek Community, "Record of withdrawal," in MS volume already described, p. 11.

before Owen visited the city in 1824. Its manifestations had all been under sectarian auspices, however, and it is little wonder that the *Cincinnati Literary Gazette* was surprised at the nonreligious character of Owen's plans. "It is true," wrote a reviewer,

> that societies have, in modern times, been formed, having a community of goods, &c.: but it has been always supposed necessary that a common religion should be the first and strongest bond of unity among them; and this idea has been so universal, that we believe Owen is the first who ever thought it practicable to dispense with it.[12b]

In point of fact, the religious background of communitarianism in Cincinnati included other sects than the Shakers and the so-called Church of God. Swedenborgianism also prepared the way, as it did for many other nineteenth-century experimental communities. At New Harmony, indeed, its adherents were accounted, by some at least, the most numerous sect.[13] In Cincinnati the minister of the Swedenborgian or New Jerusalem Church, Daniel Roe, was one of Owen's most active disciples, and his congregation formed the nucleus of the Yellow Springs Community, the Owenite enterprise organized in that city.

Owenism had reached Cincinnati through the propaganda of the New York Society for Promoting Communities, even before Owen decided to come to America. His actual arrival was duly announced in the *Liberty Hall and Cincinnati Gazette* in November 1824, and his plan received favorable editorial notice in the *Cincinnati Emporium* on December 16, 1824, a week after the visitor had passed through the city on his way to New Harmony. This interest bore fruit in an Owenite Society, formed in March 1825. Owen was at that time discoursing in Washington, but when he returned to New Harmony on April 13 he brought with him two of the Cincinnati leaders, including Daniel Roe. The latter returned to Cincinnati fired with a zeal to duplicate the promised achievements of New Harmony. Propaganda proceeded rapidly. When Owen visited Cincinnati again, on June 10 and 11, 1825, he found that half a dozen of his books and pamphlets were in print and on sale, and that arrangements were all but complete for a local community. On July 2 the new enterprise was publicly announced, and during that month communitarian life actually began on the domain which the society

---

[12b] *Cincinnati Literary Gazette*, III, 193 (June 18, 1825).

[13] "Pelham Letters," p. 377. On the connections between Swedenborgianism and various communitive movements, including the Fourierist, see Marguerite Beck Block, *The New Church in the New World: A Study of Swedenborgianism in America* (American Religion Series, V; New York, 1932), pp. 54–55, 81–82, 118–20, 130, 137–41, 150–58, 260–61.

acquired at Yellow Springs, sixty miles up the Little Miami in Greene County, a site now occupied by Antioch College.[14]

In its social and economic practices the community endeavored to be a faithful copy of New Harmony, and it succeeded in being so in its dissensions as well. Differences of social position were easier to exorcise in the lecture hall than at the community dances, and the eternal debate over the relative value of skilled and unskilled labor was repeated in precisely the phrases that were heard beside the Wabash: "Mechanics, whose single day's labor brought two dollars into the common stock, insisted that they should, in justice, work only half as long as the agriculturist, whose day's work brought but one." [15] As the year 1825 came to its end, a report echoed from New Harmony to Boston that the Yellow Springs Community had "blown out." [16]

It was actually the first failure of an Owenite enterprise in America, and the consequences to the movement as a whole looked serious. Owen himself broke his trip back to New Harmony in January 1826 to look into the matter on the spot, but he was unable to repair the damage.[17] Later in the spring Paul Brown took it upon himself to see what he could do, and, as might be expected, succeeded only in sharpening the factional conflict within the community. Finally in midsummer William Maclure journeyed to Ohio in an effort to compose the disputes and set the community going again, backed, if necessary, by additional funds from his own purse.

[14] *Cincinnati Emporium,* July 8 and Dec. 16, 1824, as cited by Irvin, pp. 4, 13; *Liberty Hall and Cincinnati Gazette,* Nov. 16, 1824, p. 2:5; March 8, 1825, p. 2:4 (the first reference to the projected community); June 3, 1825, p. 2:5; *Cincinnati Literary Gazette,* III, 86, 154–56, 161–63, 190, 193–94, 214, 245 (March 12, May 14 and 21, June 11 and 18, July 2 and 30, 1825); Washington *National Intelligencer,* July 19, 1825, p. 1:1; Oct. 22, 1825, p. 1:1; *Niles' Weekly Register,* XXVIII, 366; XXIX, 24, 133 (July 23, Sept. 10, and Oct. 29, 1825); *New-Harmony Gazette,* I, 71, 159, 310 (Nov. 23, 1825, Feb. 8 and July 21, 1826); Donald Macdonald, *Diaries,* pp. 236, 292, 296 (Dec. 9, 1824, April 13 and June 10–11, 1825); *Pears Papers,* p. 23 (Aug. 6, 1825); "Pelham Letters," pp. 374, 395 (Sept. 9 and Nov. 27, 1825). These are the principal contemporary references to the beginnings of Owenism in Cincinnati and the formation of the Yellow Springs Community. Sources covering the breakup of the latter are given in subsequent footnotes. Brief accounts, drawing upon certain additional sources, are given by William A. Galloway, *The History of Glen Helen* (Columbus, O., 1932), pp. 47–53; Noyes, *History of American Socialisms,* pp. 59–65; E. S. Dills, *History of Greene County, . . . Ohio* (Dayton, 1881), p. 665; and Block, *The New Church in the New World,* pp. 118–20.

[15] "Communism: Reminiscences of the Community at Yellow Springs, Ohio," undated clipping in A. J. Macdonald MSS, Yale University Library, folio 305.

[16] "Pelham Letters," p. 400; Boston *New England Palladium and Commercial Advertiser,* Jan. 10, 1826, p. 2:2.

[17] Donald Macdonald, *Diaries,* p. 335.

Funds were essential, for the community had paid down only half the purchase price of its 720 acres. The remaining installment of $4,000 had fallen due on January 1, 1826,[18] but the bank that held the mortgage was still willing to negotiate after the five months' default, and several members remained on the ground when Maclure undertook his mission. He left New Harmony on June 8, 1826, and on the sixteenth he interviewed the members whom he found in Cincinnati. His private opinion was that those who wanted to continue the experiment should allow the mortgage to be foreclosed and then buy in the property at the sheriff's sale, but the members were far more anxious that Maclure should put up the $4,000 and let them make a new start in their own way.[19] He balked at the proposal but agreed to see what he could accomplish at Yellow Springs itself.

When he reached the site in early July 1826 he came upon the results of Paul Brown's mission. Nine members of the "laboring class," as they described themselves, were in possession of the property, breathing fire and brimstone against the *"original purchasers* or *land-holders"* whose "selfish miserly and illiberal" object, they asserted, was *"private speculation."* The nine members had been at work for a year at the community, long since deserted by the rest, and they insisted that their contribution of labor entitled them to full partnership in the enterprise, alongside those who had subscribed the capital. Their special resentment was directed against the "opposing members" who were operating the hotel at the Springs without sharing its profits with them—an echo of the conflicts that arose at New Harmony over the control of tavern and store. Though the resident members were anxious for Maclure's $4,000, their compelling interest was compensation for the labor they had expended, a total of $655 as they reckoned it. If this sum were paid they promised to relinquish the property and depart.[20] To a modern eye there is merit in this claim to the rough equivalent of a mechanic's lien. But this concept could apply only to employees, not to partners, of the community. By insisting that they were full-fledged members, these men

[18] Deed cited by W. A. Galloway, *History of Glen Helen,* p. 52; also see his map, p. 46.

[19] Maclure to Mme Fretageot, Cincinnati, June 16, 20, and 24, 1826, MSS in Workingmen's Institute, the second of which is partially quoted in *Correspondence,* ed. Bestor, p. 339.

[20] Notice, "To the Public," signed by the nine members, dated July 3, 1826, with an addendum written subsequent to July 5, in Xenia, O., *People's Press, and Impartial Expositor,* Aug. 15, 1826, p. 2:3–4. Daniel Roe was not one of the nine signers, but he was in sympathy with them and would agree to depart only if allowed to "remain undisturbed in the manufacture of paint on the premises, until the first of December next." Maclure considered Roe the "principle agent in the dissolution of the Yellow Springs." *Maclure-Fretageot Correspondence,* p. 360.

admitted that they had risked their labor, as the others had risked their capital. Their hope had been to share in the common profit, their inescapable fate was to share in the common loss.

Maclure heard the demands of the two factions at a meeting on July 3, 1826, but could bring about no agreement. He had retained the confidence of the nine rebellious members, apparently, for they were willing to submit the whole matter to his arbitration, a proposal that was rejected by the others. In point of fact, however, Maclure had little sympathy with the recalcitrant nine and their conduct. The only man in the whole concern whom he felt he could trust was a certain Caleb Lowns, who did not belong to their faction. Maclure lingered at Yellow Springs for a few days in hope of a settlement, but by July 9 he had gone on to Columbus, his mission an acknowledged failure. Though he finally decided in December "to lend the Yellow Springs Community 4,000 dollars to be under the joint management of Lowns and others," [21] nothing came of this gesture. The community disappeared, and on January 3, 1827, its property was deeded back to the original owners.

Next to Cincinnati, Pittsburgh was the most promising center for Owenite propaganda in the west. It had enjoyed a long acquaintance with sectarian communitism through the Rappites, located first at Harmony, some thirty miles away, and latterly at Economy, only half as distant. The community that John Speakman projected at Philadelphia before Owen's arrival had found supporters in Pittsburgh, and in December 1824 Owen himself encountered a Mr. Turner who for eighteen months had been active in the latter city either in Speakman's project or one like it. The leading supporter of Owenism in western Pennsylvania, however, was Benjamin Bakewell, whose flint-glass factory was one of the industrial show-places of the region. During the earlier agitation he had become acquainted with Speakman, who, as we have seen, was the first to introduce Bakewell to Owen, on December 3, 1824. During the spring of 1825, at least, Owenism aroused almost as much enthusiasm in Pittsburgh as in Cincinnati. In May, Bakewell's nephew by marriage, Thomas Pears, together with his wife and seven children, joined the Preliminary Society at New Harmony. This migration tends to confirm the opinion of one Owenite, who had written in April 1825 that the prospect of a community near Pittsburgh was "very remote." Nevertheless, in June and July, Bakewell took the lead in organizing at Pittsburgh the Cooperating Society of Alleghany County, which

---

[21] Maclure to Mme Fretageot, Louisville, Ky., Sept. 19, 1826, MS in Workingmen's Institute. See also his other letters after the trip to Yellow Springs: Columbus, O., July 9, 1826; Springfield, O., July 21; Cincinnati, Aug. 29; partially quoted in *Correspondence*, pp. 342, 360.

published a constitution and sent out a committee to find land for a community. By September 1825, however, the project had languished, ostensibly for want of capital, but doubtless in part because of the discouraging replies that Thomas Pears was giving to his uncle's inquiries about New Harmony.[22]

From New Harmony, as from Philadelphia, New York, and Cincinnati, Owenite ideas radiated to surrounding areas. From the beginning the English Settlement of Birkbeck and Flower, across the Wabash in Edwards County, Illinois, was the most susceptible. Mention has already been made of the communitarian ideas in circulation there before Owen's first visit in December 1824. His eloquence on that occasion had its effect. A number of English farmers came to New Harmony and formed the nucleus of Feiba-Peveli, and others who remained behind became increasingly interested in the new view of society. William Hall, captivated by Owen's two addresses at Albion in December, spent two full days at New Harmony in January 1825 learning all he could from Macdonald and William Owen, and returned twice in the spring—once to witness the inauguration of the Preliminary Society in April, and a second time in May to converse at leisure with Robert Owen. Back at his home in Wanborough, Illinois, he and five other English settlers organized the Wanborough Joint Stock Society, "upon the principle of a union of Labour and Capital." Twelve members signed the constitution during July and August 1825, committees were appointed "to value the stock of the members," and a mill was acquired in exchange for shares. By September 1825 William Pelham at New Harmony had received a favorable report of the enterprise, but not until the following May did the *New-Harmony Gazette* publish any notice of what it called the Cooperative Association at Wanborough. Stedman Whitwell reported that community life was actually attempted before his departure from New Harmony in August 1826, but the evidence is too slender to warrant the belief that the Wanborough Society ever became a genuinely functioning community.[23]

[22] On Owenism in Pittsburgh, see Donald Macdonald, *Diaries*, pp. 227, 233, 297–98; William Owen, *Diary*, pp. 30, 51, 62; *Pears Papers*, pp. 20, 22–23, 27–28, 34–35, *et passim;* "Pelham Letters," pp. 374, 395; *New-Harmony Gazette*, I, 7, 159 (Oct. 1, 1825, Feb. 8, 1826); M. B. Belknap to Owen, Pittsburgh, April 6, 1825, MS no. 65 in Owen papers, Manchester (quoted). See also above, pp. 100, 109, 110, and 158.

[23] The constitution of the Wanborough Society was published in the *New-Harmony Gazette*, I, 268–69 (May 17, 1826), but without mention of names. The original MS, with signatures dated between July 26 and Aug. 15, 1825, is in the Illinois State Historical Library, and has recently been published with commentary by Walter B. Hendrickson, "An Owenite Society in Illinois," *Indiana Magazine of History*, XLV, 175–82 (June 1949). This article cites the principal additional sources: the entries from Dec. 19, 1824, to Sept. 16, 1825, in William Hall,

In the state of Indiana the example of New Harmony inspired a somewhat more substantial result. Although Bloomington was more than a hundred miles to the northeast, and on no very direct line of communication, a settler from there visited New Harmony as early as January 1825, and carried back Macdonald's statement of Owenism, promising to republish it locally. Gradually the new doctrines won the support of a number of substantial citizens of Monroe County, both in the village of Bloomington and in the surrounding country-side. As early as January 2, 1826, they entered a tract of eighty acres in the name of the Blue Spring Community, and other farms were apparently added to the domain. A constitution was drawn up on April 10, and communitarian life began in the course of the spring. More than a score of log cabins were erected, disposed in a square, possibly in imitation of Owen's elaborate parallelograms. The membership, like that of Kendal, was homogeneous, and religious radicalism seems never to have disturbed its proceedings. Under these favoring circumstances the Blue Spring Community held together for more than a year, news of its prosperity being one of the few encouraging items which the *New-Harmony Gazette* was able to publish in January 1827. Later in that same year, however, community life was abandoned in much the same quiet way as at Kendal.[24]

At New Harmony itself, as difficulties multiplied, one final project shaped itself in the minds of disaffected members—a new community in the Ohio Valley, at Neville or Nevilsville, some thirty miles above Cincinnati in Clermont County, Ohio. The proprietor of this par-ticular tract of land, General Neville, had laid out a village fifteen years before. But sales were apparently slow, and in 1826 in Cincin-nati he began to look upon the Owenites as possible prospects, offer-ing them twenty-five or twenty-six hundred acres for $15,000, on ten years' credit. Immediately the radicals from New Harmony and Yellow Springs swarmed upon him. Paul Brown tried to convince him that it was his duty to give up "all his property to be in common." He listened with well-concealed amusement, and managed to per-suade the enthusiasts that he was "a devoted community man," willing to sacrifice a heavy investment in improvements for the

"Journal," pp. 238–45; and "Pelham Letters," p. 374 (Sept. 9, 1825). See also *Co-operative Magazine,* II, 46 (Jan. 1827).

24 A carefully documented study of the Blue Spring Community is Richard Simons, "A Utopian Failure," *Indiana History Bulletin,* XVIII, 98–114 (Feb. 1941), which utilizes the documents recorded in the Monroe County archives, and the previous material gathered by local historians. The only contemporary printed references are in the *New-Harmony Gazette,* I, 159; II, 142; III, 70 (Feb. 8, 1826, Jan. 31 and Dec. 5, 1827). The visit of the Bloomington citizen to New Harmony is recorded in W. Owen, *Diary,* pp. 108–9; D. Macdonald, *Diaries,* pp. 277–79; and Macdonald to Owen, Vincennes, Feb. 7, 1825, MS no. 58 in Owen papers, Manchester.

$15,000 he was nevertheless obliged to demand. By January 1827 New Harmony was agog with the project, and in March a contingent of eighty moved off toward the promised land. They went with the blessings of Paul Brown, but apparently neither he nor they ever reached the site.[25] A few families did settle on a farm near Jefferson-ville, Indiana, in a vain attempt to continue communitarian life, but the group was soon dispersed.[26]

As might be expected, the most grandiose sequel to New Harmony was projected by Robert Owen himself. The failure of the experi-ment, it will be remembered, was not openly acknowledged by him until the spring of 1828. He had spent the second half of 1827 in England, and had returned to New Harmony by way of New Orleans instead of New York. There he apparently first became aware of the expansion that was taking place into Texas, and of the liberal land grants which the Mexican government was making in the 1820's to foreign colonists. If Stephen F. Austin could transplant the old social order there, could not Robert Owen plant the new, and con-found all opponents with its manifest superiority? By the time Owen reached England in the autumn of 1828 he was full of a new scheme. On October 10 he drew up and published a *Memorial of Robert Owen to the Mexican Republic, and to the Government of the State of Coahuila and Texas,* requesting a grant of the entire province last mentioned, to be colonized with Owenite communities. The Mexican minister told Owen, in the clearest language a diplomat is permitted to use, that the proposal was fantastic, but Owen took his words as a challenge to greater exertions. On November 22, 1828, he sailed for Mexico, armed with letters of introduction from an astonishing array of important public men—testimony to the prestige he still enjoyed in Great Britain. He spent something less than two weeks in Mexico City in February 1829, and came away proclaiming that, though the whole of Texas could nót be his, he had nevertheless received "the promise of the Mexican government, to place a district, one hundred and fifty miles broad, along the whole line of frontier bor-dering on the U. States, under Mr. Owen's jurisdiction, for the pur-pose of establishing a new political and moral system of government, founded on the laws of nature." All this was on the title page of his next publication; in the text he admitted that a legislative act or so still stood between the alleged promise and its fulfillment. One wonders whether Owen actually believed that he had received such

[25] Maclure to Mme Fretageot, Springfield, O., July 24, Aug. 2, 1826; Cincinnati, Aug. 29, 1826, MSS in Workingmen's Institute, partially quoted in *Correspondence*, p. 360; "Pelham Letters," p. 415 (Jan. 10, 1827); Paul Brown, *Twelve Months*, p. 89.

[26] Miner K. Kellogg, "Brief Notes for an Autobiography . . . 1886," MS in Indiana Historical Society.

a promise, or that he enjoyed, as he elsewhere asserted, the backing of the Rothschilds and Baring Brothers. He had an enormous capacity for self-deception, and his narrative breathed all the old assurance; on the other hand, one must note that he never betrayed the least surprise when the entire project quietly vanished into the air.[27]

Quite unconnected with the Owenite movement in the United States was a single experiment on Canadian soil in the 1820's. A retired British naval officer, Henry Jones, became a convert to Owenism, obtained from the Crown a grant of ten thousand acres at the southern end of Lake Huron, some ten miles east of the River St. Clair, in what is now Sarnia Township, Lambton County, Ontario. To this unsurveyed wilderness he brought at his own expense a party of emigrants from Scotland and in 1827 or thereabouts began an experiment on Owenite principles, calling the colony Maxwell. A missionary to the Indians stumbled upon the settlement in 1829 and found that the members had one by one abandoned their communitarian principles.[28]

Though the independent Owenite communities that sprang into

[27] Owen wrote a circumstantial account with a circumstantial title, *Robert Owen's Opening Speech, and His Reply to the Rev. Alex. Campbell, in the Recent Public Discussion in Cincinnati, to Prove That the Principles of All Religions Are Erroneous, and That Their Practice Is Injurious to the Human Race. Also, Mr. Owen's Memorial to the Republic of Mexico, and a Narrative of the Proceedings Thereon, Which Led to the Promise of the Mexican Government, to Place a District, One Hundred and Fifty Miles Broad, along the Whole Line of Frontier Bordering on the U. States, under Mr. Owen's Jurisdiction, for the Purpose of Establishing a New Political and Moral System of Government, Founded on the Laws of Nature, as Explained in the Above Debate with Mr. Campbell* (Cincinnati: Published for Robert Owen, 1829), pp. 175–226. William Maclure encountered Owen in Mexico, and there are interesting sidelights in the *Maclure-Fretageot Correspondence*, pp. 402–5. Podmore uses unpublished material from the Owen papers at Manchester in his *Robert Owen*, I, 336–40. Photostats of other relevant documents from the same collection are in the Illinois Historical Survey. Archival sources are cited in William R. Manning, *Early Diplomatic Relations between the United States and Mexico* (Baltimore, 1916), pp. 323–24; and there is a letter on the project in Eugene C. Barker, ed., *The Austin Papers* (American Historical Association, *Annual Report, 1922*, vol. II; Washington, 1928), II, 214. No new sources are utilized by Wilbert H. Timmons, "Robert Owen's Texas Project," *Southwestern Historical Quarterly*, LII, 286–93 (Jan. 1949).

[28] Peter Jones [no relative of the founder], *Life and Journals of Kah-Ke-Wa-Quo-Nā-By (Rev. Peter Jones,) Wesleyan Missionary* (Toronto, 1860), p. 244. This is apparently the only contemporary document. The recollections of descendants, together with this one reference, are woven into the account by John Morrison, "The 'Toon o' Maxwell'—An Owen Settlement in Lambton County, Ont.," Ontario Historical Society, *Papers and Records*, XII (1914), 1–12. Though published in 1914, this paper was read on Sept. 17, 1909. See Ontario Historical Society, *Annual Report, 1909*, p. 34. The identical article, but with authorship attributed to Will Dallas, was published in the *Canadian Magazine of Politics, Science, Art and Literature*, XXXIV, 323–28 (Feb. 1910).

existence or near-existence in New York and Pennsylvania and down the Ohio Valley testified to the potency of Owen's propaganda, their individual histories did little more than repeat on a smaller scale the experience of New Harmony. The impact of Owenism upon American thought, however, cannot be measured by these experiments alone. Many different movements for social reform in the years following 1825 came under the influence of the new view of society. In particular, the movement for emancipating the slaves, cross-fertilized by Owenism, produced a communitarian experiment that differed markedly in pattern from those that have been described.

The question of slavery had reached, by the middle 1820's, a stage to which the communitarian approach was particularly relevant. The militant abolitionism of William Lloyd Garrison was a thing of the future. Southern interest in ultimate emancipation was still alive. Replacement of slavery, not its violent destruction, was the objective in view, and the crux of the problem was to devise a set of relationships, economic and social, that might safely supersede the peculiar institution. A revolutionary approach was unthinkable—to array class against class in a servile insurrection was precisely the thing to be feared. A gradualist approach, by which freedmen would increase in numbers through individual manumissions, was being viewed with increasing disfavor, as discriminatory legislation against free Negroes made clear. The idea of colonization, first taken up with enthusiasm after the War of 1812, was not in itself a communitarian plan, but it did involve the very process of group migration that had engendered communitarianism in the past among the German sectarians. And after the colony of Monrovia in Liberia was finally planted in 1822 by the American Colonization Society, the absence of any clear-cut plan for the economic and social future of the settlement constituted a standing invitation to communitarian theorists.

Consequently, when Robert Owen began his propaganda in the United States only two years after the founding of Monrovia, more than one of his hearers seized upon his plan as an answer to the problem of Negro colonization. On his first trip down the Ohio to New Harmony in December 1824, one of his fellow passengers remarked that Owen's "was the only feasible plan he had ever seen, by which emancipation could be carried into effect," for all it required was a government grant of land "to the negroes to construct a settlement on this plan." [29] A variation was proposed in the columns of the *National Intelligencer* in March 1825, immediately after Owen's discourses in the Capitol. The writer, a Virginian, suggested "to the Managers of the 'American Colonization Society' the propriety of satisfying themselves of the practicability of Mr. Owen's social system,

[29] William Owen, *Diary*, p. 64 (Dec. 10, 1824).

and of inquiring into the expediency of introducing it into the colony lately established, under their auspices, on the coast of Africa." [30]

It was a young Englishwoman, Frances Wright, who saw these possibilities most vividly.[31] As a sensitive liberal she had tended to avoid the embarrassing question of slavery in her *Views of Society and Manners in America*, which embodied the observations she had made during a first tour in 1818–20. On September 11, 1824, two months before Owen, she landed for the second time in the United States, to participate in the triumphal progress of her friend and protector, Lafayette. Much of the winter of 1824–25 was spent in Washington, and before she left on February 26, 1825, she had taken part in many discussions not only of slavery but also of the ideas which Owen proclaimed in his first discourse the day before her departure and which he had been privately expounding in the capital during the preceding weeks. From Washington Miss Wright went almost directly to New Harmony, where she spent three days in March 1825 discussing the community system with the Rappites who still remained and with young William Owen.[32] Before the month was over she was at Albion, Illinois, elaborating in conversations with George Flower her plan for combining the communitarianism of his neighbors with the antislavery principles to which he was zealously

[30] Washington *National Intelligencer*, March 26, 1825, p. 4:2. The application of Owen's plan to the training of slaves for emancipation was also suggested in the *Cincinnati Literary Gazette*, III, 162 n. (May 21, 1825).

[31] The standard biography is William R. Waterman, *Frances Wright* (Columbia University, *Studies in History, Economics and Public Law*, vol. CXV, no. 1; New York, 1924). Somewhat fuller is A. J. G. Perkins and Theresa Wolfson, *Frances Wright, Free Enquirer: The Study of a Temperament* (New York, 1939), a book that is generally sound in chronology and interpretation but marred by such inexcusable inaccuracies in quotation that it must be used with caution. Both works made use of the Frances Wright MSS, then in the possession of the late Rev. Dr. William Norman Guthrie, grandson of Mme Frances Wright D'Arusmont, and not available to the present writer. The two biographies furnish copious extracts from the manuscript most significant for the history of Nashoba, the "Journal of the Plantation," or "Nashoba Book," containing entries from 1825 to 1829. There are also a number of manuscripts in the Workingmen's Institute, New Harmony. On the whole, however, the contemporary printed materials on the Nashoba experiment are the fullest and most revealing sources. Most of the documents were published or else reprinted in the *New-Harmony Gazette* and its successor, detailed references to which (as well as to other scattered sources) are given in the footnotes that follow. On Nashoba, see also Mrs. Frances M. Trollope, *Domestic Manners of the Americans* (2 vols., London, 1832), I, 37–42; and Robert Dale Owen, *Autobiography*, pp. 296–304. No additional sources are used in the two most recent articles on Nashoba: Edd Winfield Parks, "Dreamer's Vision: Frances Wright at Nashoba (1825–30)," *Tennessee Historical Magazine*, 2d series, II, 75–86 (Jan. 1932); and O. B. Emerson, "Frances Wright and Her Nashoba Experiment," *Tennessee Historical Quarterly*, VI, 289–314 (Dec. 1947).

[32] William Owen, *Diary*, p. 128 (March 19–21, 1825).

devoted. In point of fact, he may well have contributed more of the ideas than she, for it will be remembered that a similar project had been suggested to his mind six years before by his observation of the Rappites. "Mr. Flower," wrote a visitor to the English Prairie in 1819, "intends to form a society for freeing blacks, and employing free blacks. It is to be on the Harmony plan." [33]

By midsummer of 1825 Miss Wright's plan was formulated. Through the good offices of Lafayette it was communicated to Jefferson, Madison, Monroe, Marshall, and Jackson,[34] and by the end of August it had been printed at Baltimore as a pamphlet. The Moravians, Shakers, and Rappites, rather than New Harmony, were cited in the opening paragraphs, not because Miss Wright was uninfluenced by Owen, but because she wished to call attention to the undeniable successes already achieved by communitarianism. Actually she adopted the characteristic reasoning of the Owenites when she asserted "the great advantage of united, over individual labor"; when she argued "that if a more humane and profitable system should be brought to bear in any one state, the example must gradually extend through all"; when she suggested a small-scale, experimental beginning; and when she emphasized the favorite educational idea of Owen and Maclure, "a school of industry." In all these respects her plan was a communitarian one, but in its ultimate ends it was not strictly so. The communitarian ideal was a permanent reconstruction of society according to the pattern laid down in an initial experiment. Miss Wright, too, was anxious to establish a pattern, but it was not a pattern for the society of the future. On two sections of land she would gather fifty or a hundred slaves who would earn the money for their emancipation at the same time that they learned the skills and attitudes requisite for freedom.[35] Once they had done this, they would be swept into the stream of colonization and carried beyond the limits, not only of the country, but also of any social order that Miss Wright was interested in constructing.

Though Jefferson and Madison were cautious in their expressions of qualified approval, Miss Wright proceeded at once to carry out her plan. In September 1825 she stopped at New Harmony and Albion once more, and then, accompanied by George Flower, went

[33] William Faux, *Memorable Days in America* (1823), as reprinted in Thwaites, ed., *Early Western Travels*, XI, 259. Also see above, p. 49.

[34] Jefferson to Frances Wright, Monticello, Aug. 7, 1825, in his *Writings;* ed. by Lipscomb and Bergh, XVI, 119–21; Madison to same, Montpelier, Sept. 1, 1825, in his *Letters and Other Writings* (4 vols., Philadelphia, 1865), III, 495–98; Lafayette to same, Washington, Aug. 26, 1825, in Anna B. A. Brown, "A Dream of Emancipation," *New England Magazine*, XXXVI [n.s. XXX], 495 (June 1904).

[35] [Frances Wright], "A Plan for the Gradual Abolition of Slavery," *New-Harmony Gazette*, I, 4–5 (Oct. 1, 1825), reprinted from the Baltimore pamphlet.

south to pick a site for the colony. This she found along the Wolf River in Shelby County, Tennessee, some fourteen miles from Memphis. Three hundred acres of former Chickasaw land were acquired in November 1825, additional purchases soon brought the total to two thousand, and the Chickasaw name Nashoba was bestowed upon the uncleared plantation. During the winter the experiment got under way. Miss Wright was joined by her sister, by George Flower and his family, and by a certain James Richardson. Under their tutelage were a dozen or so slaves, acquired partly by purchase and partly by gift.

During May and June of 1826, however, Frances Wright visited New Harmony again. Owen and Maclure were there, as they had not been on her previous trips, and the great experiment was in full operation. She was immensely impressed by the intellectual ferment of the place, and she imbibed, apparently at this time, many of the specific radical ideas that she was to proclaim in the next few years. Frances Wright, the liberal, became Fanny Wright, the "Priestess of Beelzebub." So significant was this transformation for the history not only of Nashoba, but of the Owenite movement as a whole, that a brief digression is necessary.

Owen's critical attitude toward revealed religion had been no secret, of course, since his public addresses in London in 1817, but he had said little on the matter during his propaganda campaign in America in 1824 and 1825. Not he but his critics had raised the issue. Back in New Harmony in 1826, however, he found himself in the midst of a group who avowed their deistic views with an openness and militancy he had not met with before. Hostility to conventional religion was shared by such opposed individuals as William Maclure and Paul Brown. As the orthodox drifted off to Macluria and elsewhere, the rationalistic tone of the discussions at New Harmony became more pronounced.

Among the irrationalities that came under attack in this free-spoken society were the institutions not only of religion but also of marriage. If Owen had speculated on the latter question, he had hitherto held his peace.[36] But in the congenial atmosphere that surrounded him, and under the strong conviction that he was in truth inaugurating the millennium, Owen began to turn over in his mind all the various criticisms of society that he and his contemporaries

[36] In fact, his silence was charged against him after he had spoken his mind. "Did he invite the younger part of the females to admit to their embraces the young men as long as they shou[l]d be pleased with them, or not? . . . did he give his invitations in such language as those to whom they were addressed could not possibly mistake the entire plan of the invitor? If he fell short of this, he is chargeable with a larger share of deception that usually attaches to the old world." Shawnee-Town *Illinois Gazette*, July 15, 1826, p. 1:1–3.

were voicing. Gradually he came to see the abuses of his time as a triple-headed hydra, and the fiftieth anniversary of American independence as the appropriate time for its slaying. His Fourth of July oration in 1826 was entitled "A Declaration of Mental Independence," and in it he proclaimed his intention of freeing mankind from "a TRINITY of the most monstrous evils that could be combined to inflict mental and physical evil," namely, "PRIVATE, OR INDIVIDUAL PROPERTY—absurd and irrational SYSTEMS OF RELIGION—and MARRIAGE, founded on individual property combined with some one of these irrational systems of religion." [37]

The waves of religious disapproval beat upon him once more, but to them was now added an even darker undercurrent of suspicion and hostility. Baseless rumors of sexual infidelity at New Harmony began to circulate, and Owen himself was often the subject of those whispered tales that are too gross for print but never too gross to pass from the scandalmonger to his snickering listener. Maclure, distrustful of Owen in some matters, was not distrustful in this, and he wrote and caused to be published a letter asserting that he "never was in any place farther removed from every species of vice," or one "where the married are so faithful, or the young so chaste." [38]

Once Owen's words had been uttered, denials like these could not stem the torrent of abuse. Prior to the "Declaration of Mental Independence" the principal criticism of New Harmony, along such lines as these, had been based on the alleged immodesty of the pantaloon costume adopted there:

> In beauty there's something to hide and reveal,
> There's a thing which we decency call;
> The old system ladies display a great deal,
> But the new system ladies—*show all*.[39]

There was no humor among the grim-visaged defenders of virtue who raised their voices after the "Declaration." This was their language

[37] *New-Harmony Gazette*, I, 330 (July 12, 1826). Originally this passage was printed almost entirely in capitals and italics; I have retained Owen's emphases but in simpler typographic dress.

[38] William Maclure [to Mrs. Joseph Sistaire], Springfield, O., Aug. 4, 1826, in Washington *National Intelligencer*, Oct. 5, 1826, p. 4:3; reprinted from Philadelphia *United States Gazette*, Sept. 27; see also *Maclure-Fretageot Correspondence*, pp. 349, 355. Owen's views on marriage were defended by another contributor to the *National Intelligencer*, Sept. 21, 1826, p. 2:1.

[39] Shawnee-Town *Illinois Gazette*, July 1, 1826, p. 4:1–2. Satire of Owenism was rarer than frontal attack, but there were a few examples. James Kirke Paulding produced the most notable one in his *Merry Tales of the Three Wise Men of Gotham* (New York, 1826), which is discussed in Mentor L. Williams, "Paulding Satirizes Owenism," *Indiana Magazine of History*, XLIV, 355–65 (Dec. 1948). Quite entertaining and cleverly managed is an anonymous satire in the Washington *National Intelligencer*, Sept. 5, 1826, p. 3:1, continued on Oct. 3, p. 4:1.

now: "If we are allowed to judge of the moral character of the New Harmony society, by the licentious principles of their founder and leader, it would be no breach of charity, to class them all with whores and whoremongers, nor to say that the whole group will constitute one great brothel." [40] The diatribe was a breach both of charity and of truth. No instance of licentiousness at New Harmony was ever authenticated. It was not Owen's community but Fanny Wright's at Nashoba that confirmed the black forebodings of critics.

The young Englishwoman left New Harmony early in the summer of 1826, convinced that communitarianism had even more to offer than she had realized, and convinced also that religious and sexual emancipation was as imperative as emancipation from slavery itself. Though illness plagued her at Nashoba during the rest of the year, she was maturing in her mind a new and more radical plan for her community. On December 17, 1826, she announced it to the world.

In the first place, she superimposed upon the original experiment in Negro education a communitarian colony open to whites and "founded on the principle of community of property and labor." She had no expectation that racial equality would be realized among the existing generation of adults, but she planned to achieve it in the next by giving to the children of the community, white and colored together, an identical education. Though colonization was still mentioned in the deed of trust, Miss Wright attacked the Colonization Society in her accompanying statement, and made it clear in other ways that her earlier sympathy with the southern attitude on racial matters had disappeared. To round out the radicalism of her statement, she announced that the establishment would be free of all religious entanglements, "inasmuch as the liberty of the mind . . . can alone constitute a free man." [41]

In this comprehensive defiance of public opinion Miss Wright had the discretion to remain silent on the most unconventional of the doctrines she had imbibed at New Harmony. It remained for a colleague of hers to divulge the fact that the leaders of Nashoba harbored ideas upon sex as radical as their ideas upon race. In the spring of 1827, the situation at New Harmony having become hopeless, Robert Dale Owen joined Miss Wright at Nashoba and then accompanied her to Europe to seek support for her enterprise. In virtual charge at Nashoba was James Richardson, as methodical and uncompromising

---

[40] Indianapolis *Indiana Journal*, Nov. 14, 1826, p. 3:1. Little less restrained was a series of letters contributed by "A Christian" to the Shawnee-Town *Illinois Gazette*, May 13, 1826, p. 3:2; July 15, p. 1:1–3; Aug. 19, pp. 2:4 and 3:1–3; Sept. 30, pp. 2:4 and 3:1–2; Dec. 2, pp. 2:4 and 3:1–2.

[41] *New-Harmony Gazette*, I, 164–65 (Feb. 21, 1827).

a fanatic in his own way as Paul Brown in his. White men had had sexual intercourse with slave women before, but it had probably occurred to none of them to enter the fact in the official records of an eleemosynary institution, and having done so to publish a transcript. To James Richardson, however, this seemed the appropriate course for a reformer. The startled readers of Benjamin Lundy's *Genius of Universal Emancipation* found in the issue of July 28, 1827, a series of extracts from the "Nashoba Book," communicated by Richardson as evidence of the progress of the experiment. Two entries attracted immediate attention:

FRIDAY, JUNE 1, 1827.

Met the slaves at dinner time—Isabel had laid a complaint against Redrick, for coming during the night of Wednesday to her bedroom, uninvited; and endeavoring, without her consent, to take liberties with her person. Our views of the sexual relation had been repeatedly given to the slaves: Camilla Wright again stated it. . . . She repeated, that we consider the proper basis of the sexual intercourse to be the unconstrained and unrestrained choice of *both* parties. Nelly having requested a lock for the door of the room in which she and Isabel sleep, with the view of preventing the future uninvited entrance of any man; the lock was refused, as being, in its proposed use, inconsistent with the doctrine just explained. . . .

SUNDAY EVENING, JUNE 17, 1827.

Met the slaves—James Richardson informed them that, last night, Mamselle Josephine and he began to live together; and he took this occasion of repeating to them our views on color, and on the sexual relation.[42]

Horrified defenders of morality had already exhausted their vocabulary upon Owen. There was something a little tame and repetitious about their denunciation of Nashoba as "one great brothel." But there was nothing tame about the fury with which they turned upon Fanny Wrightism.

Miss Wright herself was too honest to disavow the basic principle of absolutely unfettered freedom which she felt was at stake. On her voyage back to America in December 1827 she penned a series of "Explanatory Notes, Respecting the Nature and Objects of the Institution of Nashoba," in which she defined, in the most sweeping possible terms, the "moral liberty" she sought: "the *free exercise of the liberty of speech and of action*, without incurring the intolerance of popular prejudice." If, she exclaimed, "the possession of the

42 *Genius of Universal Emancipation*, VII (n.s., IV), 30 (July 28, 1827). Mamselle Josephine was identified in a footnote as "a Quarteroon [*sic*], daughter of Mamselle Lolotte." On the furor that followed the publication of the article see Waterman, *Frances Wright*, pp. 117 *et seqq.*, and Perkins and Wolfson, *Frances Wright*, pp. 166 *et seqq.*

right of free action inspire not the courage to exercise the right, liberty has done but little for us." [43]

As the horizons of reform grew wider for Frances Wright, the prospects of her community at Nashoba contracted. She and Robert Dale Owen took stock of its practical affairs upon their return from Europe, and on February 1, 1828, issued a sober "Communication from the Trustees of Nashoba." In common with other attempts "to form a community of equality and of common property," Nashoba, they admitted, had encountered "many difficulties." As a consequence they were announcing "a modification of the plan originally adopted." It was nothing less than an abandonment of communitarianism:

In a cooperative community, when perfectly organized, the simple relation between the society and the individual is, that the latter devotes his time and his labor for the public good in any way the public voice may enjoin, while the society supports each individual member. . . .

In the outset of their labors the Trustees perceived, that it would be a very difficult matter to find men and women with all the qualifications. . . . Many of the individuals who were the best calculated *mentally* and *morally* for the good work, wanted physical force and practical knowledge. . . . To meet this difficulty they agreed, that where the mental and moral qualifications existed, they would receive, instead of labor, a certain sum of money yearly. . . .

The society thus assumed a mixed form. It admitted some members to labor, and others as boarders from whom no labor was required. Now the experience of the Trustees has proved to them, that they erred in so doing. . . .

It became necessary, therefore, either that physical labor should be required *from all*, or that it should be required from *none;* in other words either that the society assume the form of a simple cooperative society, or else of a society of small capitalists. . . .

Convinced that one of these modifications was necessary for the present generation of human beings, half-trained as they are, the trustees have determined to adopt the latter, and to receive those members only who possess the funds necessary for their support. . . .

The Trustees desire to express distinctly *that they have deferred for the present the attempt to form a society of cooperative labor, and they claim for their association only the title of a preliminary* SOCIAL COMMUNITY.[44]

In an accompanying editorial, signed with his initials, Robert Dale Owen restated the argument of the "Communication." [45] It was his

[43] *New-Harmony Gazette,* III, 124 (Jan. 30, 1828). The "Explanatory Notes" ran through three installments, to III, 141 (Feb. 13, 1828), and bore the date Dec. 4, 1827.

[44] *New-Harmony Gazette,* III, 172 (March 26, 1828).

[45] *Ibid.,* p. 174.

epitaph on the entire communitarian movement which his father had inaugurated in the United States.

The "Preliminary Social Community" at Nashoba was stillborn. Robert Dale Owen left less than a month after the trustees decided to establish it, and on June 4, 1828, Frances Wright herself departed. Her sister and brother-in-law were left in charge of the slaves, but in January 1830 Miss Wright sailed with them to Haiti, where their emancipation concluded the Nashoba experiment and swept away the last vestiges of communitarian life in America attributable to Owen's influence.

The voyage to Haiti constituted a brief interruption of the career, embracing reforms of a different type, which Robert Dale Owen and Frances Wright had embarked upon in 1828, after the abandonment of communitarianism at New Harmony and Nashoba. Despite the horror which new ideas on religion and marriage excited in the minds of many, there was a liberal audience in America willing to listen. Miss Wright had been unable to reach that audience from Nashoba, but in 1828 she discovered that she could reach it from the lecture platforms of the great cities. By the spring of 1829 she and young Owen were established in New York, possessed of a journal of their own—the old *New-Harmony Gazette,* rechristened *The Free Enquirer,*[46]—and of a Hall of Science, where their propaganda might take oral form. The rise of a workingmen's party in New York on the eve of the elections of 1829 provided a new outlet for the reformers' energies, and in addition furnished young Owen with a training in politics that prepared him for a public career far different from that which had been in his mind when he first came to America.

The activities of the free enquirers in New York form no real part

[46] The *New-Harmony Gazette* concluded its third volume on Oct. 22, 1828, and was succeeded by *The New-Harmony and Nashoba Gazette, or The Free Enquirer,* of which 18 numbers (described as 2d series, vol. I), were published at New Harmony, Oct. 29, 1828–Feb. 25, 1829, edited primarily by Robert Dale Owen, and "printed by William Phiquepal and his pupils." Frances Wright, nominally the co-editor, established herself in New York at the end of 1828 and on Jan. 28, 1829, began to publish a New York edition of the periodical, entitling it simply *The Free Enquirer.* The previously published numbers were reprinted, with contents considerably rearranged, at the rate of two a week. Thus no. 1 of *The Free Enquirer* was dated Oct. 29, 1828, in the heading, but carried a section at the end with the date-line New York, Jan. 28, 1829; no. 16, ostensibly for Feb. 11, 1829, concluded with a New York section dated April 19, 1829; nos. 17 and 18 were completed subsequent to April 29, as the advertisements show. Beginning with no. 19, for March 4, 1829, both series were merged in New York, under the title of *The Free Enquirer.* A file of the New Harmony edition is in the Indiana State Library, of the New York edition in the Library of Congress; photographic copies of both are in the Illinois Historical Survey. After 1832 Owen and Miss Wright ceased to be responsible for *The Free Enquirer,* but it continued as an organ of free thought until 1835.

of the history of communitarianism. They represent, in fact, a translation of Owenite social radicalism from the language of communitarian experiment into the different language of gradualist reform. This transfer is important in the history of the other movements, for into many of them it infused certain elements from Owen's wide-ranging view of society. In engrafting, for example, the "state guardianship" plan of education upon the political program of the workingmen, the free enquirers carried over into the labor movement and into politics the old communitarian ideal of a school where children would be separated from the pernicious influences of existing society by being boarded and clothed together at the common expense, raised in an atmosphere of perfect equality, trained in both manual and intellectual skills, and graduated at last as citizens capable of remaking the institutions of the old immoral world.[47]

In education, in the labor movement, in free thought, the Owenite legacy was a thing to be reckoned with in the years that followed Robert Owen's departure from America in the summer of 1829. In the end, moreover, these other reform movements each contributed something to the revival of communitive ideas after 1840. But what of the communitarian movement itself during the interval?

Owenism was in ruins when its founder sailed for England. The entire secular communitive movement, so promising when he arrived five years before, was blighted by his failure. Between 1827 and 1840 only a single experimental community came into being under purely secular auspices—the tiny settlement of Equity, in Tuscarawas County, Ohio, which the old New Harmonite Josiah Warren founded in 1835.[48] More than a decade of time, a major depression, and a shift of leaders and philosophies were needed to erase the effect of Owen's failure and to secure for communitarianism another trial as a means of secular social reform. The blight is understandable. What requires explanation is the ultimate revival. To all appearances the fate of the entire communitive movement had been staked on the experiment at New Harmony, yet in the end its failure was not accepted as conclusive.

This can be explained in part by the fact that there were too many reasons, all equally good, for the disaster. Each of Owen's personal mistakes had been sufficient in itself to wreck the experiment. If his practical management was at fault, then his basic principles may not have been. If his indiscriminate admission of members had

---

[47] Besides the biographies of Frances Wright and Robert Dale Owen, see John R. Commons and others, *History of Labour in the United States* (4 vols., 1918–35), I, 231–84.

[48] See Eunice M. Schuster, *Native American Anarchism* (Smith College *Studies in History*, vol. XVII, nos. 1–4; Northampton, Mass., 1931–32), p. 98; William Bailie, *Josiah Warren*, pp. 39–40.

doomed the enterprise, then how could one be sure that there was a fatal defect in the theory? In a firing squad, if all the guns are loaded, which man performs the execution?

In the second place, by the end of the 1820's Owenism was identified in the public mind less with communitarianism than with free thought. As early as 1826 the principal news that came out of New Harmony was concerned not with the difficulties of the community but with Owen's "Declaration of Mental Independence." Even the failure of the great experiment in 1827 attracted no such attention as the petty but sensational scandal at Nashoba. And the memory of Owen's communitarian discourses in the Capitol in 1825 was largely obliterated in 1829 by his notorious debate in Cincinnati with Alexander Campbell, designed, as Owen stated it, "to prove that the principles of all religions are erroneous, and that their practice is injurious to the human race." [49]

In the long run this was all to the advantage of the communitarian movement. Conservatives had seized upon Owen's infidel views as the handiest stick to beat the dog, and in the end they created the impression that New Harmony had failed because of its antireligious bias rather than any inherent defect in its economic principles. For the future, communitarianism had to fight the twin charges of infidelity and free love. But when in later years communitarians could prove that they subscribed to neither doctrine, they found it all the easier to dissociate their plans from the imputations of failure that clung to Owen's. In the 1840's the experience of New Harmony proved a surprisingly minor obstacle in the path of communitarian propaganda.

It was one thing to explain away the failure of New Harmony. It was another to preserve the breath of life in the communitarian movement that produced it. A social ideal cannot be nourished on

[49] *Robert Owen's Opening Speech, and His Reply to the Rev. Alex. Campbell* (Cincinnati, 1829). The quoted phrase is from the long title, which is given in full above, n. 27. Owen published only his own side of the debate, blandly explaining in the preface that his arguments sufficed to "render all the speculations on the subject of religion nugatory." His antagonist was more scrupulous and published a full report, Alexander Campbell, ed., *Debate on the Evidences of Christianity . . . between Robert Owen . . . and Alexander Campbell* (2 vols., Bethany, Va., 1829). Friendship and respect, however, always characterized the relationships between the two men. Eighteen years after the debate Campbell wrote: "I am sorry for the honor of sectarian Christianity, but glad for the honor of human nature, to state what you may have heard me say on other occasions, that, of all my opponents in debate, the infidel Robert Owen was the most candid, fair, and gentlemanly disputant I have yet met with; and a saint in morality, compared with some of my opponents." A. Campbell, "Letters from Europe—No. I," dated May 22, 1847, in *Millennial Harbinger* (Bethany, Va.), 3d series, IV, 420 (July 1847).

excuses. It was not the Owenites who kept communitarianism alive during the lean years from 1827 to 1840, it was the sectarian communities. The Shakers, the Rappites, and the Separatists of Zoar were untouched by what Owen did. Though the number of these communities did not increase in the decade after the New Harmony failure, their membership grew steadily, and their material prosperity mounted even faster. To borrow once again the metaphor of John Humphrey Noyes, they provided "the 'specie basis' that . . . upheld all the paper theories, and counteracted all the failures" of secular communitism.[50]

So long as they did so, communitarianism, even as a secular ideal, would not die. The failure of one plan was the failure of that plan alone. Someday the practical arrangements would be devised that would unite men and women as harmoniously in a community devoted to social reform as in one inspired by religious zeal. The details alone were in doubt, the ultimate results were certain. They could be seen in almost a score of trim Shaker villages, or in the prosperous settlement of the Rappites. It was only when these communities faltered and fell behind in the economic march that the communitarian faith wavered. This did not occur until the time of the Civil War, when the large scale of industrial enterprise began to render obsolete as economic units the small communities on which the communitarians had pinned their hopes. Before the coming of that fatal day, time yet remained for one last upsurge of communitarian effort. To reformers in the 1840's, as to those in the 1820's, the new society which the world awaited might yet be born in the humble guise of a backwoods village.

[50] Noyes, *History of American Socialisms,* p. 670. Also see above, pp. 53, 58–59.

APPENDIX

CHECKLIST OF COMMUNITARIAN EXPERIMENTS
INITIATED IN THE UNITED STATES
BEFORE 1860

Introductory Note

Period I. Prior to 1825
  A. Foreign-Language Sectarian Communities
  B. Shaker Villages
  C. Other English-Language Communities

Period II. 1825–1839
  A. Owenite Communities
  B. Foreign-Language Sectarian Communities
  C. Shaker Villages
  D. Other English-Language Communities

Period III. 1840–1860
  A. Fourierist Phalanxes
  B. Owenite Communities
  C. Other English-Language Communities
  D. Foreign-Language Sectarian Communities
  E. Other Foreign-Language Communities

Statistical Summary

INTRODUCTORY NOTE

The following checklist is a record of the experiments that actually began organized community life, as attested by substantial evidence. Several names, frequently given in earlier tabulations, are excluded on the ground that they probably never passed beyond the stage of projects. Though the present volume deals only with communitarianism before 1829, it has seemed best to present in the same table the data covering the period of a projected second volume on the Fourierist movement of the 1840's and 1850's.

For each community, information is given on (1) the year in which community life actually began, (2) the various names which it used, and (3) the precise geographical location in terms of modern political subdivisions. The exact sites of many Shaker villages and a few Fourierist phalanxes are perpetuated in such names as Shakers and Phalanx, found on large-scale maps like those of the United States Geological Survey. Where such is the case the place name is given in the table, together with the approximate distance from a village that can be found on maps of smaller scale. Public institutions of various kinds now make use of the buildings of many Shaker colonies, and the names of these are also recorded in the table. To show the continuity between one period and the next, earlier communities that were still in existence in 1825 are marked with an asterisk; those still in existence in 1840 with a double asterisk.

Communitarianism can be understood and evaluated, so the present writer believes, only through a careful study of the historical record, not through attempted generalization from statistical data as imperfect as that which can be compiled for the older communitarian colonies. No attempt has therefore been made to record such fluctuating data as the total membership and the extent of landholdings, or to sum up in a phrase the causes of failure, as some tabulations attempt to do. The only statistical table is one arranged to show the incidence of communitarian enthusiasm in time and place.

Classification raises a number of problems. The fundamental distinction, in the author's opinion, is not between religious and secular communities, but between sectarian communities, in which uniform adherence to a fixed body of religious doctrine was enforced, and nonsectarian communities, in which such tests were not imposed. The latter are here classified as Owenite or Fourierist only if they gave primary and avowed allegiance to the principles of one of these systems. It must be remembered, however, that the communitarian philosophies in vogue at a particular period influenced all the experiments to a greater or less degree.

Moreover, one must often be arbitrary in deciding whether to list a given experiment as one community or several. The Rappites, for example, were a single body, but they occupied three successive sites and are here listed three times. New Harmony, on the other hand, was organized into an indeterminate number of distinct communities, but is here listed only once. In general it seems more useful to disregard internal divisions of a community if confined to one location, and to make separate geographic location the test of a distinct experiment. Even this breaks down, however, in the case of the "General Economy" of the Moravians, which was for a time applied in most, if not all, the different congregations, but which must be treated, in any practicable tabulation, as a single experiment.

The first attempt to compile an inclusive table of American communitarian experiments was made by John Humphrey Noyes, whose *History of American Socialisms* (Philadelphia, 1870) includes lists of "Experiments of the Owen Epoch" and "Experiments of the Fourier Epoch" (pp. 15–17). The same two groups of experiments are tabulated in Carl Stegmann and C. Hugo, *Handbuch des Socialismus* (Zürich, 1897), pp. 202, 594–95. In 1902 William A. Hinds revised an earlier work of his, converting it into a comprehensive survey of communitive enterprises and presenting part of his material in tabular form. See his *American Communities* (revised ed., Chicago, 1902), and *American Communities and Co-operative Colonies* (2d revision [i.e., 3d ed.], Chicago, 1908). Frederick A. Bushee, "Communistic Societies in the United States," *Political Science Quarterly*, XX, 625–64 (Dec. 1905), is built around an elaborate tabulation of communities. Daniel J. Ryan, *Historic Failures in Applied Socialism* (5th ed., Columbus, O. [copyright 1920]), is a polemic work, incorporating older lists of communities. Ernest S. Wooster, *Communities of the Past and Present* (Newllano, La., 1924), is a compilation, partly tabular. In 1931 Lee Emerson Deets presented a tabulation of "American Idealistic Community Experiments" to a meeting of the Sociological Society of America. He subsequently revised and enlarged his table, which is embodied in Julia Elizabeth Williams, "An Analytical Tabulation of the North American Utopian Communities by Type, Longevity and Location," unpublished M.A. thesis, 1939, in University of South Dakota Library. The most carefully documented of all the general tabulations is Ralph Albertson, "A Survey of Mutualistic Communities in America," *Iowa Journal of History and Politics*, XXXIV, 375–444 (Oct. 1936). Also well-annotated is the regional compilation by Kenneth W. McKinley, "A Guide to the Communistic Communities of Ohio," *Ohio State Archaeological and Historical Quarterly*, XLVI, 1–15 (Jan. 1937).

Regrettably few of these compilers went back to the sources. An amusing bit of telltale evidence constantly recurs. Noyes's pioneer list included among the Owenite experiments the following four distinct colonies: Franklin Community, N.Y., Forrestville [*sic*] Community, Ind., Haverstraw Community, N.Y., and Coxsackie Community, N.Y. Actually there were only two, the Franklin Community at Haverstraw, N.Y., and the Forestville Community at Coxsackie, N.Y. Though this is perfectly clear from even the printed sources, the error is repeated in every one of the general compilations listed above, as well as in such a specialized work as G. B. Lockwood, *New Harmony Movement*, p. 177. It is only fair to say, however, that many of these tabulations are far more reliable for the period after 1860, the compilers having gathered much first-hand information from personal visits and direct correspondence.

CHECKLIST OF COMMUNITARIAN EXPERIMENTS

Period I. Prior to 1825

A. Foreign-Language Sectarian Communities

1663   PLOCKHOY'S COMMONWEALTH. At the mouth of the Hoorn Kill on the Delaware River, at what is now Lewes, Sussex County, Delaware. [1

1683   LABADIST COMMUNITY. Bohemia Manor on the Bohemia River, in what is now Cecil County, Maryland. [2

1694   SOCIETY OF THE WOMAN IN THE WILDERNESS, OR THE CONTENTED OF THE GOD-LOVING SOUL. On the Wissahickon Creek, near Germantown, Pennsylvania (within the present limits of Fairmount Park, Philadelphia). [3

1697   IRENIA, or TRUE CHURCH OF PHILADELPHIA or BROTHERLY LOVE, or BRETHREN IN AMERICA (an offshoot of the Society of the Woman in the Wilderness). Plymouth, north of Germantown, Pennsylvania. [4

1732 ** EPHRATA CLOISTER, or EPHRATA COMMUNITY. Ephrata, Ephrata Township, Lancaster County, Pennsylvania. [5

1744   THE "GENERAL ECONOMY" of the MORAVIAN BRETHREN. In effect at Bethlehem, Nazareth, and Lititz, Pennsylvania; at Wachovia (now Winston-Salem), North Carolina, and elsewhere. [6

ca. 1800 ** SEVENTH DAY BAPTIST CHURCH AT SNOW HILL, also called the SNOW HILL NUNNERY (an offshoot of Ephrata). Snow Hill, Quincy Township, Franklin County, Pennsylvania. [7

1805   HARMONIE SOCIETY (Rappites). Harmony, Jackson Township, Butler County, Pennsylvania. [8

1814   HARMONIE (second settlement of the Rappites). Harmonie (now New Harmony), Harmony Township, Posey County, Indiana. [9

1817 ** SOCIETY OF SEPARATISTS OF ZOAR. Zoar, Lawrence Township, Tuscarawas County, Ohio. [10

1824 ** ECONOMY (third and final settlement of the Rappites). Economy (adjoining Ambridge), Harmony Township, Beaver County, Pennsylvania. [11

B. Shaker Villages

1787 ** MOUNT LEBANON, or NEW LEBANON. Mount Lebanon, New Lebanon Township, Columbia County, New York. A branch, CANAAN, was located three miles south. Canaan Shakers, Canaan Township, Columbia County, New York. [12

1788 ** NISKEYUNA [now usually spelled Niskayuna], or WATERVLIET. Shakers (seven miles northwest of Albany), Colonie Township, Albany County, New York (now occupied by Ann Lee Home). [13

1790 ** HANCOCK, or WEST PITTSFIELD. Shaker Village (five miles west of Pittsfield), town of Hancock, Berkshire County, Massachusetts. [14

1790 ** ENFIELD (CONNECTICUT). Shakers (four miles east of Thompson-ville), town of Enfield, Hartford County, Connecticut (now occupied by Osborn State Prison Farm).   [15

1791 ** HARVARD. Shaker Village (three miles northeast of Harvard village, two miles southeast of Ayer), town of Harvard, Worcester County, Massachusetts (now occupied by Single-Tax "enclave").   [16

1792 ** TYRINGHAM. Town of Tyringham (three miles south of South Lee), Berkshire County, Massachusetts (owned by Sidney Howard, playwright, at time of his death in 1939).   [17

1792 ** CANTERBURY. Shaker Village (twelve miles north of Concord), town of Canterbury, Merrimack County, New Hampshire.   [18

1793 ** ENFIELD (NEW HAMPSHIRE). Upper and Lower Shaker Villages (on Mascoma Lake, twelve miles southeast of Dartmouth College), town of Enfield, Grafton County, New Hampshire (now occupied by Seminaire Lasallette).   [19

1793 ** SHIRLEY. Shaker Village (one mile south of Shirley village), town of Shirley, Middlesex County, Massachusetts.   [20

1793 ** ALFRED. Town of Alfred (two miles north of Alfred village), York County, Maine (now occupied by Institut de Notre Dame, which is shown on large-scale maps, with Shaker Pond near by).   [21

1794 ** SABBATHDAY LAKE, or NEW GLOUCESTER, or POLAND HILL. Sabbathday Lake (three miles south of Poland Spring), town of New Gloucester, Cumberland County, Maine.   [22

1794   GORHAM. Town of Gorham, Cumberland County, Maine.   [23

1805 ** UNION VILLAGE. Union Village (four miles west of Lebanon), Turtle Creek Township, Warren County, Ohio (now occupied by Lebanon State Prison Farm).   [24

1806 ** WATERVLIET (OHIO). Shakertown (on Little Beaver Creek, six miles southeast of Dayton), Van Buren Township, Montgomery County, Ohio.   [25

1809 ** SOUTH UNION, or GASPER SPRINGS. South Union (fifteen miles northeast of Russellville), Logan County, Kentucky.   [26

1809 ** PLEASANT HILL. Shakertown or Pleasanthill (seven miles east of Harrodsburg), Mercer County, Kentucky.   [27

1810 * WEST UNION, or BUSRO. Shaker Prairie Church (near confluence of Busseron Creek with Wabash River, sixteen miles above Vincennes), Haddon Township, Sullivan County, Indiana.   [28

1817   SAVOY. Town of Savoy, Berkshire County, Massachusetts.   [29

1822 ** NORTH UNION. Now the Shaker Heights suburb of Cleveland, Cuyahoga County, Ohio.   [30

C. Other English-Language Communities

1788   JERUSALEM (community of Jemima Wilkinson). Jerusalem, Yates County, New York.   [31

1798   DORRILITES. Leyden, Franklin County, Massachusetts, and Guilford, Windham County, Vermont.   [32

1804   THE UNION. Clark's Crossing, between Potsdam and Norwood, St. Lawrence County, New York.   [33

1817   PILGRIMS. South Woodstock, Windsor County, Vermont. (The group later migrated as far west as Missouri, but apparently established no real community elsewhere.)   [34

Period II. 1825–1839

A. Owenite Communities

1825   NEW HARMONY (including, in its various divisions and reorganizations: the PRELIMINARY SOCIETY OF NEW HARMONY; the NEW HARMONY COMMUNITY OF EQUALITY; MACLURIA, or NEW HARMONY COMMUNITY No. II; FEIBA-PEVELI, or NEW HARMONY COMMUNITY No. III; and various others described in the text). New Harmony (site of the second Rappite community), Harmony Township, Posey County, Indiana.   [35

1825   YELLOW SPRINGS COMMUNITY. Yellow Springs, Miami Township, Greene County, Ohio (site now occupied by Antioch College).   [36

1826   FRANKLIN COMMUNITY, or HAVERSTRAW COMMUNITY. Haverstraw, Rockland County, New York.   [37

1826   FORESTVILLE COMMUNITY, or COXSACKIE COMMUNITY. Lapham's Mills, Coxsackie, Greene County, New York.   [38

1826   KENDAL COMMUNITY, or FRIENDLY ASSOCIATION FOR MUTUAL INTERESTS AT KENDAL. Kendal (now part of the city of Massillon), Perry Township, Stark County, Ohio.   [39

1826   VALLEY FORGE COMMUNITY, or FRIENDLY ASSOCIATION FOR MUTUAL INTERESTS. Valley Forge, Chester County, Pennsylvania.   [40

1826   BLUE SPRING COMMUNITY. Van Buren Township (near Bloomington), Monroe County, Indiana.   [41

B. Foreign-Language Sectarian Communities

1832   NEW PHILADELPHIA SOCIETY (secession from the Rappites). Phillipsburg (now Monaca), Beaver County, Pennsylvania.   [42

1834   GRAND ECORE (continuation of New Philadelphia Society). Natchitoches Parish, Louisiana.   [43

1836   GERMANTOWN (continuation of Grand Ecore). Eight miles north of Minden, Webster Parish, Louisiana.   [44

C. Shaker Villages

1825 ** WHITEWATER. Shaker Village (twelve miles southwest of Hamilton), Crosby Township, Hamilton County, Ohio.   [45

1826   SODUS BAY. On Sodus Bay, in Sodus and Huron townships, Wayne County, New York (now privately owned as Alasa Farms).   [46

1836 ** GROVELAND, or SONYEA (new site of former Sodus Bay community). Sonyea Post Office (four miles south of Mount Morris), Groveland Township, Livingston County, New York (now occupied by Craig Colony).   [47

D. Other English-Language Communities

1825   COAL CREEK COMMUNITY AND CHURCH OF GOD. Stone Bluff, Fountain County, Indiana.   [48
1826   NASHOBA COMMUNITY. On Wolf River (thirteen miles east of Memphis), Shelby County, Tennessee.   [49
1830   KIRTLAND (communistic family established by Sidney Rigdon before his conversion to Mormonism). Kirtland, Lake County, Ohio.   [50
1831   ORDER OF ENOCH, or UNITED ORDER (Mormons). Independence, Jackson County, Missouri.   [51
1835   EQUITY (founded by Josiah Warren). Tuscarawas County, Ohio.   [52
1836   COMMUNITY OF UNITED CHRISTIANS. Berea, Cuyahoga County, Ohio.   [53

Period III. 1840–1860

A. Fourierist Phalanxes

1841   BROOK FARM (originally called the BROOK FARM INSTITUTE OF AGRICULTURE AND EDUCATION, then renamed the BROOK FARM ASSOCIATION FOR INDUSTRY AND EDUCATION, and finally reorganized as the BROOK FARM PHALANX). West Roxbury (then in Norfolk County, now in Suffolk County and within the city limits of Boston), Massachusetts.   [54
1842   SOCIAL REFORM UNITY. Near Goose Pond, in the Pocono Mountains, Pike County (now in Barrett Township, Monroe County, just south of the Pike County boundary line), Pennsylvania. (Organized in Brooklyn, New York.)   [55
1843   JEFFERSON COUNTY INDUSTRIAL ASSOCIATION. Cold Creek (two miles east of Watertown), Jefferson County, New York.   [56
1843   SYLVANIA ASSOCIATION, or SYLVANIA PHALANX. Darlingville or Darlingsville (now Greeley), Lackawaxen Township, Pike County, Pennsylvania. (Organized in New York City.)   [57
1843   MOREHOUSE UNION. Piseco, at the head of Piseco Lake, Arietta Township, Hamilton County, New York. (Organized in New York City.)   [58
1843   NORTH AMERICAN PHALANX. Phalanx (the present place name; addressed at the time through Leedsville Post Office), Atlantic Township, Monmouth County, New Jersey.   [59
1844   LAGRANGE PHALANX. Near Mongoquinong (now Mongo), Springfield Township, LaGrange County, Indiana.   [60
1844   CLARKSON ASSOCIATION (originally called the WESTERN NEW YORK INDUSTRIAL ASSOCIATION, reorganized again as the CLARKSON ASSOCIATION, or CLARKSON DOMAIN, and reorganized again as the PORT RICHMOND PHALANX). One mile from the mouth of Sandy Creek (where the village of North Hamlin now stands), in Clarkson Township (now Hamlin Township), Monroe County, New York. (Organized in Rochester, New York, as one of several successors to the projected ONTARIO PHALANX.)   [61

1844   BLOOMFIELD UNION ASSOCIATION, or NORTH BLOOMFIELD ASSOCIA-
TION. North Bloomfield, at the juncture of Monroe, Livingston, and
Ontario counties, New York. [62

1844   LERAYSVILLE PHALANX. LeRaysville, Pike Township, Bradford
County, Pennsylvania. [63

1844   OHIO PHALANX (originally named the AMERICAN PHALANX). Bell
Air or Bellaire, Pultney Township, Belmont County, Ohio. [64

1844   ALPHADELPHIA PHALANX. Near Galesburgh, Comstock Township,
Kalamazoo County, Michigan. (Apparently absorbed the WASHTE-
NAW PHALANX, projected at Ann Arbor, Washtenaw County.) [65

1844   SODUS BAY PHALANX (later reorganized as the SODUS PHALANX). Occupied the Shaker Tract (now called Alasa Farms), on Sodus Bay,
in Sodus and Huron townships, Wayne County, New York. [66

1844   MIXVILLE ASSOCIATION. Mixville (now Wiscoy), Hume Township,
Allegany County, New York. [67

1844   ONTARIO UNION [not to be confused with the projected Ontario
Phalanx], or MANCHESTER UNION. Bates' Mills (later Littleville, on
the Canandaigua Outlet), Manchester and Hopewell townships,
Ontario County. (Organized at Canandaigua, absorbing an earlier
projected ROCHESTER INDUSTRIAL ASSOCIATION.) [68

1844   CLERMONT PHALANX (originally called the CINCINNATI PHALANX).
On the Ohio River, about 35 miles above Cincinnati, where the
villages of Rural and Utopia now stand, Franklin Township, Clermont County, Ohio. [69

1844   TRUMBULL PHALANX. Phalanx Mills (post office: Phalanx Station),
Braceville Township, Trumbull County, Ohio. [70

1844   WISCONSIN PHALANX. Ceresco (so-called by the Fourierites, now
largely within the city limits of Ripon, Ripon Township), Fond du
Lac County, Wisconsin. (Organized at Southport, now Kenosha,
Wisconsin.) [71

1844   IOWA PIONEER PHALANX. On the north bank of the Des Moines
River, in what is now Scott Township, Mahaska County, Iowa.
(Organized at Watertown, Jefferson County, New York.) [72

1845   PHILADELPHIA INDUSTRIAL ASSOCIATION. Portage (a village since absorbed by the city of South Bend), German Township, St. Joseph
County, Indiana. [73

1845   COLUMBIAN PHALANX, or COLUMBIAN ASSOCIATION. On the Mus-
kingum River, seven miles above Zanesville, Muskingum County,
Ohio. (Absorbed the BEVERLY ASSOCIATION, projected at Beverly,
Washington County, Ohio.) [74

1845   CANTON PHALANX. Canton Township, Fulton County, Illinois. [75

1845   INTEGRAL PHALANX (with which was merged the SANGAMON ASSOCIA-
TION). Lick Creek (now Loami, Loami Township), Sangamon
County, Illinois. [76

1846   SPRING FARM PHALANX. About twenty miles from Lake Michigan,
in Sheboygan County, Wisconsin. [77

1846 or 1847 PIGEON RIVER FOURIER COLONY. North of the mouth of
Pigeon River, Sheboygan County, Wisconsin. [78

1853 RARITAN BAY UNION. Eagleswood (the estate of Marcus Spring, on Raritan Bay about a mile west of the center of Perth Amboy, and now within its city limits), Middlesex County, New Jersey. [79

1855 RÉUNION. Three or four miles west of Dallas, across the Trinity River (at a place now called Cement City), Dallas County, Texas. (Organized in France and Belgium.) [80

1858 THE FOURIER PHALANX. Moore's Hill, Sparta Township, Dearborn County, Indiana. [81

B. Owenite Communities

1843 SOCIETY OF ONE-MENTIANS, or PROMISEWELL COMMUNITY. Monroe County, Pennsylvania. [82

1843 GOOSE POND COMMUNITY (offshoot of One-Mentian Community). Near Goose Pond (on site of Social Reform Unity, which see in list of Fourierist phalanxes), Pike County, Pennsylvania. [83

1843 COLONY OF EQUALITY, or HUNT'S COLONY (organized and supported in England by several organizations, including the UTILITARIAN AS-SOCIATION OF UNITED INTERESTS, the UTILITARIAN CO-OPERATIVE EMIGRATION ASSOCIATION, the SOCIAL REFORMERS CO-OPERATIVE EMIGRATION SOCIETY, the EQUALITY SOCIETY, and the DEMOCRATIC SOCIETY). Spring Lake, Mukwonago Township, Waukesha County, Wisconsin. [84

C. Other English-Language Communities

1842 HOPEDALE COMMUNITY, or FRATERNAL COMMUNITY No. 1 (Practical Christians, led by Adin Ballou). Hopedale, town of Milford (near Mendon town line), Worcester County, Massachusetts. [85

1842 NORTHAMPTON ASSOCIATION OF EDUCATION AND INDUSTRY. Brough-ton's Meadows (now Florence), town of Northampton, Hampshire County, Massachusetts. [86

1843 MARLBORO ASSOCIATION. Marlboro, Stark County, Ohio. [87

1843 DR. ABRAM BROOKE'S EXPERIMENT. Oakland, Clinton County, Ohio. [88

1843 SKANEATELES COMMUNITY. Community Place, Mottville, Onondaga County, New York. [89

1843 FRUITLANDS. Harvard, Worcester County, Massachusetts. [90

1843 CONGREGATION OF SAINTS. Lexington, LaGrange County, Indiana. [91

1843 PUTNEY CORPORATION, or PUTNEY COMMUNITY (Perfectionists, led by John Humphrey Noyes). Putney, Windham County, Ver-mont. [92

1844 PRAIRIE HOME COMMUNITY. Near West Liberty, Logan County, Ohio. [93

1844 UNION HOME COMMUNITY. Huntsville (now Trenton), Randolph County, Indiana. [94

1845 FRUIT HILLS. Warren County, Ohio. [95

1845 GRAND PRAIRIE COMMUNITY. Warren County, Indiana. [96

1847   THE BROTHERHOOD. On part of site of Clermont Phalanx, Franklin
        Township, Clermont County, Ohio.   [97
1847   UTOPIA (founded by Josiah Warren). Utopia (another part of site
        of Clermont Phalanx), Franklin Township, Clermont County,
        Ohio.   [98
1848   ONEIDA COMMUNITY (Perfectionists, led by John Humphrey Noyes;
        formerly at Putney, Vermont). Kenwood, Oneida Township, Madi-
        son County, New York.   [99
1848   VOREE (settlement by schismatic Mormons under James J. Strang,
        who instituted a communistic ORDER OF ENOCH in 1848). Spring
        Prairie Township, Walworth County, Wisconsin.   [100
1848   GARDEN GROVE COMMUNITY. Garden Grove, Decatur County,
        Iowa.   [101
1851   WALLINGFORD COMMUNITY (branch of the Oneida Community).
        Wallingford, New Haven County, Connecticut. (Other branches
        of the Oneida Community were established in 1849 ff. at Brooklyn,
        N.Y., Newark, N.J., Putney, Vt., Cambridge, Vt., and Manlius, N.Y.,
        but were short-lived).   [102
1851   MODERN TIMES. Modern Times (now Brentwood), Suffolk County,
        Long Island, New York.   [103
1851   MOUNTAIN COVE COMMUNITY, or BROTHERHOOD OF THE NEW LIFE
        (the first of a series of Spiritualist communities founded by Thomas
        Lake Harris, the others belonging to the period after 1860). Moun-
        tain Cove, Fayette County, Virginia (now West Virginia).   [104
1852   CELESTA (Second Adventists). Celesta, Sullivan County, Pennsyl-
        vania.   [105
1852   HARMONIA. Kiantone Springs or Spiritualists Springs, one mile
        south of Kiantone, Chautauqua County, New York, on the Pennsyl-
        vania boundary line.   [106
1853   RISING STAR ASSOCIATION. Near Greenville, Darke County, Ohio. [107
1853   PREPARATION (schismatic Mormons). Preparation, Monona County,
        Iowa.   [108
1853   GRAND PRAIRIE HARMONIAL INSTITUTE, or COMMUNITY FARM. In
        sections 5 and 8, Township 23 North, Range 9 West, Warren County,
        Indiana.   [109
1856   MEMNONIA INSTITUTE. Yellow Springs, Greene County, Ohio.   [110
1856   UNION GROVE (offshoot of Hopedale Community). Meeker County,
        Minnesota.   [111
1860   HARMONIAL VEGETARIAN SOCIETY. Harmony Springs, Benton
        County, Arkansas.   [112

D. Foreign-Language Sectarian Communities

1843   EBENEZER COMMUNITY (established by the SOCIETY OF TRUE INSPIRA-
        TION). Former Seneca Indian Reservation, Ebenezer, Erie County,
        New York.   [113
1843   PEACE-UNION, or FRIEDENS-VEREIN. Limestone, Deerfield Post Office,
        Warren County, Pennsylvania.   [114

1844 BETHEL COMMUNITY. Bethel, Shelby County, Missouri. [115
1846 BISHOP HILL COLONY (founded by Eric Janson). Bishop Hill, Henry County, Illinois. [116
1850 GREEN BAY (Norwegian Moravians under Nils Otto Tank). Green Bay, Brown County, Wisconsin. [117
1851 JASPIS KOLONIE, or JASPER COLONY (Swedenborgian). Jasper, Lenox Township, Iowa County, Iowa. [118
1853 EPHRAIM (Norwegian Moravians under A. M. Iverson). Ephraim, Door County, Wisconsin. [119
1854 ST. NAZIANZ (Catholic). St. Nazianz, Eaton Township, Manitowoc County, Wisconsin. [120
1855 AMANA COMMUNITY (successor to Ebenezer), established by the SOCIETY OF TRUE INSPIRATION. Amana, West Amana, South Amana, High Amana, East Amana, Middle Amana, and Homestead, Iowa County, Iowa. [121
1856 AURORA COMMUNITY (offshoot of Bethel Community). Aurora, Marion County, Oregon. [122

E. Other Foreign-Language Communities

1842 TEUTONIA, or MCKEAN COUNTY ASSOCIATION. Ginalsburg (about twelve miles from Smethport), Sergeant Township, McKean County, Pennsylvania. [The place name Ginalsburg, not on modern maps, is shown in *New Universal Atlas* (Philadelphia: S. Augustus Mitchell, 1846), plate 13]. [123
1847 BETTINA. West of Fredericksburg, Gillespie County, Texas. [124
1847 COMMUNIA. Communia, Clayton County, Iowa. [125
1848 ICARIA (the first of the Icarian communities, established by Étienne Cabet and his followers). Fannin County, Texas. [126
1849 NAUVOO (the second Icarian Community). Nauvoo, Hancock County, Illinois. [127
1852 OLEANA, or OLEONA, or NEW NORWAY. Potter County, Pennsylvania. [128
1857 ICARIA (successor to the Icarian community at Nauvoo). Corning, Adams County, Iowa. [129
1858 CHELTENHAM (Icarian community founded by faction that seceded from Nauvoo). Cheltenham, six miles from St. Louis, Missouri. [130

STATISTICAL SUMMARY

NUMBER OF COMMUNITIES, BY DATE OF FOUNDING

	Colonial (prior to 1783)	1783–1824	1825–1860 by Five-Year Periods								Total 1663–1860
			1825–29	1830–34	1835–39	1840–44	1845–49	1850–54	1854–59	1860	
BY TYPE OF COMMUNITY											
Foreign-Language Sectarian Communities	6	5	—	2	1	3	1	4	2	—	24
Other Foreign-Language Communities	—	—	2	—	—	—	4	—	2	—	8
Shaker Villages	—	19	—	—	1	1	—	1	—	—	22
Owenite Communities	—	—	7	—	—	3	—	—	—	—	10
Fourierist Phalanxes	—	—	—	—	—	19	6	1	2	—	28
Other English-Language Communities	—	4	2	2	2	10	7	8	2	1	38
Total communities of all types	6	28	11	4	4	36	18	14	8	1	130
BY GEOGRAPHICAL LOCATION											
New England	—	13	—	—	—	5	—	1	—	—	19
Middle Atlantic Seaboard (eastern N.Y., N.J., eastern Pa., Del., Md.)	6	4	2	1	—	6	—	4	—	—	23
Ohio and Upper Mississippi Valleys (western Pa., W. Va., southern Ohio, southern Ind., Ky., Ill.)	—	8	6	—	—	7	9	3	2	—	35
Great Lakes Region (northern and western N.Y., northern Ohio, Mich., northern Ind., Wis.)	—	3	2	1	3	16	5	4	—	—	34
Trans-Mississippi West	—	—	—	2	1	2	4	2	6	1	18
Elsewhere (Tenn.)	—	—	1	—	—	—	—	—	—	—	1

BIBLIOGRAPHICAL ESSAY

I. Existing Studies of the Communitarian Movement as a Whole

II. Works on the Principal Sectarian Communities Founded before 1830
   Ephrata
   Moravians
   Rappites
   Zoar
   Shakers

III. Works on Owenism and the New Harmony Experiment
   Bibliographical Aids
   Collections of Manuscript Sources
   Writings of Robert Owen
   Owenite Periodicals
   New Harmony—Contemporary Sources
   New Harmony—Physical Remains and Pictorial Sources
   Reminiscence and Autobiography
   Secondary Works

NOTE ON THE BIBLIOGRAPHICAL ESSAY

References are given in the footnotes of the present study to a large number of works that are not of sufficient importance to be discussed in the following essay. They may be located through the index, which includes a reference, in small capitals, to each book, pamphlet, communitarian periodical, and contemporary newspaper cited, to each author of a manuscript, and to a number of periodical articles that rank as important primary sources. The capitalized entries in the index thus constitute a brief alphabetical bibliography of the present work.

The titles, often excessively long, of books and pamphlets are usually given more completely in the footnotes than in the following essay. Detailed bibliographical data (on editions, series, etc.) are also provided in the footnotes rather than the essay. The boldface numbers in the index refer to the pages where the fullest information is to be found.

In the second and third sections of this essay no effort is made to deal with the lesser sectarian communities or with the Owenite experiments other than New Harmony, for the literature dealing with these is meager enough to be encompassed in critical footnotes.

I. EXISTING STUDIES OF THE COMMUNITARIAN MOVEMENT AS A WHOLE

Such substantial research as has been done on the history of communitarian socialism is embodied, for the most part, in monographs on particular communities and particular leaders. General histories of the movement tend to reflect not so much the progress of historical scholarship as the changes in popular attitudes toward the communitarian idea itself. One might pass over without comment most of the secondary works of an inclusive sort, were it not for the fact that they themselves constitute the principal record of one significant aspect of the history of the communitarian idea, that is to say, the history of its subsequent influence and repute. The present section, chronologically arranged, attempts not only to criticize the works that have viewed communitarianism as a whole, but also to trace through them the evaluations which successive generations have made of the communitarian approach to social reform.

Reflection upon the past, the historian must ruefully admit, does not usually comport with vigorous action in the present. During the second quarter of the nineteenth century, communitarian energies were absorbed in practical projects, and few of the individuals concerned in the movement turned their attention to its history. As chapter III has shown, descriptive and historical accounts of the American communities were being written in increasing numbers during the period, but no comprehensive historical treatment resulted. Mary Hennell, *Outline of the Various Social Systems & Communities Which Have Been Founded on the Principle of Co-operation* (London, 1844), summarized the ideas of ancients and moderns on the subject. John Finch, "Notes on Travel in the United States," *New Moral World*, XII, 232, through XIII, 10–11 (Jan. 13–July 6, 1844), provided a comprehensive description of the American experiments at the height of the movement. And A. J. Macdonald's "Manuscripts and Collections," now preserved in the Yale University Library, comprised the raw materials for a history which the author did not live to complete. These three works, only one of them in book form, marked the beginnings of a secondary literature on the communitarian movement, but only the beginnings.

The decade and a half following the Civil War produced the first four substantial works. As an active movement of reform, communitarianism was clearly on the decline, and communitarian leaders began to turn their eyes more frequently to the past. Among them was John Humphrey Noyes, founder and leader of the Oneida Community. He became increasingly interested in the history of the movement in which he had played so successful a part, and his quest for the manuscripts assembled by A. J. Macdonald was rewarded in 1865 by their rediscovery. Three years later he began to publish extracts from them in the official organ of the Oneida Community, *The Circular*, n.s., V, 236, through VI, 140–41 (Oct. 12, 1868–July 19, 1869). Noyes's interest was originally antiquarian and he first entitled the series, rather slightingly, "Our Muck-Heap." Gradually he awoke to its significance, and with the fourteenth of the forty-one installments he changed the heading to "American Socialisms," and announced his intention of producing "a faithful history of Socialism in this country." The series of extracts was concluded on July 19, 1869, and in December the promised volume was published, with the title page dated the following year: John Humphrey Noyes, *History of American Socialisms* (Philadelphia, 1870).

Though Noyes supplemented Macdonald's data with extracts from important communitarian periodicals, he made no real effort to deal critically with the narratives of individual communities compiled by his predecessor, and these were in many instances meager, erroneous, and one-sided. Nevertheless, Noyes's *History* has been the principal quarry from which later writers on the movement as a whole have taken their material, using it even less critically than he.[1] Though Noyes was himself the leader of a sectarian community, he barely mentioned the earlier German colonies. And though he dealt extensively with Owenism and Fourierism, he obtained his information on the European aspects of these theories entirely at second- or third-hand. Despite these shortcomings, Noyes's *History* is still an important book, not so much for the sources it reprints (which the historian must check in the originals), but because the author's personal experience gave him an intuitive insight into the nature, motives, and problems of communitarianism such as no later writer possessed.

The publication of Noyes's *History* stirred the memories of many former communitarians, and a flood of reminiscences filled the subsequent volumes of *The Circular* and its successor *The American Socialist* (4 vols., 1876–79), providing a valuable body of historical sources, which has frequently been overlooked. The interest aroused also encouraged the editor of *The Circular* to try his hand at a small volume: William Alfred Hinds, *American Communities: Brief Sketches of Economy, Zoar, Bethel,* . . . [etc.] (Oneida, N.Y., 1878). Hinds paid attention to the sectarian communities that Noyes had neglected, and he incorporated first-hand observations (the results of a tour in 1876) more extensive than his predecessor had made. The work was expanded in 1902 and again in 1908. Though much was sheer compilation, Hinds's *American Communities and Co-operative Colonies* (2d revision [i.e., 3d ed.], Chicago, 1908) contains material otherwise unobtainable on many late nineteenth-century experiments.

In the course of the same decade George Jacob Holyoake, leader in the British co-operative and rationalistic movements, published *The History of Co-operation in England: Its Literature and Its Advocates* (2 vols., London, 1875–79), which contained the first comprehensive account of the communitarian movement in Great Britain, and also devoted some attention to the American communities.

The industrial transformation of the 1870's was not only bringing about

---

[1] At least one volume was an outright plagiarism: Heinrich Semler, *Geschichte des Socialismus und Communismus in Nordamerika* (Leipzig, 1880), whose author acknowledges indebtedness to Noyes in his preface (p. vii) when he should, in fact, have placed Noyes's name on the title page and described himself as translator and editor.

the decline of the communitarian movement by rendering obsolete its dream that modern economic life could be organized in village units, but was also causing the communitarian colony to be looked upon in an entirely different light. Once it had appeared to be a possible step forward in industrial and social progress. Now, more frequently, it appeared to be a retreat from the stresses of industrialization and the too-great complexities of modern social life. It was a desirable retreat, in the view of many onlookers, among them the author of the fourth significant work of the period: Charles Nordhoff, *Communistic Societies of the United States, from Personal Visit and Observation* (New York, 1875 [copyright 1874]). "Trades-Unions," asserted Nordhoff in his introduction, are "a power almost entirely for evil," for they teach every member "to regard himself, and to act toward society, as a hireling for life." Moreover, the cheap lands that hitherto "have acted as an important safety-valve" are in danger of exhaustion. Communitarian colonies, he believed, may provide the best remaining "way to exchange dependence for independence." Motivated by this idea, Nordhoff undertook to visit all the existing communities and to study carefully the literature of each. His ability as a serious journalist had been demonstrated by long service as managing editor of the *New York Evening Post,* by several substantial travel narratives and books on public issues, and by his recent appointment as Washington correspondent of the *New York Herald.* His book on the American communities was easily the most thorough and objective piece of reporting ever done on the subject. Its treatment of the history of the individual communities was sound, but the fact that the author chose not to discuss the communitarian experiments that had already passed away kept his book from being a comprehensive history of communitarianism.

By the decade of the 1880's Nordhoff's underlying assumptions were gradually being discarded by serious students of the contemporary scene. Trade unions and socialism clearly had to be reckoned with as permanent elements in social reform. The significant writings of this decade were those that fitted the earlier communitarianism into the history of these two portentous movements. Richard T. Ely, newly returned from study in German universities, accomplished this task in two volumes: *French and German Socialism in Modern Times* (New York, 1883), which discussed communitarian along with other socialist theories; and *The Labor Movement in America* (New York, 1886), which placed the sectarian, Owenite, and Fourierist experiments in the perspective of the history of organized labor. Just after the beginning of the new century Morris Hillquit provided a similar survey, more extensive than that of Ely but derived essentially from Noyes, in his *History of Socialism in the United States* (New York, 1903).

European writers at the turn of the century were likewise taking an all-inclusive view of the socialist movement. Socialists themselves began to look for origins as far back as the sects of the Reformation, as did Eduard Bernstein, Karl Kautsky, and their colleagues in the co-operative *Geschichte des Socialismus in Einzeldarstellungen* (Stuttgart, 1895–98).[2] All varieties of socialism were embraced in the encyclopedic reference book of Carl Stegmann and C. Hugo, *Handbuch des Socialismus* (Zürich, 1897). Several important

[2] See the discussion of works in this tradition, p. 39, n. 7, above.

scholarly works on the history and philosophy of socialism were written in these years: Otto Warschauer, *Geschichte des Socialismus und neueren Kommunismus* (3 vols., Leipzig, 1892–96); H. P. G. Quack, *De Socialisten: Personen en Stelsels* (3. Druk, 6 vols., Amsterdam, 1899–1901); and Vilfredo Pareto, *Les Systèmes socialistes* (2 vols., Paris, 1902–3). European scholarship, moreover, produced two indispensable bibliographical guides during this period: Joseph Stammhammer, *Bibliographie des Socialismus und Communismus* (3 vols., Jena, 1893–1909), a comprehensive listing of communitarian and other socialist books, pamphlets, and periodicals of Western Europe and Great Britain; and H. S. Foxwell, "Bibliography of the English Socialist School," appended to Anton Menger, *The Right to the Whole Produce of Labour,* translated by M. E. Tanner (London, 1899), pp. 189–267.

By the early years of the twentieth century the principal comprehensive accounts of communitarianism which are still generally relied on had been written. Moreover, the movement had begun to receive attention in general histories of the United States, notably Edwin Erle Sparks, *Expansion of the American People* (Chicago, 1900), pp. 376–401; and John Bach McMaster, *A History of the People of the United States,* V (New York, 1900), 88–108. Already, however, the most marked characteristic of modern historical scholarship was becoming evident—its tendency to extreme specialization. Monographs on particular communities, biographies of individual leaders, and carefully edited collections of sources are the most valuable fruits of twentieth-century research in the history of the communitarian movement, and these must be reserved for treatment in other sections of this bibliography.

The works that remain to be discussed in the present section are in general of much less consequence than those already mentioned, precisely because of this widening of the gap between exact and detailed scholarship on the one hand, and, on the other, the historical treatment of communitarianism as a whole. Narratives of the latter kind have tended to be mere compilations from the earlier works. Several of these have been mentioned in the introduction to the Checklist of Communitarian Experiments. The others require only a brief chronological listing here: A. Holynski, "Le Communisme en Amérique," *Revue socialiste,* XII, 312–26, to XVI, 296–307 (12 installments, sept. 1890–sept. 1892); George N. Tricoche, "Le Communisme en action: Étude des Communistic Societies aux États-Unis," *Journal des Économistes,* 5e série, XXV, 321–53 (mars 1896); W. J. Kerby, *Le Socialisme aux États-Unis* (Bruxelles, 1897); François Sagot, *Le Communisme au Nouveau-Monde* (Dijon, 1900); "A Brief History of Socialism in America," *Social Democracy Red Book,* Jan. 1900, pp. 3–75; Charles M. Skinner, *The American Communes (Brooklyn Eagle Library,* no. 50, [vol. XVI, no. 2]; Brooklyn, Feb. 1901); Alexander Kent, "Cooperative Communities in the United States," U.S. Department of Labor, *Bulletin,* vol. VI, no. 35, pp. 563–646 (July 1901); Montgomery E. McIntosh, "Co-operative Communities in Wisconsin," State Historical Society of Wisconsin, *Proceedings,* LI, 99–117 (1903); F. Lepelletier, "Les Sociétés communistes aux États-Unis," *La Réforme sociale,* LI, 551–64 (avril 1906); W. H. Mallock, "A Century of Socialistic Experiments," *Dublin Review*, CXLV, 79–106 (July 1909); Michaël Tugan-Baranowsky, *Die kommunistischen Gemeinwesen der Neuzeit*, translated by Elias Hurwicz (Gotha, 1921); Robert Liefmann, *Die kommunistischen Gemeinden in Nordamerika* (Jena, 1922); Harry W. Laidler, *A History of Socialist Thought* (New York, 1927); Charles Gide, *Communist and Co-operative Colonies*, translated by Ernest F. Row (London, 1930); Henrik F. Infield, *Co-operative Communities at Work* (New York, 1945).

Besides these rather pedestrian surveys, a few popular books have appeared that are challenging in interpretation even if limited in documentation: Lewis Mumford, *The Story of Utopias* (New York, 1922); J. O. Hertzler, *The History of Utopian Thought* (New York, 1923); Frances Theresa Russell, *Touring Utopia: The Realm of Constructive Humanism* (New York, 1932); Edmund Wilson, *To the Finland Station: A Study in the Writing and Acting of History* (New York, 1940); V. F. Calverton, *Where Angels Dared to Tread* (Indianapolis, 1941); Charles A. Madison, *Critics & Crusaders: A Century of American Protest* (New York, 1946); Freeman Champney, "Utopia, Ltd.," *Antioch Review*, VIII, 259–80 (Fall 1948). At the extreme of subjective interpretation are such books as Gilbert Seldes, *The Stammering Century* (New York, 1927); and Arthur E. Morgan, *Nowhere Was Somewhere: How History Makes Utopias and How Utopias Make History* (Chapel Hill, N.C., 1946); together with a number of semifictional books, of which Marguerite Young, *Angel in the Forest: A Fairy Tale of Two Utopias* (New York, 1945), is the most recent.

Aside from monographs on individual communities and scholarly biographies, the most important recent contributions to an understanding of communitarianism have been made by studies in the related fields of literary, intellectual, religious, economic, and social history: John R. Commons and others, eds., *Documentary History of American Industrial Society* (10 vols. and supplement, Cleveland, 1909–11); William F. Kamman, *Socialism in German American Literature* (Philadelphia, 1917); John R. Commons, ed., *History of Labour in the United States*, vol. I (New York, 1918); Norman J. Ware, *The Industrial Worker, 1840–1860* (Boston, 1924); Gildo Massó, *Education in Utopias* (New York, 1927); Clarence Gohdes, *Periodicals of American Transcendentalism* (Durham, N.C., 1931); J. Russell Andrus, "The Economics of the Utopian Socialists, 1800–1850" (unpublished Ph.D. dissertation, 1934, University of California Library, Berkeley); Elmer T. Clark, *The Small Sects in America* (Nashville, Tenn., 1937); J. F. Normano, "Social Utopias in American Literature," *International Review for Social History*, III, 287–300 (1938); David Ludlum, *Social Ferment in Vermont, 1791–1850* (New York, 1939); Carl Wittke, *We Who Built America: The Saga of the Immigrant* (New York, 1939); Merle Curti, *Growth of American Thought* (New York, 1943); Albert Post, *Popular Freethought in America, 1825–1850* (New York, 1943); L. L. and Jessie Bernard, *Origins of American Sociology* (New York, 1943); Arthur A. Ekirch, Jr., *The Idea of Progress in America, 1815–1860* (New York, 1944); Herbert W. Schneider, *History of American Philosophy* (New York, 1946); Vernon L. Parrington, Jr., *American Dreams: A Study of American Utopias* (Providence, R.I., 1947).

General histories of economic thought and of socialism usually devote space to such communitarians as Owen and Fourier. On the whole the most satisfactory are Charles Gide and Charles Rist, *History of Economic Doctrines*, translated by R. Richards (London, 1915); and Alexander Gray, *The Socialist Tradition, Moses to Lenin* (London, 1946). The articles in *The Encyclopaedia of the Social Sciences* (15 vols., New York, 1930-35) are valuable both for content and bibliography. Other useful bibliographies include: Frederick B. Adams, Jr., *Radical Literature in America* (Stamford, Conn., 1939); Raymond Adams, "Booklist of American Communities" (Chapel Hill, N.C., 1935), mimeographed; Library of Congress, Division of Bibliography, "Select List of References on Communistic Societies in the United States" (Washington, 1909), typewritten; and the catalogues issued annually by Leon Kramer, bookseller, of New York City.

The need for a fresh historical interpretation of the communitarian movement and a scholarly synthesis of the available material has begun to be met in the most recent years. An important start was made in the chapters in Alice Felt Tyler, *Freedom's Ferment: Phases of American Social History to 1860* (Minneapolis, 1944). The symposium at Princeton University on "Socialism and America," held in 1946-47 under the auspices of the Program of Study in American Civilization, was a major effort in this direction, and the two volumes of papers and bibliographies now being edited by Stow Persons and Donald B. Egbert, with the collaboration of T. D. Seymour Bassett, promise to be of the greatest value.

II. WORKS ON THE PRINCIPAL SECTARIAN COMMUNITIES FOUNDED BEFORE 1830

EPHRATA. An exhaustive bibliography of printed sources and secondary works has been compiled by Eugene E. Doll and Anneliese M. Funke, *The Ephrata Cloisters: An Annotated Bibliography (Bibliographies on German American History*, no. 3; Philadelphia: Carl Schurz Memorial Foundation, 1944). This includes (p. 6) a brief note on manuscript collections, which are more extensively covered in an unpublished "exploratory list" by the same compilers, filed with the Pennsylvania Historical Commission at Harrisburg. Of general value for the sectarian communities as a group are: Emil Meynen, compiler, *Bibliography on German Settlement in Colonial North America* (Leipzig, 1937), with separate title page in German; and Peter G. Mode, *Source Book and Bibliographical Guide for American Church History* (Menasha, Wis., 1921).

Of the historical publications of the community itself the most important is the *Chronicon Ephratense*, by Brothers Lamech [identity uncertain] and Agrippa [i.e., Johann Peter Miller] (Ephrata, 1786), of which there is an English translation by J. Max Hark (Lancaster, 1889). Early printed accounts include those of Israel Acrelius, originally published in Swedish (1759), translated by William M. Reynolds as Acrelius, *A History of New Sweden; or, the Settlements on the River Delaware* (Historical Society of Pennsylvania, *Memoirs*, XI; Philadelphia, 1874), pp. 373–401; and William M. Fahnestock, "An Historical Sketch of Ephrata," *Hazard's Register of Pennsylvania*, XV, 161–67, 208 (March 14 and 28, 1835).

The most extensive secondary work is by Julius Friedrich Sachse, in three volumes: *The German Pietists of Provincial Pennsylvania, 1694–1708; The German Sectarians of Pennsylvania, 1708–1742;* and the same, *1742–1800* (Philadelphia, 1895–1900), a thorough study, but somewhat antiquarian in approach and often lacking in clarity. It does not entirely supersede Oswald Seidensticker, *Ephrata: Eine amerikanische Klostergeschichte* (Cincinnati, 1883). Two substantial historical accounts, more recent than these, are: Corliss F. Randolph, "The German Seventh-Day Baptists," in Seventh Day Baptist General Conference, *Seventh Day Baptists in Europe and America* (2 vols., Plainfield, N.J., 1910), II, 933–1257; and Edwin M. Williams, "The Monastic Orders of Provincial Ephrata," in H. M. J. Klein and E. Melvin Williams, eds., *Lancaster County, Pennsylvania: A History* (4 vols., New York, 1924), I, 384–476. There is a scholarly biography of the founder by Walter C. Klein, *Johann Conrad Beissel, Mystic and Martinet, 1690–1768* (Philadelphia, 1942), containing an extensive bibliographical note.

The cloister buildings at Ephrata are preserved by the Pennsylvania Historical Commission, and books and artifacts of the community are on display. Its press is in the Franklin Institute, Philadelphia.

MORAVIANS. The General Economy of the Moravians constituted, of course, only a brief phase in the long history of the sect. That phase is definitively covered in two monographs: Hellmuth Erbe, *Bethlehem, Pa.: Eine kommunistische Herrnhuter Kolonie des 18. Jahrhunderts* (Stuttgart, 1929), and Jacob John Sessler, *Communal Pietism among Early American Moravians* (New York, 1933). Both works emphasize the Moravian experi-ments in Pennsylvania. For the important activities in the south, see the publications of Adelaide L. Fries, notably her edition of the *Records of the Moravians in North Carolina* (North Carolina Historical Commission, *Publications;* multivolume work in progress, Raleigh, 1922–). See also the Moravian Historical Society, *Transactions, 1857–* (Nazareth, Pa., 1876–). The bibliography of Sessler's study is an adequate guide to materials bearing on the General Economy. Mention should also be made, however, of four important guides to the Moravian archives. For those at Herrnhut, Germany, see Marion D. Learned, *Guide to the Manuscript Materials Relating to American History in the German State Archives* (Carnegie Institution of Washington, *Publication* 150; Washington, 1912), pp. 314–17. For archives at Bethlehem, Pa., see William H. Allison, *Inventory of Unpublished Material for American Religious History in Protestant Church Archives and Other Repositories* (same series, 137; Washington, 1910), pp. 147–65; and Archer B. Hulbert, "The Moravian Records," *Ohio Archaeological and Historical Publications,* XVIII, 199–226 (April 1909). For the Wachovian Archives at Winston-Salem, N.C., see Historical Records Survey, North Carolina, *Guide to the Manuscripts in the Archives of the Moravian Church in America, Southern Province* (Raleigh, 1942).

RAPPITES. Manuscript records of the Rappites, preserved at Economy, are briefly described in Historical Records Survey, Pennsylvania, *Guide to De-positories of Manuscript Collections in Pennsylvania* (Pennsylvania Department of Public Instruction, *Bulletin,* no. 774; Historical Commission series, no. 4; Harrisburg, 1939), pp. 2–3. Other manuscripts are in the Historical Society of Western Pennsylvania, Pittsburgh (see *ibid.,* p. 82); the Workingmen's Institute, New Harmony; and the Indiana University Library. A number of letters from the last-mentioned collection have been translated and published by John C. Andressohn in the *Indiana Magazine of History,* XLII, 395–409; XLIV, 82–108; XLV, 184–88 (Dec. 1946, March 1948, June 1949) .

The Rappite community, though probably the most prosperous of the sectarian colonies, showed far less evidence of literacy than the others, publishing little even of a religious character. Their pamphlet entitled *Thoughts on the Destiny of Man* ([Harmony, Ind.], 1824) is the most important. The most extensive early account is Ernest Ludwig Brauns, *Amerika und die moderne Völkerwanderung, nebst einer Darstellung der gegenwärtig zu Ökonomie—Economy—am Ohio angesiedelten Harmonie-Gesellschaft* (Potsdam, 1833). Other printed sources, especially descriptions written by visitors, are fairly numerous; the most important are cited in chapter III.

Aaron Williams, *The Harmony Society, at Economy, Penn'a* (Pittsburgh, 1866), is a valuable narrative based on first-hand acquaintance. The standard monograph is John A. Bole, *The Harmony Society: A Chapter in German American Culture History* (Philadelphia, 1904), which contains a bibliography. John A. Duss, *The Harmonists: A Personal History* (Harrisburg, 1943), is an important narrative by the last survivor, who was Trustee when the affairs of the community were wound up. It draws heavily on Bole for the earlier history, however. A number of articles have been published, easily located through the various periodical guides, and not requiring discussion here. See also [Rose Demorest], *The Harmonists: A Bibliography of the Collection on the Harmony Society in the Carnegie Library of Pittsburgh* ([Pittsburgh], 1940).

Many Rappite buildings still stand at the three locations of the community: Harmony, Pa., New Harmony, Ind., and Economy (now part of Ambridge), Pa. The latter are preserved by the Harmony Society Historical Association, functioning under the Pennsylvania Historical Commission. Numerous objects collected by Mr. and Mrs. Duss are on display. The remains at New Harmony are discussed in the section on Owenism, below.

ZOAR. Extensive manuscript records are preserved by the Zoar Historical Society in the old home of the founder, Joseph Bimeler, at Zoar, Ohio. The community buildings are maintained as the Zoar Village State Monument. Two scholarly monographs appeared almost simultaneously: George B. Landis, "The Society of Separatists of Zoar, Ohio," American Historical Association, *Annual Report, 1898*, pp. 163–220; and E. O. Randall, *History of the Zoar Society from its Commencement to its Conclusion: A Sociological Study in Communism* (3d ed., Columbus, O., 1904), originally published in *Ohio Archaeological and Historical Publications*, VIII, 1–100 (July 1899). Both works contain documentary appendices, and the former a bibliography. An unpublished doctoral dissertation by Edgar B. Nixon is in the library of Ohio State University; its author has published "The Zoar Society: Applicants for Membership," *Ohio Archaeological and Historical Quarterly*, XLV, 341–50 (Oct. 1936). A recent account is Catherine R. Dobbs, *Freedom's Will: The Society of Separatists of Zoar, an Historical Adventure of Religious Communism in Early Ohio* (New York, 1947). Useful articles include E. J. Bognar, "Blast-Furnaces Operated by the Separatist Society of Zoar, Ohio," *Ohio Archaeological and Historical Quarterly*, XXXIX, 503–13 (July 1930).

SHAKERS. The principal collections of Shaker manuscripts in public repositories are described by Charles C. Adams in New York State Museum *Bulletin*, no. 323 (Albany, March 1941), pp. 123–28. Besides reporting the holdings in considerable detail, Adams cites published descriptions of the various collections and notes the existence of unpublished card catalogues and checklists. A collection not mentioned by him is in the Western Kentucky Teachers College at Bowling Green, and is described in Julia Neal, *By Their Fruits* (cited below), pp. 271–73. Adams' brief note on the holdings of the Library of Congress should be supplemented by the description in its own *Handbook of Manuscripts* (Washington, 1918), pp. 365–66; in Librarian of Congress, *Report, 1930*, pp. 79–80, and American Historical Association, *Annual Report, 1937*, I, 124; and in the unpublished checklist available at the Library. Important private collections include that of Clara Endicott Sears, housed in her Wayside Museums at Harvard, Mass., and that of Edward D. Andrews, described in the bibliographies of his works cited below.

The publications of the Shakers are listed with reasonable completeness in John P. MacLean, *A Bibliography of Shaker Literature* (Columbus, O., 1905). Supplementing this, and providing a completer record of secondary works, are: "List of Works in the New York Public Library Relating to Shakers," New York Public Library, *Bulletin*, VIII, 550–59 (Nov. 1904); and Esther C. Winter, compiler, *Shaker Literature in the Grosvenor Library: A Bibliography* (Grosvenor Library *Bulletin*, vol. XXII, no. 4, pp. 65–119; Buffalo, 1940).

The Shakers paid more attention to their own history than most of the communitarian sects. Especially important for historical information and interpretation are the following official publications of the church, listed in chronological order: [Benjamin S. Youngs], *The Testimony of Christ's Second Appearing* (Lebanon, O., 1808), of which there were revised editions in 1810, 1823, and 1856; [Calvin Green and Seth Y. Wells], *A Summary View of the Millennial Church* (Albany, 1823), revised in 1848; Frederick W. Evans, *Shakers: Compendium of the Origin, History, . . . and Doctrines of the United Society of Believers* (New York, 1859), frequently reprinted, sometimes with altered title; and Anna White and Leila S. Taylor, *Shakerism: Its Meaning and Message, Embracing an Historical Account* (Columbus, O., 1904).

The beginnings of the sect are recorded in: [Rufus Bishop and Seth Y. Wells], *Testimonies of the Life, Character, Revelations and Doctrines of . . . Mother Ann Lee* (Hancock, Mass., 1816), reprinted in 1888; [Seth Y. Wells], *Testimonies Concerning the Character and Ministry of Mother Ann Lee* (Albany, 1827), not to be confused with the preceding or with Youngs's similarly titled volume; and Henry C. Blinn, *Life and Gospel Experience of Mother Ann Lee* (East Canterbury, N.H. [1901]). The basic source on Shaker expansion to the west is Richard M'Nemar, *The Kentucky Revival* (Cincinnati, 1807), reprinted in 1808, 1837, and 1846. Of great importance for the nineteenth-century movement is F. W. Evans, *Autobiography of a Shaker* (Albany, 1869), of which there was an enlarged edition (Glasgow, 1888).

Two useful pamphlets, summarizing Shaker beliefs and history for outsiders, are: [Calvin Green and S. Y. Wells], *A Brief Exposition of the Established Principles and Regulations of the United Society, Called Shakers* (Albany, 1830), reprinted many times, as late as 1879; and Giles B. Avery, *Sketches of "Shakers and Shakerism": Synopsis of Theology of United Society of Believers in Christ's Second Appearing* (Albany, 1883), reprinted 1884, containing views of many of the Shaker villages. The principal Shaker periodical appeared under varying titles from 1871 to 1899: *The Shaker* (vols. 1–2, 6–7); *Shaker and Shakeress* (vols. 3–5); *The Shaker Manifesto* (vols. 8–13); *The Manifesto* (vols. 14–29). It was preceded by the *Western Review*, circa 1834–37, and *The Day-Star*, 1845–47. They printed little on the history of the sect. Some extracts from personal papers of Shakers have been put in print, notably Clara E. Sears, compiler, *Gleanings from Old Shaker*

Journals (Boston, 1916), and Nancy L. Greene, *Ye Olde Shaker Bells* (Lexington, Ky., 1930), pp. 34–83.

The contemporary sources published by non-Shakers comprise travel books and articles written by visitors, bitter attacks from opponents of the sect, and a number of literary treatments. Several important ones are cited in chapter III. Most books and articles on the sect published during its century and a half of existence have been based upon some first-hand observation, and to that extent rank as primary sources. It is proper, however, to deal with them critically as secondary works.

The most substantial scholarly contributions to the history of the Shakers have been made by John Patterson MacLean in his bibliography (already cited) and in his *Shakers of Ohio: Fugitive Papers* (Columbus, 1907), originally published as articles in the *Ohio Archaeological and Historical Publications*, 1900–1904; and by Edward Deming Andrews in his *Community Industries of the Shakers* (New York State Museum *Handbook* 15; Albany, 1932 [copyright 1933]); *Shaker Furniture: The Craftsmanship of an American Communal Sect*, in collaboration with Faith Andrews (New Haven, 1937); and *The Gift to Be Simple: Songs, Dances and Rituals of the American Shakers* (New York, 1940). These cover special aspects of the subject. The best work on the movement as a whole is Marguerite Fellows Melcher, *The Shaker Adventure* (Princeton, 1941). On the Shakers in Kentucky, underemphasized in the works already cited, see Julia Neal, *By Their Fruits: The Story of Shakerism in South Union, Kentucky* (Chapel Hill, N.C., 1947). The doctoral dissertation by Edward F. Dow, *A Portrait of the Millennial Church of Shakers* (Orono, Maine, 1931), is of inferior quality.

Among earlier works the most valuable are: Charles Edson Robinson, *A Concise History of the United Society of Believers Called Shakers* (East Canterbury, N.H., 1893), and the section in Charles Nordhoff, *Communistic Societies of the United States* (New York, 1875), pp. 115–256. Constance Rourke has a stimulating interpretation in her *Roots of American Culture, and Other Essays* (New York, 1942), pp. 195–237. A multitude of periodical articles, many of them rather routine, can be located through the standard indexes.

Shaker buildings still stand in considerable numbers at the sites of the various communities. Some are now occupied by public institutions, as noted in the Checklist of Communitarian Experiments. The furniture and other products of Shaker craftsmanship have attracted widespread interest in recent years. They are discussed most fully in the volumes by Andrews, already cited, but a number of articles have also appeared in art journals and in the bulletins of museums where exhibitions have been held. The largest permanent collection is in the New York State Museum at Albany, described in the well-illustrated report of Charles C. Adams, "The New York State Museum's Historical Survey and Collection of the New York Shakers," New York State Museum *Bulletin*, no. 323 (March 1941), p. 77–141, a publication which also lists other public collections and several special exhibits in museums (pp. 128–30).

Colored drawings of many Shaker objects form part of the Index of American Design, produced by the Federal Art Project and now deposited in the

National Gallery of Art, Washington. Reproductions have been published in *House & Garden*, July 1938 (All America Issue), pp. 13–43; *ibid.*, March 1945, pp. 35–37, 103–34; and in Elizabeth McCausland, "The Shaker Legacy," *Magazine of Art*, XXXVII, 287–91 (Dec. 1944). The photographs of William F. Winter, Jr., have been used in many of the publications already cited, especially those of E. D. Andrews. See also C. C. Adams, *op. cit.*, pp. 132–37, 140–41, and plates.

III. WORKS ON OWENISM AND THE NEW HARMONY
EXPERIMENT

BIBLIOGRAPHICAL AIDS. Owen's separate publications number well over a hundred, many of them with confusingly similar titles. The definitive guide is a bilingual product of Japanese scholarship, Shigeru Gotô, *Robert Owen, 1771–1858: A New Bibliographical Study* (Osaka University of Commerce, *Studies*, no. 1 [Osaka, ca. 1935]), which gives line-by-line transcriptions of the title pages in English, and elaborate notes, partly in English and partly in Japanese. Though far less exhaustive, the bibliography appended to Frank Podmore, *Robert Owen: A Biography* (2 vols., London, 1906), II, 655–67, lists all his important works, and gives the wording of the title pages more completely than does National Library of Wales, *A Bibliography of Robert Owen, the Socialist* (2d ed., Aberystwyth, 1925). The latter is useful, however, for contemporary Owenite writings, as is also H. S. Foxwell, "Bibliography of the English Socialist School," appended to M. E. Tanner's translation of Anton Menger, *The Right to the Whole Produce of Labour* (London, 1899), pp. 189–267. Two general works of reference are especially valuable on Owenism: Joseph Stammhammer, *Bibliographie des Socialismus und Communismus* (3 vols., Jena, 1893–1909); and *London Bibliography of the Social Sciences* (4 vols. and 2 supplements, London, 1931–37). On the American side the most useful bibliography is that contained in Richard W. Leopold, *Robert Dale Owen: A Biography* (Cambridge, Mass., 1940), pp. 417–40. See also Rena Reese, compiler, *List of Books and Pamphlets in a Special Collection in the Library of the Workingmen's Institute* ([New Harmony], 1909), which should be brought up to date. Quite inadequate is Roger A. Hurst, "The New Harmony Manuscript Collections," *Indiana Magazine of History*, XXXVII, 45–49 (March 1941).

COLLECTIONS OF MANUSCRIPT SOURCES. The bulk of Robert Owen's personal papers are in the library of the Co-operative Union, Ltd., Holyoake House, Manchester, England. The collection comprises some three thousand letters and documents, of which 2204, dating from 1821 to 1854, have been numbered and calendared in a 120-page typewritten list, a copy of which has kindly been furnished me by the librarian, Mr. D. Flanagan. Documents nos. 1–53 belong to the years 1821–23, before Owen thought of coming to America; nos. 54–81, dated 1825, relate directly to New Harmony and Owen's propaganda in America; nos. 82–127, dated 1828, include a number of papers connected with his Mexican project and his activities in the United States; nos. 129–1321 belong to the years 1830–1843, when Owen was active in England, and contain only a few scattered letters on American affairs; nos. 1322–1556, covering the period 1844–1847, throw light not only on Owen's visits to the United States in those years, but also on Fourierism and other communitarian movements of the time; nos. 1557–2204 (the last letter calendared) belong to the years 1848–1854 and have little bearing on the history of American communitarianism.

Over thirty MS letters of Robert Owen are in various collections in the British Museum, and there are a few papers in the Robert Owen Memorial Museum, Newtown, Montgomeryshire, Wales.

The Illinois Historical Survey of the University of Illinois has assembled photostats of most of the documents relating to New Harmony in British repositories, and will shortly acquire a microfilm of the entire body of papers at Manchester. Photographic reproductions of many of the American manuscripts mentioned below are also in its possession.

The chief collection of Owenite manuscripts in America is in the Workingmen's Institute, New Harmony. Besides several books of account of the New Harmony Community, it contains a number of important collections of personal papers, notably: the Maclure-Fretageot correspondence, 1820–1833, from which a considerable selection has been published by the present writer; a large collection of other papers of William Maclure; scattered letters and transcripts of Robert Owen; considerable bodies of correspondence and papers of Robert Dale Owen, Frances Wright, Josiah Warren, Thomas Say, Charles A. Lesueur, William Phiquepal d'Arusmont, William Amphlett, and others connected with the community.

In the Indiana Historical Society are three collections containing manuscripts bearing upon Owenism: the Owen-Dorsey correspondence, the Miner K. Kellogg papers, and the William Augustus Twiggs papers. The Indiana State Library owns a MS by Richard Owen entitled "Brief History of the Social Experiment in New Harmony," several scattered letters relating to the community, and a MS volume containing records of the Rational Brethren of Oxford, Ohio, 1816–1817, and of the Coal Creek Community, Indiana, 1823–1832.

In addition to the Maclure MSS in the Workingmen's Institute, there are 42 letters from him (one from New Harmony in 1826, and the balance from Mexico, 1830–39) in the Samuel G. Morton papers, American Philosophical Society, Philadelphia. Other correspondence of his is in the Benjamin Silliman papers, of which the largest collections are in the Yale University Library and the Historical Society of Pennsylvania. There are also some letters in the Thomas Jefferson papers, Library of Congress (listed in the published *Calendar*, I, 284; II, 379).

The Purdue University Library possesses a diary of 1824 and other papers of Robert Dale Owen. The Illinois State Historical Library owns an unpublished MS volume by Paul Brown entitled "The Woodcutter or a Glimpse of the 19th Century at the West." The records of the Kendal Community in Ohio, preserved in the McClymonds Public Library, Massillon, Ohio, have been published in full. Considerable information collected at first hand in the 1840's is in the A. J. Macdonald MSS in the Yale University Library. Scattered letters of Robert Owen and his family are in the Indiana University Library, the Chicago Historical Society, and the William L. Clements Library at the University of Michigan.

The archives of Posey County in the courthouse at Mount Vernon, Indiana, contain not only the recorded deeds, but also records of the litigation in which the New Harmony experiment terminated.

The manuscript volume of minutes of the Preliminary Society and of the constitutional convention at New Harmony, 1825–26, are owned by Mr. Thomas C. Pears III of Pittsburgh, who also owns the original letters published as the *Pears Papers*. The manuscripts of William Owen's diary, Donald Macdonald's diary, and the Pelham letters—all of which have been published in full—are owned, respectively, by Mrs. James H. Genung of Bryn Mawr, Pennsylvania, Mrs. Helen MacDonald Hollymount of Carlow, Ireland, and Mr. Wilbur Pelham of New Harmony. I am indebted to Mr. Wright Howes, bookseller, of Chicago for permission to quote a MS letter owned by him, James O. Wattles to Azariah Smith, Albion, Ill., Jan. 15, 1825. Certain other manuscript collections, relating incidentally to the Owenite movement, are described in the recent biographies of Robert Dale Owen, Frances Wright, David Dale Owen, and Thomas Say, mentioned below.

Writings of Robert Owen. Owen's publications up to and including the *Report to the County of Lanark,* written in 1820, were collected by him as appendices to the *Life* . . . *Written by Himself* (2 vols., London, 1857–58), from which quotations are uniformly taken in the present study. His subsequent writings have never been collected, the selection by G. D. H. Cole in Everyman's Library, *A New View of Society & Other Writings* (London, 1927), having been drawn exclusively from the works that Owen himself republished in the *Life*. The ideas embodied in these later writings are analyzed in chapter IV, where the principal titles are cited.

Owenite Periodicals. From 1821 until Owen's death in 1858 a practically unbroken succession of Owenite journals, many of them weeklies, were published. The series began with *The Economist: A Periodical Paper Explanatory of the New System of Society Projected by Robert Owen* (2 vols., London, Jan. 27, 1821–March 9, 1822).

When Owen shifted his activities to America, a weekly periodical was launched at the new community, *The New-Harmony Gazette* (3 vols., New Harmony, Oct. 1, 1825–Oct. 22, 1828), continued as *The New-Harmony and Nashoba Gazette, or The Free Enquirer* (2d series, vol. I, nos. 1–18, New Harmony, Oct. 29, 1828–Feb. 25, 1829), and as *The Free Enquirer* (2d series, 5 vols.; 3d series, 2 vols.; New York, Oct. 29, 1828–June 28, 1835). The organ of Owen's associate in the New Harmony experiment, William Maclure, was *The Disseminator of Useful Knowledge* (several series, some in magazine and some in newspaper format; New Harmony, Jan. 16, 1828–March 4, 1841).

The leading British organ of Owenism during the time of the New Harmony experiment was *The Co-operative Magazine and Monthly Herald* (later *The London Co-operative Magazine,* then *The British Co-operator;* 5 vols., London, Jan. 1826–Oct. 1830). The leading communitarian experiment in Great Britain also published a journal, *The Register for the First Society of Adherents to Divine Revelation,* at Orbiston (34 nos., Edinburgh, Nov. 10, 1825–Sept. 19, 1827).

From 1832 to 1846 Owen edited, or was closely associated with, a succession of periodicals that constitute the most important series in the history of the British Owenite movement: *The Crisis; or The Change from Error and Misery to Truth and Happiness* (4 vols., London, April 14, 1832–Aug. 23, 1834); *The New Moral World* (13 vols., in 3 series; London, Manchester, Birmingham, Leeds, and Harmony Hall, successively; Aug. 30, 1834, Nov. 1, 1834–Aug. 23, 1845); *The Moral World* (11 nos., London, Aug. 30–Nov. 8, 1845); and *The Herald of Progress* (16 nos., London, Oct. 25, 1845–May 23, 1846). Nominally this periodical was succeeded by the *The Reasoner*, ed. by George Jacob Holyoake (30 vols., London, June 3, 1846–1872), but this was primarily a rationalist organ. Several co-operative and workingmen's journals, more or less imbued with Owenism, were published between 1828 and 1845. See Foxwell, "Bibliography," pp. 254–60.

In America, during the 1840's, the revival of Owenism produced *The Herald of the New Moral World and Millennial Harbinger* (2 vols., New York, Jan. 6, 1841–Aug. 1842). In Great Britain the Owenite community at Manea Fen published its own weekly, *The Working Bee, and Herald of the Hodsonian Community Society* (2 vols., Manea Fen, Cambridgeshire, July 20, 1839–Jan. 2, 1841).

In the 1850's the octogenarian Owen founded a succession of personal organs: *Weekly Letters to the Human Race* (17 nos., London, 1850); *Robert Owen's Journal* (4 vols., London, Nov. 2, 1850–Oct. 23, 1852); *Robert Owen's Rational Quarterly Review and Journal* (1 vol., London, Feb.–Nov. 1853); and *Robert Owen's Millennial Gazette* (16 nos., London, March 22, 1856–June 21, 1858).

NEW HARMONY—CONTEMPORARY SOURCES. The official documents of the New Harmony Community give a very incomplete and one-sided view of its history. The surviving manuscript records include a single volume of minutes of the Preliminary Society and the constitutional convention, which cover only the brief period from Nov. 2, 1825, to Feb. 28, 1826, and a few books of account, which form too incomplete a series for economic analysis. The various constitutions of the community and a few optimistic statements and reports concerning its progress were published in the *New-Harmony Gazette*. These are of course indispensable, and they have been cited in detail in the footnotes. But the official organ was largely silent, not only on the dissensions that arose, but also on day-to-day events at New Harmony that could have been reported without discrediting the movement.

Six major bodies of contemporary personal papers, all of them now in print, therefore provide the bulk of what we know about the New Harmony experiment from its inception to its failure. Only one of these covers the entire time-span, *Education and Reform at New Harmony: Correspondence of William Maclure and Marie Duclos Fretageot, 1820–1833,* ed. by Arthur E. Bestor, Jr. (Indianapolis, 1948), usually cited herein as *Maclure-Fretageot Correspondence.* The two complementary diaries of William Owen (Nov. 10, 1824–April 20, 1825) and Donald Macdonald (Oct. 2, 1824–June 3, 1826), edited respectively by Joel W. Hiatt and Caroline Dale Snedeker, cover Owen's propagandist activities in America and early phases of the effort at New Harmony itself. Two collections of personal correspondence, likewise complementary, record the life at New Harmony from the summer of 1825 to the early months of 1826: "Letters of William Pelham," in Harlow

Lindley, ed., *Indiana As Seen by Early Travelers* (Indianapolis, 1916), pp. 360–417, and *New Harmony, An Adventure in Happiness: Papers of Thomas and Sarah Pears*, ed. by Thomas Clinton Pears, Jr. (Indianapolis, 1933); briefly cited as "Pelham Letters" and *Pears Papers*, respectively. The final year of the New Harmony experiment, April 2, 1826–June 2, 1827, is covered in Paul Brown, *Twelve Months in New-Harmony* (Cincinnati, 1827), the chronological accuracy but extreme bias of which is discussed in chapter VII. Fortunately many of its statements can be critically compared with those in the *Maclure-Fretageot Correspondence*, already mentioned.

For the disintegration of the community one must turn largely to unpublished sources, particularly the Owen-Dorsey papers in the Indiana Historical Society, and the Posey County archives.

Supplementary information on many specific points is furnished by contemporary documents in the collections of personal papers in the Workingmen's Institute and other manuscript repositories. A general description of these has already been given, and detailed references are provided in the footnotes.

From contemporary published sources much valuable, albeit disconnected, information on New Harmony is obtainable. The Owenite *Co-operative Magazine* in London, which relied on private letters for much of its information because the *New-Harmony Gazette* arrived so irregularly, published articles in 1826 and 1827 which are frequently more illuminating than those in the official organ of the community. There are several descriptions by travelers, of which the most valuable is that by Karl Bernhard, Duke of Saxe-Weimar-Eisenach, reprinted in Lindley, ed., *Indiana As Seen by Early Travelers*, pp. 418–37; see also [Charles Sealsfield], *The Americans As They Are* (London, 1828), pp. 66–71; Timothy Flint, *A Condensed Geography and History of the Western States, or the Mississippi Valley* (2 vols., Cincinnati, 1828), II, 154–56; Simon A. Ferrall [i.e., O'Ferrall], *Ramble of Six Thousand Miles through the United States of America* (London, 1832), pp. 92–108; and Maximilian, Prince of Wied-Neuwied, *Reise in das innere Nord-America in den Jahren 1832 bis 1834* (2 vols., and vol. of plates by Karl Bodmer, Coblenz, 1839–41), I, 164–214, and plates, Tab. II; English translation (London, 1843), pp. 74–92; reprinted in *Early Western Travels*, ed. by Reuben Gold Thwaites (32 vols., Cleveland, 1904–7), XXII, 163–97; XXV, plate 35.

American newspapers occasionally published first-hand descriptions of New Harmony, but their files are mainly valuable as a reflection of contemporary attitudes toward Owenism in general. For the present study the following newspapers were fully checked for the periods indicated: *Niles' Weekly Register*, Baltimore, vols. XXVII–XXXIII (1824–27); Washington *National Intelligencer*, Sept. 1, 1824–Oct. 31, 1826, April 14–July 31, 1827, April 1–Aug. 30, 1829; Philadelphia *National Gazette and Literary Register*, Nov. 1–Dec. 8, 1825, Oct. 14, 1826–Feb. 24, 1827; *New-York Advertiser*, Oct. 30–Dec. 4, 1824, Feb. 26–March 16, 1825, Sept. 14–21, 1825, Nov. 19–Dec. 3, 1825, May 29–June 8, 1827, July 6, 1827; *Liberty Hall and Cincinnati Gazette*, Oct. 1, 1824–May 22, 1827; *Cincinnati Literary Gazette*, Oct. 30, 1824–Sept. 10, 1825 (vol. II, no. 18–vol. III, no. 34); *Ohio State Journal and Colum-*

bus Gazette, Jan. 11–July 26, 1827; Xenia, Ohio, *People's Press and Impartial Expositor,* May 24, 1826–Jan. 4, 1827; Zanesville *Ohio Republican,* Jan. 24, 1824, Feb. 19, 1825, Feb. 24, 1827 (the only extant issues for these years); Indianapolis *Indiana Journal,* Jan. 18, 1825–Nov. 13, 1827; Vincennes, Ind., *Western Sun and General Advertiser,* Jan. 7–Dec. 15, 1826; *Western Register and Terre Haute* [Ind.] *Advertiser,* March 31–Dec. 27, 1826; Shawnee-Town *Illinois Gazette,* Aug. 7, 1824–Dec. 23, 1826; London *Times,* Aug. 20–Oct. 6, 1824, March 9, 1825, Aug. 6–Oct. 6, 1825 (also *Palmer's Index to The Times Newspaper,* 1817–1858). I am indebted to my research assistants, Mr. Claude E. Fike, Jr., and Mr. Philip I. Mitterling, for performing much of the labor involved. Additional scattered references to these and other newspapers are given in the footnotes. In a few instances where the original files were not available, references are taken (with due acknowledgment given) from Mary Louise Irvin, "Contemporary American Opinion of the New Harmony Movement" (unpublished M.A. thesis, 1932, in the University of Illinois Library).

Contemporary writings that illustrate the influence of Owenism upon the American labor movement and upon Jacksonian democracy have been assembled in John R. Commons and others, eds., *A Documentary History of American Industrial Society* (10 vols. and supplement, Cleveland, 1909–11), vols. V, VII; and Joseph L. Blau, ed., *Social Theories of Jacksonian Democracy: Representative Writings of the Period 1825–1850* (New York, 1947).

New Harmony—Physical Remains and Pictorial Sources. A very important contemporary pictorial record was made by Charles Alexandre Lesueur, whose sketches are preserved in the Museum of Natural History at Le Havre, France. Photographs of over eight hundred of these, representing American subjects, are in the American Antiquarian Society, and are described in detail by Robert W. G. Vail, "The American Sketchbooks of a French Naturalist," American Antiquarian Society, *Proceedings,* n.s., XLVIII, 49–155 (April 1938). Sketches nos. 94–218 (according to the numbering of Vail's checklist) picture the voyage of the *Philanthropist* to New Harmony; nos. 222–242, 741–754, and 814 are scenes in and about the community; no. 572 shows Nashoba. A number of the sketches are reproduced in *Dessins de Ch.-A. Lesueur, exécutés aux États-Unis de 1816 à 1837* ([Paris, ca. 1933]), and others in Vail's article and in the biographies of Lesueur mentioned below.

Many of the buildings erected by the Rappites and used by the Owenite community are still standing in New Harmony, among them three of the large brick rooming-houses: Community House No. 2 (preserved as a museum), the Tavern (or Community House No. 3), and Community House No. 4 (subsequently a theater and now a garage). Also surviving are a large brick granary of the Rappites, constructed in 1818 in such a way as to serve also as a fort if necessary, and a considerable number of smaller brick and frame houses built by the Rappites and used by the Owenites. The most notable of these, by reason of its personal associations, is the so-called Fauntleroy House. Unfortunately the most important building of all, the brick church completed by the Rappites in 1822, and renamed New Harmony Hall by the Owenites, who used it for their most important public discussions and other functions, was almost entirely razed in 1873, and the last vestiges were removed in 1913, except for the doorway, which has been built into the present high-school building. The earlier frame church of the Rappites, used by Maclure's School of Industry, was taken down in 1836. Several present-day landmarks, though connected with the history of New Harmony, are of later date than the community. These include the house built by Alexander Maclure in 1844 on the site of the house earlier occupied by Father George Rapp and then by William Maclure; the home and laboratory of David Dale Owen, erected in 1859; and the library and museum of the Workingmen's Institute, built in 1893. The Rappite cemetery, fenced by brick taken from their church but with graves unmarked, is another memento of the past.

A guidebook with maps and illustrations has been prepared by Nora C. Fretageot, *Historic New Harmony: A Guide* (3d ed. [New Harmony], 1934). The New Harmony Memorial Commission, established by the state of Indiana in 1939, has undertaken certain restorations, and has issued several publications, including two volumes of a somewhat antiquarian character by its director, Ross F. Lockridge: *The Old Fauntleroy Home* ([New Harmony], 1939), and *The Labyrinth: A History of the New Harmony Labyrinth* ([New Harmony], 1941). Thomas James de la Hunt is the compiler of a *History of the New Harmony Working Men's Institute . . . 1838–1927* (Evansville, Ind., 1927).

REMINISCENCE AND AUTOBIOGRAPHY. The charm that Robert Owen exercised over his contemporaries is alive in the pages of his autobiography, *The Life of Robert Owen, Written by Himself* (2 vols., London, 1857–58), but the incurable optimism is there also, and many of his statements must be subjected to more rigorous historical criticism than they have ordinarily received. Moreover the narrative ends in 1820, four years before his first trip to the United States. As a matter of fact, Owen experienced a psychological block whenever in his autobiographical writing he reached the period of his American venture. For example, he brought the story of his life down to 1823 in the first five parts of his *New Existence of Man upon the Earth* (8 parts, London, 1854–55), then in Part VI he jumped to the year 1854. Consequently the only narrative of the American period for which Owen was in any way responsible is an anonymous series of "Memoranda Relative to Robert Owen," *New Moral World*, I, 332–34, through pp. 409–11 (8 installments, Aug. 15–Oct. 24, 1835), based, so the introductory note asserts, on outlines furnished by Owen himself. The account is useful at some points but unreliable.

Robert Owen's eldest son, Robert Dale Owen, contributed his reminiscences to the *Atlantic Monthly* in 1873–75 (XXXI, 1–16, to XXXV, 660–70), and gathered the earlier installments, including all on New Harmony, into his *Twenty-Seven Years of Autobiography: Threading My Way* (New York, 1874), the most important of the autobiographical sources dealing with that community.

Two pupils in the New Harmony schools left reminiscences of the community, namely Victor Colin Duclos, whose "Diary and Recollections," transcribed by Nora C. Fretageot, are published in Lindley, ed., *Indiana As Seen by Early Travelers*, pp. 536–48; and Miner K. Kellogg, whose MS reminiscences are in the Indiana Historical Society. Richard Owen, youngest son of Robert Owen, produced a "Brief History of the Social Experiment in New Harmony," MS in the Indiana State Library, and revised J. Schneck's pamphlet, *The Rappites: Interesting Notes about Early New Harmony* (Evansville, Ind. [1890]), more accurately described by its cover title: *The History of New Harmony, Ind.*, written by Dr. J. Schnack [*sic*] and Richard Owen. A. J. Macdonald visited New Harmony in 1842 and collected information from former members of the community and other sources, embodied in his "Manuscripts and Collections" in the Yale University Library, folios 501–614, partly reprinted in J. H. Noyes, *History of American Socialisms,* pp. 34–58.

First-hand accounts of Owenism in Great Britain from the 1840's onward are to be found in Thomas Frost, *Forty Years' Recollections, Literary and Political* (London, 1880), and in two works by George Jacob Holyoake, *The History of Co-operation in England* (2 vols., London, 1875–79; revised ed., 1906), and *Sixty Years of an Agitator's Life* (2 vols., London, 1892).

SECONDARY WORKS. The standard biography of Robert Owen is by Frank Podmore (2 vols., London, 1906). It is by no means superseded by G. D. H. Cole's (London, 1925), though the latter offers some illuminating interpretations. The earlier biographies by G. J. Holyoake (London, 1859), William L. Sargant (London, 1860), Frederick A. Packard (Philadelphia, 1866), Arthur J. Booth (London, 1869), and Lloyd Jones (London, 1889–90) incorporate a certain amount of first-hand material on Owen's later career, but are valueless so far as his American experiences are concerned. A scholarly biographical study in French is that by Édouard Dolléans (Paris, 1905). There is a paucity of documented articles on Owen's personal career; only two require mention: Albert T. Volwiler, "Robert Owen and the Congress of Aix-la-Chapelle, 1818," *Scottish Historical Review*, XIX, 96–105 (Jan. 1922), and Paul H. Douglas, "Some New Material on the Lives of Robert and Robert Dale Owen," unpublished paper presented to the Chicago Literary Club, Feb. 2, 1942 (typescripts in the Library of Congress and the Newberry Library).

There are excellent biographies of several persons connected with the New Harmony experiment: Richard W. Leopold, *Robert Dale Owen: A Biography* (Cambridge, Mass., 1940); Harry B. Weiss and Grace M. Ziegler, *Thomas Say, Early American Naturalist* (Springfield, Ill., 1931); A. J. G. Perkins and Theresa Wolfson, *Frances Wright, Free Enquirer* (New York, 1939); William R. Waterman, *Frances Wright* (New York, 1924); Walter B. Hendrickson, *David Dale Owen, Pioneer Geologist of the Middle West* (Indianapolis, 1943); E. T. Hamy, *Les Voyages du naturaliste Ch. Alex. Lesueur dans l'Amérique du nord (1815–1837)* (Paris, 1904); Mme Adrien Loir, *Charles-Alexandre Lesueur, artiste et savant français en Amérique de 1816 à 1839* (Le Havre, 1920); and Victor L. Albjerg, *Richard Owen* ([Lafayette, Ind.], 1946). A biography of William Maclure is being written by Dr. Mary E. Cameron James of Philadelphia.

Owen's ideas and activities are discussed in all the standard histories of socialism, and in most histories of economic thought and of the British labor movement, but the treatment is usually perfunctory and conventional. Two very significant historical essays on Owenism and the radical Owenite thinkers should not be overlooked, however: Anton Menger, *The Right to the Whole Produce of Labour,* translated by M. E. Tanner (London, 1899), and the long introduction by H. S. Foxwell prefixed to this translation. One phase of Owenism in Great Britain is treated by Alex. Cullen, *Adventures in Socialism: New Lanark Establishment and Orbiston Community* (Glasgow, 1910).

The only book-length history of the New Harmony experiment is George B. Lockwood, *The New Harmony Communities* (Marion, Ind., 1902), republished in revised and augmented form as *The New Harmony Movement* (New York, 1905). Its value today is sharply limited by the fact that many of the fundamental sources bearing on the history of the community have become available only since the book was written. The best brief account of New Harmony is to be found in the opening chapters of Leopold, *Robert Dale Owen.*

Useful information is to be found in histories of related movements: Will S. Monroe, *History of the Pestalozzian Movement in the United States* (Syracuse, N.Y., 1907); Albert Post, *Popular Freethought in America, 1825–1850* (New York, 1943); John R. Commons and associates, *History of Labour in the United States,* vol. I (New York, 1918); George Flower, *History of the English Settlement in Edwards County, Illinois* (Chicago, 1882).

The published articles on New Harmony are not very weighty, but a few should be mentioned: David Starr Jordan and Amos W. Butler, "New Harmony," *Scientific Monthly,* XXV, 468–70 (Nov. 1927), reprinted in Indiana Academy of Science, *Proceedings,* XXXVII, 59–62 (1928); Charles Albert Browne, "Some Relations of the New Harmony Movement to the History of Science in America," *Scientific Monthly,* XLII, 483–97 (June 1936); Elfrieda Lang, "The Inhabitants of New Harmony According to the Federal Census of 1850," *Indiana Magazine of History,* XLII, 355–94 (Dec. 1946); Richard E. Banta, "New Harmony's Golden Years," *ibid.,* XLIV, 25–36 (March 1948).

Of the unpublished theses on New Harmony, that of Mary Louise Irvin, already mentioned, is valuable for its newspaper citations. Sister Juliana Baldwin, "Constitutional History of the New Harmony Experiment" (unpublished Ph.D dissertation, 1937, University of Oklahoma Library), abstracted at considerable length in University of Oklahoma *Bulletin,* n.s., no. 780, Abstracts of Theses Issue (May 22, 1939), is vitiated by major errors of chronology. Helen Elliott, "Development of the New Harmony Community with Special Reference to Education" (unpublished M.A. thesis, 1933, Indiana University Library), deals ably with procedures in the schools, but gives less attention to the broad social implications of the educational philosophies of Owen and Maclure.

A number of historical novels have been written about New Harmony, notably by Mrs. Caroline Dale Snedeker, and there have been some semific-tional interpretations, of which the most recent is Marguerite Young, *Angel in the Forest: A Fairy Tale of Two Utopias* (New York, 1945).

The literature dealing with the American Owenite communities other than New Harmony is meager. Sources and secondary works are therefore discussed in the bibliographical footnotes assigned to each in Chapter VIII.

INDEX

NOTE. Incorporated in this general index is an author index, printed in SMALL CAPITALS, to the books, pamphlets, articles, contemporaneous periodicals, and manuscripts cited in the present work, whether in text, footnotes, or bibliographical essay. The **boldface numeral** indicates the page that furnishes the most complete bibliographical data on the given work. Under the most important authors, separate titles, in shortened form, are listed in chronological order, and there are subheadings for letters and manuscripts other than letters (MSS). Newspapers are indexed under place of publication, not title.

Regular subject entries are in upper- and lower-case letters. Where an individual or an organization figures both as author and subject, the two types of entries are frequently combined in one. The subject entries are given at the end and are introduced by such phrases as "personal references" or "history of." The subject entries are omitted entirely, however, if they merely duplicate the page references in the bibliographical part of the entry.

The "Checklist of Communitarian Experiments" is fully indexed herein, the serial number from the appendix being added (in parentheses) to the page reference.

81; William Thompson, 84-85; John Gray, 85-86; C. C. Blatchly, 97-99; William Maclure, 148-52, 184; Paul Brown, 165, 182, 187-89, 215. *See also* Owen, Robert, views concerning community of goods.

Competition, *see* Community of goods

Concordium (Eng.), 140

Congregation of Saints (Ind.), community, 240 (no. 91)

CONSIDERANT, VICTOR, *Exposition abrégée*, **9 n,** 15-16; other publications, **89 n;** personal references, 57. *See also* Réunion (Tex.)

COOPER, JAMES FENIMORE, 43 n

Cooper, Thomas, 37

CO-OPERATIVE MAGAZINE, 48, 129 n, 169 n, 176-78, 183-85, 189 n, 195, 197 n, 215 n, **261,** 263

Co-operative movement, 87-88, 248

Co-operative Union, Manchester (Eng.), MSS in, ix, **112 n,** 114-15 n, 121 n, 122, 128 n, 130, 155-56, 162-63, 179-81, 186-87, 213-14, 215 n, 217 n, **259**

Cornelius, Peter, *see* Plockhoy, Pieter C.

Cornell University, MSS in, 33 n

CORRESPONDENT (periodical), 101, 178 n, 197 n, 203

Coxsackie (N.Y.), Forestville Community, 204-5, 206, 234, 237 (no. 38)

CRANE, VERNER W., 36 n

Crawford, William H., 108

CREDIT FONCIER OF SINALOA (periodical), 57 n

CRISIS (periodical), 88, 90-91, **261-62**

CULLEN, ALEX., 267

CURTI, MERLE, **14 n,** 251

DALLAS, WILL, 217 n

DANCKAERTS, JASPER, *Journal*, 28 n

DAY-STAR (periodical), 256

D'Arusmont, *see* Phiquepal, William S.; Wright, Frances

DEETS, LEE L., 234

DE LEON, DANIEL, 11 n

Democratic Society, Owenite organization, 240 (no. 84)

DEMOREST, ROSE, 255

Depravity of man, *see* Religious controversies

Determinism, historical, not characteristic of communitarianism, 14-15

De Tocqueville, *see* Tocqueville

DIAL (periodical), 43 n, 51 n, 140 n

DICKENS, CHARLES, 2

Diggers, 21, 27

DILLS, E. S., 211 n

DISSEMINATOR OF USEFUL KNOWLEDGE (periodical), 200, **261**

Distribution of Wealth, *see* Community of goods

DOBBS, CATHERINE B., 255

DOHERTY, HUGH, 16 n

DOLL, EUGENE E., 253

DOLLÉANS, ÉDOUARD, 266

DOMBROWSKI, JAMES, 39 n

Dorrilites, community of, 34, 236 (no. 32)

Dorsey, James M., 199-200, 207; MSS of, 162 n, 198 n, 199-200 n, 260, 263

DOUGLAS, PAUL H., 199 n., 266

DOW, EDWARD F., 257

DOWNIE, JOHN, 27 n

Duane, William, 96

DUCLOS, VICTOR C., "Diary," **158 n,** 266

Dukhobors, 98

DUSS, JOHN S., *The Harmonists*, **12 n,** 36, 40, 255; Rappite collection of, 255

Dwight, Theodore, 105

DWIGHT, TIMOTHY, *Travels*, 42 n

DYER, MARY M., **41, 41-42 n**

Eagleswood (N.J.), Fourierist community, 240 (no. 79)

Ebenezer Community (N.Y.), 51, 53, 241 (no. 113)

ECLECTIC REVIEW, 95

Economic ideas, not the primary feature of communitarianism, 3, 77-79, 83 n, 92-93, 107. *See also* Community of goods

Economies in co-operative living, *see* Waste

ECONOMIST (periodical), **83 n,** 103 n, 144, **261**

Economy (Pa.), Rappite community, 1-2, 35, 40, 44-45, 50, 55 n, 109, 213, 235 (no. 11); MSS at, 254

Edinburgh (Scotland), newspapers cited, 110 n

EDINBURGH REVIEW, 95-96, 138-39, 142, 145

Education Society, William Maclure's part of New Harmony Community, 179, 182-85, 191-93, 197-200

Educational philosophy, connections with communitarianism, 67, 78, 107,

SHAKERS (*continued*)
  publications of, **5, 26 n, 31 n,** 40-41,
  42 n, 256; MS records, 255; bibliography of, 255-58
Shakers, contemporary descriptions of,
  1-3, 34, 41-46, 52; development of
  communitarianism among, 5, 6, 24-26,
  31-32, 40-41; expansion of, 31, 32-33,
  39, 58-59, 229; connections with other
  communitarian movements, 47-48,
  50-56, 58-59, 95-96, 98, 106, 123, 203,
  207, 220, 229; buildings and artifacts,
  59, 233, 257-58; list of communities,
  235-36 (nos. 12-30), 237 (nos. 45-47)
SHAW, ALBERT, 56 n
Shawnee-Town (Ill.), newspapers cited,
  112 n, 115 n, 122 n, 125-26, 131 n, 166-
  67, 184-85, 221-23, 264
SHEPARD, ODELL, 51 n
Shirley (Mass.), Shaker community, 32,
  236 (no. 20)
SILBERLING, E., 9 n
SILLIMAN, BENJAMIN, 42 n; MSS, 260
SIMONS, RICHARD, 215 n
Skaneateles Community (N.Y.), 50-52,
  55, 240 (no. 89)
SKINNER, CHARLES M., 250
Slavery, *see* Antislavery
Small-scale experimentation, fundamen-
  tal to communitarianism, 3-4, 13-14,
  18-19, 69, 72, 135, 152, 229
SMITH, ADAM, 82 n
SMITH, JAMES, 41
SNEDEKER, CAROLINE D., 47 n, 262, 268
Snow Hill Community (Pa.), 30, 235
  (no. 7)
Social classes, *see* Classes, social
Social Reform Unity (Pa.), Fourierist
  community, 238 (no. 55)
Social Reformers Co-operative Emigra-
  tion Society, 240 (no. 84)
Socialism, terminology of, vii-viii. *See
  also* Communitarianism
Sodus Bay (N.Y.), Shaker community,
  32, 59, 237 (no. 46)
Sodus Bay Phalanx (N.Y.), 59, 239 (no.
  66)
SON OF THE MIST, *Letter to Robert Owen,*
  131 n
Sonyea (N.Y.), Shaker community, 32,
  237 (no. 47)
South Union (Ky.), Shaker community,
  32, 236 (no. 26)
Southey, Robert, 37

Spackman, Samuel, 108 n
Spain, Maclure's school in, 148, 152
SPARKS, EDWIN E., 250
SPEAKMAN, JOHN, letters, 112 n; personal
  references, 100, 108-10, 112 n, 154-55,
  202, 213
Spiritualism, Robert Owen's interest in,
  90
Spring, Marcus, 50
Spring Farm Phalanx (Wis.), 239 (no. 77)
STAMMHAMMER, JOSEPH, *Bibliographie
  des Socialismus,* **89 n,** 250, 259
State guardianship plan of education,
  227
STAUFFER, DAVID MCN., 200 n
STEGMANN, CARL, *Handbuch des Socialis-
  mus,* **100 n,** 234, 249
STEIN, LORENZ VON, 45-46 n
STEWART, WATT, 2 n
STORY, JOSEPH, letters, 106
Strang, James J., 241 (no. 100)
STUART, JAMES, 45 n
Swedenborgianism, 210, 242 (no. 118)
Sylvania Phalanx (Pa.), 57, 238 (no. 57)

Tank, Nils Otto, 242 (no. 117)
TAYLOR, LEILA S., *Shakerism,* **32 n,** 203 n,
  256
Taylor, William G., 195
Taylor, Fauntleroy & Co., 165 n
Terre Haute (Ind.), newspapers cited,
  264
Teutonia Community (Pa.), 242 (no.
  123)
Texas, Owen's project in, 216-17
THOMAS, DAVID, 44 n
Thompson, Jeremiah, 105
THOMPSON, WILLIAM, *Inquiry into the
  Distribution of Wealth* (1824), **83 n,**
  108, 170; *Practical Directions* (1830),
  77 n, **83-85**
THOMPSON, ZADOCK, 34 n
THWAITES, REUBEN G., **34 n,** 263
Tiebout, Cornelius, 200
Time stores, 185. *See also* Labor notes
TIMES, *see* London (Eng.), newspapers
TIMMONS, WILBERT H., 217 n
TOCQUEVILLE, ALEXIS DE, **2, 17 n**
Topolobampo (Mexico), community, 57
TORRENS, ROBERT, 95-96
TOYNBEE, ARNOLD J., 3
Trades unions, *see* Labor movement
TRICOCHE, GEORGE N., 250
TROELTSCH, ERNST, 5